Photo: Swaine

BRIGADIER-GENERAL W. L. OSBORN, C.B., C.M.G., D.S.O.

Frontispiece

THE HISTORY
OF THE
SEVENTH (SERVICE) BATTALION
THE
ROYAL SUSSEX REGIMENT
1914—1919

COMPILED BY A COMMITTEE OF OFFICERS OF THE BATTALION

EDITED BY OWEN RUTTER

WITH AN INTRODUCTION BY GENERAL SIR HUBERT GOUGH
G.C.M.G., K.C.B., K.C.V.O.

PREFACE BY BRIGADIER-GENERAL W. L. OSBORN
C.B., C.M.G., D.S.O.
(COLONEL OF THE ROYAL SUSSEX REGIMENT)

Made and Printed
in Great Britain

*TO THE MEMORY OF
OUR COMRADES*

BATTLE HONOURS
of
THE 7th (SERVICE) BATTALION
THE ROYAL SUSSEX REGIMENT

"Loos."

"Somme, 1916, 1918."

"Albert, 1916, 1918."

"Bazentin."

"Pozières."

"Le Transloy."

"Arras, 1917."

"Scarpe, 1917."

"Arleux."

"Cambrai, 1917."

"Bapaume, 1918."

"Ancre, 1918."

"Amiens."

"Hindenburg Line."

"Epehy."

"St. Quentin Canal."

"France and Flanders, 1915-1918."

INTRODUCTION
by
GENERAL SIR HUBERT GOUGH,
G.C.M.G., K.C.B., K.C.V.O.

This is not the first book to be written which recounts the deeds of Englishmen who, brought up in a happy land of peace without a thought of war and military matters, became England's soldiers just for the period of the great struggle. But although it is not the first of these individual histories to be written it is, none the less, an absorbingly interesting narrative. The stories it tells are tales of heroism, of suffering, of hardships in miserable conditions cheerfully borne, of the undying confidence of the home-bred Englishmen in this country, and its eventual victory in the face of terrible losses and of many discouraging failures. None of these things can be told too often. Besides, though other posthumous honours were denied them, in these pages are recorded the names of brave men and their heroic actions, which are worthy to be praised and remembered, and thus at last justice and a greatly merited honour are accorded to them.

Moreover, here is history; just plain hard facts, which, for all future time, as long as the English race supports its great Imperial burden, can be read and referred to by the men of Sussex and their descendants, wherein can be seen what manner of men their forbears were and what they accomplished.

The characters of these men are plainly to be seen in these pages, and it is important to record them as examples and guides to Englishmen yet unborn. And in doing this the authors have performed a great service to their country and in particular to their own county.

As one who participated in these terrible struggles, who saw and admired these men of Britain, and who has thought much on all he saw, let me strike one note, point one moral. When a Nation takes up the gage of war (and God knows when we may have to do it again), when it enters the battlefield, when it steps into the ring, if it should be against a brave, a powerful, a thoroughly efficient foe, be under no illusion that the victory

INTRODUCTION—*continued.*

can be won by easy means. Neither good tactics nor good strategy is sufficient to gain a cheap success against an efficient enemy; for his tactics and strategy will be at least as good as yours and he will often counter your best moves. Then it will be necessary to call in to one's aid, besides sound tactics and strategy, those great qualities of undaunted courage, of patient endurance, of absolute steadfastness.

Without these great qualities, which are so apparent in the tale here unfolded of these men of Sussex, in common with the others of their countrymen, military efficiency alone would not have availed to ensure their victory.

The moral I wish to point is that to enter on a war with a great people is no light nor easy undertaking and can only be successfully carried through by brave men of a firm moral fibre. Such were the men of this generation of Englishmen who faced up to all the terrible consequences of the national decision to go into this war with a steadfast courage and a cheerfulness for which no words of mine can adequately express my love and admiration. With Polonius, we can say for the guidance of future generations: " Beware of entrance to a quarrel; but, being in, bear't that the opposed may beware of thee."

PREFACE

by

BRIGADIER-GENERAL W. L. OSBORN,
C.B., C.M.G., D.S.O.,

Colonel of the Royal Sussex Regiment

The 7th (Service) Battalion of the Royal Sussex Regiment started life with the " First Hundred Thousand " in August, 1914. From its inception there existed a strong bond of unity between all ranks. This happily still holds together the numerous survivors, and their demand for a permanent record of the battalion's history has resulted in the production of this book.

Unfortunately the suggestion was not made in a practical form until the middle of 1925, by which time many irreplaceable records of the battalion had been wantonly destroyed by those responsible for their custody. Much time was lost in attempting to trace the missing records, and it was not until two years later that the guilty secret of their destruction was disclosed. It was then found that the only available material consisted of Part II Orders and the War Diary. Part II Orders were of no assistance in the writing of the narrative, though they were later most useful when the appendices were compiled; the War Diary, though valuable as a whole, proved to be seriously deficient in operation orders and to be lacking exact information whenever it was most wanted.

The absence of the full records of the battalion—for instance, Part I Orders, the Battalion Recommendation Book, and the Address Books—necessarily makes our history incomplete in many ways. It is generally impossible to give fighting strengths for comparison with casualties suffered and results achieved in any battle. Except in a few instances, only the bare fact that a decoration was awarded can be mentioned (and that not always with certainty), whereas the deed which earned the award cannot be recorded. Again, the exact rôle of the battalion in several actions in which the survivors were few (and they now no longer traceable) is still largely a matter of conjecture.

PREFACE—*continued.*

In the end, the story has mainly been told by various members of the battalion, whose experiences were laboriously collected, pieced together and added to by Lieutenant-Colonel G. H. Impey, D.S.O. He took over the compilation of the history at its most unpromising moment, in 1930, and worked incessantly to produce the completed chronicle—a labour of love for the battalion with which he served so long, but none the less a most arduous one.

In 1933 we were fortunate in obtaining the expert services of Major Owen Rutter, who has skilfully arranged our loosely-strung narratives into uniform shape and balance.

The other two members of the editorial committee, Lieutenant-Colonel W. H. C. Le Hardy, M.C., and Captain G. L. Reckitt, M.C., have from the first been the chief organisers of this history and have worked hard in tracing and collecting material, in compiling narratives, and in preparing the book for, and seeing it through, the press. Lieutenant-Colonel Le Hardy has acted as the committee's secretary throughout, and Captain Reckitt has compiled the index and the appendices, the latter with the assistance of Captain J. R. Wilton, who also undertook the considerable task of drawing all the sketch maps.

With regard to the 7th Battalion itself, it is no exaggeration to say that, in spite of its short life of four years or so and its official disbandment, it is still in being so far as the personnel is concerned. This is in a great measure due to the various annual reunions, which keep us in touch with each other, but it is also the result of the unity existing between all in the battalion, the pride of the officers in the fighting qualities of their men and the confidence of the men in their officers.

We have the honour of an introduction by General Sir Hubert Gough, G.C.M.G., K.C.B., K.C.V.O., under whose able command the battalion served in many hard-fought actions, and we thank him for his kind remembrance.

Our grateful acknowledgments are also due to many friends, without whose aid this book could not have been written.

First, we are deeply indebted to the staff of the Historical Section (Military Branch) of the Committee of Imperial Defence, and especially to Captain W. Miles and Mr. E. A. Dixon. They have, during several years, given us ready access to a mass of documents and maps and have always been eager to assist and advise us in any way.

PREFACE—*continued.*

Colonel H. P. Hancock, D.S.O., lately in the charge of the Infantry Record Office at Hounslow, and Mr. J. R. Nelson, M.B.E., of the War Office, Disposal of Records Section, Isleworth, and their staffs, gave much sympathetic assistance when we were attempting to trace our battalion records.

Various departments of the War Office have given us help and advice whenever asked, and the Geographical Section, and especially Captain W. W. Cowan, R.A., did us a considerable service in providing us with the copies of the general map at the end of our volume and in arranging for us the formalities necessary for its reproduction.

In this connection it should be noted that, for the sake of uniformity, the spelling and accentuation of place names used in this general map (which is a part of " North-West Europe, 1 :250,000 ") have been followed throughout the narrative and in all the sketch maps, except in one or two cases of obvious misprints. In cases where a place name does not appear on this map, " France and Belgium, 1 :100,000," has been followed.

Last, but by no means least, the thanks of the battalion are given to those whose generous financial assistance has made it possible to publish the history.

CONTENTS

	PAGE
DEDICATION	iii
BATTLE HONOURS	v
INTRODUCTION	vii
PREFACE	ix
ORDER OF BATTLE OF THE 12TH DIVISION	xvii

CHAPTER

		PAGE
I.	FORMATION AND TRAINING	1
II.	ARMENTIÈRES	13
III.	LOOS AND AFTER	33
IV.	FESTUBERT AND GIVENCHY	46
V.	THE HOHENZOLLERN CRATERS	55
VI.	THE SOMME	77
VII.	THE BATTLE OF ARRAS	109
VIII.	THE DEFENCE OF MONCHY	133
IX.	THE BATTLE OF CAMBRAI	147
X.	FLEURBAIX	180
XI.	AVELUY WOOD	189
XII.	MAILLY AND BOUZINCOURT	210
XIII.	THE BATTLE OF AMIENS	220
XIV.	THE BREAKING OF THE HINDENBURG LINE	235
XV.	THE FINAL ADVANCE	253
XVI.	AFTER THE ARMISTICE	265

APPENDICES

		PAGE
Note		272
A.	Diary of Movements, 1915-1919	273
B.	Summary of Casualties	
	(i) Killed and died, 1915-1919	279
	(ii) Killed and wounded in main engagements	280
C.	Roll of Honour	
	(i) Officers	281
	(ii) Other Ranks	283
D.	Honours and Awards Gained by Members of the Battalion	304
E.	Officers and Senior N.C.O.s who Proceeded Overseas with the Battalion in May, 1915	311
F.	Names and Service of Officers who Served with the Battalion	313
G.	Particulars of Re-Union Dinners	322
	Index	323

ILLUSTRATIONS

1. BRIGADIER-GENERAL W. L. OSBORN, C.B., C.M.G., D.S.O. - - - - *Frontispiece*

facing page

2. OFFICERS OF THE 7TH ROYAL SUSSEX AT ALDERSHOT, MAY, 1915 - - - 11

3. THE 7TH ROYAL SUSSEX AT ALDERSHOT, MAY, 1915 - - - - - 12

4. ESSEX SAP, 20th OCTOBER, 1915 - - 40

5. HOHENZOLLERN CRATERS, MARCH, 1916 - 72

6. HEADQUARTERS AND SENIOR N.C.O.s AT LAPUGNOY, JUNE, 1916 - - - 80

7. D COMPANY IN THE BROWN LINE NEAR MONCHY, 10th APRIL, 1917 - - 120

8. PRESENTATION OF THE KING'S COLOUR AT ERRE BY H.R.H. THE PRINCE OF WALES, 4th FEBRUARY, 1919 - - - 264

MAPS

Drawn by CAPTAIN J. R. WILTON

		facing page
1.	ARMENTIÈRES AREA, 1915	13
2.	BETHUNE AREA	33
3.	FESTUBERT AND GIVENCHY, 1915	47
4.	HOHENZOLLERN AND QUARRIES SECTORS, 1916	55
5.	THE SOMME—NORTHERN AREA	77
6.	OVILLERS	83
7.	POZIÈRES	97
8.	GUEUDECOURT	105
9.	ARRAS AREA, 1917	109
10.	ARRAS, FRONT LINES, 1917	119
11.	SCARPE	125
12.	MONCHY LE PREUX	133
13.	CAMBRAI AREA, 1917	147
14.	CAMBRAI, TRENCH MAP	153
15.	FLEURBAIX AREA	181
16.	AVELUY WOOD	189
17.	MAILLY AND BOUZINCOURT	211
18.	THE SOMME—SOUTHERN AREA	221
19.	NURLU	235
20.	EPEHY	239
21.	COURCELLES	255
22.	CHÂTEAU L'ABBAYE	259

ORDER OF BATTLE
OF THE 12th (EASTERN) DIVISION

35TH INFANTRY BRIGADE.

7th Battalion the Norfolk Regiment.
7th Battalion the Suffolk Regiment.[1]
9th Battalion the Essex Regiment.
5th Battalion the Royal Berkshire Regiment (Princess Charlotte of Wales's).[2]
1/1st Battalion the Cambridgeshire Regiment (T.F.).[3]
35th Light Trench-Mortar Battery.[4]

36TH INFANTRY BRIGADE.

8th Battalion the Royal Fusiliers (City of London Regiment).[5]
9th Battalion the Royal Fusiliers (City of London Regiment).
7th Battalion the Royal Sussex Regiment.
11th Battalion the Middlesex Regiment (Duke of Cambridge's Own).[6]
36th Light Trench-Mortar Battery.[7]

37TH INFANTRY BRIGADE.

6th Battalion the Queen's Royal Regiment (West Surrey).
6th Battalion the Buffs (East Kent Regiment).
7th Battalion the East Surrey Regiment.[8]
6th Battalion the Queen's Own Royal West Kent Regiment.
37th Light Trench-Mortar Battery.[9]

PIONEER BATTALION.

5th Battalion the Northamptonshire Regiment.

---

[1] Disbanded April, 1918, and absorbed into 1/1 Cambs.
[2] Transferred to 36th Brigade February, 1918.
[3] Joined Division April, 1918.
[4] Formed March, 1916.
[5] Disbanded February, 1918, and absorbed into 9th Royal Fusiliers.
[6] Disbanded February, 1918.
[7] Formed March, 1916.
[8] Disbanded February, 1918.
[9] Formed March, 1916.

ORDER OF BATTLE OF THE 12TH (EASTERN) DIVISION—*continued.*

MACHINE-GUN CORPS.
12th Battalion the Machine-Gun Corps.[10]

THE ROYAL ARTILLERY.
62nd, 63rd, 64th and 65th Brigades, Royal Field Artillery.[11]
Divisional Ammunition Column.
X, Y and Z Trench-Mortar Batteries.[12]

THE ROYAL ENGINEERS.
69th, 70th and 87th Field Companies.
Signal Company.
"A" Squadron 1st King Edward's Horse.[13]
9th Motor Machine-Gun Battery.[14]
12th Cyclist Company.[15]

THE ROYAL ARMY SERVICE CORPS.
116th, 117th, 118th and 119th Companies.

THE ROYAL ARMY MEDICAL CORPS.
36th, 37th and 38th Field Ambulances.
23rd Sanitary Section.

THE ROYAL ARMY VETERINARY CORPS.
23rd Mobile Veterinary Section.

---

[10] When the Division left for France, the Machine-guns were organised in sections by battalions; in February, 1916, each Brigade formed a Machine-Gun Company from those sections and the battalions were given Lewis guns instead; in July, 1917, a fourth company, the 235th, was added as a Divisional Company; and in March, 1918, these companies were organised as a battalion.
[11] 64th became an Army Brigade in December, 1916; 65th (Howitzers) was distributed among the other Brigades in August, 1916.
[12] Formed March, 1916.
[13] Became Corps Troops, 1915.
[14] To M.-G. Corps, 1916.
[15] Became Corps Troops, 1915.

CHAPTER I

FORMATION AND TRAINING

AUGUST, 1914—31ST MAY, 1915

Shortly after the declaration of war on the 4th August, 1914, that far-seeing soldier and statesman Lord Kitchener, then Secretary of State for War, realised that it must be a long and arduous struggle and called on the 7th August for a " New Army " of a hundred thousand men. The 2nd Battalion of the Royal Sussex Regiment then formed part of the 1st Division and was completing its mobilisation at Inkerman Barracks, Woking, when it was ordered to send a captain, two subalterns and fifteen N.C.O.s to the Regimental Depot at Chichester to form the nucleus of the regiment's first battalion under this scheme.

AUGUST 1914

Captain J. L. Sleeman, who had served with the 1st Battalion in the South African War and in India, and also with the 2nd Battalion in Ireland, was selected for this duty owing to the fact that he had recently rejoined after having formed the first units of the Officers Training Corps in Ireland. He left for Chichester on the 8th August with Lieutenant E. W. T. Rowe and 2nd Lieutenant J. S. Magrath, and the following N.C.O.s : A. Basson, A. Betts, H. L. Faircloth, E. Godfree, P. J. Hanlon, E. Hulkes, J. King, C. Lord, C. Maidment, W. Raby, A. Richold, B. Songhurst, F. Taylor, E. N. Venn, and T. Weller. It is worthy of mention that two of these, Hanlon and Raby, remained with the battalion without interruption throughout the war.

On the 12th August this little party was joined by Captains E. C. Beeton and R. M. Birkett, and Lieutenants R. J. A. Betham and J. A. Thompson, who were home on leave from abroad.

Colonel Sleeman gives the following description of the very earliest days of our formation :—

" The scene for the following fortnight almost baffles description. A depot filled beyond capacity with recruits and more arriving every few hours, most of them with nothing more than the clothes they stood in, and without documents to show to what regiment, or even corps, they had been posted ; all joyfully

FORMATION AND TRAINING

expecting to be immediately issued with rifle and bayonet and sent to France. Stereotyped regulations, hopelessly inelastic to deal with such abnormal problems; undisciplined humanity, drilled for ten hours daily, many unaccustomed to hardship and lacking even toilet essentials; order preserved from chaos by the tact of the soldier and the splendid spirit of the recruits."

AUGUST 1914

It was then decided that all the Commanding Officers and Regimental Sergeant-Majors of regimental depots should become the Commanding Officers and Quartermasters of the first Service Battalions of their regiments, and the battalion was most fortunate in obtaining Major W. L. Osborn and Regimental Sergeant-Major J. E. Clarke as its first Commanding Officer and Quartermaster. No better selections could have been made. Major Osborn had served with both the 1st and 2nd Battalions in the Tirah Campaign and Tibetan Expedition; he had been Adjutant of the 2nd Battalion and also Brigade-Major to one of the most efficient brigades in India, and was universally popular with all ranks, while Regimental Sergeant-Major Clarke speedily gathered up the threads of his new work and, with the exception of a brief spell at home when wounded, remained with the battalion throughout the war.

On the 21st August the nucleus of the new battalion left Chichester for Sobraon Barracks, Colchester, where Lieutenant-Colonel W. L. Osborn (as he had then become) took over command and the battalion was officially designated the 7th (Service) Battalion the Royal Sussex Regiment, and was posted to the 36th Infantry Brigade of the 12th (Eastern) Division.* The Brigade Commander, Brigadier-General H. B. Borradaile, D.S.O., Indian Army retired, was himself a Sussex man, while the first Divisional Commander was Major-General J. Spens, C.B.

Strenuous training was carried out from the first day of formation and a large number of recruits had joined the battalion, but unfortunately the ex-N.C.O.s of the regiment, naturally wishing to rejoin the battalions with which they had served, did not respond to the call of the New Army, although they were vital to its efficiency. It was then that Colonel Osborn inserted an appeal in the Sussex newspapers, signed by himself and Captain Sleeman, urging those ex-N.C.O.s who had served under them in the 1st and 2nd Battalions to rejoin for service with the 7th Battalion and promising them the ranks they had held on

---

* The order of battle of the 12th Division is given on pp. xvii and xviii.

retirement. The response was immediate and the battalion soon obtained the services of many excellent ex-N.C.O.s, amongst them Colour-Sergeants F. C. J. Coley, T. Solomon, W. Long, H. Page, A. F. Lusted, and G. Burr, all of whom proved invaluable in this emergency. An advertisement (reproduced below) was also inserted in the local papers.

AUGUST 1914

Several successful recruiting tours through Sussex were made with the generous co-operation of local car-owners. Amongst

---

APPEAL.

**7TH SERVICE BATTALION
THE ROYAL SUSSEX REGIMENT.**

THIS BATTALION OF
**LORD KITCHENER'S
SECOND EXPEDITIONARY FORCE OF
100,000**
Is forming at COLCHESTER, and is Short of Men.
Major W. L. OSBORN, Royal Sussex Regiment, who is in Command,
APPEALS TO ALL SUSSEX MEN,
Including EX-N.C.O.'s and SOLDIERS,
TO COME FORWARD NOW, WITHOUT ANY DELAY,
To join the Battalion and
FILL THE RANKS WITH SUSSEX MEN,
Who will sustain the honour of the Regiment Abroad.
The Four Double Company Commanders are Captains
**E. C. BEETON, J. L. SLEEMAN,
R. M. BIRKETT, G. H. IMPEY,**
ROYAL SUSSEX REGIMENT.
Report at nearest Recruiting Office, and
INSIST ON SERVING IN THE 7th BATTALION
FOR PERIOD OF WAR.
GOD SAVE THE KING!

---

them may be mentioned Major M. F. S. Jewell, the captain of the Worcestershire County Cricket Eleven, who then lived at Selsey.

Lieutenants Rowe and Magrath left the battalion, but numerous other officers joined, including Captain G. H. Impey and 2nd Lieutenant G. F. Osborne, both from the 1st Battalion (the former having been serving at the depot and the latter being home on leave from India), and Lieutenants J. G. Bussell and S. G. Evans, who had both seen service in the South African War. The

Formation and Training

battalion was also equally fortunate in securing a splendid supply of junior officers, principally from the Senior Division of the Officers' Training Corps, gentlemen of the finest type who had in times of peace realised their duty to the country and had passed the necessary examinations fitting them for commissions. Only those responsible for creating the " First Hundred Thousand " can sufficiently appreciate what that meant in those times of stress. New as these young officers were to commissioned rank they ably took their place in the battalion and performed their duties as efficiently as those from Sandhurst. It would be difficult to give higher praise.

<small>August 1914</small>

A most important addition to our ranks on taking over barracks at Colchester was the discovery of a puppy dog of unknown breed but genial aspect. A label tied round his neck made it clear that his name was " Harold," and added the injunction : " Please take care of me." He soon became the battalion mascot, and served continuously throughout the war, with the exception of a period of three weeks when he was absent without leave. Harold early showed that he was well able to take care of himself, and that his talents lay rather in the direction of " Q " than " G " Branch, for after attaching himself first to A Company he transferred to the Transport, and was seldom seen in the trenches. He disliked all civilians and possessed an uncanny instinct for distinguishing members of the battalion (especially the cooks), and it was popularly believed that he could recognise the Royal Sussex badge. On the march he would often walk along the whole length of the battalion, as though inspecting it. Harold eventually earned two wound stripes (one as the result of a shell-splinter while parading with the Transport on the Hulluch Road) and three medal ribbons (1914-15 Star, War and Victory Medals). He also had a Conduct Sheet, a document upon which much humour of a broad description was lavished, one of his crimes being . " Making love in the presence of the battalion." On his demobilisation (via the Blue Cross Kennels) in 1919 he was handed over to Captain H. Sadler and thus retired on a pension in the shape of a good and well-earned home on a farm.

The task of turning the splendid material into trained soldiers proceeded apace. Such was the inrush of recruits everywhere and the temporary confusion resulting therefrom that the battalion was very nearly filled up with some 1,200 men from the London district. However, matters righted themselves, and except for an excellent group of about thirty men from the Newcastle and Sunderland districts, it remained almost entirely Sussex.

The formation of companies and platoons began at once and the efficiency of the battalion progressed rapidly, while its numbers grew to such proportions that early in September it stood at full war strength. No one will ever forget the sight of those splendid men, from all grades of society and in every description of clothing, as they appeared on parade for the first time. There was soon an enormous surplus of recruits, who were ultimately drafted out to form the 8th Battalion of the regiment. Unfortunately the supply of man-power was too great for the administrative services to cope with, and the result was that the men suffered much discomfort and hardship from lack of clothing and equipment. After fruitless efforts to procure these necessaries Colonel Osborn demanded that either they should be supplied immediately by the War Office or that he should be given powers to purchase them from civilian sources ; his energy resulted in the necessary sanction to purchase them at 20 per cent. over army contract rates, and Captain Sleeman was sent to London, where he succeeded in buying the many thousands of articles required—such as hairbrushes, shirts, knives, spoons, towels, razors, braces, and socks— at considerably less than the contract rates. That this was possible is a commentary on the contracts entered into ; that it was necessary shows the straits to which the New Army were reduced. But for Colonel Osborn's insistence the battalion would have gone about ragged for many weeks more. The fact that recruits had been required to work for two months without these articles is a proof of the difficulties which had to be overcome by those responsible for forming the New Armies, and mention should also be made of the cheerfulness with which the men bore these inconveniences.

SEPTEMBER 1914

Training now went on rapidly, in spite of the inevitable vaccination and inoculation. There was a shortage of senior N.C.O.s, and it was a strange sight to see company commanders personally giving out the details for " Slope Arms " and " Right Turn," but good progress was made and the new N.C.O.s soon picked up their jobs.

Another spectacle not readily forgotten was that of Sergeant-Drummer Aylmore, clad in a bowler hat, black coat, khaki breeches and leggings, confronting a number of youthful enthusiasts and instilling into them at close range the arts of

Formation and Training

drumming, bugle-blowing and fife-playing, with results which in due course blessed the battalion with a corps of drums second to none in the Division. Drill parades were varied by route marches, range work, elementary field exercises, and night operations.

On the 2nd October the battalion left Colchester by train for St. Martin's Plain, Shorncliffe, a place well known for its annual Territorial camps. Here an admirable training-ground was available, but winter was approaching and the battalion suffered much from cold and wet. To make matters worse the shortage of tents caused overcrowding, but late in October we moved into hutments at Sandling. After tents these huts should have proved a welcome change, but unfortunately they were hardly completed when we arrived and had been built on swampy ground, which quickly became a morass. However, owing to its closer proximity to Hythe Ranges, Sandling was perhaps a more convenient place as a training-ground.

OCTOBER 1914

It was about this time that the battalion had its first taste of a mild form of active service, since reports were received that a German raid on the coast near Hythe was anticipated and we received orders to prepare a defensive position to resist it. We dug trenches and strong-points along the coast and near the military canal at Lyminge, and although it was the men's first experience of trench-making the result was good. In addition to these precautions patrols of two or three officers were sent out at night to ascertain the source of the various light-signals to German submarines alleged to have been seen, but nothing suspicious was ever found by these patrols. At this period the shortage of serviceable rifles was so great that none of the battalions in the Brigade possessed more than 200 for its 1,100 men, and when this raid was threatened the authorities showed their confidence in the battalion's efficiency by ordering the other three battalions in the Brigade to hand over all their serviceable rifles to us so that we might form the defending force, an order which, needless to say, was not at all popular with the other units concerned. The threatened raid, however, never took place.

During our tour at Sandling a most important unit came into being—namely, the Transport, and it would take many pages to

Formation and Training

do justice to its achievements. For our first (and last) Transport Officer we were very fortunate to possess 2nd Lieutenant R. C. D. Hind, who had given up a good job on a horse ranch in the Argentine to take a commission. His experience served him well and, with the assistance of Sergeant A. Lee, his organisation was admirable. It is not too much to say that, no matter what the conditions, the Transport never failed to deliver rations and stores, while many officers have happy memories of the Transport Mess.

NOVEMBER 1914

Captain Hind gives the following description of his early experiences :—

"When the Transport was first formed we took over the stabling of the Folkestone Race Course at Westenhanger; we then had five officers' chargers, ten light-draught horses and one old G.S. wagon. On moving into billets at Folkestone, the village of Newington was taken over as a billeting area and the farm buildings of Mr. Graves' Pound Farm as our transport lines, Mr. Graves being most genial and helpful.

"It was from here that I was ordered to meet a trainload of about 200 mules at Shorncliffe Station at 11 p.m., and to unload and divide them amongst the units of the Brigade. The train arrived at midnight, and we then found that all the mules were loaded in cattle trucks, with their tails towards the loading-platform. This created an awkward situation, as only Sergeant Lee and myself had any previous experience with mules, Lee having been Transport-Corporal with the regiment in India. No lights were allowed, owing to the danger of hostile aircraft. Since all the other men looked upon mules as man-eaters, it was left to the two of us to enter each truck first and unload the entire train. Everything went well until the last truck, when Lee, not being quick enough in entering, was met by a double-barrel kick in the stomach and lifted over the platform, fortunately without much damage.

"The hardest work during our early training was the riding school at Newington with semi-broken mules, without saddles and with untrained men. For the first week there was considerable soreness around the camp."

The hutments at Sandling had been more or less completed, but continual rain and sickness were beginning to make the place impossible, and a rumour went round that a move to billets in

Folkestone was contemplated. Probably what decided matters was an especially stormy night during which the whole camp was entirely flooded out. On that occasion a certain young officer, who shared a water-logged hut with a number of his contemporaries, completely saved the situation at about 3 a.m. by remarking, as the rain poured in cascades through the roof, " Well, they may say what they like, but I know they don't have a worse time than this in the trenches," a remark which proved an excellent moral-raiser at an hour when medical science tells us human vitality is at its lowest ebb.

DECEMBER 1914

Orders for the Brigade to be billeted in Folkestone were issued just before Christmas, and a party under Captain Impey proceeded there to arrange for our billets. Of this particular experience Major C. D. Jay has a vivid remembrance and describes it as follows :—

" When the billeting party of A Company arrived in Folkestone they were given their allotted area and told to carry on. Being doubtful as to the correct procedure, they considered themselves lucky to come across a former officer of A Company, Lieutenant S. G. Evans, who was now Staff Captain and was engaged in finding billets for Brigade H.Q., so they attached themselves to him for experience. Evans approached a large house, in more peaceful times a boarding establishment, and loudly rang the bell. It was answered immediately by the landlady herself. With the correct military air he informed her he was going to billet a certain number of men in her house. She looked at him scornfully, snapped, ' Young man, you will do nothing of the sort ! ' and banged the door in his face.

" Three officers, Richards, Nagle and myself, took up their abode with two old maiden ladies, in whose house things were rather *difficile* ; smoking indoors could only be accomplished surreptitiously up the dining-room chimney, and the final straw came at 10 p.m., when we were handed round tumblers of warm milk. The next day we told our tale of woe to a doctor whose house was in the same street, and he willingly took us in, although medical men were exempted from having troops billeted on them."

The town of Folkestone was divided up into areas, the officers at first being billeted with their companies ; later a battalion mess was established at the West Cliff Hotel and finally at the Leas Hotel, where it remained most comfortably until our departure, while the troops were accommodated in the area on the north-east side of the Central Railway Station and near the viaduct at the

Formation and Training

back of the town. Considering that it was the men's first experience of billets and the townspeople's first experience of providing them (there had been no billeting in England since the seventeenth century), it says much for the adaptability of both sides that matters went off as smoothly DECEMBER 1914
as they did ; and though a few were unlucky, the great majority of the battalion was received with the utmost hospitality and kindness, and many friendships were formed which outlasted the war period.

Once Christmas was over, training was renewed with redoubled energy, special attention being paid to trench-digging and field exercises. Much valuable experience was gained through the Commanding Officer insisting that the trenches must be dug under all conditions—rain, cold and darkness—and of those who took part in them few are likely to forget those hectic early morning digging-operations on the hilly ground alongside the Dover Road just above Folkestone Junction Station. Besides this we obtained our first experience in combined field exercises with the other battalions in the Brigade on the excellent training-ground near such well-known haunts as Caesar's Camp.

During January, 1915, an historical event occurred, for the 3rd, 7th and 10th Battalions of the Royal Sussex Regiment met on the same day during JANUARY 1915
a route march on the Dover Road, the only time in the three hundred years' history of the regiment when three of its battalions had come together.

It was while we were at Folkestone that the dog Harold was reported an absentee and shown as Guilty of losing by neglect his kit and regimental necessaries, *i.e.* :—

Collars, Dog, 1 ;   Discs, Identity, 1.

How Harold was recovered is related by Captain J. R. Wilton, who was then Signalling Officer :—

" I had been detailed to take the signallers for a route march. We went towards Hythe, the general topic of conversation being the disappearance of Harold, and just before getting into Sandgate we saw something move in some shrubs at the bottom of an embankment. One of the men said ' Good Lord, I believe that's Harold ! ' and, sure enough, Harold it proved to be. He was very exhausted, as thin as a rake, and had been so badly knocked about that he could scarcely walk. We had to carry him the rest of the way out and all the way back to Folkestone. I shall never forget our delight in finding him, nor his joy when he realised he was back once more with the battalion."

FORMATION AND TRAINING

While we were in these billets an epidemic of spotted fever broke out in the Division. All leave was cancelled and some of the platoons were put into quarantine. Although there were not many cases in our battalion, we had to mourn our first casualty when Private A. W. George, of D Company, died on the 28th January. Though not as the result of this epidemic, five other men were to die before we went overseas—Privates S. Arnell (B), C. Bowley (C), C. R. Glue (A), R. Hollingdale (D) and T. Owen (B).

Towards the middle of February rumours were afloat that the Division was to move to Aldershot. We started by route march on the 3rd March. The reason for this march was a sound one. Sir John French had refused to have any New Army troops out in France unless they had had previous experience of moving and working by divisions, doing their own billeting and being supplied by their own supply columns. Our Brigade, being in the Folkestone area, was given the route via Ashford, Maidstone, Edenbridge, Dorking and Guildford, and halted for the night at each place. The whole operation went off well, and fulfilled its object by giving us valuable experience in working by division. The attitude of the inhabitants in the various towns and villages through which we passed was most friendly, everyone showing us great kindness and hospitality. During our longest march—25 miles from Edenbridge to Dorking—the whole Division had the memorable experience of marching past Lord Kitchener.

MARCH 1915

Before the battalion left Folkestone the following Divisional Order was issued:—

"The Major-General Commanding has great pleasure in publishing for the information of all concerned the following letter received from the Mayor of Folkestone:—

> 'Now that the troops billeted in Folkestone are about to leave us, I should like to say, on behalf of the inhabitants of this Town, how much we appreciate the splendid behaviour of the men whilst they have been here. I hear on all sides from those who have had men billeted on them of the quiet, considerate conduct of the men and how they have tried to cause as little inconvenience as possible, and the Chief Constable also speaks in high terms of the men's behaviour. Our hearts go out in feeling of deepest gratitude to all

THE OFFICERS OF THE 7TH BN. THE ROYAL SUSSEX REGIMENT AT RAMILLIES BARRACKS, ALDERSHOT, IN MAY, 1915

TOP ROW—2/Lt. R. T. MAY; 2/Lt. G. A. THOMPSON; Lt. A. K. TROWER; 2/Lt. T. A. HILL; 2/Lt. J. R. WILTON; 2/Lt. W. K. SUTTON; 2/Lt. E. G. SUTTON; 2/Lt. D. F. WOODFORD; 2/Lt. J. F. E. WORLLEDGE; 2/Lt. H. S. STOCKS

MIDDLE (Standing)—Lt. R. C. D. HIND; 2/Lt. B. T. M. HEBERT; 2 Lt. R. G. WELLS; Lt. C. W. BEALE; 2 Lt. D. L. COX; 2/Lt. G. G. STOCKS; 2/Lt. N. J. COX; Lt. C. D. JAY; Lt. G. L. RECKITT; 2/Lt. E. G. C. RICHARDS; Capt. L. F. CASS; 2/Lt. W. CHAMPNEYS

MIDDLE (Sitting)—Capt. G. F. OSBORNE; Capt. J. A. THOMPSON; Capt. J. G. BUSSELL; Capt. R. J. A. BETHAM (Adjutant); Maj. J. L.* SLEEMAN (Second-in-Command); Maj.-Gen. J. C. YOUNG (Col.-in-Chief, R. Sussex Regt.); Lt.-Col. W. L. OSBORN (Commanding); Maj. R. M. BIRKETT; Capt. G. H. IMPEY; Capt. H. S. BOWLBY; Lt. J. E. CLARKE

FRONT ROW—Lt. R. J. RICHARDSON; 2 Lt. G. NAGLE

ABSENT—Capt. G. WOODHAMS; 2/Lt. F. H. BICKERTON

(From a photograph by Messrs. Gale and Polden)

Facing page 11

Formation and Training

officers, N.C.O.s and men for what they are doing and are prepared to do and suffer for King and Country, and that God may bless, protect and prosper them and bring them back safely is the earnest prayer of myself and the people of Folkestone.'"

On arrival at Aldershot the battalion was quartered in Ramillies Barracks, Marlborough Lines, which were shared with the 11th Middlesex, while the Transport lived under canvas in Camp 40 adjoining the Royal Pavilion.

From this time forward the training and equipping of the battalion went on quickly, and as the Division was now concentrated we were initiated into the mysteries of division organisation. Our new Divisional Commander, Major-General F. D. V. Wing, C.B., C.M.G., took over, and having just returned from France APRIL 1915 was able to put us up to all the latest tips. Company and battalion training began at once, succeeded in due course by brigade and divisional manoeuvres, and many interesting field exercises, including night operations, took place in the vast training area available and also farther afield in the neighbourhood of the Fox Hills, Farnham, Hartley Row, and Eversley Cross. It was during brigade and divisional training that we had our first taste of night bivouacs and of occupying a trench line by day and night on Hartford Bridge Flats. The experience was made all the more realistic by the fact that the battalion sustained some casualties during the march back to barracks through a motor cyclist running into the rear platoon and knocking out several men, some of whom had to go to hospital. Courses in machine-guns, bombing and signalling were carried out, and with the introduction of poison gas by the Germans at the Second Battle of Ypres (the 22nd April, 1915) we had to cope with this new form of warfare.

Thus, within nine months, a magnificent fighting battalion was evolved from 1,100 raw civilians, a feat made possible only by the untiring efforts of the few experienced officers and N.C.O.s and by the fine spirit of all those who had joined up for the duration.

An inspection was carried out by Lord Kitchener on Queen's Parade, and shortly after this the battalion was honoured by a visit from the Colonel of the Regiment, the late Major-General J. C. Young, C.B., who inspected it on parade, addressed all ranks, and was afterwards photographed in a group with the officers.

FORMATION AND TRAINING

Our training was now drawing to a close, time was getting on, and all ranks were anxious to go overseas. Two of our sister divisions, the 9th (Scottish) and the 14th (Light), were also concentrated in the neighbourhood, and rumours were rife as to which would be the first to go. All wondered, but the veil of secrecy was impenetrable until at length we woke up one morning and found that the 9th Division had departed. After a short spell the 14th followed. When would our turn come was the question on all lips. But before further orders were received a great and final honour awaited us all, and that was the attendance of His Majesty the King, accompanied by Her Majesty the Queen and Her Royal Highness Princess Mary, at a divisional church parade, and the following gracious message, dated the 29th May, 1915, was received from His Majesty prior to the Division's departure :—

MAY 1915

" You are about to join your comrades at the front in bringing to a successful conclusion this relentless war of over nine months' duration. Your prompt and patriotic answer to the Nation's call to arms will never be forgotten. The keen exertions of all ranks during the period of training have brought you to a state of efficiency not unworthy of my Regular Army. I am confident that in the field you will nobly uphold the traditions of the fine regiments whose names you bear. Ever since your enrolment I have closely watched the growth and steady progress of all units. I shall continue to follow with interest the fortunes of your Division.

" In bidding you farewell, I pray that God may bless you in all your undertakings."

At last the great day came when the long-expected orders were received, and the first units of the Division began to move on the 29th May, 1915.

The 7th Bn. The Royal Sussex Regiment being inspected by Major-General J. C. Young, C.B., at Ramillies Barracks, Aldershot, in May, 1915.
(From a photograph by Messrs. Gale and Polden)

1. ARMENTIÈRES AREA, 1915

CHAPTER II

ARMENTIÈRES

31st May—29th September, 1915
[Sketch Map, No. 1]

The first units of the battalion to move were the Transport and the Machine-gun sections. They left Farnborough, strength 3 officers and 102 other ranks,* under Major J. L. Sleeman, the Second-in-Command, together with Lieutenants C. D. Jay and R. C. D. Hind, on the 30th May and proceeded via Southampton by S.S. *City of Dunkirk* to Havre. The main battalion, strength 26 officers and 888 other ranks,* left the troop-siding at Aldershot on the 31st May by two trains, at 7.20 p.m. and 7.55 p.m., and reached Folkestone Pier about 11 p.m., embarking on the S.S. *Victoria.* Those who may have looked forward to a departure gladdened by flag-wagging and music, cheers and waving handkerchiefs, were disappointed. Whatever may have happened in the South African War, on the departure of our troopship there was not a soul to see us off. No band played us on board. In the darkness we marched up the gangway grimly, almost stealthily, no one talking, no one smoking; beyond the tramp of our feet the only sounds were the rattle of equipment and the gurgling of our waterbottles.

MAY 1915

The *Victoria* reached Boulogne after a smooth and peaceful crossing at 1 a.m. on the 1st June, thus causing considerable argument between those who had wagered that the battalion would, or would not, be "overseas" before the end of May.

JUNE 1915

After disembarkation we marched up the steep hill to Ostrohove Camp and settled down for the remainder of the night. This camp was situated on the heights overlooking the town and harbour, and when daylight came we saw that we were quite close to the column, which was begun in 1804 but not completed until 1841, to commemorate the projected invasion of England by Napoleon, whose bronze statue stands upon the top, facing our

---

* The names of the officers and senior N.C.O.s who proceeded overseas are given in Appendix E.

shores. It was here that our French interpreter, Captain Raoul Vassas, joined us.

We paraded at 4.25 a.m. next day, marched to Pont de Briques and entrained at 6.30 a.m., being joined by the Transport and Machine-gun sections, which had left Havre the previous day.

This was our first experience of French railway transport, the officers being accommodated in old second-class carriages and the troops in wagons and trucks bearing the well-known inscription *Hommes* 40, *Chevaux* 8. Before leaving we made our first acquaintance with the French Army in the shape of a trainload of Territorials, oldish men who looked very picturesque in their képis, dark jackets and red trousers, and gave us a rousing welcome. In order to cement the *entente cordiale* still further, they offered our men drinks out of their water-bottles, which are of a peculiar design, and our men, since they were unacquainted with the correct method of using them, only succeeded in pouring the contents down their necks—to the great delight of the donors.

JUNE 1915

After passing through St. Omer (at that time G.H.Q.) we reached Arques about 11.15 a.m. and, having detrained, made a short march to Blendecques, where we occupied our first billets in France.

Blendecques was a large and somewhat scattered village, intersected by a number of streams. The men were billeted for the most part in factories and outbuildings and the officers in private houses. It was clear that the advent of British troops was (at that time) welcomed by the local inhabitants, who seemed anxious to do all they could for us.

We took full advantage of the facilities for bathing and devoted some time to training in the use of anti-gas respirators, the earliest type of which consisted of a strip of gauze and a pad soaked with chemicals—useful but uncomfortable. The early type of smoke-helmet was issued to us shortly afterwards.

On the 5th we started a long trek up to the front line area, during which we experienced for the first time the extreme discomfort of marching by brigade in full equipment over hard and slippery *pavé* roads and under a blazing sun.

Our first march of some 12½ miles brought us to Les Cinq Rues, about a mile west of Hazebrouck, where the battalion bivouacked in a field with H.Q. in a farm near by. During this march 37 men fell out but rejoined later. The next day was even more trying. Parading at 6.10 a.m. we marched by brigade 15½ miles to Steenwerck, being inspected at Merris by the III Corps Commander, Lieutenant-General Sir William Pulteney. The day was again intensely hot, and in spite of extra halts many men fell out exhausted, our unofficial rearguard eventually increasing to numbers which, though imposing, were, we believe, exceeded by each of the other battalions in the Brigade.

However, although we reached Steenwerck 156 men short at 2.30 p.m., all the stragglers had rejoined in billets under their own steam by 6 p.m. Two-thirds of the casualties took place in the last $1\frac{1}{2}$ miles, and a contributory cause was that, owing to no webbing equipment being available, we were forced to wear a very uncomfortable brand of American manufacture against which vigorous comment was levelled, particularly by our veteran N.C.O.s. This experience taught us the futility of trying to march the regulation $3\frac{1}{2}$ miles an hour in full equipment, and later on we found $2\frac{1}{2}$ miles to be our correct pace, while later still our longer moves were usually made by bus.

JUNE 1915

The battalion was billeted just outside Steenwerck, a large village about five miles west of Armentières. Accommodation was not very plentiful, the men living mostly in barns ; a certain number were forced to bivouac in the fields, but owing to the warm weather this was no great hardship.

On the 10th the battalion, less the majority of the Transport, which remained at Steenwerck, marched by brigade to Armentières to undergo its first training in trench warfare in the form of an instructional tour with the 82nd Brigade of the 27th Division. On reaching Armentières we were billeted in the neighbourhood of Rue des Jesuits, and a very unhealthy spot it was to prove.

Armentières had been a manufacturing town of some 28,000 inhabitants, containing many factories, and at this period most of the inhabitants were still in residence in spite of the town being less than three miles from the front line. Although many of the principal buildings, including the *Hôtel de Ville*, were intact, the Cathedral and the neighbourhood of the railway station had been severely damaged. Yet the inhabitants seemed to carry on their normal life and, ignoring the spasmodic shelling, kept most of their shops open. It must indeed have surprised some of our South African veterans to find a branch of Burberry's, a Félix Potin and many cafés and restaurants where all sorts of luxuries unknown in earlier campaigns could be obtained.

The 11th June saw the beginning of our attachment to the 82nd Brigade, regular troops who had arrived in France from

Armentières

foreign stations in December, 1914, and had seen such hard fighting at St. Eloi and throughout the whole of the Second Battle of Ypres that in spite of drafts they were far below our strength.

JUNE 1915

The 2nd Duke of Cornwall's Light Infantry and the 2nd Royal Irish Fusiliers, in trenches in front of Le Touquet and Houplines respectively, gave us instruction in front line work, the 1st Leinsters in close billets at Le Bizet provided technical instruction in the support line, and the 1st Royal Irish Regiment at Houplines introduced us to the doubtful pleasures of night digging and carrying-parties. Our four companies were attached in rotation to these battalions for periods of twenty-four hours, while Battalion H.Q., with its details and the Machine-gun section, received similar attention.

This part of the line, which had remained practically unaltered since the previous November, was on the whole very quiet, and as our tutors were most helpful and hospitable the four days passed pleasantly enough. None the less, on the 13th the battalion had to mourn its first casualty, for early in the morning Private G. King, of C Company, was killed while working in the Royal Irish Fusiliers' trenches in front of Houplines. On the same day D Company, then attached to a company of the Cornwalls in the front line at Le Touquet, received their first real taste of war through the Germans exploding a small mine on the company front, followed by some heavy shelling, with the result that three more casualties were sustained, Sergeant C. E. Lewis and Privates Marshall and Waller, all of 15 Platoon, being wounded by shrapnel.

On that day also Major Sleeman, the Second-in-Command, and Captain A. M. Thomson, the Medical Officer, had a narrow escape when visiting the trenches held by the Cornwalls. A shell pitched in the centre of a group of officers of which they formed part, killing one and seriously wounding two. Captain Thomson showed great coolness in binding up the wounds, although shelling continued for a considerable time afterwards.

On the evening of the 14th the Germans sent five shells into C Company's billet in a school in Rue de Quesnoy, but owing to the absence of the company in the trenches there were no casualties. The next day saw the whole battalion reassembled in billets, everyone full of his new experiences, and in the afternoon we returned to Steenwerck. Our total casualties during the period of instruction were 1 man killed and 6 wounded.

We now took over our old billets at Steenwerck where we spent eleven days, which were employed in various forms of

Armentières

training. During our moments of leisure time was found for company sports and for exploring Steenwerck, which possessed a café and a few quite good shops. However, this state of affairs could not continue, for, having served our probationary period, we were now to enter upon our novitiate, which was to last for three months and to prove of immense value in the more stormy future.

JUNE 1915

The 12th Division had been lucky in the time of its arrival in France, since a temporary lull had set in on the British Front after the German attacks in the Second Battle of Ypres and the British assaults on the Aubers Ridge. Except for fierce local fighting at Givenchy, Bellewaarde and Hooge, this period of quietness was to remain more or less unbroken until the Battle of Loos. Consequently, unlike the early Territorial units and our two sister divisions of the New Army, the 9th and 14th, we were allowed the golden opportunity of settling down gradually to the conditions of modern warfare, which were almost impossible to grasp in England and very difficult to assimilate during the stress of an action or of a heavily engaged sector.

And here let a tribute be paid to the efficiency of the Army Postal Service, both during this period and that which was to come. No army could have been served better. Not only letters, but parcels containing such delicacies as fruit pies and pots of jam, invariably reached us, both in billets and in the front line. The regularity of this service was one of the solaces of the war.

On the 25th June the battalion marched to billets in Pont de Nieppe, with the exception of A Company, which went to Oosthove Farm, and the Transport, which proceeded to Pontceau.

The 27th June was a memorable day in the battalion's history, for it then made its first appearance in the front line as a complete unit. The relief started at 8.30 p.m. with B Company, which relieved the 2nd Cornwalls in Le Touquet and Lys Farm. The farm was situated alongside the Armentières-Comines railway, near the bank of the River Lys, and in full view of the enemy. The inhabitants were still in residence, carrying on quite unconcernedly with their farm duties; even cattle grazed round about, but it was strictly forbidden for any troops to show themselves in the daytime.

In the meantime Battalion H.Q. had established itself in a farm known as H.Q. Farm, about 1,500 yards from the front line, a ready target for artillery and machine-guns. The other three companies proceeded to relieve the Leinsters in the front line via Motor Car Corner and the road as far as the railway crossing, where they entered a remarkable communication trench, called House Avenue, which ran nearly the whole distance through the houses on the right of the road. C Company took over the right sector, with A in the centre and D on the left. Of these sectors there is no doubt the centre was the worst, consisting as it did of various small houses on both sides of the lines, which in some places were only ten yards apart, thus rendering it very difficult for newcomers to avoid exposure to the enemy's snipers. So close were the lines that it was possible at one point to see the eyes of the enemy sentry gazing through his periscope. This cost us dearly next morning, for Captain J. G. Bussell, who was commanding A Company, was killed by a sniper in an advanced salient while inspecting the line. One of the finest officers in the battalion, a clergyman, a master at Marlborough and a famous Rugby footballer, he was a great loss to all ranks, to whom his irresistible cheeriness had always endeared him. Captain L. F. Cass succeeded him in command.

JUNE 1915

We found that the grass between the trenches here was so long that it gave patrols good cover from view, and a large tract in front of our own trenches was kept mown nightly by " reaping parties," a job which came easy enough to the Sussex men.

Lieutenant H. S. Stocks gives the following description of this sector :—

" The trenches would not have taken a prize for the excellence of their sanitary arrangements. On one occasion Nagle and I were not at all satisfied with the flavour of some Bovril made by my batman and sent it back. Later on we heard that a sergeant of A Company had tasted the rejected concoction, which he pronounced delicious, and then and there scoffed the lot. Next day the highly decomposed remains of a horse were exhumed from quite near our well ! "

The Le Touquet area was just inside the frontier of Belgium, and in view of the wanderings of the battalion it is remarkable that it was more than three years before we again set foot in that country, and then only for about an hour. The strangest feature of the sector was the presence of inhabitants living quite close to the front line. At Le Touquet railway station there was, in addition to a derelict train, an estaminet still open and carrying on business within 1,200 yards of the enemy. With reference to this tour in the trenches Regimental Sergeant-Major Hanlon makes the following comment :—

"Many will remember the shock we all got during our tour of instruction with the Cornwalls owing to the explosion of the mine just before morning stand-to, but I really think an even greater one was when, about midday, we were asked who wanted beer and found it was obtainable from an estaminet so close to the line."

On the 30th June, however, all the inhabitants were evacuated from the Le Touquet area. Their presence had been responsible, probably quite unjustly, for reports of signalling and sniping behind our lines, although on one occasion while in billets at Le Bizet a report of signalling from an unoccupied farm led to the discovery of a pair of binoculars, but not its owner.

JUNE 1915

It was during this period, too, that someone started a scare that messages were being sent to the enemy concealed in the dead bodies of animals which were floated down the River Lys. Consequently a net was placed across the river, and in the early hours of the morning a party (drawn from the resting company) went down, hauled in the net and collected a weird array of carcasses. They were removed and cut open by the local butcher and their insides were examined for hidden messages. Some of these carcasses had been dead for a long time, and the effect in the early morning on an empty stomach was not agreeable. History does not relate if any hidden secrets were ever discovered.

Captain A. K. Trower recalls one night when C Company found this carcass-hunting fatigue :—

"Beale and I were out in a carrion-smelling old punt, rain falling and occasional extreme-range bullets droning past, when Beale suddenly doubled up with laughter. He had just remembered the date, which was the anniversary of the last day of Henley, 1914, when he had stroked the Caius boat to victory in the Thames Cup, and the contrast between the two river parties appealed to his sense of humour."

On the 1st July we were relieved by the 8th Royal Fusiliers and went back to billets in Le Bizet, the whole battalion being in a large disused factory on the bank of the River Lys, and the officers in the various workmen's cottages close at hand. Our casualties during our first tour were 1 officer killed, 1 man killed, and 10 wounded.

During our spell at Le Bizet we had our first opportunity of fully grasping the significance of the word "rest" in its military sense. Each night we had to find parties of between 600 and 700 strong for work in the second line. Owing to the daylight it was impossible to start work before 9 p.m., so that there was little enough rest for anyone, and it was quite a relief to take over our old sector in the front line on the 6th July.

JULY 1915

The Germans, on the 7th July, sent some kites over our trenches. One, which a patrol of D Company secured, carried the following message :—

" You can fill your trenches with devils. We Germans fear nothing in this world, and we Germans await victory, which has already long been evident. Englishmen ! How badly you shoot. You will be served as the Russians. The Russians are defeated ; so will you be. We Germans can hold out longer, as with the German Army there are no rabble who surrender and desert like the English soldier army crowd.

" You Englishmen, we have wine, sausage and meat ; you English are hungry and thirsty. Not yet will you understand who will be victorious. We Germans must be victors. If you still wish to fight it will go with you as with the Russians. You stupid soldiers ; do not let yourself be misled and do not believe your superiors that Russia and France have up to now been victorious. They have been defeated by the Germans. The writing of this has been done by two German soldiers, which we are."

Judging from the last sentence, this effort was the work of a propaganda department, anxious to conceal its identity. Read to-day, it shows clearly the misrepresentations of fact and the wild beliefs which were part of the military education of the soldiers on both sides. Here was a writer who thought our men starving —at a time when they were particularly well fed, comfortable and happy ; whilst doubtless the German soldier—living equally as well—was receiving messages couched in the same language from our side.

During this period Private J. King, of A Company, started a series of similar exploits by carrying out a daring patrol. In broad daylight he made a long reconnaissance of the enemy's front line and wire entanglements, and secured from a dead body the identification of the *104th Regiment, XIX (Saxon) Corps*. Later he went out again and brought in a German flag as well as the bomb to which its base was attached.

On the 9th July there was considerable shelling upon our support line and Battalion H.Q. in the farm, which sustained several direct hits, but luckily there were no casualties. Directly in front of H.Q. Farm, situated between it and the enemy, was a large barn in which some of the scouts and signallers were living, and concerning this General Osborn contributes the following reminiscence :—

"I don't know why, but prior to my starting for the front line that morning I had a presentiment that something was going to happen, with the result that I ordered all the men to vacate the place as soon as possible. I remember Sergeant Russell asking me if they could wait until later on, but I said 'No, it must be done at once.' Sure enough, when I returned I found the barn had been hit by several shells and some equipment destroyed, but no casualties ; and there is no doubt that if the men had not cleared out at once the casualties would have been very heavy."

JULY 1915

Major Sleeman and Captain Betham were alone in H.Q. during this "hate," which coincided with a telephone message from Brigade H.Q. asking what had happened to five blankets, lost some months before—a typical "Bairnsfather" interlude which relieved the tension of an unpleasant situation.

It was about this time that we had our first meeting with a war-correspondent, and with the details of his visit as set down in a book published in 1920 we have no cause to be dissatisfied. Perhaps this famous and always sympathetic writer went beyond his brief in describing the officers of the battalion as "men of old county families," but none will fail to recognise and applaud the pen-portrait of our Colonel as "a bronzed man with a grizzled moustache and light blue eyes, with a fine tenderness in his smile," and the jest recorded from the mouth of one of our wags, "I like Germans more'n Sergeant-Majors," never quite lost its point throughout the war.*

About 12.30 a.m. on the night of the 9th we had our first alarm, owing to a report of a big German concentration at Perenchies. As the result the battalion stood-to most of the night and all possible precautions were taken. Nothing materialised, although a thick fog through which Verey lights could not penetrate lasted until 6 a.m. It was perhaps fortunate that the battalion was not called upon, for, although no doubt it would have given a good account of itself, ammunition, especially for the covering artillery, was woefully short, and the rear defences were inadequate. Later on the same morning we were relieved by the 6th Queen's and moved into billets at Pont de Nieppe.

---

* *Realities of War*, by Sir Philip Gibbs, pp. 59-63.

Armentières

On the 14th Major J. L. Sleeman, who had for some time past been suffering from a most serious internal injury but had refused to go sick, was compelled to do so, greatly to the regret of all ranks. His condition was such that he was immediately invalided and—upon recovery—was appointed Director of Military Training to the New Zealand Forces and remained with them until the end of the war. Major R. M. Birkett took Major Sleeman's place as Second-in-Command, and Captain G. Woodhams took over B Company.

JULY 1915

As the 14th July happens to be a French national fête day, the Germans celebrated it by heavily shelling Armentières, especially in the neighbourhood of the *Grande Place*, and caused numerous casualties amongst the civil population.

On the 15th July we relieved the Royal Irish Fusiliers in Houplines. A, B and C Companies went into billets there, and D Company took over S.S. 88, the second support line, from the Royal Irish Regiment, with its company H.Q. in a ruined château called Le Ruage, which in the days of peace had evidently been the residence of some Armentières business magnate. The Transport moved to Pont d'Achelles on the Armentières-Bailleul road, about five miles away. Battalion H.Q. was established in Château Rose, a charming house at that time quite intact and situated very prettily on the banks of the River Lys. Unfortunately the gate of the drive opened out on to the main road in full view of the enemy; as the distance to the front line was only about 1,600 yards observation was very easy, and consequently it came in for a certain amount of shelling, while the machine-gun bullets down the drive were distinctly unpleasant. Notwithstanding these disadvantages it was a very good H.Q. and was retained as such during the whole of our tour in the sector.

The 36th Brigade held this front on a two-battalion frontage, with two battalions in support, the 9th Royal Fusiliers and the 11th Middlesex in the right sector, and the 8th Royal Fusiliers and ourselves in the left sector, exchanging every six days.

Houplines, another suburb of Armentières, and about two miles from it on the southern bank of the River Lys, was almost intact at this time, except for the church and a few houses, and was full of civilians, who were always ready to help in any way. Its disadvantage was that the road from Armentières, shortly after leaving Nouvel Houplines and right up to the factory (in which two companies were billeted), was in full view of the enemy. JULY 1915

Consequently movement by day had to be much restricted until we had constructed another road out of observation on the bank of the river to bridge the gap. It was, however, possible to carry out the reliefs of the front line in daylight owing to there being some very good communication trenches, particularly Irish Avenue and River Avenue; the latter ran along the banks of the river for some distance in the open but quite out of hostile observation.

At 5 a.m. on the 19th we were aroused by the Germans firing a hundred whizzbangs into Houplines. They were evidently searching just behind the factory for an anti-aircraft battery which had previously hit one of their planes, but beyond one unfortunate civilian no casualties resulted. On the 21st we took over the left sector of the front line (Trenches 85 to 89) from the 8th Royal Fusiliers, the companies taking up their positions from the right in the order A, B, C, D, an arrangement which remained unaltered during subsequent tours.

Our new sector, from which a good view of our old position at Le Touquet could be obtained, was situated on the opposite bank of the Lys and had an original and fascinating character of its own. A Company's front included Hobbs' Farm, a favourite target for whizzbangs and aerial torpedoes, or " sausages," as they were called by the troops. B Company's trench was more conventional, but both positions gave admirable opportunities for patrolling both by day and by night. The battalion's champion in this art was Private J. King, of A Company, who had already distinguished himself at Le Touquet. He carried out many daring and successful patrols in search of identifications and was later awarded the Distinguished Conduct Medal and promoted Sergeant for his excellent work.

C Company occupied a small rise, behind which flourished a number of unprotected sheds and shelters quite out in the open, but in apparent security. Its left approached closer to the enemy and contained the mining system of the sector—a somewhat doubtful blessing. Of their support trench, S. 88, the less said the better. On low and marshy ground, it stubbornly resisted the combined efforts of R.E. brains and infantry muscle to turn it into a tenable position. Hours of labour and tons of material were wasted upon this ungrateful trench in accordance with an order from Corps H.Q., which prophetically stated: " It is necessary to make the line as comfortable and safe as possible in case we have another winter."

D Company's trench, Number 89, approached still closer to the German positions in the Crater, the Chicken Run and Frélinghien Brewery; here the trenches were about sixty yards apart at their nearest point. There were many houses in this sector, and one called Buck House was actually in the front line and used as a sniper's post; eventually, after several attempts, it was blown up by the Royal Engineers, as it formed too good a range mark for the German gunners, but not before our snipers had claimed quite a number of victims. Perhaps the chief attraction of this trench was its left flank, which rested on the River Lys, and many a bathing party assembled at D Company's H.Q. for a bathe in the river no more than a hundred yards from the enemy. The trench was very short of shelters in the front line, especially in the sector held by 16 Platoon. Captain Impey, together with Lieutenant R. G. Wells, the commander of 16 Platoon, selected a suitable spot for three small shelters to be built. Then the question of names for them arose. D Company contained most of the men who had joined the battalion from the Newcastle and Sunderland districts, and, hoping to remind them of the pleasant moments spent at the various football grounds in their district, Captain Impey suggested that they should be called Roker Park and St. James's Park, the names of the grounds of the Sunderland and Newcastle United Clubs respectively; but, lost for a name for the third one, he asked the men for a suggestion, and they at once plumped for Hetton-le-Hole, the village where many of them lived.

JULY 1915

Although this sector was a quiet one we again began by finding the enemy on the top of us in sniping, and at first casualties were frequent, but eventually we got the upper hand, largely as the result of our excellent scouts and snipers under Lieutenant C. W. Beale, that ingenious and independent spirit, who had the able assistance of Sergeant F. J. Russell. From the ruined houses in which the whole sector abounded constant observation and accurate sniping were carried out with very satisfactory results. It was only a lack of targets which caused the roll of hits claimed to dwindle, for after a short time no German dared to show his head above the parapet, while the enemy's loopholes were quickly spotted by our scouts and severely dealt with by our snipers. The battalion will always remember the debt of gratitude it owes to Beale and his efficient band of assassins.

Sergeant-Major Hanlon relates the following incident, which took place during one of the frequent sniping combats about this time:—

"There was a number of periscopes on top of the parapet of the German trenches, including one very large one, obviously a dummy, just in front of the brewery at Frélinghien. This particularly attracted me, JULY 1915 so one afternoon I went round with a rifle fitted with a sniperscope and had a shot at it. Immediately after firing the Germans turned it sideways and waved a flag, signalising a washout. I fired another round and a large broom was waved to and fro and then lowered. I was firing from the left of Lumbago Walk (so called because of the struts across it, which necessitated one's bending almost double for some yards) when suddenly a shot from the crater on my right front went straight through the top sandbag not far from my head."

The condition of our trenches in this sector has evoked the following note from Captain D. L. Cox:—

"The Germans lacked little in thoroughness—for instance, they very wisely came to the conclusion that the outline of their trenches should be as untidy and as irregular as possible; also that a variety of colour was advisable. Our trenches, on the other hand, were 'dressed from the right,' so to speak: a stretch of sandbags in perfect alignment, with the result that any projecting object was immediately observed.

"G.H.Q. eventually came to the conclusion that a too rigid sense of order and tidiness, although perhaps pleasing to the eye, was costing a considerable number of casualties. Their next move, therefore, was to send the battalion a consignment of paint and brushes. It was naturally left to the discretion of the company commanders as to when the paint should be applied.

"Two of our company, presumably decorators by trade, took kindly to the idea, and, without waiting for the necessary orders, they acquired the said material and utensils and in broad daylight proceeded to daub our trenches in full view of the astonished Germans. They were left in peace for a short time, until the enemy, presumably having had his amusement, considered that such an excellent target should not be disregarded.

"We were therefore awakened by a few rounds of rapid and with considerable difficulty reclaimed our two enthusiasts. They were indeed lucky, for one escaped intact, and the other was only slightly wounded."

An instance of the accuracy of the German snipers is given by Major Jay :—

JULY 1915

"The shooting of the German snipers at this period was excellent, as the following incident will illustrate. The well-known firm of whisky distillers, John Dewar and Sons, Limited, sent out as an advertisement some highly polished metal squares, which made splendid mirrors for periscopes. Having acquired one of these squares we put it in a board and held it over the parapet of our front line trench. In less than no time the mirror was struck twice by a German sniper, one bullet remaining in the metal. On sending this back to Messrs. Dewar we were rewarded by a case of half-a-dozen of their best."

One evening a large flight of wild duck flew over C Company's trench from the direction of the German lines. Both C Company and the enemy fired rapid; one duck became a casualty and, falling in our lines, was promptly and rightly appropriated by C Company and consigned to the cooking-pot.

On the afternoon of the 26th an intense bombardment of the brewery at Frélinghien and the crater near the Chicken Run, where much hostile work was suspected, was carried out by 4.5″ howitzers and heavy 50lb. trench-mortars (commonly called plum puddings), while our field-guns swept the communication trenches with shrapnel. Much damage was reported to be done. Except for a few rifle-grenades during the evening there was no retaliation, and later on Private King went out on patrol and brought in a German hand-grenade, attached to a flag placed near their trenches, inscribed " *Gott strafe England.*"

The 8th Fusiliers relieved us on the 28th and we returned to Houplines, but not before receiving a parting greeting from the enemy in the shape of some aerial torpedoes, which fell mostly on A Company in Hobbs' Farm and in D Company's Trench 89. These missiles appeared to be fired from some form of gun or small mortar, since a distinct " pop," reminiscent of pleasanter sounds, was first heard; their range appeared to be about 400 yards, and one " dud " recovered consisted of a small cylinder of sheet iron plugged with wood and a slow match at one end; they caused a considerable explosion but little damage. After this all sentries were warned to watch for these " sausages," which, directly the pop was heard, could be seen turning over and over in the air, and after a little practice it became possible to judge quite accurately the spot where they would fall. Their prevalence inspired a wag to invent the following addition to the sentry's orders :—

> Just keep my eyes towards the skies
> And see which way the sausage flies,
> Then on my whistle give one blast,
> Or some one's future will be past.

On the 4th August the Royal Engineers exploded a small mine on C Company's front to counteract extensive German sapping operations, but with doubtful results owing to the quick repairs effected by the enemy during the night. The next day Lieutenant-General Sir Charles Fergusson, the Corps Commander,* together with the Divisional and Brigade Commanders, paid us a visit and inspected the battalion front.   AUGUST 1915

During the month of August we received two more machine-guns, bringing our total number up to four.

On the 6th we heard sounds of hilarity coming from the German lines, and eventually a notice-board was put up informing us that Warsaw had fallen. We were able to retaliate with an account of a successful naval action in the Baltic, and the next evening Private King brought in the German notice-board† with the inscription " *WARSCHAU DEUTSCH* " painted on cloth, as well as a roughly-made German flag.

Two days later the front line and communication trenches were unpleasantly shelled by heavy artillery and D Company suffered some casualties. This shelling was evidently registration, for at 4.45 a.m. on the 9th, when we were back again in billets, the Germans opened a bombardment on the 8th Royal Fusiliers in Trenches 88 and 89 with heavy guns and *minenwerfer*, while their field-guns put down a curtain of shrapnel over a line about 800 yards in rear. Our guns retaliated as far as ammunition would permit, but there was no rifle-fire on either side. The battalion stood-to for over an hour, but no attack developed. The Fusiliers had 25 casualties.

During this bombardment all telephone wires, including the cable in the River Lys, were cut, and great credit was due to Lieutenant J. R. Wilton and the battalion signallers that touch was maintained with C Company in S.S. 88, which also came in for the bombardment.

---

* We were now in the II Corps owing to a readjustment of Corps boundaries.
† This relic is in the possession of Lieutenant H. S. Stocks, to whom King presented it the day he removed it from the German parapet.

Having read the above passage while it was in typescript, Wilton wrote:—

"I do not think that much credit was due to me. When I arrived on the scene I found that a number of volunteers were already parading under Sergeants Lord and Catchpole, and I merely accompanied them. It is, however, worth mentioning that when we returned Colonel Osborn ordered me to put in a list of the names of the men who had formed the party, but Sergeant Lord told me that the men especially asked that their names should not go in. I could give very many other instances where signallers volunteered for unpleasant duties and carried them out without waiting for any orders. I have no hesitation in saying that what counted with the signallers, with whom I am very proud to have been associated, was the honour of the battalion: the individual counted not at all."

AUGUST 1915

He also mentions that after this episode he met one of the Artillery Forward Observing Officers coming back from his observation post, very distressed because he had just been told on the telephone that he was under arrest for having fired the whole of the ammunition that his battery possessed or was likely to possess for some time—a total of thirty-five rounds!

During our next front line tour we played the part of teachers, for two platoons from each company of the 10th Royal Fusiliers (our old friends and neighbours at Colchester) were attached to each of our companies for a twenty-four hours' spell of individual instruction; although we did our best, excessive crowding made matters difficult.

On the 19th the Germans introduced a new form of abomination in the shape of incendiary shells, which they poured into Armentières and Houplines; several houses and a large factory in Nouvel Houplines were burnt.

On the 23rd Lieutenant N. J. Cox was killed between S. 88 and River Avenue by a chance bullet through the head. One of two brothers with the battalion, a very keen officer and a great footballer, he was popular with everyone, and his loss was a sad one to us all.

While we were in the front line on the 26th and during the two following days, the enemy, who were evidently Saxons, made distinct attempts at fraternisation. They inquired whether we had been there last Christmas and made apologies for recent "strafing," with an invitation for a half-way meeting in No Man's Land, but strict orders were issued to prevent anything of the kind.

Armentières

Referring to this episode, Captain Wilton writes :—

"On one of these occasions I was having tea with A Company when we heard a lot of shouting and went out to investigate. We found our men and the Germans standing on their respective parapets. Suddenly a salvo arrived but did no damage. Naturally both sides got down and our men started swearing at the Germans, when all at once a brave German got on to his parapet and shouted out : 'We are very sorry about that; we hope no one was hurt. It is not our fault, it is that damned Prussian artillery.'"

AUGUST 1915

On the 28th a bathing-party at D Company's headquarters came in for some unpleasant attention. The party, consisting of about six officers, was spotted by the enemy, who started sniping with rifle-grenades and bullets, and Captain G. F. Osborne (then commanding C Company, as Captain Thompson had gone sick), while emerging from the water, was hit by a sniper in a part of his anatomy which must have awakened memories of his school days, but fortunately the wound, although severe, allowed him to return to the battalion five months later. Captain H. S. Bowlby took over command of C Company.

The 5th September saw the beginning of leave, and it was only fitting that the Commanding Officer should go first. During his week's absence Major Birkett assumed temporary command and Major Impey became Second-in-Command.

While the Colonel was in England General Sir Herbert Plumer, G.O.C. Second Army, inspected the battalion. A, B and C Companies paraded near our billets, and D Company was visited in S.S. 88. Sir Herbert afterwards expressed his satisfaction with everything he saw.

At about this time our Divisional Sign, an Ace of Spades, was painted on all vehicles in the Division.* The sign was adopted in conformity with the order that each division was to choose a distinguishing mark, which was to be substituted on all transport vehicles for the names and numbers of the individual regiments. In view of the enormous amount of digging undertaken by all units of the Division during their rests, no more appropriate sign could have been invented. However, since it happened also to be the sign of the Penal Battalions of the French Army, it at first caused some surprise to our Allies, and was responsible on more than one occasion for providing us with a chilly reception in a new billeting area.

---

* Motorists are well acquainted with this device in these days, for the "Ace of Spades" road-houses are directed by a late member of the 12th Division.

Armentières

Continual rumours were now coming through about momentous future events farther south, and it was doubtless on this account that the civil inhabitants of Houplines were evacuated on the 9th September. For many reasons we were sorry to see them go. They had done all that was possible to make us comfortable, and it was also a great convenience to have shops and estaminets close at hand. On the other hand, it was a relief to be clear of all possible chances of espionage, and although the Houplinois did not seem to offend in this way, many will remember the famous howling dog which always gave tongue whenever a relief was going on. This creature could never be traced, but it was suspected that some local inhabitant devised a means of causing his dog to howl at the appropriate times, and since the Germans passed through Houplines in 1914 there may have been grounds for this suspicion.

September 1915

On the 11th the Commanding Officer returned from leave, and the following day, as the result of mining being heard opposite C Company's front, a small mine was blown by the newly formed Brigade Mining Section under Lieutenant T. H. Carlisle, R.E. One of the miners was gassed in the shaft and Lieutenant E. G. Sutton, of B Company, who had just been attached to the Section, immediately went to his assistance, entirely unprotected from gas and without knowing how far down the man was, and was successful in saving him. For this very gallant action he received the Military Cross, the first decoration to be gained by any officer serving with the 12th Division.

We now received information that our rôle in the coming operations was to be an attempt to delude the enemy into thinking we were going to attack, by employing large quantities of incendiary and smoke-producing devices and also a new form of catapult to hurl missiles into the enemy's trenches. In order that everyone should grasp the correct methods to be employed a party from each company attended an unintentionally hilarious demonstration organised by the Corps in the use and abuse of these materials, when a Corps Staff Officer disclosed the astounding fact that " water poured on the top of fire is liable to extinguish it ! "

With reference to the new catapult, Sergeant R. Ellis writes :—

" I actually have a sketch of one of these uncertain weapons which, unfortunately, was placed just outside my shelter. However, it caused a lot of fun. The great thing was to make a quick ' get-away ' after releasing the spring, as the bomb was liable to fall back into the trench, or rather, in this case, the entrance to my shelter. Tins of bully beef, however, always seemed to make beautiful flights into the German lines ninety yards away."

On the 19th the battalion went up for what proved to be its last tour spent in the front line at Houplines, and the first few days were spent in preparation for the coming operations. In the meantime Houplines was getting a very bad time from the German artillery. Château Rose came in for special attention on the 22nd and 23rd and had to be temporarily evacuated after being struck several times.

SEPTEMBER 1915

On the 24th, Battalion H.Q. moved into its battle position in S.S.88 (appropriately enough called Goodwood), Brigade H.Q. taking over Château Rose. Increased hostile artillery activity continued over the whole area, while D Company, in Trench 89, got the better of a bomb and rifle-grenade contest.

The same evening, as a start for the morrow's operations, an ingenious attempt was made to blow up the bridges over the River Lys behind the German lines. Charges of explosive with a clockwork fuse were put into the middle of a large wooden framework shaped like a wheel and the whole contraption was floated down the river from D Company's H.Q. This was Lieutenant Beale's suggestion, and the idea was that even if these floating mines caught against the banks of the winding river they would easily float clear again through the action of the current. Some did, indeed, successfully reach their destination, but one eased up against the end of 14 Platoon's trench and gave Lieutenant G. L. Reckitt and Sergeant J. Joy, his platoon sergeant, a shock by blowing up just before they arrived to push it off.

The morning of the 25th saw the start, farther south, of the battle of Loos, and at 5.56 a.m. we began to offer up our burnt sacrifice for its success by setting fire to damp straw on the top of the parapet and further increasing our smoke curtain by means of threlfallite and phosphorous bombs. Our artillery, trench-mortars and machine-guns also joined in, but in spite of all our efforts it is very doubtful if the enemy was in any way deceived, although he retaliated strongly with all the weapons at his disposal. Later on in the day things quietened down and a dead calm set in. Our total casualties this day were 3 killed and 9 wounded, mostly in D Company.

The next day proved a very quiet one; even a low-flying aeroplane only attracted a few solitary shots from a " caretaker " in the German lines, and at 7.30 p.m. we were relieved by the 7th Durham Light Infantry (50th Division) and moved into billets in Armentières.

Armentières

September 1915

Our new billets were in a very unhealthy area around the *Grande Place* and came in for some heavy shelling by 4.2 howitzers on the afternoon of the 27th. All the battalion billets were hit, except those of Battalion H.Q. and D Company; these escaped, although the houses on the opposite side of the street were struck. The Machine-gun section in an old school building in Rue de Quesnoy suffered most, for Sergeant A. Basson and 2 men were killed and 9 others wounded, including Sergeant J. Baldwin, who was very severely hit and eventually perished when the Hospital Ship *Anglia* was mined by the Germans in the Channel.

Our total casualties were 4 killed and 18 wounded. It was fortunate that two companies were at the time attending the baths at Pont de Nieppe, otherwise our casualties must have been far heavier. It must be admitted that for once the numerous spy rumours were justified, for there is little doubt that such accurate shooting could not have taken place without some information having reached the enemy, and, as Colonel Osborn truly remarked at the time, " Their shooting could not have been better if they had actually had an F.O.O. on the tower of the *Mairie*."

During our two days at Armentières the Transport remained in the streets of the town, hooked-to with poles dropped and drivers sleeping on the pavement all night, ready to move at a moment's notice. On the 28th the battalion paraded at 5.45 a.m., and marching to Steenwerck entrained there for Chocques, on its way to the battle area of Loos. The Transport started before dawn and proceeded by forced marches towards the same area.

Our long tour in these quiet sectors proved of great value to the battalion and was a period which will, on account of its comparative pleasantness, long be remembered by those who have survived. Pleasant though it may have been, the wastage of war even in a " peace-time " sector is clearly shown by the fact that, apart from losses from sickness, the battalion lost 2 officers killed and 2 wounded, and 28 other ranks killed and 81 wounded, of whom 10 died of wounds: a total of 113 casualties from the 11th June to the 28th September.

2. BETHUNE AREA

CHAPTER III

LOOS AND AFTER

28TH SEPTEMBER—3RD DECEMBER, 1915
[Sketch Maps, Nos. 2 and 4]

We reached Chocques just before noon on the 28th September, three days after the opening of the Battle of Loos.

The British offensive, made in conjunction with important French operations farther south, had been rendered possible only by the enormously increased output of shells in the United Kingdom and by the arrival in France of several Territorial and New Army divisions. The task given to the I Corps and the IV Corps had been to attack on the front between La Bassée and Lens, the principal immediate objectives being, to the north, the Hohenzollern Redoubt (a famous strong-point in the German front line), Fosse 8 de Bethune (a large slag-heap) and the Quarries, and, to the south, Hill 70 and the mining village of Loos.

SEPTEMBER 1915

The attack had been launched on 25th September, after a preliminary discharge of gas—in retaliation for the gas used by the enemy at the Second Battle of Ypres. In the first onslaught the objectives had been taken, and the two Scottish divisions of the New Army, the 9th and the 15th, had covered themselves with glory. But it is easier to take trenches than to hold them, and in those early days the difficulties of supporting front line units in the chaos of a modern battle had yet to be mastered; so that the inevitable counter-attacks, which the enemy delivered with the utmost fury, had won back Fosse 8, most of the Hohenzollern Redoubt, the Quarries, and Hill 70, but nevertheless had left in our hands an area of captured ground from 2,000 to 3,000 yards in depth, including the village of Loos.

This, then, was the position when we reached the battle area. Leaving Chocques we billeted for the night at Busnettes, and early on the 29th marched about nine miles to Verquigneul, near Verquin, where the whole battalion was billeted in the buildings of a coal mine south of the village. This proved a welcome but somewhat grimy residence, although there were many spots where it was forbidden to enter. The D Company men from the Newcastle district, who were mostly miners, enjoyed a return to peace-time labour, for they spent much of their time wheeling heavy trucks of coal from the pithead.

Verquigneul was about five miles from the new front line, and we were now for the first time in the French mining country, the greater part of which was either in the enemy's hands or so well within range of his guns as to be unworkable. The first signs of battle we saw were numerous ambulances and German prisoners.

SEPTEMBER 1915

On the following day we received a visit from Lieutenant-Colonel E. W. B. Green, D.S.O., and Captain T. A. Jones, D.C.M., the Commanding Officer and the Quartermaster of the 2nd Royal Sussex, which was resting out of the line at Noeux-les-Mines. Colonel Green had commanded an independent force, called " Green's Force," during the battle, while Major E. F. Villiers, D.S.O., had led the 2nd Battalion in its attack with the first wave of the 2nd Brigade (1st Division). It had suffered very heavily and had lost nearly 500 officers and men. Colonel Osborn and the company commanders, when they went up later in the day to reconnoitre the front line, were saddened to see the bodies of many of the gallant men of the 2nd Battalion in and around the German wire near the solitary cherry tree in No Man's Land known as " Lone Tree."

In the late afternoon we started up to relieve the 3rd Coldstream Guards (1st Brigade of the newly formed Guards Division) in the front line opposite Hulluch. It was a long and trying relief which was not completed until after midnight, and full packs made the march extremely tiring. On our way up we passed through the village of Vermelles, which had suffered greatly in the early days of the war. It was almost in ruins, the most interesting of which was the château, where a ferocious combat was said to have taken place between a party of French on the ground floor and some Germans who were defending the storey above. The inhabitants had long since left the town, but it was still possible to use the cellars as billets, especially the large one in the brewery, and a few intact houses on the outskirts.

Vermelles was being heavily shelled as we passed through. It was dark and rain had started to fall. There was much confusion and congestion owing to the movement of many troops and a large amount of guns and transport. We were glad to emerge from Vermelles and proceed along a muddy country road to Le Rutoire, a cluster of ruined farm buildings about two miles from the front line; its cellars and dug-outs served as the H.Q. of various units. The ground rose gently towards the old front line and then fell gradually towards Hulluch. To the south-west lay the famous heights of Notre Dame de Lorette and the pit-heads of numerous collieries, including that well-known feature the "Tower Bridge" at Loos—actually a pair of iron winding-towers, one of which had been wrecked in the recent fighting. But undoubtedly the most sinister feature overlooking all was the Slag Heap, officially known as Fosse 8 de Bethune, but commonly called the Dump, which was to remain in the possession of the enemy as an invaluable observation post for three more years of war.

SEPTEMBER 1915

After crossing the old front line we came under long range rifle and machine-gun fire from the direction of the Hohenzollern Redoubt and suffered some casualties, including the guide to D Company, which had some difficulty in finding its ultimate position. The battalion was finally installed after having had 1 man killed and 9 wounded during the relief.

We had the 8th Royal Fusiliers on our left and the 11th Middlesex on our right, and when daylight came we could see that our position overlooked Hulluch (from which there came a considerable amount of enfilade fire) and consisted of the back communication trenches of the old German position. One company was actually in a trench running at right-angles to the enemy, while Battalion H.Q. was under an old trench bridge in the second line. There was no dug-out accommodation, the only shelter being small traverses and scrapes in the side of the trench. We were thus confronted with a formidable amount of consolidation work, which was begun at once.

OCTOBER 1915

Included in the defences near our forward line were two German gunpits, containing two field-guns and about 1,000 rounds of ammunition which the enemy had abandoned. This proved a very awkward position to hold, exposed as it was to accurate sniping from the direction of Hulluch, and it cost us several casualties, including Captain H. de B. Grant, commanding one of the howitzer batteries in the 65th Brigade, R.F.A., who was killed while reconnoitring for an observation post.

Our communications were very bad, and there was no other road for the transport but the main Hulluch-Vermelles Road, which, under direct observation from the Dump, could be used only by night, so that the congestion was very great. There was equal congestion in Vermelles, especially at the Brewery Cross-Roads, which were frequently shelled. The highest praise is due to Lieutenants Clarke and Hind and the men who were responsible for bringing up stores and rations under these trying conditions.

OCTOBER 1915

In spite of all our efforts the shortage of water proved acute, for every drop had to be carried by hand from the nearest refilling point, the water-carts about a mile away on the Hulluch Road. Some parties ventured as far as Le Rutoire in search of water, and there were several casualties from shelling as the result.

On the evening of the 2nd all units in the Brigade had to find large working-parties to dig a new forward trench with the object of advancing and shortening our front line. The work continued until just before daylight, covered by a shrapnel barrage, one gun firing all the time short, but just clear, of our party. Frequently the men had to stop digging to remove the bodies of those who had fallen in the first attack; and it was an eerie experience working in the glare of the Verey lights and of the villages which were burning behind the German lines. Fortunately only 3 men were wounded.

Sergeant Ellis, of C Company, recalls that " on the departure of the working parties small groups of men were left in charge of the partially-dug trench until the following night. As the trench after the first night's digging was not more than three feet deep, holding it was a job which had to be carried out lying down, no periscopes, no smoking, and, in my particular sector, no communication with other groups. However, the Germans were probably equally well employed and the day passed quietly."

Large working-parties were again found on the next night, and they had a disturbing experience as the result of an attack in the neighbourhood of the Dump, which started heavy shelling by both sides. After about an hour things quietened down, but the whole battalion area was searched throughout the night by a heavy howitzer battery.

The sad rumour which had reached us during the day of the death of Major-General F. D. V. Wing, the Divisional Commander, only too unfortunately proved to be true, for he and Lieutenant C. C. Tower, his A.D.C., had been killed by a shell while inspecting a battery position on the Bethune-Lens

Road. He was succeeded by Major-General A. B. Scott, C.B., D.S.O., another Gunner, who had come out with the Indian Corps and had been Major-General, R.A., Third Army.

On the 4th there was a considerable amount of shelling at intervals and our ration parties came in for a bad time; consequently we went very short of water. The usual working-parties were again found and the two German guns were removed from our forward position by a party of Royal Engineers and 5th Northants. The 5th proved a quieter day all round, and our working-parties had a more peaceful time, probably because the enemy were also working on a new front line, with a covering-party within a hundred yards of ours. This was an extraordinary sight and one not likely to be forgotten by those who saw it.

OCTOBER 1915

Hostile shelling increased in volume the next day, but work went on as usual, and on the 7th our line was taken over by the 1st Cameron Highlanders, the 8th Royal Berks and the 10th Gloucesters of the 1st Brigade, but as the detachments of these units had to come from various places the relief could not start until 10 p.m., and we did not reach Verquin until 3.45 a.m. next morning, our total casualties during the tour having been 3 killed, 32 wounded, and 1 missing.

It was during this tour that the misplaced enterprise of the spy-maniacs reached its height, as the following episode will show. Major Impey, commanding D Company, received a slight wound in the neck from a piece of shrapnel, and as soon as darkness set in was sent off by our Medical Officer for an anti-tetanus inoculation. On reaching the aid-post at Lone Tree, he was directed to proceed on the long and muddy trek to the forward dressing-station at Le Rutoire. Since the dressing-station could not provide the inoculation he had to go by motor-ambulance to the 36th Field Ambulance at Philosophe, which he reached after a disagreeable drive through heavy shelling at the Brewery Cross-Roads in Vermelles, and finally obtained the inoculation. In the meantime a dark plot had been hatched by the R.A.M.C. representatives at Lone Tree and Le Rutoire, with the result that the following message was received at the 36th Field Ambulance :—

" Tall, formidable-looking person dressed in a Burberry coat, covered with chalk and mud, appears not to have shaved for several days, is masquerading as a British Officer and reported to 36th F.A.; circumstances most suspicious. He should be arrested at once and sent under armed escort to Brigade H.Q."

In spite of Major Impey's protests, this remarkable order was carried out. He was deprived of all his equipment, some of which, including his revolver, was never seen again, and then this desperate spy, accompanied by his orderly and escorted by three unarmed R.A.M.C. men, began the return journey. Before reaching Le Rutoire it was considered necessary, as a further precaution, to requisition an armed escort from a working-party returning from the line. On his arrival at Le Rutoire no one knew the whereabouts of Brigade H.Q., and he was able to demonstrate his efficiency as a spy by disclosing it. Once there, everything was cleared up.

OCTOBER 1915

Thus ended a most regrettable occurrence, reflecting little credit on those responsible, since it would be difficult to imagine anyone less like a spy than Major Impey. It was, however, suggested that his well-known grasp of the niceties of the English tongue during his unpleasant walk from Lone Tree to Le Rutoire was not understood by the medical staff and led to his undoing.

We did not remain long in peace at Verquin, for during the afternoon of the 8th the enemy made a big counter-attack on the front line, which was driven off with heavy losses by our troops. We were put on an hour's notice that day and the next, but were not called upon to move.

On the 12th we marched to Noyelles, a village about a mile behind Vermelles, where most of the companies were billeted in some farm buildings near the château. The next day saw the Brigade in Divisional Reserve, while the 35th and 37th Brigades, together with the 46th Division, attacked the Quarries at 2 p.m., after two hours' intense bombardment. Unfortunately this attack was only partially successful. Most of the German retaliation fell on or in front of Vermelles, so that the battalion had a quiet time in billets until 7 p.m., when orders were received to occupy the Railway Trenches near Vermelles. This proved to be an impossibility owing to the proximity of the artillery positions, and so a number of ruined houses at Philosophe on the Bethune-Lens Road were taken over as billets for the night. These were in a dreadful state and had been used for all sorts of purposes. The worst experience befell those at Battalion H.Q. During the night they had been puzzled by the damp and slippery state of their billet, but not until daylight did they discover that the rooms on the ground floor were covered with pools of blood, and that the house had evidently been used as a collecting place for dead and wounded.

On the 14th we relieved the 6th Queen's in the front line immediately south of the Hulluch Road. This was a most unpleasant relief, which started at 5 p.m. and did not finish until 3 a.m. next morning owing to the mud and the mass of telephone wires in all the communication trenches.

OCTOBER 1915

Our trenches were about 400 yards from the enemy and there was very little rifle fire, but considerable shelling with field-guns and howitzers. The heavy trench-mortars which fired one afternoon from our support line brought down on us severe retaliation from the German artillery. During this tour much was done to improve the trenches and communications, and also the wire, and we were able to take advantage of the early morning mist. Much work, too, had to be done burying the dead.

We were interested to find that the 2nd Battalion occupied the sector on our right, but there was no time for liaison.

On the evening of the 20th we were relieved by the 7th Royal Scots (15th Division) and moved into the old British front line and assembly trench north of the Hulluch Road, our last tour having cost us in casualties 9 killed and 36 wounded.

Here it becomes necessary to contradict the following inaccurate statement which appears in the *History of the 12th Division**:—

" On the following day† some German bombers captured a post held by the 7th Royal Sussex, but they were promptly counter-attacked by the bombers of D Company, 11th Middlesex, under Lieutenant [J. O.] Leach, who were in support, and driven out in confusion."

Now the facts are these. On the 19th the 9th Essex had repulsed with heavy loss an enemy attack on some posts near the Quarries. But the Essex had suffered severely themselves, and next day we were ordered to relieve their bombers. About 6 p.m. 2nd Lieutenant D. F. Woodford‡ and 16 bombers reported for

---
* *History of the 12th (Eastern) Division in the Great War*, by Major-General Sir Arthur B. Scott and the Rev. P. Middleton Brumwell, p. 24.
† The 20th October.
‡ From whose private diary these details have been taken.

this duty to Lieutenant-Colonel C. G. Lewes, commanding the 9th Essex, and arrangements were made with Captain C. D. Jay for co-operation with two machine-guns in the event of further attack.

The posts were situated in an old German communication trench which ran diagonally across the front and well in advance of the main line. The conditions were chaotic; trenches were blown in and every kind of litter lay about together with a number of unburied dead. The posts were taken over and the bombers were posted, the Essex sentries remaining as well. About 10.15 p.m., without the slightest warning, a shower of bombs began to fall at the end of the trench near a barricade, and, although it was difficult to tell from which direction they came, our bombers at once retaliated, while Captain Jay opened a heavy fire with his machine-guns. For some fifteen minutes a stiff bomb fight ensued, eventually dying down as suddenly as it had begun, without a single German having succeeded in gaining a footing in the trench. Later on the bombers of the 11th Middlesex relieved our men, who handed over the positions exactly as they had found them. The operation cost us 3 killed, including Corporal A. N. De St. Croix, of D Company, and 9 wounded amongst the bombers, as well as 5 casualties in the machine-gun section.

OCTOBER 1915

Should it have been necessary at any time to recapture these posts some other unit must have been responsible for their loss, and it is to be regretted that the facts should have become so distorted.

Having spent the 21st in the old British front line, we moved out of the line next day, marched to Noyelles and embussed there for Fouquereuil, which we reached late at night.

A new form of protection, destined to be the means of saving many lives, was now issued for the first time. These were steel helmets, commonly called " tin hats " or " battle bowlers." Only a very few were available to start with, and these were issued first to the bombers when posted in the saps.

Major-General Scott paid us his first visit when he inspected the battalion on the 23rd. On the following day an unfortunate accident took place at bombing practice, when 2nd Lieutenant D. L. Cox and one man were wounded by splinters while throwing live bombs.

Essex Sap, Hulluch Road, on the 20th October, 1915
(From a photograph taken at the time by Major C. D. Jay)

Loos and After

Major Birkett proceeded to the 36th Brigade for attachment on the 25th, and on the same day we marched to Annequin, where we took over billets in the miners' cottages.

Annequin was a small village a mile north-east of Vermelles, consisting almost entirely of miners' cottages. There was also a big fosse, or slag-heap, known as Fosse 9 de Bethune, with colliery works and buildings, which had the great advantage of possessing some good baths. Considering its proximity to the line, it was a fairly peaceful spot, but a battery of 9.2 howitzers, known as Mother, near the slag-heap, brought it periodical attention and a few of the houses were badly knocked about.

October 1915

We left on the 28th to take over some reserve trenches between Noyelles and Vermelles. They had no trench boards and were in a dreadful state, but as the only alternative was the heavily shelled ruins of Vermelles it was better to take the lesser of two evils.

While in these trenches we lost Private Cain, of D Company, known to his intimate friends as Barney, and also a boxer of some repute, who was wounded when he lit a Mills bomb detonator in mistake for a cigarette. It should be mentioned that Mills bombs had only just been issued, and up to that time it had not been possible to train everyone in their use.

Winter was now beginning; the weather had become very wet and we were getting our first real experience of French mud. On the afternoon of the 29th Noyelles came in for a brief but sharp spell of shelling, most of which fell near the cross-roads at the south end of the village. Unfortunately, Battalion H.Q. and the Transport were situated close by, the latter being in a field alongside the road to Mazingarbe, with the result that Lieutenant Clarke and Captain Woodhams, together with 4 privates, were wounded by shrapnel. The former had to go home for about three months, which, with the exception of normal leaves, was his only period of absence from the battalion throughout the war. One horse and two mules were also wounded and the Transport had to be moved temporarily. Lieutenant Hind now took over the duties of Quartermaster in addition to those of Transport Officer.

Orders had been received from the Corps for an attack on Little Willie and Cross Trench, in the Hohenzollern Redoubt, to be undertaken by three of our companies, assisted by the 11th Middlesex, and practice assaults were accordingly carried out for the next two days in a section of trenches especially dug to represent these objectives.

Loos and After

During the afternoon of the 1st November we relieved the 6th Buffs in the Hohenzollern trenches, Battalion H.Q. being near the junction of the Annequin-Vermelles mine railway. The weather was very wet and the trenches were deep in mud. Working-parties for the front line were found for the next three days and an R.E. dump near Battalion H.Q. came in for frequent attention from the German artillery owing to the continual movement about it. This movement was eventually stopped by the Commanding Officer, but not before we had sustained several casualties.

On the 5th November we relieved the 11th Middlesex in the front line, the Germans keeping up the ancient tradition of that date by heavily shelling all the communication trenches during the relief, and we were lucky to escape with 1 killed and 1 wounded. Battalion H.Q. in the Quarry came in for special attention, in the course of which a member of a certain Highland battalion, to escape the shelling, jumped from a trench above right on the top of the Commanding Officer, who was standing outside the H.Q. dug-out. No doubt he felt afterwards that the fire of the enemy would have been preferable to the frying-pan of the Colonel's indignation.

November 1915

For the first time we now occupied part of the famous Hohenzollern Redoubt, that extensive German strong-point which protected the Dump, or Fosse 8. The Redoubt consisted of three faces, the north and south face being called Big and Little Willie respectively, while, owing to the middle or west face remaining in our possession, another trench known as the Chord had been dug by the enemy; our patrols found the Chord only lightly held, the main positions being Cross Trench, Big and Little Willie.

It was an unpleasant position in every way. There were dead bodies—both ours and the enemy's—scattered about most of the parapets in the front line. Several of the communication trenches, particularly Cork Street, were also in an appalling state. No Man's Land was piled with corpses (mostly belonging to the 9th, Scottish, Division) which had been lying there since the attack on the 25th September.

The distribution of the companies was as follows:—C Company in the front line in Sticky and Mud Trenches, D Company in support in Northampton Trench, and A and B Companies in reserve in the old British line just above the Quarry. Mining operations had not yet begun, but it was on the old British line

Loos and After

and Battalion H.Q. in the Quarry that the enemy chiefly concentrated his shelling, A Company having an especially bad time, with intense shelling almost every day.

Sergeant-Major Hanlon gives the following personal account of the situation at this time :—

"The trenches were in an awful state, and what with mud and rain I remember it took the platoon commanders and sergeants the whole afternoon to get to the front line in order to make the preliminary reconnaissance for the proposed attack. It was cancelled owing to the weather, and we had to remain in the line for the best part of three weeks, and many men got trench feet. My platoon (Number 13) was reduced from 52 to 17. The distance between our lines and the enemy's was about forty yards, and 2nd Lieutenant F. H. Bickerton suggested that we should try to bury some of the corpses which were lying in No Man's Land. We managed to do this by scraping holes and rolling the bodies into them, after removing the identity discs. Some weeks later we were called upon to explain why we had not brought the bodies down for burial in the cemetery, and were also asked to give exact map reference for each grave."

NOVEMBER 1915

The weather had now finally broken and was wet and cold throughout the whole tour. The trenches were partly new and partly old ones. The new trenches, Guildford, Northampton, Sticky and Mud, had been completed only about a week before we took over, and not being properly constructed were frequently falling in and having to be cleared. We felt the absence of duck-boards severely, and from the 28th October to the 12th November the battalion lived in mud and water and for the most part without dug-outs, with the result that, in spite of the daily use of whale-oil, anti-frostbite grease and massage of the feet, the sick rate was a heavy one. Altogether about 200 sick were evacuated for trench feet and rheumatism. Gum-boots were provided for the troops in the most exposed positions, and they were also relieved every 48 hours; nevertheless, many had to go sick. In fact, trench feet was still a new ailment, and any organisation such as the adequate provision of dry socks and hot soup had not yet been developed to combat it, although a part of the trench was reserved for men to go to two at a time, at least once a day, and rub each other's feet with grease. It was neatly labelled, "This bay is reserved for the greasing and rubbing of feet." Then some wag posted a notice in the next fire-bay, "This bay is reserved for wailing and gnashing of teeth."

Loos and After

It was doubtless for these reasons that the proposed attack on Little Willie and the Chord was definitely cancelled, to our very great relief.

The increased rate of sickness from trench feet was now beginning to trouble our superiors, for on the 10th we received a visit from Lieutenant-General H. de la P. Gough, the G.O.C. I Corps, who made a thorough inspection of all the trenches in order to acquaint himself with the conditions, and on the 12th we were relieved by the 8th Royal Fusiliers and proceeded to Sailly Labourse, another village about two miles behind Vermelles on the main Bethune-Lens Road, where we remained for three days.

NOVEMBER 1915

In addition to the large number of sick, our casualties for the last tour amounted to 3 killed and 18 wounded, bringing our total casualty list for the Battle of Loos and its aftermath up to 108—3 officers wounded ; 20 other ranks killed and 85 wounded, of whom 10 died. Previous to the relief we made the acquaintance of our new Brigade Commander, Lieutenant-Colonel L. B. Boyd-Moss, of the South Staffordshire Regiment.

On the 16th the Brigade marched to Bethune (the railhead of the district) and all its battalions were billeted in the Orphanage in Rue Michelet. This was our first experience of Bethune. It was a country town much the same size as Armentières, but, being farther from the line, it had up to that time escaped any severe damage. There were those who maintained that there was a sort of tacit understanding that if we did not shell La Bassée the enemy would not shell Bethune, but, if it did exist, it was rudely broken later on.

In the town there were plenty of good shops, hotels, restaurants and cafés. Many will remember the Globe Restaurant in the *Grande Place*, famous for its champagne cocktails at five francs a glass, and no description of Bethune is complete without mentioning the boot shop and the " Red Lamp." There was also a good theatre, where our excellent Divisional Theatrical Troupe, later known as " The Spades," staged many good shows, including a pantomime, " Aladdin."

Drill and cleaning up started at once, but there were strong rumours that a real rest and refit were in store for us. This materialised when, on the 18th, the Brigade marched to the St.

Loos and After

Hilaire district, four miles on the farther side of Lillers. The battalion was billeted in St. Hilaire itself, a quiet little village on the main road to Aire and about thirteen miles from Bethune, far removed from the sounds or signs of war.

We took over billets from the Indian Corps and were for the most part quite comfortable in houses and farms, so that our stay there from the 18th November to the 2nd December was the nearest approach to rest we had yet had. There was, however, plenty of work to be done and, after a thorough clean up, we turned seriously to training.

NOVEMBER 1915

As a further protection from the cold the troops were issued with leather jerkins, waterproof capes, mitts and vests. The jerkins were mostly made of dogskin of all varieties, with the result that each company had a bobbery pack consisting of fox-terriers, collies, retrievers, and even airedales.

Our stay at St. Hilaire did the battalion a great deal of good. Besides the training we had found time for all kinds of recreation, football especially being in great favour. Health improved and the men's spirits were high. Then on the 3rd December we received orders to move once more.

CHAPTER IV

FESTUBERT AND GIVENCHY

3RD DECEMBER, 1915—10TH FEBRUARY, 1916
[Sketch Maps, Nos. 2 and 3]

On the 3rd December we marched again in the direction of the line and in the afternoon reached Hingette, a hamlet on the outskirts of Hinges, a mile and a half from Bethune. During this period the Corps organised a spy-hunt in Bethune and allotted a definite area to each battalion to clear up; we found ourselves in some very queer parts of the town.

DECEMBER 1915

On the 8th Colonel Osborn went on leave to England, and as Major Birkett was employed at the Divisional School Major Impey temporarily took command. On the 10th we relieved the 19th Royal Fusiliers (33rd Division) in the village line near Festubert, between Rue du Bois and Le Plantin. The next evening we relieved the 21st Royal Fusiliers of the same division in the front line.

Festubert was a small village on Rue de l'Epinette, the road connecting Rue du Bois with the Bethune-La Bassée Road. It had been in ruins ever since the severe fighting in the autumn of 1914. The conditions in this sector were unusually trying. The front line was a mile east of the village, and the country, consisting principally of water-meadows, was entirely water-logged. All the trenches were filled with water and quite untenable, and the front line was composed only of an intermittent sandbag parapet, standing above the surrounding mud and water and held wherever possible by a series of posts on small islands suitably known as " grouse butts," the garrisons varying from six to twenty-four according to the amount of space available.

These posts, numbered 1 to 16, were relieved every forty-eight hours, and all reliefs had to take place by night along certain defined tracks, for it was impossible to reach the islands by daylight owing to all the old communication trenches being full of water. One man was discovered in the darkness close to the so-called front line just after a relief, having slipped off the track

3. FESTUBERT AND GIVENCHY, 1915

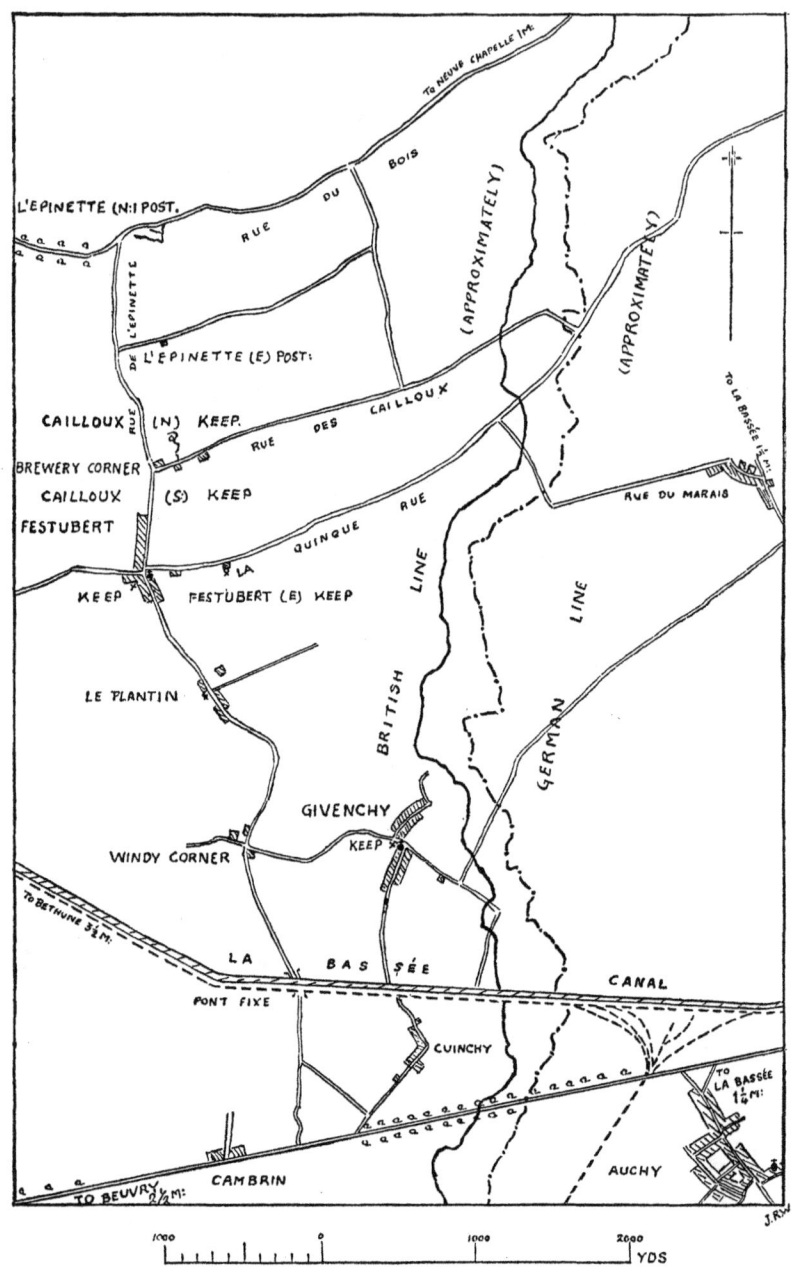

and having abandoned his gum-boots and trousers in the mud in his efforts to extricate himself. Cold and half-naked, he was warmed by some rum, and as he made his way to the Transport for an issue of trousers he was a strange apparition in the flickering glare of a Verey light.

It was impossible to support the front line, and the main line of defence was the old British line, 800 yards in rear, with several derelict British and German lines in between. The Germans, although on slightly higher ground, were in much the same plight as we were, so that beyond sniping there was not much other activity. It was a case of live and let live.

DECEMBER 1915

At first A and B Companies garrisoned the islands with two platoons each, their other two platoons being billeted in the ruins of Festubert, while C and D Companies were with Battalion H.Q. in the old British line. The Royal Fusiliers had told some of our men that there was any amount of rum buried under the water, and great was the disgust when salvage operations produced nothing more stimulating than thirteen S.R.D. jars containing lime juice.

On the 13th the battalion sustained a severe loss when Captain L. F. Cass, commanding A Company, was shot by a sniper, thus suffering the same fate as his old friend and predecessor in the company, Captain Bussell. Lieutenant R. T. May took over the Company.

The next day passed quietly, and on the 15th we were relieved by the 8th Royal Fusiliers and went into the village line again, where the battalion was distributed as follows :—C Company in Festubert Central and East Keeps, B Company in various keeps on Tuning Fork Road leading to Gorre, A and D Companies and Battalion H.Q. in Rue de l'Epinette, a post being found by one of the companies in Rue des Cailloux, where there was a somewhat unhealthy spot called Brewery Corner which came in for periodical shelling. The Transport was at Le Touret, about two miles away.

This period was quiet on the whole, but the accommodation was none too good, consisting as it did of ruined or dilapidated houses. C Company had the worst time, since the enemy shelled Festubert nearly every day, the chief targets being the divisional gum-boot store and soup kitchen. These were both excellent institutions and much appreciated, but for some reason they were always established at cross-roads (as in Festubert) or in some other conspicuous position. B Company's officers had quite a homely H.Q. in a ruined house along Tuning Fork Road. They shared it with a large rat, which had become very tame. He was christened Herbert, and the house was called Herbert Villa in his honour.

Numerous fatigue parties for the Royal Engineers and work on keeps occupied our time during this tour, until the 6th Royal West Kents relieved us on the 19th and we returned to Hingette.

DECEMBER 1915

The next day a large carrying-party of 18 officers and 720 other ranks had to be found to take gas-cylinders up to the Givenchy line for the 35th Brigade. The Commanding Officer returned on the 21st, but owing to the temporary absence of the Brigadier he took over command of the Brigade.

On the 23rd we relieved the 7th Suffolks in the right sector in front of Givenchy. The trenches were full of mud and water, with gas-cylinders sticking out at all angles, usually in the most narrow parts; some of them were even leaking and it was difficult for the men to squeeze by them in full equipment. We found that the gas-cylinders had been loosed off the previous day, and the inevitable retaliation made things very lively; we were heavily shelled throughout the relief, but fortunately with few casualties.

Givenchy was another small village on the banks of La Bassée Canal, in front of Rue de l'Epinette. It was almost a mile south-east of Festubert and had also suffered severely in 1914. The famous keep situated about the ruins of the church, which had saved the day then, was still in existence. Our front was held from the Sap H, south of Rifleman's Crater, to just south of the Duck's Bill by C, B and D Companies, A Company being in support in Gunners' Siding and Mairie Redoubt, while Battalion H.Q. was in a house on Rue de l'Epinette about 1,000 yards back. There were many other houses near by in a tolerable state of repair and we used some of them for the company cookers, so that it was possible to send the men's food already cooked up to the front line, thus ensuring a regular service of hot meals, a great advantage at that time of year. A trench tramway ran from Rue de l'Epinette up to Givenchy Church and was very convenient for transporting dixies and other heavy stores, but it was regularly shelled at fixed times, especially at its terminus in Givenchy. After we had suffered several casualties meal and dump times were altered, with good results.

One unusual feature of this sector was that we had the advantage in observation, for the village was situated on a slight rise overlooking the enemy. The front line had been badly cut up by the recent shelling and by mining operations, while bad weather had churned everything into liquid mud, which in places was waist deep.

At 7.15 a.m. on the 24th the enemy exploded a mine opposite G and H Saps, blowing in the ends of both of them and burying most of the bombers there. A heavy barrage put down at the same time caused us many casualties, 16 Platoon being the chief sufferers. Our artillery also put down a barrage, but in the afternoon the enemy occupied the newly-formed crater and could not be attacked overland owing to the depth of the mud, while the number and proximity of the craters made it impossible to use either trench-mortars or machine-guns against him. Finally, however, the enemy's position was rendered untenable by bombs and rifle-grenades.

DECEMBER 1915

Sergeant C. W. Butcher, of D Company, contributes the following notes, which elaborate the record of this operation :—

" About 7 a.m. on the 24th December the Germans blew a mine under my company front, causing us heavy losses in killed and wounded. I was in charge of the bomb saps and immediately after the explosion found that the Germans were trying to occupy them. Captain Woodhams, who was commanding B Company on our right, the D Company bombers and myself drove them back after heavy bomb-fighting and rifle-grenading, and eventually they evacuated the new crater. During this stunt I consider I had the narrowest escape during the whole of my time at the front. Captain Woodhams asked me to look out for the effect of his bombing, and as I peered over the sap-head I saw a German about 80 yards away in the mine crater at the kneeling position. He fired the instant he saw my head, but luckily I ducked the instant I saw him and the bullet ripped the sandbag over my head, so I shall always remember Christmas, 1915."

Sergeant-Major Hanlon also contributes a reminiscence of the " Lilliputians," a section of men in 13 Platoon, small in stature, but great in heart :—

" The Lilliputians had a bad time that day, for although hot food was available in the village, few managed to get any. However, they did manage to produce some tea by the aid of four candles and little pieces of wood. I can see them even now, Corporal W. Baker, Lance-Corporal E. Stoner and Private

T. Scutt, huddled up in a small shelter, with an old sheet to keep the light from showing. I doubt if the dixie ever boiled, but I have never tasted better tea since."

There was a great deal of shelling by both sides during the night of the 24th and also on Christmas morning, when we were relieved by the 8th Royal Fusiliers, our casualties having been 3 killed and 23 wounded.

On going back we took over the keeps, being distributed as follows :—B Company, Givenchy Keep ; A Company, Le Plantin Keep ; D Company billets, Windy Corner. C Company was near Battalion H.Q. and was used for bomb carrying parties.

The Germans seemed quite determined that our first Christmas in the trenches should be a merry one. Shelling continued most of the day, being especially heavy on all roads leading to the line, consequently the Transport had a lively time.

DECEMBER 1915 Rue de l'Epinette, in the neighbourhood of Battalion H.Q., was also an unhealthy spot, since the enemy made continual, but unsuccessful, attempts to destroy the brewery with its tall chimney on the banks of La Bassée Canal, just near Pont Fixe. At the other end of the street was Windy Corner, another spot where loitering was inadvisable. Here (almost needlessly to say) the soup kitchen and gum-boot store were situated.

We returned to the line on the 27th, taking over from the 8th Royal Fusiliers ; this time A, B and C Companies were in the front line and D Company in Gunners' Siding.

The next day Colonel Osborn resumed command of the battalion. There was less shelling, but a great deal of rifle-grenading, during which a disastrous accident occurred, Company Quartermaster-Sergeant H. L. Faircloth being killed and several men severely wounded by the accidental explosion of one of our own rifle-grenades, owing to the safety pin being inadvertently removed before the grenade had been inserted in the rifle. Faircloth was one of the N.C.O.s originally sent from the 2nd Battalion, and his death was much regretted.

The next day, prior to our relief by the 8th Royal Fusiliers, the Germans exploded a second mine, close to the previous one. Sap H was again damaged and four of our bombers were buried, but enough of the sap remained to prevent the enemy occupying the crater ; the buried bombers were extricated and, under

Festubert and Givenchy

Lance-Corporal J. Austin, of A Company, did fine work in keeping back the enemy.

The total casualties during this tour were 3 killed and 14 wounded. Once again special mention must be made of the work done by the Transport. The approaches, especially Rue de l'Epinette, Brewery and Windy Corners, and the tracks leading to them, came in for frequent shelling at dumping times, but, as usual, our rations never failed to arrive in the front line. The tour had proved a trying one; it was our first experience of serious mine fighting, and the lessons learnt were to stand us in good stead during the coming Battle of the Craters.

DECEMBER 1915

The battalion now went into Brigade Reserve at Le Quesnoy, whence a large fatigue party, consisting of the whole battalion, was found on the night of the 30th to remove the gas-cylinders from our old sector.

On the 31st December we were relieved by the 6th Royal West Kents and returned to Hingette for four days before taking over from the 7th Suffolks on the 4th January in our old position in front of Festubert. This time C and D Companies found the island parties, while A and B remained with Battalion H.Q. in the old British line.

JANUARY 1916

On the 8th we changed places with the 8th Royal Fusiliers in the village line, and the battalion was distributed as follows:—Battalion H.Q. in Rue de l'Epinette with half A and B Companies, the other half occupying Epinette West Keep and Rue des Cailloux Keep respectively, D Company in Festubert Central and East Keeps, and C Company in billets about Le Plantin. The 6th Royal West Kents relieved us on the 13th, and the battalion took over billets in the tobacco factory at Bethune, where we spent the next two days on heavy fatigues for the Royal Engineers. Our casualties in the Festubert and Givenchy area had amounted to 55 (1 officer killed, 8 other ranks killed, and 46 wounded, of whom 2 died).

Before we left these parts a mishap befell two members of the Transport which might have had more serious consequences. The quickest way into Bethune from Hingette was by a path on the banks of La Bassée Canal, along which one night two of the Transport, brothers and Sussex men, were wending their way back from Bethune after a cheery evening. Finding the surface of the path was rough and not realising in the darkness that they were on the banks of the canal, one brother remarked to the other, "Let's walk on the *road*, Herb, it will be softer for our feet." Accordingly they stepped together on to the faintly gleaming surface of what they imagined was a tarred roadway, only to find themselves a second later struggling in the waters of the canal. Fortunately they could swim and were lucky to get off with merely a good wetting.

JANUARY 1916

On the morning of the 16th the battalion entrained, and on reaching Lillers marched to Ham-en-Artois for a long rest. Ham was a small village quite close to our previous billets at St. Hilaire, and the accommodation was very good. We spent the first three days practising ceremonial drill for a brigade inspection by General Joffre. This inspection took place on the 20th in a field near Lillers, and for the first time we were all able to see the famous French Commander-in-Chief. He was dressed in black patrol jacket, red riding-breeches and dark-blue képi, and looked magnificent. He carefully inspected all ranks, accompanied by our new Commander-in-Chief, General Sir Douglas Haig, and numerous officers of the French and English Staffs.

The time up to the 29th was spent in battalion and brigade training, varied by periods of company training, in which special attention was given to rapid firing and firing in smoke helmets. This work was varied by sport and games of all descriptions, and there was an inter-regimental football tournament, which created a lot of interest and was won by the 9th Royal Fusiliers. We also had many pleasant contacts with the 2nd Battalion, which was at Lillers, where we had an exciting football match on the afternoon of the 22nd, the 2nd Battalion winning by 3 goals to 1.

These days of unaccustomed ease were broken on the 26th, when the whole Division was placed under two hours' notice to march. This order remained hanging over us for three days. It was apparently due to the German artillery celebrating the birthday of the Kaiser by continuous and heavy shelling of the Loos salient, but nothing further came of it. It was about this time that our Quartermaster, Lieutenant Clarke, returned to the battalion, completely recovered from his wounds.

On the 30th the battalion marched with the rest of the Brigade for divisional manoeuvres in the neighbourhood of Rely and Estrée Blanche, billeting for the night at Blessy, and returning to Ham the following day. Orders previously issued for a move to

Bethune were now cancelled; the battalion remained at Ham until the 5th February, when our Brigade exchanged billets with the 37th Brigade, and we proceeded to L'Ecleme.

Before we left Ham the 36th Brigade Machine Gun Company was organised under the command of Captain A. G. Astley, 8th Royal Fusiliers, and 2nd Lieutenants F. H. Bickerton and T. A. Hill, both of D Company, together with 33 N.C.O.s and men, were transferred to that unit of the newly-formed Machine Gun Corps. The 36th Company (which in March, 1918, became B Company of the 12th Battalion the M.G.C.) did excellent work in close liaison with us during the remainder of the war.

FEBRUARY 1916

Shortly before this we had been very sorry to have to say goodbye to Captain C. D. Jay, our Machine-gun Officer, who left us to become Brigade M.G.O. in another division.

In place of our 4 machine-guns we received 8 Lewis guns, and men had been specially trained in their use before the change was effected. They were originally organised as a battalion unit under a Lewis Gun Officer, 2nd Lieutenant E. A. Montesole being the first to act in that capacity. It cannot be said that we welcomed the change at first, for the Lewis gun seemed very fragile after the Vickers and most difficult to keep in action when conditions were muddy—as they generally were during the fighting in 1916. However, the gun itself and our management of it were improved gradually.*

Another new unit came into being about this time and we had to part with more men for the ranks of the 36th Light Trench Mortar Battery, commanded by Captain E. M. Barlow, 8th Royal Fusiliers.† Before the formation of these batteries trench-mortars had not been popular with the front line troops, who had little chance of co-operating with the trench-mortar personnel. The infantryman's unfortunate impression was of the sudden invasion of his otherwise peaceful trench by a band of strangers, who fired off a weapon of doubtful offensive value from a most inadequately concealed position, and then left him to bear the unpleasant retaliation. The new battery, armed with the most efficient Light Stokes Mortar and manned by properly trained teams

---

* The number of guns was doubled before the Somme battle in July, 1916, and early in 1917 they were distributed so that each platoon had its own Lewis gun section. In March, 1918, we received 20 more guns, of which 4 were for anti-aircraft use at Battalion H.Q. or with the Transport, so that for the rest of the war there were 2 guns with each platoon.

† Captain S. Neale, 11th Middlesex, took over the battery early in 1917 and commanded it until the end of the war.

drawn from the ranks of our own Brigade, soon won a well-deserved popularity and was of the greatest assistance to us both in attack and defence.

On the afternoon of the 8th Major-General Scott, at a special parade of the whole battalion, presented the ribbon of the Distinguished Conduct Medal to Sergeant J. King, of A Company, for his magnificent work on patrol. No honour could have been more thoroughly earned.

FEBRUARY 1916

We had been nearly a month out of the line, so that it was no surprise when, on the 10th February, the Commanding Officer and company commanders received orders to inspect our old Hohenzollern Redoubt trenches. Early next day we started for Sailly Labourse, bound for what was to prove the severest ordeal the battalion had yet endured.

4. HOHENZOLLERN AND QUARRIES SECTORS, 1916

CHAPTER V

THE HOHENZOLLERN CRATERS

11TH FEBRUARY—27TH APRIL, 1916
[Sketch Maps, Nos. 2 and 4]

We reached our billets at Sailly Labourse in the afternoon of the 11th February, and the final preparations for the relief of the morrow were put in hand. Continuous rain throughout the day made the prospect of another tour of the Hohenzollern Redoubt none too alluring. FEBRUARY 1916 An early start was made next day, and the relief of the right sector of the Hohenzollern trenches was complete by 9.45 a.m. The unit we relieved, a composite battalion mainly composed of the 15th Hussars under Colonel F. C. Pilkington, D.S.O., and forming part of the Dismounted Cavalry Division, which had been created from all the units of the Cavalry Corps, gave us a bad account of the sector owing to hostile mining operations. This we soon found to be only too true, and we were now in for a trying period of mine fighting which, owing to the Germans having got about six weeks' start, had given our predecessors a bad time.

Mining had become a science. Its main object was to blow up the enemy and his trenches and to protect commanding ground, while preventing him from doing the same. Secrecy was the essence of the work. A series of shafts had already been sunk from our lines, and galleries were already being driven forward towards the enemy with all possible speed by the 170th Tunnelling Company, Royal Engineers, which did magnificent work for us during the ten weeks of our occupation of this sector. This was very anxious and jumpy work for the tunnelling companies, and the greatest care had to be taken to avoid any noise when approaching the enemy's galleries. When, as often happened, only a thin partition separated them, it became a race as to which side could blow the sooner. The strain on the tunnellers must have been terrible, and it was unnerving for the troops in the front trenches to realise that they were possibly standing on the top of a volcano which might explode under them at any moment of the day or night. As one man put it light-heartedly to his pal, "A transfer to the R.F.C. is possible any time."

Anyone in the listening shaft could hear the dull "tap, tap, tap," followed by a pause (while the soil was removed), then "tap, tap, tap," again. The only consolation about this sinister sound was that while the enemy was still working there was no immediate prospect of being blown up. As soon as the tapping ceased we knew that danger was imminent; the alarm would be given and sentries would be withdrawn from the sap-heads. A few moments later one would hear and feel the awful explosion, which shook everything throughout a large area and caused the dug-out frames, even as far back as the reserve line, to sway as if in an earthquake. Then would follow a period of intense and bitter hand-to-hand fighting, during which both sides endeavoured to seize the crater that had been formed.

FEBRUARY 1916

Another important factor was the disposal of the soil excavated from the workings. Since it was chalk and easy to see, it had to be removed altogether and placed somewhere out of the enemy's view; and as all this work of removal had to be done by hand it entailed large and continual carrying-fatigues.

During this time the use of the rifle as a long-range weapon was almost forgotten. All the fighting was done with bombs, rifle-grenades and trench-mortars, the last a far heavier species than our old friends the "sausages" of Houplines. We would crouch in our trenches watching them coming over and wondering how close they would fall, and although they could be seen in the air quite easily the way they seemed to follow one about was uncanny.

Compared with the previous November, we found a great difference in the trenches. The front line was no longer continuous between Guildford Trench and Sap 9, but consisted almost entirely of positions on the lips of the various new craters, which were reached by means of saps. In one way, however, there was a marked improvement, since all trenches had been drained and boarded. Battalion H.Q. was situated in a very shallow excavation alongside the Vermelles-Violaines mines railway, just in front of Brigade H.Q. The roof of this shelter consisted only of corrugated iron and one layer of sandbags. One morning General Sir Hubert Gough, the I Corps Commander, accompanied by a Staff Officer, arrived without warning, and, not knowing where the entrance was, proceeded to walk over the roof in search of it. He then noticed Private F. H. Souch, the

The Hohenzollern Craters

Adjutant's servant,* who was cooking breakfast on a stove down below, and (not realising he was standing on the roof) asked, "How do I get into this dug-out, my man?" Souch, not recognising him, replied, "Through the bloody roof, sir, if you don't look out." The Colonel then appeared and, not recognising the G.O.C. either, made some similar observation. However, the General took it all in very good part and seemed much amused.

FEBRUARY 1916

Except for a few trench-mortars our first day in the sector was quiet. At 5.30 p.m. on the 13th the enemy opened an intense bombardment with howitzers, field-guns and trench-mortars on the 11th Middlesex on our right. The right platoon of A Company on that flank also suffered. Our artillery at once retaliated, and half-an-hour later the Germans blew a small mine in front of one of our saps, but the activity of our bombers prevented the enemy from attempting to occupy the crater.

Sergeant-Major Hanlon recollects an unfortunate sniping incident which took place during this tour:—

"Sergeant A. E. Webb and Private W. Pratt were trying to get a sniper who was pulling their legs by waving a large black and white flag. Just previously, Pratt's name had been submitted for work on roads some way back as a steam-roller driver, which was his job in civil life. I happened to be near them, and suddenly I heard a shot with the usual smack which tells you that it has got someone, and sure enough poor Pratt had got it through the head."

This German sniper was a particularly clever one and had claimed a large number of victims, to which he nearly added Lieutenant-Colonel A. C. Annesley, the Commanding Officer of the 8th Royal Fusiliers, who had his cap shot off. It is believed the man was eventually blown up on the first day of the Battle of the Craters.

On the 16th we were relieved by the 8th Royal Fusiliers and went into the reserve trenches. On the 20th Colonel Osborn went on leave and Major Impey took over command, and next day, after being relieved by the 6th Royal West Kents, the battalion moved to Fouquereuil, leaving behind garrisons for the keeps at Vermelles, Noyelles and Sailly Labourse. These were relieved

---

* A great battalion character who was afterwards killed by a stray shell near Monchy le Preux in August, 1917.

The Hohenzollern Craters

on the 25th. The weather had again become bad, with continuous snow and sleet, which made a relief all the more welcome.

On the 27th Major Birkett, who was still on duty at the Divisional School, was ordered to proceed to England to take command of the 2/17th Battalion of the London Regiment. We wished him much luck, but parted from him with many regrets.

FEBRUARY 1916

On the 28th we moved to Annequin. The weather now showed signs of improvement, and after spending one night at Annequin we relieved the 6th Royal West Kents in the left sector of the Hohenzollern trenches opposite Little Willie, in preparation for the coming battle.

The events which led up to the Battle of the Craters were these. Since it was impossible to locate the German mine system with any certainty, it was necessary to hold the front line by posts in order to minimise casualties. The Germans had already blown four large craters in No Man's Land, known as Craters 1 to 4, and had occupied the near lips of them; owing to the western face of the Hohenzollern Redoubt passing into our possession after the Battle of Loos they had dug a trench called the Chord, which became their front line; and since our line was slightly below it, they thus obtained the advantage in observation. To counteract this advantage three large mines* had been completed under the shallow German mining system by the 170th Tunnelling Company, Royal Engineers, after four months' work; and the authorities recognised that unless these mines were fired soon it would only be a matter of time before they were discovered. The plan was to explode them simultaneously, and immediately after the explosions the 8th and 9th Royal Fusiliers were to occupy the Chord, together with all the craters it was intended to hold. Once we had obtained command of the enemy's trenches in this way we could counteract the advantages he had in observation from Fosse 8; at the same time it was hoped to destroy the main galleries of his mining system.

The night of the 1st-2nd March was spent in the unpleasant task of clearing all the wire from in front of our lines, and in the morning we were relieved by the 8th Royal Fusiliers and distributed as follows:—B and C Companies in Reserve Trench, and one platoon in Central Keep; D Company in Railway Reserve Trench; A Company in Lancashire Trench, with one platoon in Junction Keep.

---

* One mine contained over 10,000lbs. of explosive and the other two 7,000lbs. each. They were larger than any blown by the British until the Battle of the Somme in July, 1916.

The Hohenzollern Craters

Major Impey commanded the battalion, with Lieutenant Wilton acting as Adjutant, until Colonel Osborn and Captain Betham returned from leave on the morning of the 3rd. The usual commanders of A, B and C Companies (Captains R. T. May, G. Woodhams and H. S. Bowlby) were away for various reasons, and their companies were temporarily commanded by 2nd Lieutenant G. Nagle, Lieutenant R. J. Richardson and Lieutenant G. L. Reckitt respectively. D Company was led by Captain G. F. Osborne, who had returned to us during the previous month.

MARCH 1916

At 5.45 p.m. the action began with the explosion of the mines and a heavy barrage, to which the enemy soon replied. The details of the attack made by the 8th and 9th Royal Fusiliers are to be found well described in the *History of the 12th Division*.* It is enough to say here that the old German craters and those newly-created by the mines (known as A, B and C) were carried, occupied and held, with great gallantry, though not without severe loss,† and their possession gave us the desired advantage in observation of the enemy position as far as Fosse 8. How much the enemy resented this advance was clear from his determined efforts to dislodge us subsequently. As regards the part played by the battalion, D Company was ordered up at 5.45 p.m. to hold Mud Trench and placed under orders of the 8th Royal Fusiliers; all the other companies, with the exception of three platoons of A (left in Lancashire Trench), were employed in bomb-carrying and other fatigues throughout the whole night. We were lucky to get off with only one casualty.

At 2.30 a.m. next morning (the 3rd) B and C Companies of the 6th Connaught Rangers (16th Division) were ordered up as reinforcements from Annequin and occupied Reserve Trench, while at 7 a.m. we received orders to relieve the 8th Royal Fusiliers in the front line; the 11th Middlesex were to relieve the 9th Royal Fusiliers. The Commanding Officer and the company commanders proceeded to reconnoitre the new positions, and the same morning Colonel Osborn returned. The relief was complete by 4.30 p.m., the battalion being distributed as follows:—
A Company, Craters 3, 4, B and C; B Company, West Face and Northampton Trench; C and D Companies, two platoons each in Mud and Sticky Trenches, and two platoons each in Northampton

---

* *Op. cit.*, pp. 35-7.
† The 8th Royal Fusiliers lost 7 officers and 247 other ranks; the 9th Royal Fusiliers lost 5 officers and 155 other ranks.

The Hohenzollern Craters

Trench. B and C Companies of the Connaught Rangers were in Mud Trench, with one platoon in Northampton Trench.

Immediately after the relief the enemy opened an intense bombardment with large trench-mortars, howitzers and field-guns on all the craters, West Face and Northampton Trench. Our artillery at once retaliated, an especially heavy barrage being put down on Cross Trench. Towards 7 p.m. there was a great deal of bomb-fighting, in which we held the advantage. At 10.15 p.m. the bombardment ceased, but intermittent shelling continued throughout the night.

MARCH 1916

At 6 a.m. next morning the enemy again opened a violent bombardment, and at 6.45 a.m. bombing-parties tried to debouch from Little Willie and the Chord, but were stopped with heavy losses by fire from Sticky Trench and from Crater 4. After repeatedly unsuccessful attempts to drive us out the enemy abandoned the attack soon after 9 a.m., leaving us in possession of all the positions we had taken over.

During the morning's fighting reinforcements were sent up to the craters from C and D Companies, and bomb-carrying parties from the three rear companies were continually bringing up fresh supplies to A Company. The snow which fell during the morning added considerably to the mud and the general discomfort.

After this action Colonel Osborn was awarded the Distinguished Service Order for " his conspicuous ability in the performance of his duties. The excellent training of his Battalion, and the careful attention paid to all details of organisation of defence, ensured that the captured position he took over on relief was securely held, in spite of constant counter-attacks. He showed great initiative in launching counter-attacks."*

This is but a succinct account of the heaviest fighting the battalion had yet seen. It is for Colonel Impey, who was Second-in-Command at the time, to elaborate it with the following personal description of the battle :—

" The Germans were most anxious to gain positions of observation corresponding to those destroyed by the mines, and they made tremendous efforts to do so. On the afternoon of the 3rd March, almost directly the relief was over, they opened a very heavy bombardment with artillery and trench-mortars, and later

---

* *London Gazette*, 14th April, 1916.

on, under its cover, tried to bomb our front posts out of the craters, when some bitter fighting took place, rendered all the more difficult by the appalling state of the ground as the result of wet weather, on the top of the destruction caused by the explosion of the mines. Our own gunners supported us splendidly, and the Commanding Officer, quickly spotting that Cross Trench was the only possible assembly-place for the enemy, had a continuous barrage kept on it, a fact which greatly contributed to the enemy's repulse. Eventually, towards 10.20 p.m., the attack petered out. We spent a very anxious night, rendered none the less so by a message which reached us that considerable movement of vehicular traffic and reinforcements had been seen moving towards the line, so we felt that we were for it again in the near future.

MARCH 1916

" The night passed quietly, except for some spasmodic shelling, but at 6 a.m. next morning an intense bombardment opened again, even heavier than on the previous day. Battalion H.Q. was in a small shelter which faced the wrong way, and its only head cover was a single layer of sandbags. It was situated in the old British line, which invariably came in for most of the shelling, and it is a wonder that any of us survived. Perhaps the only reason was that that particular part of the trench ran just on the reverse slope of a slight rise, consequently most shells went skimming over it without landing in the trench. Time after time shells just missed the roof, and the concussion and noise made it impossible to hear anything; reports kept reaching us of attempts by the enemy to debouch from their trenches.

" During the height of the attack I have a vivid recollection of going down to the front line to organise working-parties to keep communication between the craters and Sticky Trench. West Face had become a shambles, but the troops were behaving splendidly, and if it were possible to individualise any, it would be the garrison of the various craters on whom the brunt of the attacks fell.

" I also well remember meeting Wells, one of my own platoon commanders in D Company, just as I was leaving one of the craters. He was returning to his post in it, and his last words to me were ' I'm having the time of my life ! ' Shortly afterwards he was killed. He had done great work that morning, and his death came as a great blow to us.

" The state of the craters was awful; deep mud, little or no cover, and the way the posts stuck it was wonderful. In one crater

The Hohenzollern Craters

I saw the bodies of several Germans, including one very tall officer. Eventually the attack died down about 9.30 a.m., leaving us in full possession of all our positions."

Another personal narrative comes from Sergeant-Major Hanlon :—

"D Company was in Railway Reserve Trench, and we had a good view of the explosion of the mines at 5.45 p.m. Directly afterwards we received orders to occupy the front line. I was acting Company Sergeant-Major and took command of 13 and 14 Platoons, making my way up Quarry Alley, which was being heavily shelled. On reaching the Quarry I decided to go round instead of through it, which was just as well, for three large shells landed inside it as we wended our way along. On reaching the front line we found it badly knocked about and had to get it into ship-shape order again; soon afterwards we were employed helping the Pioneer Battalion, the 5th Northamptons, to dig a communication trench from the front line to the craters.

"Next afternoon (the 3rd March) the battalion relieved the 8th Royal Fusiliers in the craters and front line, and the same evening and early the following morning we were heavily attacked. It was a very tough fight, and I remember Private J. Bird received the Military Medal, but never lived to wear it, as he was killed on the Somme. Lance-Corporal E. Stoner managed to get a bottle of rum up to Crater C by crawling the whole way from the front line."

According to Captain W. S. Till, the most comfortable place during the crater battle was in the old front line.

"The support line was absolutely pulverised by continuous shelling," he writes in a personal reminiscence, "and in the craters themselves things were very hot. My platoon in C Company was in the old front line on the left of the entrance to Russian Sap, which was simply a shallow communication trench that joined the old front line to the left crater (C), and although a great deal of stuff passed over us going in both directions, we ourselves were hardly shelled at all.

"It was our business to keep the enemy in his trenches, bringing fire to bear upon him if he attempted to retake the craters; we were also to supply reinforcements to the craters if they were needed. There was a light fall of snow on the ground, so that any movement in No Man's Land was easily spotted. We saw two small parties of the enemy try to leave their trenches, apparently with the object of retaking the craters, but the field-artillery and our own rifle-fire were on to them at once, scattering them almost as soon as they appeared.

"In the craters on our right the bombing was fairly heavy. It was impossible to tell what was really happening, and all kinds of rumours reached us to the effect that one or other of the craters had been retaken by the enemy. We heard that casualties were heavy and that Montesole* had been killed in the crater on our immediate right. Wells, who was near us, went up, and was killed soon after in the same spot. Foster,† of C Company, then took charge of this crater, and when he was wounded I relieved him, and so was in Crater C during the last twenty-four hours before the battalion was relieved.

MARCH 1916

"As one emerged from Russian Sap one found oneself looking straight down into the crater, which was an inverted cone, 35 feet deep, 130 feet across, and almost exactly circular. We were holding the lip to the left and front, while our right was covered by the adjoining crater, B. The sides of our crater were steep, and near the bottom were the bodies of three Germans who had been blown out of their line when the mine went up. (Only the other day I came across some picture-postcards and a notebook that I took from the pocket of one of these Germans.) German bombs, of the tin-can type with wooden handles, were dropping into the crater at two points, and it was evident that these were being thrown from two bombing-saps.

"With a periscope I could see the enemy in one of these saps, not more than twelve yards from the lip of the crater. The crater was an easy target, and by the nature of things it was difficult to construct a parados. For this reason any enemy bombs that fell into the crater stood a good chance of getting someone in the back; this was how most of our casualties had occurred, but the danger-points were now known, and by avoiding the two spots on which the bombs actually dropped casualties were largely avoided.

"The obvious thing to do was to keep on bombing the two points from which the enemy was throwing his bombs and so prevent him from getting near enough to lob them into the crater; but the end of a sap is not an easy mark to hit, and probably only one in ten of our bombs actually went in, whereas if the other fellow could get near enough he was almost sure of getting all his bombs into the crater; he could hardly miss it.

---

* 2nd Lieutenant E. A. Montesole, Battalion Lewis gun officer.
† 2nd Lieutenant P. G. Foster.

The Hohenzollern Craters

"With this advantage in his favour, the enemy had certainly established superiority of fire, so far as bombs were concerned, and as our stock of bombs was far too small a messenger was sent back for more. Since such messages had a way of failing to get to the right place (communication trenches were being heavily shelled) this one was repeated at intervals until the bombs arrived, which was none too soon, as the enemy was far too uppish and was getting enough bombs into the crater to make it unhealthy.

MARCH 1916

"There was one amusing little scene. One of our men had been down to the bottom of the crater, and as he was scrambling up again a German bomb dropped in front of him and rolled down the side of the crater almost to his feet. In the effort to avoid it he slipped and fell on his knees, almost on top of the bomb. There was no time to waste in getting up again, so he stayed where he was, with his head in the mud and his hinder parts in the air. The bomb was not a yard from his head, and everyone watched and waited. To insure his life at that moment would have meant a heavy premium. At last the bomb exploded and our friend seemed to jump sideways like a cat—he then picked himself up, brushed the mud off his knees, blushed furiously and rejoined his pals, who greeted him with hoots of laughter, in which he joined.

"At last our bombs arrived, and it seemed that all our messages must have got through and been dealt with separately, for when the bombs did come they came in no small numbers. We needed them; not so much because of any fear of attack, since, from what we had seen, our artillery was well able to keep the enemy in his trenches during daylight, but I knew it would be a different story when night came, for unless we wanted heavy casualties we should have to make the enemy's bombing-post unhealthy for him to occupy.

"Meanwhile, a party of three or four Royal Engineers had started to make a dug-out almost at the bottom of the crater—Heaven knows why, because it seemed obvious that it would be submerged after the first heavy rain. With these Royal Engineers was a Scotsman of gigantic size and great strength, who invited us to see what he could do with a Mills bomb. The distance that man could throw was something to marvel at, and there is no doubt that it surprised our friends on the other side. As our problem was really one of long-distance throwing this was exactly what we wanted, and the Scot was delighted to break bomb-throwing records in preference to building dug-outs. Before

The Hohenzollern Craters

nightfall we had definitely made the enemy's saps too hot for him and his bombs practically ceased to arrive—in fact, he was rather unnaturally quiet, and we assumed that a night attack was almost a certainty. We knew it would not be easy to deal with, so we did all we could to discourage it by intermittent rifle-fire and by continuing to bomb the enemy's saps.

"The attack did not come, and we got through the night without casualties. The morning broke in sunshine, and the enemy was so quiet that we had a nasty feeling that he must have withdrawn his men with the idea of shelling us out—it is difficult to understand why he did not do so. One of his planes came over to have a good look at us, and we expected the shells at any moment after that. The prospect of being inside a large tea-cup in which shells were bursting was not exhilarating, but our luck held.

MARCH 1916

"Various people came to visit us that morning. The first arrival appeared round the end of Russian Sap with a cocked revolver held well in front of him—he had heard that we had lost the crater and expected to find the enemy in it! Someone from H.Q. came to tell us that we were to be relieved, and after watching us silently for some time he called to me and said, ' Do you know that you are using 3,000 bombs a day ?' I was not certain whether this was intended as a rebuke or a piece of interesting statistical information. No doubt we had been rather extravagant, but on the other side of the account was the fact that we still held the crater and that our casualties had been small.

"The relief went off quietly and we were out before the shells arrived, although I heard afterwards that the unit which relieved us got it hot and strong."

Our casualties during the operation of the 3rd and 4th March, out of a strength of 18 officers and 625 other ranks, were as follows:—

	Officers	Other ranks
Killed and missing	3	24*
Died of wounds	1	11*
Wounded	5	175*
Totals	9	210*

Officers killed : Lieutenant C. W. Beale (C, attached 36th Trench-mortars); Lieutenant R. G. Wells (D); 2nd Lieutenant E. A. Montesole (Lewis gun officer).

„ died of wounds : 2nd Lieutenant P. G. Foster (C).†

* Approximate. † On the 2nd April, 1916, in England.

The Hohenzollern Craters

Officers wounded : Captain G. F. Osborne (D) ; Lieutenant H. S. Cousens (A) ; Lieutenant J. R. Wilton (H.Q.) ; 2nd Lieutenant S. N. Bourne (A) ; 2nd Lieutenant G. Nagle (A).
N.C.O.s killed : Sergeants J. King, D.C.M. (A) ; R. Brewster (A) ; F. S. Gilham (C).
„ wounded : Sergeants C. Lower (A) ; F. J. Ransom (B) ; Corporals W. Golds (C) ; F. Picton (D) ; T. W. Soames (C).

Mention must be made of the splendid work done by 2nd Lieutenant G. Nagle, Officer Commanding A Company, who, although wounded early in the operations, carried on with great courage, and was largely responsible for repelling the counter-attack on the morning of the 4th. For this gallantry he was awarded the Military Cross and promoted Captain. Sergeant G. Langley, of C Company, performed magnificent work in organising reinforcements and bomb-carrying parties under heavy shell-fire, thus keeping the posts in the craters continually supplied, while Lance-Corporal H. Short (who was wounded) and Private R. Cheesman, also of C, remained at their bombing-posts for twenty-seven hours at a stretch, refusing relief because, owing to casualties, no other reliable bombers were available. All three were awarded the Distinguished Conduct Medal.

MARCH 1916

Many other recommendations for bravery were sent in, but it was not until later in the year that any further awards were announced. In the *London Gazette* of the 14th September, 1916, the names of 14 N.C.O.s and men of the battalion appeared as having been awarded the Military Medal, which had been instituted by Royal Warrant on the 26th March of that year. The names were :—
Sergeants E. R. Bankes (B), A. W. Beale (A), A. J. Evans (A), A. N. Peacock (B), and J. G. Peacock (D) ; Corporal F. Picton (D) ; Lance-Corporals E. Dudman (A), W. Hendry (B), and A. Turton (B) ; Privates J. Bird (D), F. Gratwicke (D), E. Harman (D), H. J. Lawrence (B), and J. Wilson (D).

When these awards were announced only a few of the recipients were still with us ; two had been killed in action at Ovillers on the 7th July—Sergeant Evans and Private Bird. Private "Joe" Wilson, one of D Company's most gallant stretcher-bearers (who all volunteered to stay in the front line and clear the wounded after the battalion was relieved on the 5th March), was put in a strange predicament by this Gazette, for he had already been awarded a Military Medal on the 1st September in recognition of his good work at Ovillers. However, the difficulty was settled in the following January, when a subsequent Gazette transformed the second award into a bar to his medal.

The following free translation from the history of the *III Battalion* of the *18th Infantry Regiment* (*3rd Bavarian Division*), who opposed us in this sector, gives a picture of the situation in the enemy lines during this fight:—

"On the 2nd March, after increased artillery activity, which eventually reached drum-fire, two large earth tremors were felt about 7 p.m.* and two large fountains of earth went up in the air underneath our front trench (the Chord), tearing up and destroying the various sections of trench around; drum-fire extended over the whole position, on which also fell the flying stones and debris vomited out of the mines. For a moment there was a paralysing calm, and then two English companies, with field equipment just recognisable in the last moments of dusk, marched in close formation towards our position, occupied the craters, and tried to enter our front line.

MARCH 1916

"The explosion of the mines came as a complete surprise and had a paralysing effect. The terrible cries of the wounded and buried men could be heard above the din of the fighting, and heavy clouds of smoke and dust blinded the Verey lights.

"It is impossible on these occasions for a commander to help everyone, but some brave men from the front companies at once started organising trench blocks and stopping the attacks by bombs and rifle-fire. Two privates especially distinguished themselves by hurrying forward and stopping the English from penetrating any further into the Chord; they were assisted by another private who, although wounded, was very conspicuous in cheering up the remainder and encouraging them to keep up a stiff resistance. It was entirely owing to the tenacity of these three men from the Palatinate that no further advance was made.

"All communications to Battalion H.Q. went at once, and at 7.30 p.m. the battalion commander went up to the front line. It was not until 9 p.m. that any messages were received from the front line. The situation was considered serious, as it was thought that the English would not be satisfied with only occupying the two craters, but would try to further extend their gains.

---
* The German time varied from the British by about an hour.

The Hohenzollern Craters

"Reinforcements, consisting of the *13th Company* from the *23rd Regiment*, took over shortly after midnight, followed soon after by two other companies of the same regiment. The trenches were very overcrowded as the result of reliefs losing direction, owing to the broken state of the ground. The Officer Commanding the *18th Regiment* arranged with the Officer Commanding the *23rd Regiment* for a counter-attack before daybreak the next day. This was carried out by three companies of the *18th Regiment* and one company of the *23rd Regiment*, but it met with a very stiff resistance and was repulsed with heavy casualties.*

MARCH 1916

"Day broke, and no further fighting was possible, as troops were very exhausted. However, some bomb fighting went on, but the English could not extend their gains. The Battalion Commander of the *III Battalion, 23rd Regiment*, after an inspection, decided to postpone any further counter-attack until the next day, the 4th March. Harassing fire and bomb-fighting were carried out vigorously, but no further counter-attack took place that day.

"The counter-attack began at about 7 a.m. and was carried out by the *III Battalion, 23rd Regiment*. It was met by heavy machine-gun fire from the English position, which made it impossible to advance across the open, and companies had to withdraw without making any progress. After this failure the Higher Command decided that a special and well-organised scheme must be made to regain commanding positions for observation on the craters, and work was at once started in the assembly positions.

"The *III Battalion* of the *18th Infantry Regiment* admit the following casualties:—

	Officers	Other ranks
Killed and missing	2	72
Wounded	4	41

The losses of the *23rd Infantry Regiment* were far heavier.

"Several missing men of the *11th Company, III Battalion, 18th Infantry Regiment*, turned up. It appeared that immediately after the explosion of the mines they were trying to rescue some of their comrades when the English entered the trench and they were obliged to hide, which they did in a dug-out, blocking up the entrance with sandbags and remaining there for four days,

---

* It is interesting to note that when we took over, the Officer Commanding the 8th Royal Fusiliers described this counter-attack as a very half-hearted affair.

while an English post was above them in the trench. However, they succeeded in the end in getting away."

On 5th March we were relieved by the 7th East Surreys and moved to Annequin, where we spent a quiet night. Next day, in very bad weather, we marched to Fouquereuil, but at 11.30 p.m. the same evening we were ordered to return to Sailly Labourse the following morning. We spent two days there, and each day two companies had to be found for bomb-carrying in Vermelles.

MARCH 1916

On the afternoon of the 8th we were inspected by Lieutenant-General Sir Hubert Gough, G.O.C. I Corps, who addressed all ranks and complimented the battalion on its defence of the craters.

On the 11th we returned to the trenches and took over from the 7th Suffolks in the left of the Quarries sector, C and D Companies being in the firing-line, B in the old British line, A in Curley Crescent.

The Quarries sector included the remains of the Hairpin, which consisted of a trench in that shape, making a sharp re-entrant towards the German lines. As a result of a large mine explosion near its base the previous December it had been considerably reduced in size, and we occupied the crater at the end of it. The rest of the sector was similar to our recent position in the Hohenzollern Redoubt. We also occupied a large chalk mound, known as the Pulpit (from its shape), which had been thrown up as the result of countless mining operations and formed a good observation post.

On the 12th Captain R. J. A. Betham left the battalion for attachment to the Divisional Staff, and Lieutenant H. S. Stocks took over the duties of Adjutant.

On the 14th the 8th Royal Fusiliers relieved us, and we proceeded to billets in Vermelles and Noyelles. Conditions in Vermelles were none too good ; it was shelled continually, and the only billets available were in the cellars of the ruined houses, Battalion H.Q. being in the cellar of the devastated brewery at the cross-roads. The troops were employed the whole time on fatigues and carrying-parties, and we were well out of it with no more than 1 man killed.

The Hohenzollern Craters

We relieved the 8th Royal Fusiliers again in the front line of the Quarries sector on the 17th. During the day there was considerable trench-mortar activity on our front line about Hairpin Crater, but the real resumption of the Battle of the Craters began the next day. All the morning the enemy poured an intense trench-mortar fire into the front line on our left and followed it up at 5 p.m. by a crashing bombardment of the whole Hohenzollern sector, as well as on Vermelles and the communication trenches. It was all too clear that a fresh attack on the craters was at hand. The 37th Brigade, which was holding the sector, was then taken by surprise by the explosion of two enemy mines which had been driven through the clay on the top of the chalk. This was the first experience of these surface mines, and our listeners deep down in the galleries had failed to hear the noise of working. The enemy followed up these demonstrations by attacking strongly, and the fighting continued throughout the day. The 37th Brigade put up a fine defence in spite of very heavy casualties, with the result that next morning we still held Craters 3 and 4 and the near lips of Craters 1, 2, A, and B. At 10.30 p.m. the near lip of Crater C was regained, and the 5th Northamptons had joined it up again with our line. The battalion was just outside the heavily shelled area and only sustained 9 casualties, all wounded.

MARCH 1916

This attack virtually ended the Battle of the Craters, which had cost the Division over 3,000 casualties.

After this no further attempt was made to capture the Chord. It was found that the holding of the interior of the craters was very costly in men. The crater bottoms were a mass of liquid mud, the sides were impossible to revet, and no shelters could be constructed; in fact, the interior of a crater was a death-trap into which any shell or trench-mortar could be easily lobbed. There were two alternatives to holding the interiors: to occupy either the near lips of the craters or a line in front of them. The former course was adopted.

On the evening of the 19th our tunnellers had to blow a camouflet, or small mine, near the left leg of the Hairpin in order to destroy a German gallery. This resulted in a small crater being formed, which was not worth holding except as a sap-head. The enemy retaliated with rifle and machine-gun fire, and unfortunately it was near here that Captain G. Woodhams, commanding B Company, was killed, and Lieutenant R. J. Richardson slightly wounded while helping a wounded man.

The Hohenzollern Craters

Captain Woodhams had been with the battalion since August, 1914, and was a most promising officer with a fine future before him. He had already passed into the Indian Civil Service, but had obtained special sanction to take a commission. Captain R. T. May and
Lieutenant G. Nagle took over the com- MARCH 1916
mand of B and A Companies respectively.

The 8th Royal Fusiliers relieved us on the 20th, having been terribly bombarded in Vermelles during the attack of the 18th, and we were glad to find that we were to occupy the support trenches instead of going there. Our casualties during the last tour were 1 officer killed and 1 wounded; 28 other ranks wounded.

During this period in support we were called upon to find excessive fatigue parties; 350 men out of a duty strength of 450 were employed for the greater part of twenty-four hours, and no less than 20 men were wounded.

On the 23rd we took over from the 8th Royal Fusiliers. There was a heavy fall of snow next day and the weather was bad throughout the whole of this tour; in spite of all efforts a few more cases of trench feet occurred. It was a great relief, therefore, to hand over to the 6th Royal West Kents on the 27th and proceed to Annequin.

Our two days' rest was disagreeably interrupted on the morning of the 28th, when the German artillery started searching for the battery of 9.2 howitzers near Fosse 9 and struck the Lewis gunners' billet with a shell, killing
1 man and wounding 7. On the 30th we APRIL 1916
exchanged billets with the 8th Royal Fusiliers
in Bethune, and on the 2nd April General Sir Charles Monro, G.O.C. First Army, attended a church parade held in the theatre, and the next day, at a special parade held at Sailly Labourse, presented the medal ribbons for the honours awarded for the recent fighting in the Hohenzollern Redoubt.

On the same day we relieved the 7th Suffolks in the Hohenzollern Reserve trenches. Colonel Osborn and Captain Nagle proceeded to England on the 5th April for an investiture at Buckingham Palace, Major Impey taking command. Captain Nagle became Assistant Adjutant about this time, and Captain May returned to command A Company, Lieutenant Richardson taking over B Company.

We went into the front line of the Hohenzollern on the 7th April, and a small defensive mine was blown on the sector on our right, with the result that Sergeant A. Skerrett and 3 Lewis gunners were wounded during the retaliation. Sergeant Skerrett, who was another of the original N.C.O.s, unfortunately died of wounds.

The next day passed quietly until 6.30 p.m., when the Germans blew a large mine just west of Crater A. West Face and the mine shafts there were blown in, 17 miners being buried in the shaft and dug-outs. All these miners were extricated except one man, who went mad under the strain of this ordeal and shot himself. The support company (D) was at once ordered to reinforce B, which was holding the position affected; but the enemy made no attempt to occupy this new crater, so Sap 9 was extended to its lip and West Face was cleared where it had been blown in by the explosion. Our casualties were heavy, and included Lieutenant E. G. Sutton, who was shot by a sniper when climbing over the filled-in portion of West Face, just after the explosion, to find out what had happened. He was a very gallant young officer, the first in the Division, it will be remembered, to receive a decoration for bravery. In addition to his loss we had 8 other ranks killed and 39 wounded.

APRIL 1916

The Commanding Officer returned on the 10th, and the next day we were relieved by the 8th Royal Fusiliers. During the relief of A Company a surface mine was blown by the Germans near Craters A and 3, with the result that 2nd Lieutenant J. M. Field, who had only just joined the battalion from the Honourable Artillery Company, was killed, and Sergeants A. Williams and P. W. Wood wounded by lumps of falling chalk.

During our tour in the reserve trenches decoy screens were put up on the spare ground between the trenches in order to draw hostile fire. This move was the result of a visit by Major-General Scott and proved remarkably successful.

By this time the defence of the front line was causing anxiety, since the trenches opposite the Hohenzollern group of craters had gradually become mere communication trenches to the sap heads and crater lips and could not be defended by rifle-fire. A number of new trenches and works were dug, so that the position could be held with more confidence in case of attack.

To illustrate the nature of the ground between the trenches it may be mentioned that after three small mines had been blown by our tunnellers near Crater C, on the 13th, it was seen that the chasm formed between Craters C and 4 had become so enlarged that it was now 200 yards long and from 60 to 100 yards wide.

As the result of all these mining operations the whole front system had become a complete labyrinth of craters, and its

One of the Hohenzollern Craters in March, 1916
(From a photograph taken by Captain D. F. Woodford)

extraordinary aspect was well described by an officer who said it looked like " the craters in the moon."

Some excitement was caused when we were again in the front line on the 16th by an officer of the Tunnelling Company reporting that his men had broken into a German shaft under the far lip of Crater 3 and had withdrawn a charge of 2,000lbs. of explosive.

A good description of this incident is given by Major Osborne:—

" We all had an immense admiration for the miners. Day after day they would go down their shafts tunnelling out towards the enemy's line. Frequently they could hear the Germans working at a counter-mine, and then would ensue a race to finish the work first and blow up the other. They never knew when they would break into a German gallery or whether the Germans were sitting quietly listening to them and waiting for the appropriate moment to launch them into eternity ; yet they were always cheerful and seemed no more perturbed than if they were doing their ordinary coal-mining in Yorkshire. I remember the occasion when Reckitt and I were sitting in our dug-out and the Mining Officer came in about midnight and announced quite quietly and imperturbably that while digging a gallery under our front line his men had broken into a German mine, all tamped and ready to go off. He added that he was preparing a camouflet to destroy the German mine, but did not know which would go off first ! We cleared the part of the trench affected and waited in suspense. There was nothing else to be done, but I well remember the anxiety of those few hours sitting helplessly and wondering who would win the race. Actually we won, and the German mine was effectively destroyed."

APRIL 1916

On the 13th the 6th Royal West Kents relieved us and we went back to Annequin, our casualties for this last tour having been 2nd Lieutenants R. C. S. Johnstone (B) and E. G. Pepper (D) wounded, as well as 3 other ranks killed and 14 wounded.

During our stay at Annequin we handed back to the Ordnance all our winter equipment of leather jerkins and fur coats. On the 20th we again exchanged billets with the 8th Royal Fusiliers in Bethune, this time taking over the tobacco factory, but our stay there was only a short one, for on the 22nd we relieved the 9th Essex in Noyelles and Vermelles. Here we carried out a test gas alarm, which was to prove timely practice for events to come.

The Hohenzollern Craters

On the 23rd the Commanding Officer and company commanders visited the trenches in the Quarries sector, which we were to take over, and found that the 35th Brigade had started another big "strafe" by exploding three large mines the evening previous to the relief, leaving us once more to bear the inevitable retaliation.

APRIL 1916

We relieved the front line next day and found the trenches in a very water-logged condition as the result of the previous week's rain. Shortly afterwards officers of the 7th Cameron Highlanders (15th, Scottish, Division) arrived to arrange details for a divisional relief on the 26th April, and it was heartening to feel that at last we were going to have a rest after our long tour.

The 25th was quiet except in the Hulluch sector (south of us), where the German artillery bombarded systematically with field-guns and 5.9 and 4.2 howitzers, beginning with two targets in one sector, then shifting to two targets in another sector, and then to two more in a third. There seemed little doubt that this was registration.

On the 26th the Camerons relieved us and took over their duties in a delightfully efficient manner. There was, however, a slight check just as Battalion H.Q. was about to move out, for at that moment our Tunnelling Officer reported that he had broken into a German gallery and found a heavy charge of gelignite. He had disconnected the firing cable and now wanted a fatigue party to clear the explosive, which amounted to something like 1,000lbs. Since we could not leave so unpleasant a legacy to newly arrived troops, our runners, signallers and batmen formed a fatigue party and shifted it.

The battalion returned to Annequin, which was still in pretty good condition, although its only occupants were a few French miners with their families, who formed a maintenance party for the mine-shaft and machinery. We had been detailed to remain at Annequin in reserve to the 44th Brigade of the 15th Division until relief arrived. The rest of the 12th Division, except Divisional H.Q. at Château des Prés, Sailly Labourse, left the fighting line for a rest in reserve.

As the weather had suddenly become agreeably hot and summer-like we were anticipating an enjoyable time. There were, however, signs that this would be denied to us. The large increase in the number of German observation balloons, the uncanny quietness of the past two days, and the unusual behaviour of the German artillery caused a presentiment of coming trouble.

The Hohenzollern Craters

Sure enough, our slumbers were rudely broken at 5 a.m. on the 27th April, when the enemy opened a furious bombardment of all gun positions surrounding Annequin with high explosive and gas-shells, and put down a heavy barrage on the front system. However hard those of us who were resting comfortably in bed on that brilliant spring morning might try to attribute the noise to the local " Archies " firing at early morning planes, it became all too clear that something far more serious was maturing. Further consideration brought to mind the 9.2 howitzers behind Annequin slag-heap, and it seemed certain that sooner or later the German gunners would try to find them. Consequently C Company was ordered to clear out of the school-house billets and to move to the open fields north of the village. Hardly had this order been complied with when the school building was wrecked by a 5.9 shell; the other companies followed into the fields, away from the slag-heap and adjacent gun positions. How timely these precautions were may be judged from the fact that although the enemy shelled the slag-heap and the southern end of the village for over an hour only 1 man of the battalion was wounded.

April 1916

Then, at 7 o'clock, the dread sound of Strombos horns from the direction of Vermelles warned us of an impending gas attack. A few moments later we saw a blue cloud approaching from far away. The battalion stood-to and all ranks put on their smoke helmets without an instant's delay. The helmets in use at this time consisted of grey flannel bags soaked in chemicals and fitted with a talc window; they had a somewhat suffocating effect.

The conditions for a gas attack were ideal, for there was no wind but only a slow movement of the air. We had scarcely got into our helmets when the gas cloud, as thick as a London fog, gradually enveloped us, making it impossible to see more than a few yards. It lingered until 7.45 a.m., when it began to clear. Helmets were removed at 8 a.m., but the enemy bombarded the gun positions with lachrymatory shells for another hour. Our helmets proved quite effective and no one was at all affected by the gas, but all equipment such as brasses and buckles, rifles, Lewis guns and all metals were, in spite of immediate attention, corroded by a thick coating of verdigris. It says much for the discipline of the battalion that out of 700 men we should have had no casualties through carelessness or disobedience to orders during the strain of this morning.

The Hohenzollern Craters

In the meantime a message came through from the 12th Division H.Q. at Sailly asking how we fared and telling us that the attack was on the right of the 15th Division, which had relieved us, but chiefly on their neighbours to the south, the 16th (Irish) Division. The *II Bavarian Corps* had sent over two separate gas clouds, with half-an-hour's interval between them, had exploded some mines, and had attempted an attack. All assaults had been driven off and the front line reported that all was quiet after 7.30 a.m.

April 1916

After this attack we learnt that a shell had landed right through the entrance of our late Battalion H.Q. dug-out in St. Elie Avenue, which, being an old German dug-out, faced the wrong way, and practically the whole of the H.Q. staff of our successors was killed as the result.

As all was quiet we were relieved during the afternoon of the 27th, company by company, by the 6th Cameron Highlanders, and after assembling west of Sailly marched as a battalion to Lapugnoy, a distance of twelve miles. No one fell out, but the horses and mules were very slack and seemed to have been affected by the gas. We were perhaps lucky to get away from this sector when we did, for two days later the Germans renewed their gas attacks on the 16th Division, which suffered even more seriously than on the 27th.

We were now to have a well-deserved holiday after an exhausting tour of duty. Constant mining and counter-mining, and the resultant bomb and crater fighting, had severely tested the courage and endurance of both officers and men, but never once had they failed. The heavy cost of this defence of the Hohenzollern and Quarries sectors since the 11th February had amounted to 6 officers killed and 10 wounded; 52 other ranks killed and 345 wounded, of whom 20 died of wounds.

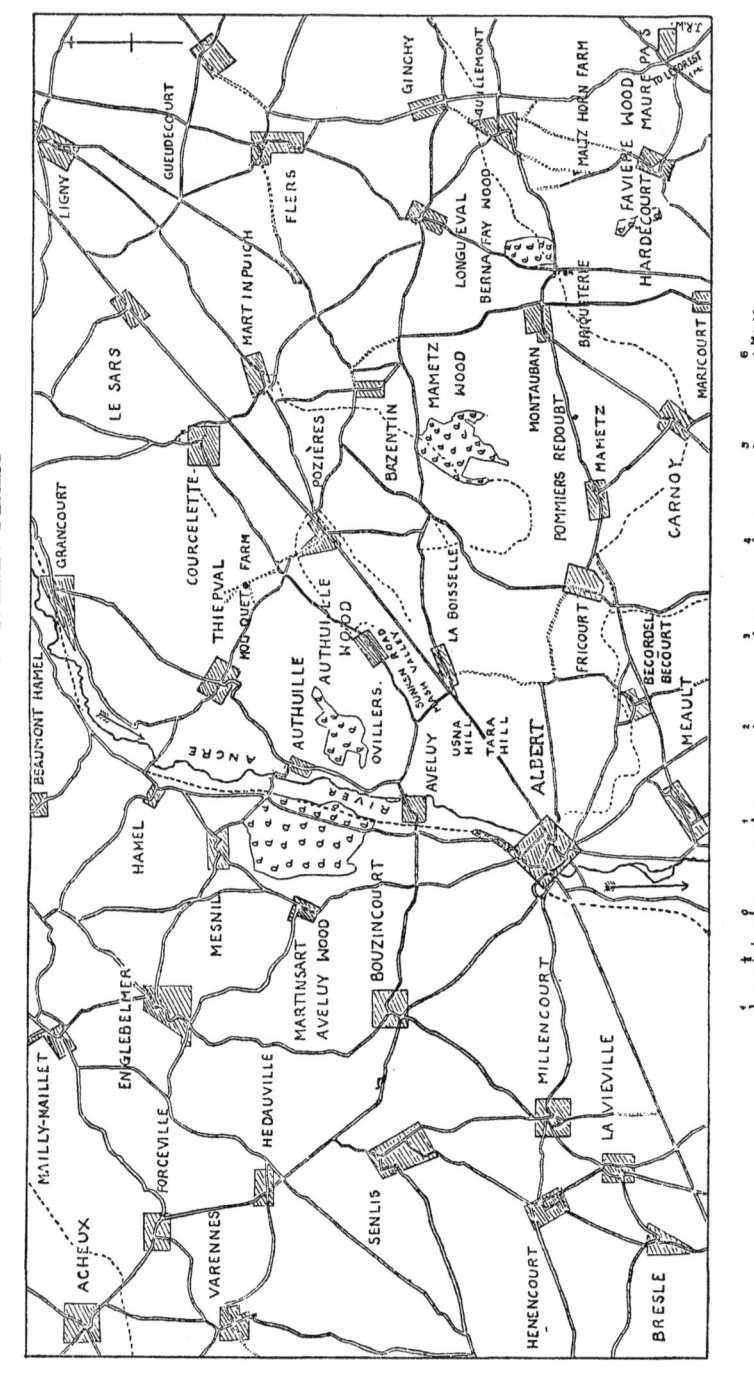

5. SOMME—NORTHERN AREA

CHAPTER VI

THE SOMME

27TH APRIL—17TH DECEMBER, 1916
[Sketch Maps, Nos. 5, 6, 7 and 8]

At Lapugnoy we enjoyed the most splendid period of rest we ever experienced in France. The village, which we shared with the 9th Royal Fusiliers, was a delightful one, situated about five miles south-west of Bethune, and was traversed by a trout stream which wound into it through green fields in a valley bordered by woods. APRIL 1916 The inhabitants were kindly disposed, the weather perfect, and no sounds of battle reached the peaceful village; in fact, our only reminder of war was an order to be ready to move at three hours' notice.

On the 30th April Major Impey left the battalion to take command of the 12th Royal Sussex (39th Division) at Givenchy, Major J. R. Torrens, who had joined us from the 13th Battalion, becoming Second-in-Command. The next day saw a notable addition to our ranks in the arrival of the Rev. W. J. Williams, who was attached to the battalion and remained with it until the end of the war. "Padre Bill," as he was very soon called, at once made friends, and by his invariable cheerfulness and readiness to help in any way speedily endeared himself to all ranks.

Our first days were spent in fitting out with clean clothing, bathing, inoculation, and route marches to get boots and feet in order. These matters were part of army routine, but they had a wider usefulness, too, for the constant activity tended to keep our thoughts occupied with MAY 1916 useful affairs and to prevent us brooding over things which were best forgotten. On most days training was begun early and finished soon after noon to allow for sports and recreation in the afternoon. In the evenings concerts were arranged. Brigade athletic sports were held on the 20th May and five first prizes were gained by members of the battalion.

Many were the lectures and demonstrations, among them one given by Major R. B. Campbell, of the Army Gymnastic Staff.

The Somme

MAY 1916

It was entitled " Bayonet-fighting and the application of the bayonet in open fighting." Though slightly blood-thirsty in tone it was a masterly exposition of ju-jutsu mixed with what soldiers call " rough-housing," but at the close of the lecture, when questions were asked for, one man stood up and said, " Please, sir, can you tell me how I can get a transfer to the A.S.C. ? "

We spent from the 22nd to the 29th May at Estrée Blanche and Floringhem for brigade training. On the 29th the whole Division was placed under one hour's notice to act as reserve to the First Army, and between the 28th and the 31st the Commanding Officer and company commanders reconnoitred the areas occupied by the 1st, 2nd, 16th and 23rd Divisions.

It now dawned on us that we were having the kind of training and rest which was the prelude to some hard fighting. In fact, we began to realise that we were going through what is commonly known as the process of being " fattened up." This seemed confirmed by the nightly passage of many railway-trains southwards. We then found that we were about the only people who were not in the know about the coming Battle of the Somme. Indeed, the French inhabitants of Lapugnoy were the first to reveal the position to us. This was a typical example of the " secrecy " observed at this and most other periods of the war.

On the 31st May the battalion celebrated the completion of one year's service in France. The original officers of the battalion, who had come out with it a year before, held a most cheerful dinner in a marquee near Battalion H.Q. Special menus were designed by Sergeant R. Ellis, and music was supplied by D Company's gramophone until the operator—who shall be nameless—found the task of changing records and needles more than he could manage after dinner.

An extra reason for celebration was the mention of the battalion in Sir Douglas Haig's despatch, published on the 29th May, for " good work in carrying out or repelling local attacks and raids." Besides ourselves, the other units of the 12th Division to be mentioned were the 62nd Brigade, R.F.A., the 70th Field Company, R.E., the 7th Suffolks, the 8th and 9th Royal Fusiliers, the 7th East Surreys, and the 5th Northamptons ; and, we were very glad to notice, our old friends the 170th Tunnelling Company, R.E. The 8th Royal Sussex, in the 18th Division, was also mentioned. This was Sir Douglas Haig's first despatch, and it was also the last despatch which contained a list of this nature.

The Somme

On the 1st June we received warning to be ready to reinforce at short notice. It appeared that German deserters had been telling the Higher Command that an attack was impending in the Loos salient. Whether this was so or not is uncertain, but these warnings (which may have been inspired by the German Intelligence) were constantly being received.

It was not until a week later that we actually did move—to Bully-Grenay and Maroc, in relief of the 9th Essex. Here we were attached to the 1st Division and were given the task of restoring some rear lines of defence known as the Maistre and Bajolle lines. Rain interfered a good deal with work, which was mostly done by night. At Bully-Grenay we met the 2nd Battalion from Les Brebis and fraternised with them for a day. Our stay was soon cut short by preliminary movements towards the Somme battle area, for on the 13th June we went to billets in Drouvin and Vaudricourt, and on the 16th to Fouquereuil. The train left at noon and arrived at Longueau, near Amiens, at 7.45 p.m. From there we had a long march of fifteen miles to Vignacourt, which we reached at 4 a.m. There was not much rest for Battalion H.Q. officers and company commanders, who had to proceed by bus at 5.30 a.m. next day to reconnoitre the rear of the line north of Albert and did not return until 5.30 p.m.

JUNE 1916

It was at Vignacourt that we began to find the French peasant antagonistic to the troops. There was no serious trouble, but we had to cope with constant demands for *réclamations* for minor damage and grumbles about waste of well-water, and so on. The French interpreter with Brigade H.Q. said this attitude was quite usual even with the French troops manoeuvring in the area in peace time.

We spent most of our time at Vignacourt in practising attack formations by battalion, brigade and division. We frequently combined with the 8th Royal Fusiliers, the idea being to teach the rank and file of both units to carry on after reinforcements and casualties had intermingled their personnel. This practice was to prove of great value later on. The country round Vignacourt provided a delightful training ground—woodland, pasture and arable land. The last was not always treated with the respect due to it. Captain Sadler observes : " We actually trained day after day through the best crops of standing wheat that I have ever seen. Transport, guns and all the lot simply stamped miles of it flat ; and being a farmer it made one feel quite sick to see such wanton damage to badly needed crops."

The Somme

The dog Harold enjoyed himself thoroughly hunting partridges on the wing and an occasional roe-deer, but he never put up a wild boar, which were said to be plentiful. Perhaps it was a sense of self-preservation that prevented him. The curious thing about Harold was that he never went to another battalion by mistake. He seemed to know the 7th from any distance.

JUNE 1916

Now began lectures on the duties allotted to us as part of an army of pursuit should the line be broken, also reconnaissance of the approach lines to the battle area and study of the country east of the German lines.

It was during our stay at Vignacourt that a most important institution came into being. This was the Regimental Canteen. The idea originated with the officers of our " Q " Department, Captains Clarke and Hind, mainly because the men had great difficulty in buying cigarettes. The canteen was started with a capital of about 200 francs, put up by Clarke and Hind; from these humble beginnings it developed into a miniature Harrods. The profits not only paid for Christmas dinners, but also for newspapers and various other items. Early in 1917 a further addition was made in the shape of a wet canteen, which supplied beer to all transport lines in the vicinity of Chichester Paddock at Faubourg de Ronville, in the Arras sector, and consequently made a considerable profit out of other units as well as our own. It would be difficult to speak too highly of this undertaking and the way it was run. The whole battalion benefited by it, and the greatest praise is due to the officers concerned for their untiring efforts to make it such a success.

On the 27th June we marched three miles to Flesselles, our first move in the Battle of the Somme.

On the 30th Brigadier-General Boyd-Moss presented red and green cards to the N.C.O.s and men who had been recommended for distinguished conduct during the Hohenzollern fighting. The cards had been instituted by the Divisional Commander to assure the men concerned of his appreciation before the actual publication of the honours awarded, which often took place after the men had left the Division. A red card signified that the recommendation had been passed on by the Divisional Commander to the higher authorities, and a green card that, while it had not been possible to forward the recommendation, the Divisional

HEADQUARTERS AND SOME SENIOR N.C.O.s AT LAPUGNOY, JUNE, 1916

TOP ROW—Sgt. P. J. HANLON (D); Sgt. G. PANNICK (Provost); Sgt. G. WARD (B); Sgt. W. E. CHALK (A); Sgt. F. MAUDLING (Shoemaker); Sgt. H. EASTON (C); Sgt. H. ROWE (D); Sgt. F. TAYLOR (C); Sgt. E. HULKES (L.G.); Sgt. F. J. RUSSELL (Scouts)

MIDDLE (Standing)—Sgt. J. P. CATCHPOLE (C); Sgt. A. LEE (Transport); C.Q.M.S. C. LORD (A); C.Q.M.S. E. SIMMINS (B); C.S.M. J. JOY (B); C.S.M. A. RICHOLD (C); C.S.M. J. HAYES (D); C.Q.M.S. J. E. VINALL (D); C.Q.M.S. B. SONGHURST (C)

MIDDLE (Sitting)—C.S.M. A. WHAPHAM (A); R.S.M. H. PAGE, D.C.M.; Lt. J. E. CLARKE (Quartermaster); Capt. G. NAGLE, M.C. (Ass. Adjutant); Capt. A. M. THOMSON, R.A.M.C. (Medical Officer); Lt.-Col. W. L. OSBORN, D.S.O. (Commanding Officer); Lt. R. C. D. HIND (Transport Officer); R.Q.M.S. W. LONG; C.S.M. G. BURR (D) (awaiting commission)

FRONT ROW—Sgt. Dr. A. AYLMORE (Drums); Sgt. W. BAKER (Orderly Room); Sgt. C. MAIDMENT (C); Sgt. T. LEACH (D); Sgt. G. LANGLEY, D.C.M. (C); Sgt. E. HARRIS (Mess); Sgt. W. RABY (Cook) "HAROLD" (Regimental Mascot)

Facing page 80

THE SOMME

Commander had taken note of it for a future occasion or for a mention in despatches. Fourteen men of the battalion were eligible to receive red cards, but owing to wounds or other causes only eight of them were present. As mentioned above, all of them were later awarded the Military Medal. The following were presented with green cards:—Sergeants W. H. Budgen and J. Simmonds, Lance-Corporal Woolgar, and Private F. V. Nichols, all of B Company.

JUNE 1916

That evening billeting parties left for Fréchencourt, ten miles distant. The battalion marched at 7.30 p.m. and billeted at 12.45 a.m., with orders to be ready to move at 7 a.m. The old French peasant in whose house the Commanding Officer was billeted insisted on giving him clean sheets and a bed for the night, saying that her son was also marching up to the battle, and she hoped that he, too, would get the best of everything on his way.

At 7.10 a.m. on the 1st July, the opening day of the great Somme battle, the battalion marched three miles to Baizieux Wood and bivouacked with the 8th Royal Fusiliers and 11th Middlesex. The same afternoon orders came to move to Millencourt, leaving packs stored at Baizieux. Here we received a liaison officer from the 2nd Cameronians, 8th Division.

Company commanders went on to reconnoitre the trenches which the 35th Brigade was taking over from the 8th Division. On the march our destination was changed, and we proceeded by brigade to the Albert-Bouzincourt line and got into new reserve trenches there at 1.30 a.m. That morning (the 2nd July) we sent back those who were to be kept out of action to form a nucleus to reform the battalion in case of heavy losses. From our position we had a good view of the German and British trench systems, extending from the Albert-Bapaume Road on the south up to Thiepval on the north.

JULY 1916

On the 1st July, after a prolonged bombardment of six days, the Fourth Army had attacked on a twenty-five mile front, from Maricourt in the south to Gommecourt in the north. The first task allotted to the III Corps, to which we were now attached, had been the capture of La Boisselle and Ovillers; when the 8th and 34th Divisions had taken these villages the 19th and 12th were to pass through, the rôle of the 12th Division being the capture of Martinpuich.

The Somme

Unfortunately the attack of the 8th and 34th Divisions had been a failure. Although the 34th had established a footing in the German line, the 8th had suffered over 5,000 casualties and was back in its original trenches. Consequently the plan of battle had to be changed, and at 10 p.m. on the night of the 2nd particulars were received of a fresh attack to be made on Ovillers by the 35th and 37th Brigades at 3.15 a.m. next morning. At midnight the battalion joined the 8th Royal Fusiliers and formed a reserve in the railway cutting north of Albert railway station. The other two battalions of our Brigade were holding the trenches for the two Brigades attacking Ovillers.

JULY 1916

The cutting would have been a quiet spot but for the presence of a 12-inch howitzer carrying out counter-battery work in collaboration with an aeroplane. The concussion made the already hard floor of the rail-track a most uneasy bed. The plotting of the shots fired and the wireless direction from the observer in the air interested those of us invited into the dug-out. It was not all straightforward, owing to constant jamming of the wireless by a high-power German station.

No call was made on the battalion, except to provide two bomb-carrying parties of fifty men each to the 35th and 37th Brigades, and at 9 a.m. we were ordered back to the Albert-Bouzincourt line. On our arrival we heard of the failure of the 35th and 37th Brigades to take Ovillers.

The attack had cost them in casualties 97 officers and 2,277 other ranks, and *The History of the 12th Division* states that " the failure was undoubtedly affected by the flanking machine-gun fire, which was unmolested, and raked the excessive distance between the opposing front lines over which supports had to cross. Also by the attack being carried out in the dark by troops who were hurried into the fight without being well acquainted with the terrain, leading to loss of cohesion ; by the artillery bombardment destroying the wire and trenches, yet failing to reach the deep dug-outs, which remained unharmed ; and by the recent storms making shell holes and trenches in places almost impassable."*

We found various working-parties during the next three days, chiefly for preparing and carrying bombs. The more expert bombers usually undertook the detonating of the Mills bombs. The practice was to make a circular hole in the ground a couple of feet deep. Round this the bombers sat

---
* *Op. cit.,* p. 54.

6. OVILLERS

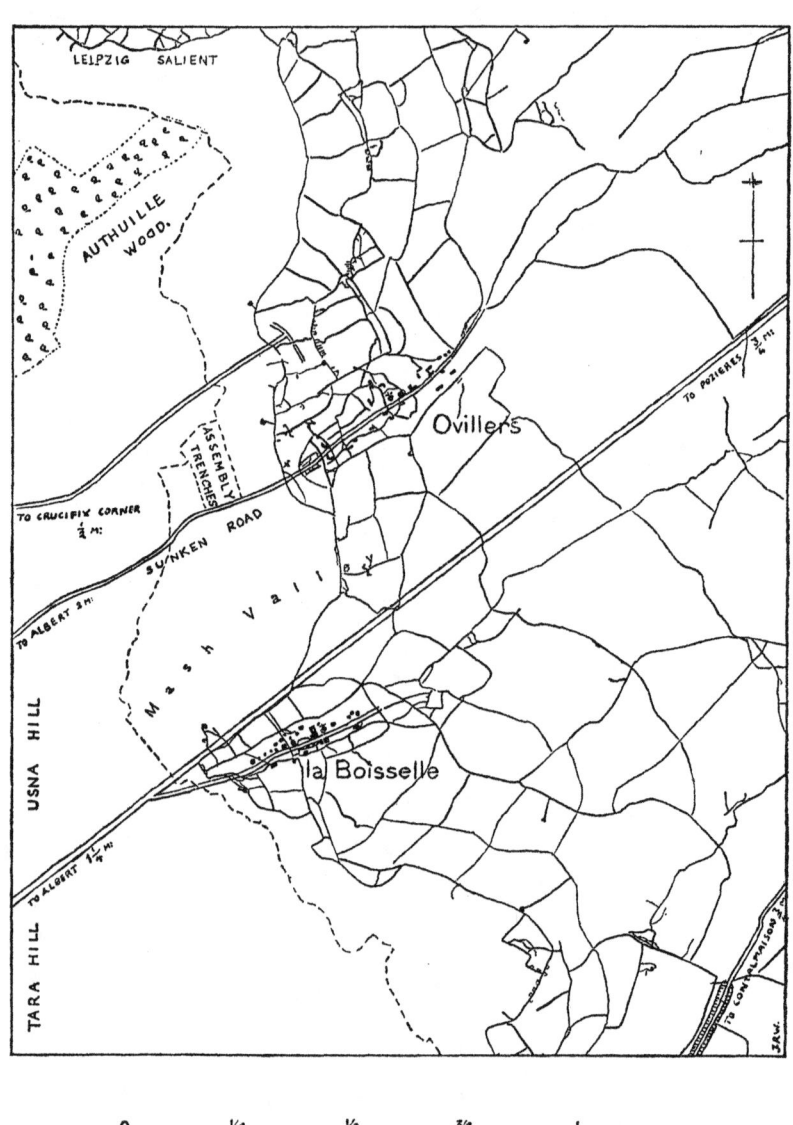

in a circle fixing detonators. In case of a slip the faulty bomb was dropped into the hole, and if it exploded the fragments either went into the earth or straight up into the air. Rain began on the 4th July and lasted all day. We seemed fated to have rain in France whenever a big operation was planned. Coming on top of soil powdered by continual explosions, the rain made a kind of porridge into which men in fighting order sank often to the knees.

JULY 1916

On the 5th, B Company had 1 man killed and 8 wounded on a brigade working-party—our first casualties for over two months. On this day, owing to a reorganisation of the attack, we came under the orders of the X Corps of the Fifth Army.

Lieutenant W. D. Allan relates the following incident, which occurred during this period :—

" Just before we went into the Somme show, Taylor, one of C Company's subalterns, returned from leave with a case of wines, amongst which was a particularly good brown sherry, and a tumbler of this nectar was sent to the Colonel's dug-out with C Company's compliments. Unfortunately for the Colonel, Thomson, our Medical Officer, arrived first, and, feeling perhaps that a little refreshment would relieve the stress of war, he gulped it down at one draught, remarking afterwards that it was ' damned funny whisky.' This was poor old Thomson's last crime, however, for he was killed a few days later."

At 8 a.m. on the 6th July orders came for the 36th Brigade to relieve the 37th in the trenches facing Ovillers. The Commanding Officer and one officer from each company went to Brigade H.Q. to receive instructions from Brigadier-General Boyd-Moss for an attack on Ovillers the following day. Undaunted by the frightful casualties suffered in the actions of the preceding days the battalion was on its toes, knowing that the 36th Brigade was to attack where first a whole division and then two brigades had failed.

At 11.15 a.m. we relieved the 7th Norfolks in the trenches in front of Ovillers, A and B Companies in the front line, with C and D and Battalion H.Q. in the reserve line close up.

At 7 p.m. Colonel Osborn issued his orders for the attack, which was to begin at 8.30 a.m. the following morning. The battalion was ordered to advance with its right resting on the sunken road leading into Ovillers from the west. The 8th and

9th Royal Fusiliers were to be on our right and left. The whole Brigade was to move on the southern slope of the spur ending in Tara and Usna Hills, whereby it was hoped to avoid observation and fire of enemy machine-guns from the Leipzig salient, a mile distant to the north. These guns had been the direct cause of the 8th Division's failure.

JULY 1916

The 74th Brigade (34th Division) was to co-operate by attacking from La Boisselle at 8 a.m. to capture Mash Valley.

Five lines of German trenches were included as objectives, the farthest being just east of Ovillers Church. The attack had to cross 400 yards of No Man's Land and penetrate 1,200 yards into the German trench system. Luckily, one gable of the church survived and remained standing until after the attack was launched. It formed a valuable landmark in what was otherwise a tangle of shell-holes. The movement was to be a " leap-frogging " one, on a one company front. A Company was to take the first two objectives, B to pass through and take the third, C the fourth, and D the fifth. Companies were to follow each other as closely as possible, so as to get over No Man's Land before the German barrage began.

Captain R. T. May led A Company; Captain W. J. Borlase had taken over B after Captain R. J. Richardson had gone to England to a Training Reserve Battalion; Captains H. S. Bowlby and G. F. Osborne were both left out with the battle reserve, and their companies, C and D, were commanded by Captains A. E. T. Cleaver (who had come to us from the 2nd Royal Scots Fusiliers on the 3rd July) and G. L. Reckitt.

With his orders the Commanding Officer issued the following general instructions :—

1. Block every possible exit to a trench.
2. As many bombs as possible to be taken over.
3. Lines to be as thick and as close as possible.
4. Bombs are to be economised. It may be possible to arrange a supply by the sunken road.
5. No bombs to be wasted over making a barrage. No bomb attack to be made along long trenches. Instead, make counter-attack over the open, shooting into trenches.
6. German trenches have practically no wire, but are very deep and offer serious obstacles. Front and rear line dug-outs are connected. To make a block, destroy about 20 yards of the trench.
7. First line to go over at the double. Rest at a steady advance.

The Somme

8. Each captured trench is to have a garrison told off to it, who must remain there at all costs and guard the trench and exits of dug-outs, and must provide a blocking party on the flanks, who must destroy the trench to avoid being bombed.

9. Attacking waves are to follow as quickly and as close as possible—even 10 yards apart.

10. Select front you have to attack on to-night, before dark.

11. Twenty bombs per man to be carried, except leading line, who may take 10. Co-operate with right and left. Two Lewis guns per company to go over. One pick and shovel to every fourth man, except first assaulting line.

JULY 1916

12. At 8.30 a.m. the artillery barrage will lift on to third objective, and will remain there for 10 minutes. At 8.40 a.m. artillery barrage will lift on to Church Line objective for 10 minutes.

13. The direction of the original assault will be due east. After passing first objective, the general line will be north-east.

14. Get companies out two minutes before Zero.

15. Highest ruin visible is the Church.

16. Map of Ovillers 1/10,000 will be used.

17. Order men to stick where they get to. They must not go back.

18. Slightly wounded men are not to return. Collect badly wounded in dug-outs or shell holes.

19. Look for water, and if found communicate to battalions on right and left. Dumps of water will be arranged on our own front line after dark.

20. Make bomb stores at the junction of communication trenches and collect German bombs if possible.

21. Start establishing reserves by companies when the line is taken.

22. When Ovillers is reached communication must be by visual signalling.

At 6.45 a.m. on the 7th July the intensive bombardment by our guns began, and later the German artillery started on our assembly trenches, causing heavy casualties. A Company reported about 40. In the whole Brigade there were about 350 casualties before zero hour.

The Somme

The attack of the 74th Brigade on our right at 8 a.m. also brought retaliation on our heads. This assault made some progress, but unfortunately it did not succeed in reaching or silencing the machine-gun posts in Mash Valley which had done so much damage on the 1st and 3rd July.

In spite of this the attack of the 36th Brigade started punctually and well, but that very gallant officer Lieutenant-Colonel A. C. Annesley, D.S.O., of the 8th Royal Fusiliers, was wounded three times and then killed while leading his men across No Man's Land.

JULY 1916

The fortunes of the battalion are best told by Brigadier-General Osborn, who accompanied the battalion in the attack.

"On leaving the front British line with Battalion H.Q.," he writes, "I noticed that besides the artillery fire there was a very heavy machine-gun barrage which seemed to come from the north. The Adjutant, Lieutenant Stocks, Regimental Sergeant-Major H. Page and some signallers and bombers were hit and fell immediately, some ten in all.

"On looking back when about half-way over No Man's Land I saw to my horror that two platoons of D Company had lain down in an old trench made in some previous attack. They said they had been told to take the first trench they came to and stay there!* When they saw my signal they came on at once. Two other platoons of this company went astray and only rejoined at night time.

"On approaching the German lines after this delay I found most of Battalion H.Q. and some stragglers had dropped into two enormous shell-holes. I joined them, and we re-organised for a further rush into the front German line. Before we got off Lieutenant Gordon, the Bombing Officer, was killed, and Lieutenant Wilton, the Signals Officer, wounded; also three of the men were killed.

"In the German lines things were a little chaotic. Some shots were being exchanged and bombs thrown on the flank and into dug-outs. A few German snipers had stuck to their posts. I shot one and frightened off another with a rifle I picked up from a casualty.

"Our own liaison aeroplane then came over to look us up and flew most gallantly right into the barrage of shrapnel. We tried to signal him, but I don't think he saw us. Our flares were

---

* Captain Reckitt writes: "By that time all the company officers save one had been hit, and most of the senior N.C.O.s too. The surviving officer stated that he did not hear the whistle signal to go over the top and stopped his and the adjoining platoon from attacking."

ready, but we had not time to light them before he was gone. When there is hand-to-hand fighting it is impossible to light flares at a fixed hour.

"Captain Cleaver and 2nd Lieutenant Sadler now came to meet me, and we collected men and organised a firing line and began to find out what had happened.

"Our leading company (A) had lost all its officers but one, 2nd Lieutenant Broughall, who had reached the farther objective, the fourth line, with a weak platoon. The other three lines were held in a somewhat scattered way. Altogether I found I had six officers—Captain Cleaver, 2nd Lieutenants Sadler, Taylor, Burdett, Fortescue and Broughall—and about 250 men. The 8th Royal Fusiliers on my right had no officers and only 40 other ranks, so I joined them on to my platoons. This worked quite well owing to the practice Colonel Annesley and I had given them in training-time, and all ranks amalgamated quite easily.

JULY 1916

"While going round the lines organising the defences I went into a German dug-out occupied by some nine or ten *Guard Fusiliers* who had surrendered to our men and the 9th Royal Fusiliers. I was questioning them about water-supply and bombs when the Germans rushed the trench above from a flank. After five minutes or so our men drove them off and my orderly (Private Charman) and I were released, but 2nd Lieutenant Sadler, who led the counter-attack, was wounded. This dug-out was well found with rations, soda-water, Iron Crosses and Guards' helmets.

"After that episode I found Company Sergeant-Major J. Joy and made him temporary Regimental Sergeant-Major (*vice* Page, wounded), and formed a small Battalion H.Q. in a central spot. Here, also, I collected Company Sergeant-Major A. Whapham, Sergeant H. Payne, Corporal R. Prevett, and Sergeant F. J. Russell. The new Battalion H.Q. was a deep dug-out, two-storeyed; from the lower storey a gallery led out towards the British line ending in a shaft, the top of which issued into No Man's Land. The roof of the shaft was turfed over and formed an all-round loop-hole. Undoubtedly this was a machine-gun post which had caused a number of casualties to the 8th Royal Fusiliers and ourselves.

"The troops on our left, the 9th Royal Fusiliers under Captain E. T. Beck, M.C.,* had now only three officers and 90 men in action, so I took over command of all the units of the three

---

* The Officer Commanding 9th Royal Fusiliers had made his H.Q. in the front British line. Captain Beck received the D.S.O. for his work in this action.

battalions. It seemed impossible to reach the Brigadier, for no messengers could get over No Man's Land, although many tried.

"There was a good deal of bombing and numerous small attacks on our left flank. Fearing that a wedge might be driven into our thinly-held captures I ordered two of the objectives to be strongly held, outposts placed in the third, and the fourth to be abandoned except by patrols.

JULY 1916

"There was still much machine-gun fire from the north, and our firing-line had to make traverses and cut recesses in the parados of the trenches to enable the men to line the parapets. 2nd Lieutenant Taylor's platoon was badly harassed by this fire, but stuck to its post.

"About 3 p.m. Lieutenant E. A. Moore, of the 11th Middlesex, arrived with a Lewis gun and 20 other ranks of his battalion. My own two lost platoons also arrived with Captain I. A. Crombie (11th Middlesex) and a detachment with another Lewis gun.

"Matters were by now much more satisfactory but for the heavy rain, which, starting at noon, made movement difficult. The reinforcements secured our left flank, and by 6 p.m. the Brigadier was informed of the position.

"Soon afterwards we were reinforced by the 9th Essex (Major C. I. Ryan) and the 7th East Surreys (Lieutenant-Colonel R. H. Baldwin). We were now pretty sure of holding the footing we had gained in the German trench system—a depth of about 300 yards. From 9 a.m. until nightfall, when reinforcements of men, ammunition and bombs came, we had been rather hanging on by our eyelids, but now had a chance of pushing north and of gaining touch to the south with the 74th Brigade. We had also received artillery liaison officers, and a large dump of water, bombs and small-arms ammunition was made by working-parties of the 11th Middlesex.

"The situation in the morning, when Brigadier-General Boyd-Moss came over to visit the fighting troops, was that we held strongly two objectives in the Ovillers-La Boisselle trenches, with two more up to Ovillers Church held lightly and patrolled. Our left did not quite reach a gallery called Rivington Tunnel, which had been dug for rapid conversion to a communication trench after the capture of the German trenches.

"In reconnaissance for the capture of this tunnel-head Major Ryan (9th Essex) was killed in a bombing affray with the Germans. The position on this flank fluctuated considerably with bombing attacks and counter-attacks.

The Somme

"Nothing particular occurred on the 8th, and in the evening the remnants of the 8th and 9th Royal Fusiliers and the 7th Royal Sussex, together with the 9th Essex, were relieved by the 2nd Manchesters (32nd Division) and moved out of the fight to near Albert.

"Luckily the relief got clear before a heavy German barrage descended between the old and front lines. I had waited with Company Sergeant-Major Joy, a signaller and a couple of runners to clear up some points with the new Commanding Officer, Lieutenant-Colonel N. Luxmoore, of the Devonshire Regiment,

JULY 1916

who was commanding the 2nd Manchesters. We were caught before we could cross, having to take cover for about an hour till the barrage abated. Arriving at Crucifix Corner, near Aveluy, where the relieved troops had collected for hot tea and soup from the cook-wagons, I found that out of 25 officers and 650 rank and file who had gone into action on the 7th there remained myself, 2nd Lieutenants Taylor, Fortescue, Day and Broughall, and 220 other ranks, of whom some 12 were lightly wounded. And so to bed in a comfortable loft, with orders to move at 10 a.m. next morning."

Colonel Osborn was himself slightly wounded during the action, but remained at duty.

Captain J. R. Wilton, then the Signalling Officer, who was wounded before reaching the German front line, adds the following notes on the gallantry displayed by the N.C.O.s and men in one of the shell-holes mentioned by General Osborn:—

"Corporal Chevis was badly wounded as he was getting into the shell-hole. At the time he was carrying one of the two large signalling shutters on a pole. This was smashed by the piece of shell which went through his thigh, while shortly afterwards he was wounded again in the same leg, and died the following morning. No words could express his bravery during the pain he suffered. I should also like to add that Sergeant Russell, the Scout Sergeant, was also in the shell-hole and was doing all he could for the wounded. I remember saying to him later, ' You are lucky, Russell, you are the only one of us who has not been hit.' Then, and only then, did he tell me that he had been, and pulled up his sleeve, displaying a nasty wound through the upper part of his right arm.

"I took one of the signalling shutters on my knees, and as our contact aeroplane came over I kept sending our battalion call-sign —R.S.U.G.—which I think was seen, because the plane came down quite low, and the observer waved what looked like a muffler before flying away. This may have been after the Colonel left us to try and get up to the battalion."

No mention of casualties would be complete without an account of the gallant death of our Medical Officer, Captain Thomson. Lieutenant Stocks thus describes the facts:—

"Thomson and I went with Colonel Osborn when the battalion attacked on the 7th July. When half-way across No Man's Land I was hit by a bullet in the right leg and immediately put *hors de combat*.

JULY 1916

Thanks to Thomson's presence of mind my wound was speedily dressed; indeed, he used his own cane as a temporary splint on my broken leg. By this time our casualties had reached a considerable number, and for the next few hours Thomson was continuously at work attending to the wounded. With my badly-fractured femur I found it impossible to move, and it must have been after midday when Thomson came to me again and said he was going to drag me back to a shallow assembly trench not far from where I lay. With an entire disregard for the enemy's heavy shell and machine-gun fire he managed to haul me on to a groundsheet, and was having me pulled to cover on this improvised sledge when he suddenly fell forward almost on top of me, without uttering even a groan, apparently shot through the heart by a sniper.

"At the first opportunity after my arrival at King Edward VII. Hospital in London I wrote to Colonel Osborn and told him of Thomson's gallant action, or, rather, series of gallant deeds, which he performed that day. It has always grieved me to think that no posthumous award was ever granted to one who so splendidly and gallantly made the supreme sacrifice, though I understand Colonel Osborn strongly recommended one."

Another personal account of the battle comes from Captain H. Sadler, who was with A Company:—

"A Company was the first wave starting from the British front line. We were badly shelled for about two hours before Zero by the guns that practically enfiladed the trench from the north (our left). We actually lost more men then, I think, than in getting across No Man's Land. Captain May, my company commander, got a shrapnel bullet through his tin hat about fifteen minutes before we went over; although this was, I think, the wound which killed him, he kept on his feet and walked up and down the trench talking to the men till we attacked. He must have held out till Zero and then dropped.

"In the actual attack we—my platoon, anyway—lost very few men. I had previously impressed on them that speed was the essence of the contract and that the German trench was the best place after we had left ours. I myself went across like a scalded cat, and when I got to the German front line I had to wait for a moment for our guns to lift.

"As I was travelling light and the men were loaded with all sorts of junk, I got to the enemy line all alone. It was blown all to hell, but the dug-outs were obvious. There was not a soul in the trench and I realised I had got there before the Germans had come out of their burrows. I sat down facing the dug-out doors and got all the Germans as they came up. They had no idea I was there even, the ground was so blown up and I was in a hole; they never knew what hit them. Broughall, a plucky little Canadian, was about the next of our people to arrive; he was very excited at my bag, but disgusted at their "hats," as they all had steel helmets or flat caps, and he had promised himself the best spiked helmet (*pickelhaube*) in France.

JULY 1916

"This craving for a trophy was the cause of his getting to the fourth line, as related by General Osborn. While we were cleaning up the front line we put up a big German wearing a very smart spiked helmet. Broughall, unaware that there were dozens of other helmets in the dug-outs, at once gave chase to the wearer. His platoon rallied to the cry of 'Get that bloody hat' and followed him. The quarry ran up a communication trench and was finally pulled down in the German fourth line, where Broughall and his platoon settled him and held their own against repeated counter-attacks.

"While we were rounding up the prisoners I came upon one of the Fusiliers being embraced round the knees by a trembling Hun who had a very nice wrist watch. After hearing the man's plea for mercy the Fusilier said, 'That's all right, mate, I accept your apology, but let's have that ticker.'

"We had cleaned up things in the first line by the time I saw the Commanding Officer again, and I showed him the best dug-out for Battalion H.Q. and left him examining German prisoners.

"I started five men making a block on our left and told them to hold on there. While I was busy on our right the enemy attacked on our left, captured our block, killing the men I had left, and occupying the trench where the Battalion H.Q. dug-out (with Colonel Osborn inside it) was situated.

"German stick-bombs were going off all over the place and things were a bit windy for a moment, but directly the men knew the Colonel was 'in the ditch' they wanted no leading. We just went for the Germans, and they could not withstand the combination of Mills bombs and the 7th Battalion bereft of their Commanding Officer.

"When we had cleared them well back and made good the line again, I hared to the top of the steps of the dug-out where the Colonel was; there was someone lying dead at the bottom, and I thought for the moment it was the Colonel and shouted, 'They have got the C.O.' He heard me and, sticking his head round the corner, said, 'Oh, no they haven't!'

JULY 1916

"He then explained that the Germans had wounded his runner, who had been sitting on the steps, and had rushed on. He had been watching the different coloured legs go by in the trench as the scrap went on.

"I then went into the dug-out myself and the Commanding Officer tied up my head. I did not take any further part in the show, as I found I was full of little bits of bomb. When it got dark I was told to get myself back if I could, and I started. I crawled and hobbled about for hours and twice ran into bits of trench which the Huns held, but luckily heard them talking and lay low till I could sneak away again, until finally I found my way back to our old front line."

The History of the 12th Division refers to this fighting as some of the most severe the Division was called upon to take part in and records the losses as follows :—

"The casualties of the three battalions making the attack on the 7th were very heavy. Out of 66 officers, 60 became casualties. In other ranks, out of a total of 2,100, 340 were hit by shell fire before leaving our trenches, 1,260 were hit by machine-gun fire in No Man's Land, and of the 500 who reached the village, 150 became casualties during the subsequent fighting. The total casualties of the Division from 1st to 8th July inclusive were officers 189, other ranks 4,576."*

Altogether it had been a pretty rough thirty-six hours, during which the personnel of the 36th Brigade had behaved with extraordinary gallantry, especially the rank and file when deprived of their leaders.

The casualties suffered by the battalion on the 7th and 8th July, out of a strength of 25 officers and 650 other ranks, were as follows :—

	Officers	Other ranks
Killed and missing	7	119
Died of wounds	1	15
Wounded	13	306
Totals	21	440

* *Op. cit.*, p. 61.

THE SOMME

Officers killed : Captain R. T. May (O.C. A Company); Lieutenant H. B. Gordon (Bombing Officer, H.Q.); 2nd Lieutenants C. I. Dadswell (D), J. C. R. Godwin (B), R. Kenward (A), F. R. Waring (A), and Captain A. M. Thomson, R.A.M.C. (attached H.Q.).

„ died of wounds : 2nd Lieutenant C. M. Sing (B), on the 7th July.

Officers wounded : Lieutenant-Colonel W. L. Osborn (H.Q.); Captains W. J. Borlase (O.C. B Company), A. E. T. Cleaver (2nd Royal Scots Fusiliers attd., O.C. C Company), and G. L. Reckitt (O.C. D Company); Lieutenant and Adjutant H. S. Stocks (H.Q.), Lieutenant J. R. Wilton (Signals Officer, H.Q.); 2nd Lieutenants W. D. Allan (C), S. L. Burdett (A), D. F. Christie (C), R. Cornford (D), W. G. Hall (C), and H. Sadler (A), A. E. Warren (D).

JULY 1916

N.C.O.s killed : Sergeants A. J. Evans (Signals), J. C. Kent (B), W. Madge (D), W. Unsted (C); Corporals W Cheesman (B), G. E. Chevis (Signals), J. Crawley (B), and E. Wadey (B).

The honours awarded for the action were :—

Military Cross : Captain A. E. T. Cleaver (C); 2nd Lieutenants H. S. Broughall (A) and H. Sadler (A); Company Sergeant-Major J. Joy (B).

Distinguished Conduct Medal : Corporal R. Prevett (B).

Military Medal* : Corporal W. Butcher (C); Privates C. E. Brown (B), H. E. Cosham (C), and J. Wilson (D).

It may here be of interest to give a translation from the history of the *Guard Fusilier Regiment* which opposed us at Ovillers :—

I Battalion, right flank, near Thiepval (less *No. 3 Company*).

III Battalion, centre, Ovillers North.

II Battalion, left, Ovillers South (with *No. 3 Company, I Battalion*).

" Artillery fire was very heavy and troops had to stay in dugouts. *No. 3 Company* was in a re-entrant. Storm troops were kept in dug-outs ready for immediate counter-attack. Elements of other regiments were also placed under the regiment's command.

" There was a gas attack in front of *II Battalion* and also intense drum fire.

---

* Other Military Medals awarded were included in the Pozières honours shown on p. 103.

THE SOMME

JULY 1916

"The English attacked in six lines, but the attack was thrown back at first by trench fighting and machine-gun fire; an *unteroffizier* especially distinguished himself by the way in which he handled the machine-guns. The *8th Company (II Battalion)* had very heavy losses and was eventually blotted out and the officer commanding killed, and the English at length succeeded in taking possession of our trenches."

On the 9th July we marched by brigade via Millencourt to Senlis, and had dinner while the 32nd Division cleared from the village. The following officers now remained with the battalion:—

Lieutenant-Colonel W. L. Osborn, commanding; Captain G. F. Osborne,* Acting Second-in-Command; Lieutenant W. S. Till,* Acting Adjutant.

A Company : 2nd Lieutenants H. F. Broughall, C. F. Rolfe,* T. V. Wood,* and I. D. Margary.*

B Company : 2nd Lieutenants R. H. Fortescue, H. F. Cooke,* and D. S. Glenister.*

C Company : Captain H. S. Bowlby,* 2nd Lieutenants H. F. Taylor and T. Fitzsimons.*

D Company : Captain A. K. Trower,* 2nd Lieutenants J. C. Day, R. S. Browning,* and D. G. Le Doux Veitch.*

Transport Officer, Lieutenant R. C. D. Hind; Quartermaster, Lieutenant J. E. Clarke.

Captain Shaw, 38th Field Ambulance, acted as Medical Officer, until succeeded by Lieutenant E. F. Buckler on the 15th.

On the 10th, after bathing and cleaning up, we marched to Forceville and billeted, and on the 11th moved on to Bus-les-Artois via Acheux. On this last march the Divisional and Brigade Commanders reviewed the battalions and congratulated them. The Divisional Band played the Regimental March (1st Battalion) and we were made to feel we had done our job.

Major-General Scott came again on the 12th especially to congratulate the men on their gallant fight at Ovillers. We were thoroughly comfortable in the woods at Bus and started reorganising at once.

---

* These officers formed the battle reserve and did not go into action. Captain G. Nagle was attached to the 35th Brigade H.Q.

The Somme

On the 14th July a composite battalion of 350 7th Royal Sussex and 250 9th Royal Fusiliers was formed under the command of Colonel Osborn and moved forward to bivouac west of Sailly-au-Bois as reserve to the 145th Brigade, 48th Division. This composite battalion was relieved two days later by the 13th Welch Regiment (38th Division) and returned to huts and tents in Bus Wood.

The next day drafts to fill the depleted ranks of the battalion arrived from the Base, the men being members of the Royal Fusiliers, Middlesex and Queen's Regiments. It was ascertained, however, that a draft of Royal Sussex men had been posted to the Royal West Kent Regiment, and no delay ensued in obtaining authority for exchanges to be made so that the men could join their own regiments. The regimental spirit never waned.

JULY 1916

The tranquillity of the days spent in Bus Wood, out of sight and out of range of the enemy, was much appreciated, and good use was made of the time available for reorganisation and re-equipment. But on the 20th July the battalion moved to Mailly-Maillet preparatory to taking over the line. The men were mostly accommodated in cellars and the town was sporadically shelled, particularly at night. Orders to take over the line were cancelled, and on the 24th July we moved back to the Bois du Warnimont, north-west of Bus.

On this day Colonel Osborn received orders to proceed to Poperinghe to take command of the 16th Brigade (6th Division), and on the following day, after addressing the battalion, he drove away to the sound of " Sussex by the Sea," played by the band, and of the cheers of all ranks who lined the road.

Although everyone was delighted at Colonel Osborn's well-merited promotion, his loss was keenly felt. He had virtually founded the battalion in the first days of the war, had nursed it through its early training in England, had watched it grow to the fine fighting unit it became, and had announced its arrival to the M.L.O. at Boulogne. He had been with it in its baptism of fire, had led it through its hardest times of trial, and, above all, by his personality had imbued it with that *esprit de corps* which remained with it to the end of the war—and after the war—although it never came under his command again.

Captain G. F. Osborne now took command, and the battalion moved south for its second spell in the Battle of the Somme.

THE SOMME

Since we had left the sector the Australians had captured Pozières and the line on the left of the attack had moved forward; the plan now was to seize the high ground north of Pozières and to advance on Thiepval.

JULY 1916   This task was allotted to the 12th Division, in co-operation with the Australian Corps on their right. We now passed into the II Corps.

Until the 30th July we occupied support trenches between Ovillers and La Boisselle. These trenches had been part of the German front line system before the attack on the 1st July, and it was with amazement that we explored and enjoyed the spacious and comfortable deep dug-outs to which the Germans were accustomed in a stable part of the line; they were indeed a contrast to the sheet of corrugated iron set in a wall of the trench which had so often sufficed for shelter in our lines. It was even reported that a lady's trousseau had been discovered in a commodious wardrobe! Souvenir hunters had their fill, and the warning which had been issued before leaving for the Somme against loading packs with souvenirs as "there would be plenty to be found on the Somme" had indeed come true.

On the 30th we relieved the 11th Middlesex and again found ourselves in the front line occupying Third Avenue, with C Company in Pozières Trench in touch with the Australians on the right.

On the night of the relief the 11th Middlesex made an unsuccessful attack from the south against a strong-point on our left flank, under cover of a demonstration by our D Company operating from the north. Our casualties were 5 killed and 24 wounded. On the following evening a similar attempt was made in conjunction with the Middlesex, but met with little success, though our bombing-attack gained fifty yards, which were held and consolidated. This attack cost us 7 killed and 11 wounded.

On the night of the 3rd August an attack on a larger scale was organised with the object of capturing Fourth Avenue. At 11 p.m., after heavy artillery preparation, the 8th Royal Fusiliers, with the 6th Buffs on their left, reached their

AUGUST 1916   objective, penetrating to Ration Trench, which was reported to be captured. A Company was then sent forward with instructions to get into touch with the 8th Royal Fusiliers in Ration Trench and to work down towards Point 77, on the right, while a platoon of C Company was despatched to bring pressure to bear on Point 77 by an attack up Pozières Trench.

7. POZIÈRES

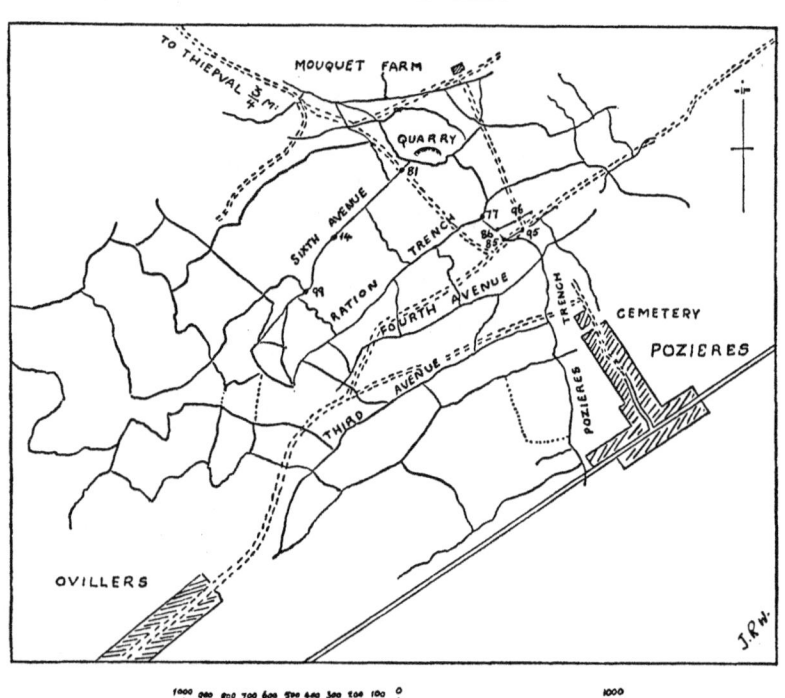

A Company lost direction in the dark, and it was a matter of luck that they were not fired on by the 8th Royal Fusiliers, who saw them charging down on the right flank.* Eventually, however, they reached the south-west portion of Ration Trench and reported to Lieutenant-Colonel T. G. Cope, commanding the 6th Buffs, who ordered two officers' patrols (one from his own battalion and the other from A Company under 2nd Lieutenant Rolfe) to push out towards Sixth Avenue from Point 99 to Point 81. These patrols reported that Sixth Avenue was thinly held and without wire or dug-outs, also that there were many dead and wounded Germans lying about, which evidently showed the accuracy of our artillery preparation. Colonel Cope then ordered A Company to push forward and capture Sixth Avenue on the ridge. They reached this objective without difficulty, but a strong counter-attack, and lack of support, led to severe losses, and only remnants of the company ever returned to Ration Trench.

AUGUST 1916

The Divisional History states : "A captured prisoner said that his company was ' half an hour ' away in Thiepval. A small gap had evidently been found, but it was impossible to exploit it further as machine-guns now opened fire from a position about 200 yards to the west, and a body of some 200 Germans advancing from Mouquet Farm forced the patrols to retire from the vicinity of Points 81 and 14. Valuable information had been gained for the future, however."†

C Company's attack against Point 77 was broken up by heavy machine-gun and rifle fire ; artillery or trench-mortar preparation was impossible owing to the closeness of our trenches to the enemy's.

During the night of the 4th a further effort was made to capture the right of Ration Trench and Point 77. B and D Companies advanced across the open, their objective being 250 yards of Ration Trench, and although they lost direction they reached part of the objective and obtained touch with the 9th Royal Fusiliers, which had attacked on the left. All objectives were gained and consolidated in this part of the attack, but the attack by two platoons of C Company on Point 77 was again abortive, the enemy holding in force Points 77, 86 and 96. One platoon attacked up Pozières Trench and the other platoon debouched from the trench held by the Australians between Points 85 and 95. The Australians holding this portion of trench spontaneously

---

* *Vide* H. C. O'Neill's *The Royal Fusiliers in the Great War*, p. 125.
† *Op. cit.*, p. 64.

joined in the attack to a man, and the trenches thus denuded were occupied again by the Australians easing up to the left, and by the remaining platoon of C Company easing up to the right.

What had probably incensed the Australians was the fact that at the spot where our C Company joined up with them the German snipers had been shooting the wounded; in broad daylight Australian stretcher-bearers had gone out to get one man in, and just as they got him both had been killed by the snipers.

AUGUST 1916

During this attack one of the "Lilliputians," Lance-Corporal Peters, in jumping into the German trench, landed straight on the head of a huge German, who promptly surrendered; the little corporal, with fixed bayonet, escorted him and nine others back to our lines. Sergeant-Major Hanlon relates that he saw Regimental Sergeant-Major Joy smoking a big German cigar as he brought in three prisoners whom he had captured by pointing an empty Verey light pistol.

The 5th August was noteworthy for the surrender of 2 officers and 100 men of a *Jäger* battalion who had been lying out in shell-holes between Ration Trench and our original front line; they were encouraged to come in by the assurance of some of the 8th Royal Fusiliers who spoke German that they would not be shot.

Our casualties on the 3rd and 4th August amounted to a total of 165.

A personal narrative of these operations is given by Sergeant-Major Hanlon :—

"About 6 p.m. on the 4th August we were ordered up to the front line, and about 8.50 p.m., Captain A. K. Trower, commanding D Company, informed me that Zero was at 9.15 p.m. (*i.e.*, 25 minutes to go) and that the company was going over in two lines, 13 Platoon on the right and 14 on the left, with 15 and 16 in support. A small party was sent off to collect what they could from the dump near Battalion H.Q. in the way of bombs and Verey lights, with orders to get into touch again as soon as possible. This party we never saw again until we came out. The Australians were on our right and the 9th Royal Fusiliers on our left. At 9.10 p.m. the intense bombardment started, lasting for five minutes, and as soon as it lifted over we went. The orders for the attack were very vague. I had been ordered to go straight ahead, across the Albert-Bapaume Road, and continue on for about 400 yards. We soon began to get thinned out. Number 13 was not in touch on the right, while on

The Somme

our left was a gap of about forty yards between Number 14 and the Fusiliers. But we met with very little resistance and soon occupied our objective in Ration Trench. We collected about a dozen prisoners—Brandenburgers—who were sent back to Battalion H.Q.

"We then began to consolidate, but our right gave us some trouble until, under the command of an officer of the Royal Fusiliers, we built a barricade and blocked an adjoining communication trench. Shortly afterwards orders were received to place alternate sentries on the back of the trench, facing the rear, for apparently during the attack we had passed over some of the enemy who had come out of the trenches to escape our bombardment and they were now sniping us from the rear.

AUGUST 1916

"About dawn the enemy counter-attacked with liquid fire, but Sergeant F. Tooms (A), who was attached to us, got both of the *flammenwerfer* carriers with the first burst of his Lewis gun and the counter-attack failed. The rest of the morning was most unpleasant, as our sentries were being continuously sniped from the rear, and several were killed. A few of the enemy crawled in and surrendered, and one, a Sergeant-Major, was told to stand up and try and persuade the others to do so, but he was killed by a German bullet. However, about 2 p.m., the remainder did surrender.

"Towards dusk I was ordered to withdraw my platoon (only about four were left) as the battalion was being relieved. We made our way to Crucifix Corner, where we found the cookers and had a most welcome hot meal; we then occupied some disused gun-pits, where we were gas shelled and had to wear our respirators most of the night."

Second Lieutenant C. F. Rolfe, who was wounded and taken prisoner in these operations, adds the following personal recollections :—

"The night of the relief, when the 11th Middlesex made the unsuccessful attack against a strong-point on the left flank, was one of the very worst I have ever experienced, not even being equalled by the attacks I had taken part in previously in the Ypres salient in 1915. Many of our men had not been in the firing line before, and our particular trench was crowded out with the Middlesex men, poor fellows, who were engaged in the abortive attack. Several of my men were killed by one shell, and I shall never forget the scene which met my eyes when I arrived at the spot. Among them was Sergeant Tyrrell, a fine chap only recently promoted. That ghastly night will ever live in my memory. I have never been so near murder as when Lieutenant Broughall fired his revolver just behind me! I imagine he was in good spirits, having just had a good night's rest in a luxurious dug-out which had been built by the enemy.

"Soon after this we were moved into the last trench I was to occupy. It was a poor affair, giving little cover. On our left it was held by the enemy, who were separated from us by a neutral length of trench of about 30 yards. Having been taught that it was my duty to harry the enemy whenever possible, I engaged in a little bombing practice early one morning. I then retired and lay down in the open trench for a well-earned sleep, not having had any for some days. Imagine my disgust when the Brigadier arrived and demanded to know who was the officer in charge and why the devil he couldn't let the enemy alone!

AUGUST 1916

"On August 4th I received orders at 3.30 a.m. to attack as soon as possible and consolidate the position in Ration Trench, which had been captured.

"We moved forward just as it was becoming light, passing over several wounded men lying in shell-holes. In the half light we moved too far to the left, getting into touch with the 6th Buffs, whose Commanding Officer directed me to what he believed to be Ration Trench. Many prisoners were then passing down through our lines.

"We pushed on for some 800 yards till we came to an imposing-looking trench, which we entered with little opposition and, I think, few casualties. Leaving Lieutenant Wood there (he was shortly afterwards killed), I pushed up the trench to the left in pursuit of the retiring Germans. Having no bombs of our own left we collected some of theirs and used them with good effect. By this time enemy shelling had begun and, coming to a deep communication trench, I climbed up on the top to view the position when something like a steam roller hit me—actually a sniper's bullet. That was the end so far as I was concerned.

"My stretcher-bearers stripped off my tunic and shirt and bound me up as best they could. It was impossible for them to get me away, and they had to retire as best they could in face of a counter-attack. I was lying out from 4.30 a.m. to 8 p.m. in a kind of little No Man's Land all to myself and thought I was finished when a 12-inch shell (one of ours, I suspect) fell within inches of me, but luckily it failed to explode.

THE SOMME

"Eventually I was found by the Germans and taken down to a first-aid post, where I was relieved of my watch and boots, the only things remaining to me then being a pair of trousers. On the whole I was then well treated. My great regret is that I have never been able to thank those stretcher-bearers who attended me when I was wounded, and I have always hoped they got back safely."

AUGUST 1916

Rolfe was reported "missing, believed killed" after this attack, as there seemed little chance of his survival. There was no trace of him when Ration Trench was eventually taken, and it was known that the enemy's communications were so bad that they had not received any supplies in the front line for several days.

After the action of the 4th August the following message was received by the G.O.C. Fifth Army (Gough):—

"The Commander-in-Chief warmly congratulates you and the commanders, staffs and troops of all arms under you who organised and carried out the attack last night. The success gained is of very considerable importance and opens the way to further equally valuable successes to be obtained by similar careful methods of preparation and gallantry and thoroughness in execution.

"The 12th Division and 2nd Australian Division have not been mentioned by name in the congratulations telegraphed to you this morning in accordance with the Commander-in-Chief's instructions.

"The reason for not mentioning them is that there is a risk of conveying information to the enemy.

"The Commander-in-Chief desires, however, that the divisions concerned may be informed that they are specially included in his congratulations.

"5.8.16.   Chief, General Staff."*

On the evening of the 5th August the battalion was relieved by the 9th Royal Fusiliers and moved back to old gun positions in the Tara-Usna line, where Major H. A. Carr, D.S.O., from the 4th Worcestershire Regiment, greeted the remnants of the battalion and took over command. Captain Osborne became Second-in-Command and Captain Nagle Adjutant. The company

---
* Quoted from *The History of the 12th Division*, pp. 65-6.

commanders were Lieutenant H. S. Cousens, A; 2nd Lieutenant H. Sadler, B; Captain H. S. Bowlby, C; 2nd Lieutenant H. F. Taylor, D.

The fighting from which we had emerged had been designed to exploit earlier successes and to discover the weak spots in the enemy's defence. Orders to this end were often received at notice which did not allow of adequate reconnaissance and preparation, with the result that direction was lost, effort was not synchronised, and confusion ensued. It was typical of the nature of the operations that one of the original stalwarts of the battalion, a platoon sergeant of A Company, when sorely wounded and undiscovered by stretcher-bearing search parties, was able to crawl to safety after days of wandering from trench to trench and shell-hole to shell-hole—only to be killed when being carried to the advanced dressing-station.

<small>AUGUST 1916</small>

Nevertheless, the outcome of this fighting was the complete capture of Fourth Avenue and the majority of Ration Trench, the surrender of over 100 Germans and, by justifiable inference, the infliction of heavy casualties on the enemy, who at this period defended stubbornly every yard of ground; moreover, it paved the way to the subsequent capture of all this ground, including Mouquet Farm, the focus of the enemy's strength in this sector.

The casualties sustained by the Division during this second tour in the Battle of the Somme were 126 officers and 2,739 other ranks. Since the 28th July it had gained three lines of enemy's trench on a front of 1,500 yards, and on its departure from the scene of these operations a special order of the day was received from Sir Hubert Gough, the G.O.C. Fifth Army :—

" On the departure of the 12th Division to join the Third Army, the G.O.C. Reserve Army desires to place on record his appreciation of the good work done by the Division while under his command.

" On both occasions on which the Division has been in the line it has borne its full share of the fighting with gallantry and determination, and the best record of its achievements is to be found in the considerable area of ground now in our possession, in the capture of which it has played so important a part.

" The G.O.C. parts with the services of the Division with regret and wishes all ranks the best of good luck in their new sphere of action.

" 13.8.16. H.Q. Reserve Army."*

---

* Quoted from *The History of the 12th Division*, pp. 73-4.

The Somme

The casualties of the battalion in the Pozières operations between the 30th July and the 5th August amounted to:—

	Officers	Other ranks
Killed	4	38
Wounded and prisoner	1	20
Died of wounds ..	—	5
Wounded	5	151
Totals ..	10	214

Officers killed : 2nd Lieutenants H. F. Cooke (O.C. B Company), T. Fitzsimons (C), D. G. Le Doux Veitch (D), and T. V. Wood (A).

,, wounded & prisoner : 2nd Lieutenant C. F. Rolfe (O.C. A Company).

,, wounded : Captain A. K. Trower (O.C. D Company) ; 2nd Lieutenants R. D'Alton (C), D. S. Glenister (B), R. M. Howe (A), and R. S. Browning (D).

N.C.O.s killed : Sergeants E. Hulkes (B), G. Seckham (A), and G. W. Tyrrell (A) ; Corporal W. Linden (B).

The honours awarded in these operations were :—

Military Cross : Captain H. S. Bowlby (O.C. C Company).
Distinguished Conduct Medal : Sergeants G. Hodges (C) and G. Ward (B).
Military Medal* : Company Sergeant-Majors J. Hayes (D) and A. Richold (C) ; Sergeants A. W. Horne (A), R. Lawrence (A), L. Rovery (C), and A. E. Selby (A) ; Lance-Corporal C. P. Mayes (D) ; Privates H. Aungier (B), H. Glenister (A), J. H. Goddard (D), H. W. Newport (A), F. V. Nichols (B), J. R. Selsby (B), and P. A. C. White (C).

On the 6th August a move was made to the Albert-Bouzincourt line, in which the 9th Essex relieved us on the following day, and we then marched to billets in Bouzincourt, where we stayed for three days.

The 10th August was memorable for an inspection of the 36th Brigade by His Majesty the King. The Brigade lined a country road near Senlis and His Majesty walked between the ranks, accompanied by His Royal Highness the Prince of Wales, General Sir Hubert Gough (Fifth Army), Lieutenant-General C. W. Jacob (II Corps), and Major-General A. B. Scott, the Divisional Commander.

AUGUST 1916

On the following day the battalion began its march from the Somme and, halting at Varennes, Puchevillers, Sarton, Sus-St.

---
* Some of these include awards for gallantry at Ovillers.

Léger, Izel-lez-Hameau and Berneville, and picking up drafts en route, it reached Agny (just south of Arras) on the 20th and relieved the 6th Green Howards (11th Division).

The Agny sector was a quiet one; in fact a haven of rest after the Somme, and the total casualties during our stay of five weeks in this area amounted only to 2 killed and 1 wounded.

One morning a board was seen in front of the German wire stating the number of guns and prisoners captured in Roumania.

AUGUST 1916 — Lance-Corporal L. M. Barker, of D Company, brought it in, and a *Daily Mail* poster, announcing in big type "Another Two Zeppelins Brought Down," was put on the top of it. It was replaced in the enemy wire the same night.

Identification of the enemy forces was important to determine the rate of wastage of his divisions on the Somme, and to this end numerous raids were carried out by the Division. Six days in the line and six days in reserve became the routine procedure, with comparative immunity from shelling whether in or out of the line.

At Agny we could hear the ominous rumble of the incessant conflict on the Somme, and eventually the inevitable orders arrived for the battalion to be relieved by the 9th King's Royal Rifle Corps (14th Division) and to proceed for a third time to the main scene of activity. The relief was completed on the 26th September, and after billeting for a night in Berneville we embussed in French vehicles for Bouquemaison, where two nights were spent. On the 29th buses took us as far as Lavieville, and a march of ten miles then brought us to Pommiers Redoubt at 1 a.m. on the 30th. We had supposed that some accommodation, either above or below ground, would be available at this redoubt, which appeared formidable on the map, but arriving as we did in the small hours it was only with the greatest difficulty that we found anywhere to sleep at all.

The condition of the country at this time was appalling. Hardly a foot of ground had not been ploughed up by shelling, and on top of this came the rain, which was only less incessant than the shelling. The result was a quagmire.

SEPTEMBER 1916 — The roads were mere country lanes, never made to withstand the weight of heavy traffic nor to accommodate a double stream of it. Horses, men, limbers and lorries stuck in the mud, and pack-transport was generally the only practicable means of supply. According to Captain Hind the Flers road was "the worst the Transport ever had to compete with, being made entirely of dead men, mules

8. GUEUDECOURT

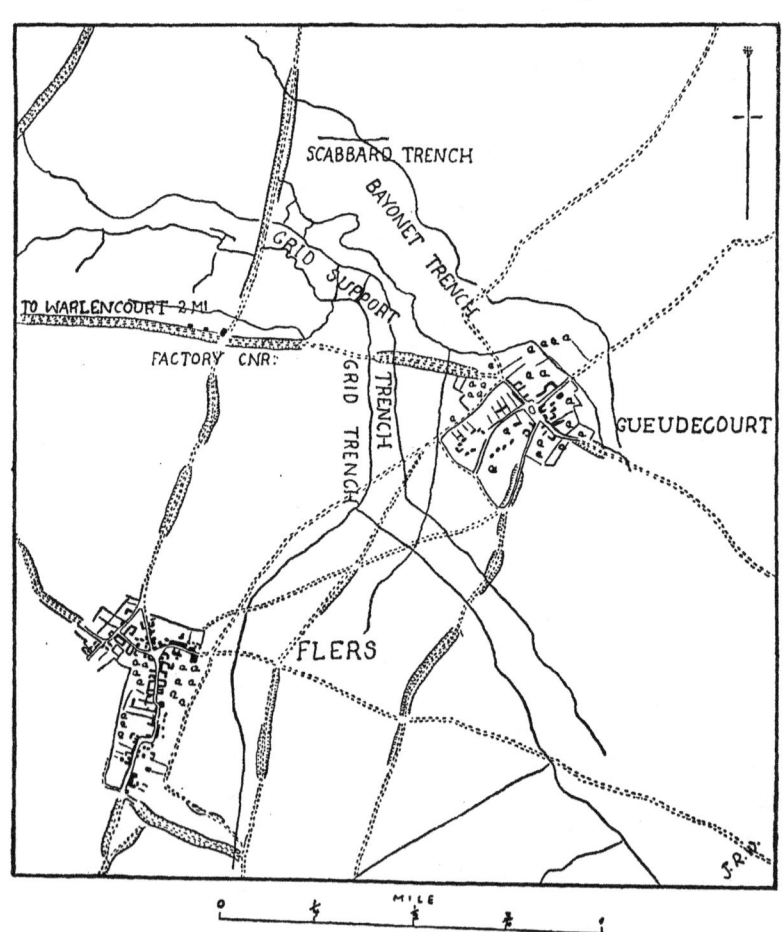

and horses; sometimes it took teams of six mules to half a limber to deliver rations."

Under such conditions the battalion entered on its third spell of the Somme battle, and during the relief of the 11th Queen's (21st Division) on the 1st October we began to wonder whether we should ever arrive at our allotted positions in support to the 8th and 9th Royal Fusiliers, OCTOBER 1916 who occupied Grid Support and Grid Trench, with the 37th Brigade on their right and Anzac Division on their left. Sundry bearded men were met on the left, and it was said that our neighbours had vowed not to shave until they came out of the line; since rumour had it that they had already been in five weeks the length of the beards seemed to corroborate the story.

The sector occupied by the 36th Brigade (now in the XV Corps) was not an easy one. The front line, Grid Support and Grid Trench, consisted of old German trenches, and the support line was some 500 yards to the rear. The communication trench between Grid Support and Grid Trench was only two feet deep and in full view of the enemy. The main approach to the trenches from the rear was down an open valley, into which shells dropped almost unceasingly. Battalion H.Q. was propped against the side of a sunken road to the east of Flers. Flers itself was constantly shelled, but as it was not occupied and was visited only occasionally by scavenging parties in search of firewood or material for shelters this attention by the enemy was a boon. Behind Battalion H.Q. was a morass in which men and animals struggled to their destinations. Throughout the time we occupied the front area the shelling was intense and our losses were very heavy, considering that we were not involved in any actual fighting.

On the 3rd October the battalion relieved the 8th Royal Fusiliers in the front line, C and D Companies being in the foremost trench, Grid Support, B in support in Factory Trench, and A in reserve behind. The German gunners knew the exact position of these trenches, and so severe were the casualties from shelling that on the night of the 5th the whole of C and D Companies went out and dug a new trench fifty to one hundred yards in advance of the front line, in the hope of reducing this wastage of men. Our casualties in killed alone amounted to 2 officers and 17 other ranks during the 5th October.

There was little rifle or machine-gun fire during this operation, and in the darkness the company sergeant-majors could be heard giving orders in stentorian tones. The trench may not have been orientated in an ideal manner, but at least it afforded some relief from shelling and was officially hailed as an advance.

OCTOBER 1916

While the trench was being dug two Germans came over and surrendered to the working-parties.

On the 6th October the 8th Royal Fusiliers relieved us and we went back to the old support trenches. One company commander, who came up in advance to reconnoitre the front line, arrived with acute shell-shock, and his substitute was killed later while traversing the shallow communication trench, so that eventually one company commander took over the entire line.

The following day the Fourth and Fifth Armies and the Sixth French Army carried out an attack which had been postponed for forty-eight hours owing to the weather. On the 36th Brigade front the 8th and 9th Royal Fusiliers attacked Bayonet Trench. Since we were in support, A and D Companies were sent forward to Grid Trench under Captain Osborne in readiness to move into the front line when the attack was launched. Shortly before Zero the Germans opened furious machine-gun fire and put down a barrage of increasing intensity, which indicated a previous knowledge of the attack and prevented the assaulting troops (whose casualties were very heavy) from gaining their objectives. So heavy was the shell-fire that only D Company was able to reach the front line. B and C Companies were moved up into support.

The same evening the whole Brigade front was taken over by the 11th Middlesex and the battalion moved back into support with the exception of D Company and the Lewis gunners, who were ordered to support the 37th Brigade and remained in the line for a further twenty-four hours. On the 10th October the 9th Essex relieved us and we moved back to Bernafay Wood, near Montauban. This area was beyond the range of any but the long-range guns of the enemy, though chances of rest were marred by heavy working-parties and by the propinquity of a battery of 6-inch guns some 150 yards to the rear. When these guns fired, which they did frequently, the blast was shattering, extinguishing all lights and making tents flutter like bellows.

Here Colonel Carr was ordered to take over command of the 1/8th Worcestershires (48th Division), and Captain A. J. Sansom, of the 5th Royal Sussex, came to us from the Staff of the VIII Corps on the 10th and assumed command.

The Somme

The casualties in the Gueudecourt area from the 1st to the 8th October amounted to :—

	Officers	Other ranks
Killed	2	31
Died of wounds	—	10*
Wounded	5	134*
Totals	7	175*

Officers killed : 2nd Lieutenants W. J. Franklin (D) and F. Golds (A).
„   wounded : Lieutenant W. S. Till (C); 2nd Lieutenants B. Martin (D), G. A. Phipps (D), H. Roos (B), and A. C. W. Uloth (C).
N.C.O.s killed : Sergeants R. Prevett, D.C.M. (B) and F. J. Russell (Scouts); Corporals R. Cheesman, D.C.M. (C), A. H. Head (D), C. Holden (A), J. A. Hulme (B), and J. C. Norman (A).

Private H. Aungier (B) was later awarded a bar to his Military Medal for his work during this fighting, and Private W. H. Hayward (C) received a Military Medal.

On the 17th October the battalion was attached to the 35th Brigade and moved forward into reserve trenches.

The same afternoon another attack against Bayonet Trench by the 9th Essex broke down owing to machine-gun fire and uncut wire. The attack was to be continued on the following day, and the battalion was ordered to go into action on the left, with the 5th Royal Berks on the right. The attack was to be a surprise one, four bombing-squads, supported by one company, attacking from each flank without any preliminary bombardment. Our bombing-parties were commanded by 2nd Lieutenants T. Clarke and R. J. Ledger, with C Company, commanded by Lieutenant C. W. Ballard, in support.

OCTOBER 1916

At 2.50 a.m., ten minutes before Zero, the Germans put down a heavy barrage, accompanied by cascades of Verey lights. Patrols reported that the enemy was holding Bayonet Trench strongly and was obviously waiting for an attack. Since any idea of surprise was thus out of the question, Lieutenant-Colonel F. G. Willan, D.S.O., commanding the 5th Royal Berks, who was in charge of the operation, decided that it should be abandoned.

At 6 a.m. next morning (the 19th) the assaulting troops were withdrawn, and at 3 p.m. we were relieved by the 1st Lancashire

---

* Approximate.

The Somme

Fusiliers (29th Division) and moved back to Mametz Wood Camp. The following day we rejoined the 36th Brigade at Fricourt Camp and turned our back on the Somme until the great German attack and our subsequent victorious advance in 1918.

From now until the end of the month we moved leisurely by foot and by bus via Buire, Gouy and Dainville, to the Agny area, where, on the 1st November, we relieved the 8th Royal Fusiliers in the front line.

We knew this sector intimately, and procedure in the matter of reliefs, raids and working-parties was much the same as it had been in September. The only event of interest, apart from normal routine, was the issue on November 23rd of the small box-respirator. This respirator was certainly a vast improvement on the piece of shirting soaked in chemicals and worn over the head, and every man's new respirator was tested in a gas chamber by the user on issue. It was during this period, too, that Brigadier-General Boyd-Moss was relieved by Brigadier-General C. S. Owen, D.S.O., who had been commanding the 6th Royal West Kents, and was to lead the Brigade until the end of the war.

NOVEMBER 1916

On the 16th December the battalion was relieved by the 5th Oxford and Bucks Light Infantry (14th Division) and, marching away westwards, arrived at Sibiville next day for a needed and well-earned rest.

9. ARRAS AREA, 1917

CHAPTER VII

THE BATTLE OF ARRAS

18TH DECEMBER, 1916—15TH MAY, 1917
[Sketch Maps, Nos. 9, 10, 11, and 12]

Although for the last month the battalion had not been engaged in an active sector, the prospect of a stay in a real rest area was extremely welcome. Since leaving Vignacourt for the Somme battle nearly six months previously the battalion had not been out of the front line area, and during that period it had suffered casualties to a total of 38 officers and 900 other ranks, a number considerably larger than its average ration strength. The conditions of the front line area, with its eternal working-parties, scattered billets, and hurried moves, were not conducive to the proper assimilation of the many drafts received, and reorganisation and training, especially of newly promoted N.C.O.s, had been impossible.

DECEMBER 1916

Sibiville, a small village about twenty miles west of Arras and five miles south of St. Pol, provided a pleasant but unremarkable billeting area, after giving us a poor welcome on arrival. Our predecessors had not made themselves much liked by the inhabitants, and it needed great tact on the part of the Commanding Officer, who went to call upon the local Mayor, and of our silver-tongued billeting corporal, Corporal Ramsay, before the battalion was comfortably settled in after its long march.

Christmas was naturally the first thought, and the arrangements made (carried out as efficiently as ever by Sergeant Raby) had successfully cheerful results on the 25th, when B and D Companies, and on the 26th, when A and C Companies, dined and wined, or rather " beered," in D Company's large barn. A large consignment of puddings arrived through the funds organised by *The Daily Telegraph*, *The Daily News*, and *The Hastings and St. Leonards Advertiser*, and they went down very well. Even more strenuous entertainment was provided by the sergeants when they gave a smoking-concert to the officers on New Year's Eve, and again when the officers returned the compliment a week later.

The Battle of Arras

JANUARY 1917

A battalion inter-company football league was formed, for the winners of which Colonel Sansom most generously gave a challenge cup and individual medals. These were won by D Company's unbeaten team, which was lucky to have the expert services of the brothers Rosier, late of the Brentford team. The D Company side also contained no less than six officers, including Captain Reckitt, who had returned in December, and the battalion football captain, 2nd Lieutenant H. J. R. Farrow. B Company were the runners-up, being beaten only by D. The efficient services of our Medical Officer, Captain A. A. Rees, who acted as referee on our extremely muddy field, were much appreciated. In the brigade and divisional competitions we did not progress very far, and we were beaten in the first round of the latter by the 8th Royal Fusiliers, when our outside-left, Sergeant Rennie, of D Company, was unlucky enough to break a leg.

Each company held an afternoon with a full programme of keenly-contested athletic sports, and a vigorous cross-country race resulted in a victory for B Company's team.

The battalion canteen was started again most successfully, and the daily ceremonial sounding of "Retreat" by Sergeant-Drummer Aylmore's troupe (now augmented by the presentation of tenor drums by the Commanding Officer and Captain Bowlby) was the admiration and inspiration of British and French alike.

Recreation has been put first, for it is more easily remembered than work. But much useful reorganisation and training were done in spite of consistently bad weather, so that the battalion began to feel itself as a whole instead of as batches of survivors and reinforcements. Of the latter we received further drafts of 2 officers and 100 other ranks while at Sibiville.

There were two ceremonial parades, at which the battalion acquitted itself well. On the 9th January the Brigadier inspected us and presented cards for gallantry to Regimental Quartermaster-Sergeant W. Long and Company Quartermaster-Sergeant P. J. Hanlon. On the 13th General Scott inspected us and presented the medal ribbons for the operations at Pozières and Gueudecourt.

Altogether it was a good month, well spent, and, when the call came for the curtain to go up on the first act of the Battle of Arras, we were well ready to answer it.

On the 18th January an intensely cold and irritatingly slippery march of fifteen miles brought us to muddy Wanquetin and very cramped and uncomfortable billets. Before these were altered Colonel Sansom was forced to adopt stern language to those who were responsible. The mighty did not appreciate being reminded of their duty, nor, as it transpired, did they forget it. The JANUARY 1917 battalion both remembered and appreciated.

It was fortunate that we had more room given us, for another draft of 135 men arrived while we were at Wanquetin.

On the 23rd we marched, again on an extremely cold day, to billets in Arras, where we were attached to the 37th Brigade, commanded by Brigadier-General A. B. E. Cator, D.S.O., whose recent death when G.O.C. London District was much mourned by all who knew him in the 12th Division. Our duties were to consist solely in night-digging and tunnelling work in preparation for the coming battle.

The history of Arras, of which the 12th Division, when it finally left the area nine months later, was hailed by the Mayor as " the defenders and the deliverers," goes back to the earliest times, and the town has seen many invaders at its gates—Romans, Huns, Spaniards and Germans. For centuries the inhabitants had quarried stone from beneath them for their houses, public buildings and churches, with the result that there were many large caves and cellars in existence in 1917, a number of which had been out of use for a long time.

General Sir Edmund Allenby, who commanded the Third Army, was denied the element of surprise in the coming attack entrusted to him, for he was ordered to prepare a long preliminary bombardment. He therefore decided to introduce one surprise element by providing cover for a large number of his reserves close up to the front line. Consequently it was arranged that as many of the larger caves as could be located should be joined up underground and linked to the extensive cellars of the *Grande Place* and *Petite Place*, and to the main sewer of the town. The whole system was to be extended so as to provide exits into No Man's Land. Cover was thus to be provided for as many as 40,000 men, and living accommodation for about a quarter of that number, who would be the reserve troops of the 3rd, 12th, and 15th Divisions of the VI Corps. Tramways, kitchens, electric light, water, and sanitation were provided in " The Caves," as they were called, and the whole system was elaborately sign-posted and was controlled by a staff of "Caves Officers." Above ground the preparations were no less extensive, and miles of communication trenches and wide cross-trenches, tramways and light railways were constructed. Such was the work on which we were to be engaged.

And work, indeed, it was. The working-parties before the Arras battle will long be remembered by those who took part in them for the intense rigour of the weather, the coldest spell for very many years. This naturally made digging a most difficult task, for the ground was frozen for a depth of more than a foot, and when a trench was left half-completed the sides of it froze also and work upon it was by no means easy. On their way to the scene of operations the troops marched through the railway station (which was intact except for the broken glass), through the booking-office, whose walls were adorned with invitations to visit the Côte d'Azur and other tourist resorts, on to the platform, across the rails and out the other side, without any sign of life but a solitary military policeman.

JANUARY 1917

The battalion worked in two reliefs, beginning at 6 p.m. and finishing when the job was completed. The latter time varied, but was usually about 3 or 4 a.m. There were many difficulties to contend with. The normal proportion of picks to shovels, as laid down in the Army Regulations, was quite inadequate to such conditions. It was not easy to get this altered, partly because it is always a super-human task to persuade the authorities to alter anything in any regulations, and partly because of the enormous demand. A great many of the tools issued were broken or otherwise unsuitable, but again, owing to the abnormal demand, it was not possible to replace them. Perhaps the greatest disadvantage was the fact that this period coincided with an attempt by an " expert " to reorganise the entire railway system of the British Army in France. Road traffic had already been cut down to a minimum owing to the frost, and many materials and large stores of ammunition were required for the coming offensive. Part of the " expert's " remedial process was to reduce the volume of traffic for a time, so that the ordinary rations for the front line troops could not be sent by rail. In the result, we lived on iron rations for several days. This was most unsuitable fare for men who were doing very heavy tasks in very cold weather, and the outcome of it was a severe epidemic of boils, which considerably reduced our efficiency and fitness.

Arras was a strange city in those days, with a routine of life peculiar to itself. Dominated by the heights known as Orange

The Battle of Arras

and Telegraph Hills, which the enemy held, and with front line trenches running through all its eastern suburbs, it showed few signs of life during the daytime, when most of its inhabitants, military and civilian, slept. No uncontrolled movement was allowed there during the daylight hours, and all persons proceeding on any duty had to have a pass and keep strictly to the inside of the pavements. After dark it had, in addition to the usual back-of-the-front bustle at night, a life of its own, for many inhabitants still remained, and the shops, with carefully screened windows, did a brisk trade. Although it was within easy bullet-range, Arras was very little shelled in those days, and there were many soldiers who found it more comfortable before the offensive than after it, when the line moved several miles eastward.   JANUARY 1917

Thanks to good and appreciative staff work by the 37th Brigade and to the efficiency of our immediate task-masters, the Royal Engineers, the 5th Northamptons and the New Zealand Tunnelling Company, we managed to perform our tasks quite cheerfully and with satisfaction to ourselves and others.

The battalion was fortunate in not having many casualties during this period and in meeting heavy enemy shell-fire on only one occasion. On the night of the 25th January A and B Companies were heavily gas-shelled, but, out of 20 men affected, only 4 went to hospital, 1 slightly wounded and 3 as gas cases.

It was remarkable that more opposition was not encountered, for the sparks thrown up by a working-party on that frozen and flinty ground could be seen from a long way off. It sometimes took the first relief an hour to make any impression on the soil, and one officer recalls a night when the first relief on one portion of the task had failed to excavate anything at all at the end of three hours' hard work. Then it was found that the men had been put to dig up the concrete bed of a dismantled factory.

On the 4th February Captain Rees, our Medical Officer, died at the Casualty Clearing Station, to the great regret of all. His place was filled by Captain E. A. Mills, who was to remain with us for a long time, and was always   FEBRUARY 1917 a success, both as a doctor and as a pianist.

During this period our front received a distinguished visitor in the person of Mr. Bernard Shaw, who, it must be admitted, did not look his best in a tin hat, which hardly suited his famous beard. It was while we were at Arras, too, that the "piano incident" occurred; it is worth relating, if only as an example of the kind of petty officialdom with which the fighting soldier sometimes had to contend at the hands of minor potentates who lived behind the line, and is best told in the words of the victim, Major G. F. Osborne :—

"On the opposite side of the street in which Battalion H.Q. was situated was a shelled and ruined house. Its walls were barely standing and its roof had completely collapsed. Various articles of furniture were exposed and someone discovered a piano. It was not in a first-class state, being covered with rubble and plaster, but it did work. One night this was 'salvaged' and transferred to the H.Q. Mess across the road. We had a professional piano-tuner in the ranks, and he got busy with whatever instruments he could raise and made a fairly respectable job of renovation, so that the piano eventually provided us with some cheery evenings.

FEBRUARY 1917

"But Nemesis, in the shape of a gendarme, suddenly descended on us. Having inspected the house and consulted his list of its contents, he discovered that there should be no piano there. This was a serious matter. Where had it come from ? It must have been 'looted.' In vain we protested that we had merely salvaged it, saved it from complete destruction, and with expert repair had made it a better piano than we found it. All to no avail. A report must be made to the Town Major, who, without even condescending to ask us for our version of the story, sent the report straight to Corps H.Q. From there eventually permeated down a very severe letter pointing out the extreme sentences which can be inflicted for looting and the serious view of the matter which those in authority took. The result was that I, who was held responsible, was marched in front of the Divisional Commander and received a severe censuring."

On the 7th we finished our first spell of digging and went to relieve the 6th Royal West Kents in front of Blangy. This was known as the I/2 sector Arras, and was the left front sector of that portion of the line which had all its trench names beginning with the letter I. A, B and C Companies were in the front line, with D in support. The enemy was very quiet; this was fortunate, for at one point the opposing trenches were reputed to be closer together than anywhere else along the whole British line. The trenches appeared to be about ten yards apart, hence the familiar tale that each side took it in turns to use the same loophole. The transport animals benefited from the discovery of a quantity of

The Battle of Arras

linseed cake near D Company's H.Q. Comfort reigned at this H.Q., which was provided with real beds, a piano and a summerhouse. The left-hand company had a post on a small island in the Scarpe, relief of sentries taking place just before dawn by means of an old punt.

Four days of this quiet were succeeded by four days' digging. Then the front line again in the I/1 (right) sector, where the enemy was also inclined to be quiet. Early in the morning of the 18th, D Company had a mild excitement. Two Russian prisoners, who had been employed on a working-party close behind the German lines, attempted to escape into our lines. Unfortunately they chose a spot where a new assembly trench was being dug in advance of our wire. The trench was overlooked by two sentries under orders to use special vigilance, and after challenging the Russians, who spoke no English, and receiving no answer, the sentries opened fire in the dusk, killing one man and wounding the other. The nationality of the survivor was not realised until he was interrogated farther back, and Captain Reckitt received a lot of chaff for having somewhat triumphantly announced the capture of a German prisoner. The words of his message to the Adjutant had been, "Herewith one Bosche slightly bent," to which the Adjutant replied, "For your message read 'Herewith one Ally rudely assaulted!'"

FEBRUARY 1917

Captain G. W. Prince contributes the following personal reminiscences relating to this period :—

"There was a lot of snow at the time, and I remember being detailed for a patrol one night. A kind and thoughtful Staff sent up some white coats and trousers so that we should blend with the landscape; needless to say, mine was for a six-foot fellow* and hampered me greatly. On returning from patrol and being pleased that all was well, we asked the sentry what the effect had been. His reply was 'Fine, Sir, you showed up lovely, and we watched you the whole way!' The Staff had forgotten the background of dark stakes and wire."

After another spell of digging we spent another four days in the I/1 sector. On the 26th the 11th Middlesex carried out a most successful daylight raid from our front. The enemy retaliation was heavy, and we had 2 men killed and 6 wounded.

After a couple of nights in Arras we moved to Lignereuil, where we were to do our final training for the offensive, spending a night at Montenescourt on the way. Lignereuil was a village about a

---

* Captain Prince was barely five foot.

The Battle of Arras

dozen miles behind the line, and close by, at Givenchy-le-Noble, we constructed an elaborate system of trenches, a replica of those which we were to attack. The château provided an excellent mess for all the officers of the battalion. This was the only occasion before the Armistice when we were able to have such an arrangement and it proved to be a great success. The long, tree-fringed avenue which led up to the château was known as "the puppy-dog's paradise."

Many hours were spent attacking over the practice trenches and in studying the small-scale sand model of the enemy lines which had been made outside the château. Whether this was actually of much value will be seen later. Other excitements were an inspection by Sir Douglas Haig on the 6th March and a tank demonstration at Erin for some of the officers on the 8th.

MARCH 1917

Two bad bombing accidents marred the enjoyment of the otherwise most pleasant period of eighteen days. On the 9th March 2nd Lieutenant R. J. Ledger was severly wounded by a bomb during practice and died of his injuries two days later. 2nd Lieutenant H. C. Bowller was also wounded at the same time. The following day 2nd Lieutenant A. E. Willard and 6 men were wounded by the premature explosion of a rifle-grenade.

The battalion moved, on the 21st, to Lattre-St. Quentin, about five miles nearer the front, and spent a very cold and snowy period of twelve days there in bad billets. On the 23rd C Company was ordered up to Arras to work under the 35th Brigade and A Company followed on the 30th to work under the 37th Brigade, an unlucky shell killing 8 men the next night. The remaining two companies of the battalion were inspected by the Corps Commander, Lieutenant-General J. A. L. Haldane, on the 31st.

On the 3rd April we marched to Arras, leaving 3 officers and 100 other ranks with the Transport at Agnez-lez Duisans as a battle reserve under the command of Captain A. L. Thomson, the newly-appointed Second-in-Command, who had come to us from the 1st Royal Sussex in India. The march was a very long and trying one in pouring rain, and the enemy was showing signs of activity. However, by 4 a.m. on the 4th, the whole battalion was safely in cellars along the Cambrai Road, east of the railway station. The preliminary bombardment began two hours later, and was to go on for the next five days. In the evening A and

APRIL 1917

The Battle of Arras

B Companies moved up into the left half of the I/1 sector, from which front we were to attack. H.Q. was in the reserve line in Ink Trench; C and D Companies remained in their cellars to provide ration and carrying parties.

It was a long and weary wait in badly damaged trenches, with the din of the bombardment going on without ceasing. On the 5th the wire was removed from in front of all trenches except the front line, and scaling-ladders and trench-bridges were brought up.

APRIL 1917

Patrols were active examining the damage caused by the bombardment, and Lieutenant N. McCracken thus describes two of these ventures :—

" On the 5th April I went out with a patrol of 6 men with orders to ascertain if the artillery had cut a lane through the wire at a certain point and whether that part of the line was being held. We found that the guns had done their job and, passing through the gap, reached the trench unchallenged. Leaving the others to cover us, I dropped in with one of the men and we made our way for some little distance along the trench without meeting anyone.

" The next night Brigade H.Q. wanted to know whether a certain post was being held, so I went out with the same party. Leaving the others, I crawled up to the wire with the Lance-Corporal and soon found that the post was occupied all right, for the occupants began shying bombs at us. Fortunately there was a shell-hole a little way back into which we slid, and the next five minutes were distinctly unpleasant. What annoyed us was that we had no bombs to retaliate with, and we thought it best not to fire, as the flash would have made us an easier target. Having obtained the information required, needless to say we lost no time in returning to our line when the excitement was over."

For this patrol work McCracken was awarded the Military Cross.

On the 7th 2 Platoon, under Lieutenant G. W. Prince, raided the German lines successfully. The enemy evacuated his trench when our men appeared, but a rifle and other things were secured for identification. The enemy opposition from his support line was severe, and the platoon lost 1 man killed and 2 wounded. The Military Cross was awarded to Lieutenant Prince for his skilful leadership. He mentions that one of his N.C.O.s, Sergeant Barnett, was to be sent home for a commission at this time, but asked permission to remain with the battalion for the attack. Unfortunately he was severely wounded in the knee and was eventually invalided out.

The Battle of Arras

On the evening of the 8th, Easter Sunday, all final arrangements were made and the front line wire was cleared away. At 3.30 a.m. on the 9th April C and D Companies moved up to take their positions in the line, 15 Platoon having many casualties from a direct hit by an 8-inch shell.

The Battle of Arras had been planned as far back as November, 1916. The intention of the Commander-in-Chief then was to attack against both sides of the salient created between the Rivers Scarpe and Ancre by the prolonged Somme fighting. The Fifth Army was to operate from the Ancre front and the Third Army from Arras, protecting its flank by securing Vimy Ridge. The enemy's retirement to the Hindenburg Line in March, 1917, did not seriously affect the programme allotted to the Third Army, for the Hindenburg Line joined the German front lines of defence in front of Arras.

April 1917

The first objective of the VI Corps, in which we were now serving, was the Wancourt-Feuchy line (the Brown Line), and the capture of this was to be followed by securing Orange Hill, Monchy le Preux, and the high ground to the east of this village. The rôle of the 12th Division was the assault, by three stages, of part of the Brown Line to the north of the Arras-Cambrai Road. The 36th Brigade was to take part in the first two stages. The 11th Middlesex, on the right, and the 7th Royal Sussex, on the left, were to take the Black Line, about 800 yards from our trenches, and the two Royal Fusilier battalions were to go through to Observation Ridge (the Blue Line), 1,000 yards beyond.

The Black Line contained the main defences of the Hindenburg Line, where it joined the German front line; the Blue Line contained the strong redoubts and observation posts supporting the Hindenburg defences; and the Brown Line, 2,000 yards behind, was the heavily wired switch line which the Germans had constructed in view of their recent retirement. Behind this last line there were no prepared positions finished, and it was hoped that the capture of the high ground on each side of the Scarpe would pave the way for further exploitation by the Cavalry Corps.

The immediate objective of the battalion was the capture of part of the Black Line, which consisted of the enemy front system

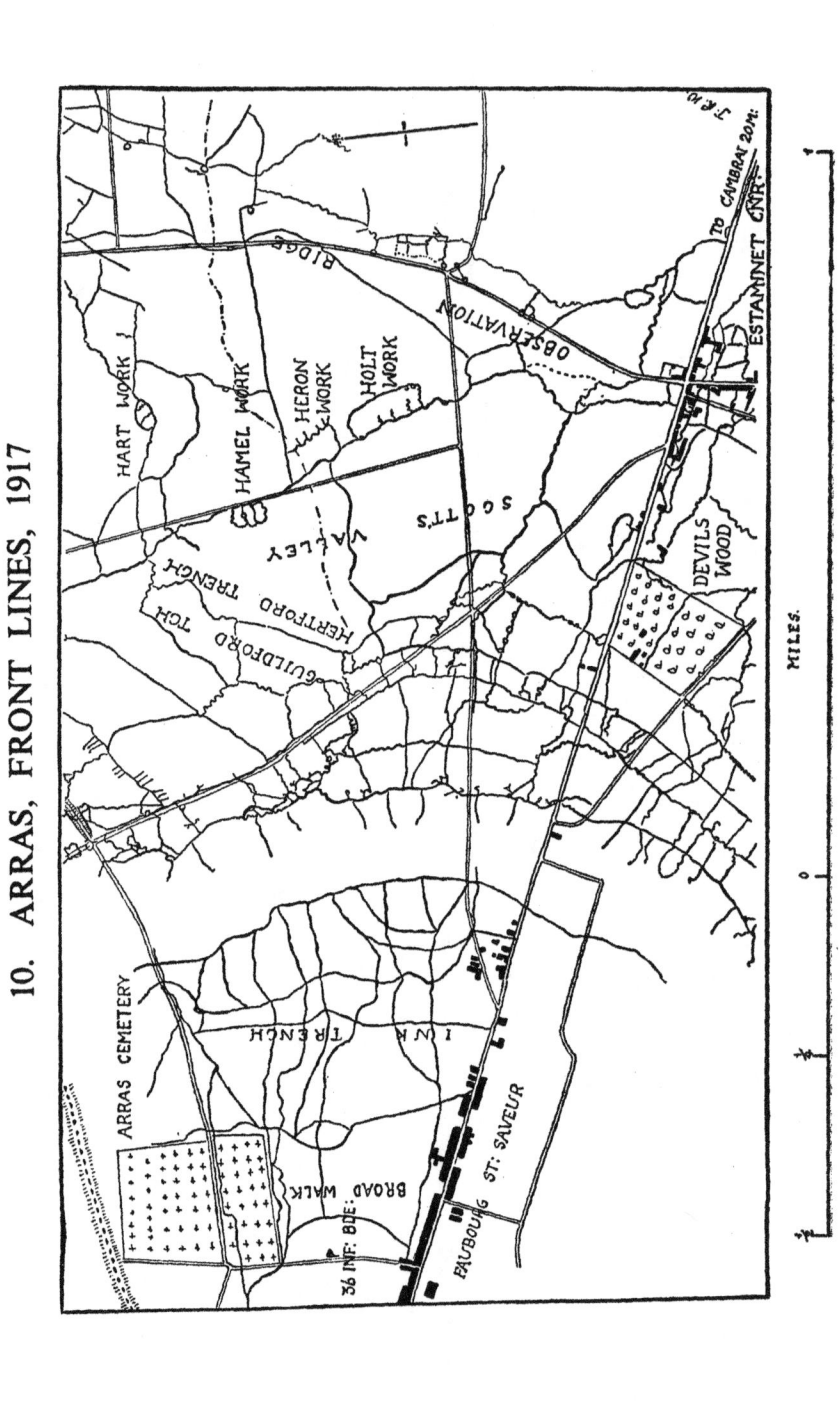

10. ARRAS, FRONT LINES, 1917

of four lines, ending with Hertford Trench—a depth of about 800 yards. The battalion was attacking on a frontage of about 250 yards, with, from right to left, A and B Companies in front and C and D in support. A Company's objective was the German front line; B was to "jump" the front line and to occupy the second and third lines. C was to mop up for A and B. The capture of Guildford and Hertford Trenches was the rôle of D Company, which would be supported by A and B after they had done their tasks. The 11th Middlesex was on our right, and the 8th/10th Gordons (15th Division) on our left. The companies were commanded by Lieutenants C. W. Ballard (A) and W. H. Sainton (B), and Captains H. F. Taylor (C) and G. L. Reckitt (D). Major Osborne acted as Second-in-Command.

APRIL 1917

At 5.30 a.m. the tremendous barrage began and the advance started. It was then that the full effect of the preliminary bombardment was realised, for little, if anything, remained of the enemy wire and trenches. In the darkness and smoke it was extremely difficult to find our way, and the ground bore no resemblance to the neat trenches over which we had practised so carefully at Lignereuil. We met with very little opposition from the dazed enemy and gained all the objectives up to time. A and B Companies entered the front line trench together and, finding little resistance, went on to the fourth line. The barrage was to pause in front of our objectives for some time to allow the reserves to come up, and it was at this period that the majority of our casualties were sustained, for enemy riflemen and machine-gunners, just out of range of the barrage, were very active and hit many who were engaged in reorganisation and consolidation. As it happened, the 8th Royal Fusiliers, which, with the 9th Royal Fusiliers, was to carry on the second stage of the attack, had been close upon our heels so as to avoid the enemy's barrage, and it arrived at its starting-point very soon after we had arrived at our objectives. On the 36th Brigade front, therefore, it would have been better if there had been no pause in the barrage, though perhaps matters were different on other parts of the long front.

At 7.30 a.m. the Royal Fusiliers advanced successfully, and from that moment all was quiet on our front. At 12.15 p.m. the 35th Brigade, and in the afternoon the 37th Division, passed through us to continue the advance.

At 5 p.m. B and C Companies were ordered up in support of the 5th Royal Berks, which was held up on the Feuchy Road in front of the Brown (Wancourt-Feuchy) Line. Later in the evening D Company was also sent up, but was unable to find the way in the darkness and a blinding snowstorm, so returned to wait until dawn.

After this action Colonel Sansom received the following letter from the Brigadier:—

"Dear Sansom,

"Please convey my very best congratulations to all ranks who took part in the attack to-day. They did magnificent work. They went forward and carried out their job as if they had been on the practice trenches at Lignereuil. Whilst one cannot but regret the number of casualties experienced, yet considering the successful results achieved they have on the whole proved remarkably small. I hope you will bring to my notice all officers and other ranks who distinguished themselves.

"Yours sincerely,

"C. Owen."*

April 1917

At 6 a.m. on the 10th B, C and D Companies, with three companies of the 11th Middlesex, advanced in support of the 5th Royal Berks to attack the enemy position from the flank, passing to the north through the front of the 15th Division, which had obtained a footing in the Brown Line during the night. The attack of the Royal Berks was immediately successful, and our companies were not called upon to take an active part. The rest of that day the three companies spent sitting in the Brown Line, very cold in the snow, and watching the attacks of the 37th Division and the 8th Cavalry Brigade on Monchy. A photograph of a section of D Company in this position is reproduced opposite.

The casualties in this attack were very heavy. The wire defences of Monchy had not been destroyed, with the result that the cavalry, faced by uncut wire, became an easy target for the enemy. Few who saw it will forget the scene of carnage in and round Monchy. Dead horses littered the ground, and many weary and unpleasant hours were spent by the working-parties which had to bury the carcasses.

On relief, C and D Companies went back to their old cellars on the Cambrai Road, while B Company joined Battalion H.Q. and A Company in the old British line, where they had moved early in the afternoon. This respite was to be a short one, for soon we

---

* Quoted from *Letters from France*, by A. J. Sansom, p. 310.

MEN OF NO. 13 PLATOON, D COMPANY, IN THE BROWN LINE NEAR MONCHY DURING THE BATTLE OF ARRAS, ON THE 10TH APRIL, 1917

On the right of the trench (from front to rear)—Cpl. A. H. HEAD and Pte. SEARLE
On the left of the trench (from front to rear)—L/Cpl. PETERS, Pte. J. HUMPHREY, Sgt. W. BAKER, and Pte. RAPLEY

(From a photograph by "Realistic Travels")

Facing page 120

The Battle of Arras

received orders to relieve the 5th Royal Berks next morning in the Brown Line near Feuchy Chapel. This relief was completed by 12.30 p.m. on the 11th, and at 9 p.m. we were ordered to relieve elements of the 37th Division, mostly the 112th Brigade, in the front line on the south-east outskirts of Monchy. We had at first been ordered to continue the attack in which these troops had just been engaged, but these orders were cancelled later.

APRIL 1917

This relief was a difficult one, for the troops in the line had suffered very heavy casualties and were not in any definite formation. The front line consisted of an irregular chain of muddy shell-holes, about knee-deep, the snow lay thick upon the ground, and the enemy shelling was severe. Luckily a large German engineers' dump, containing quantities of tools, sandbags, wire and stakes, was found near Battalion H.Q. at Les Fosses Farm on the Cambrai Road. These were issued to the three front companies, who soon made good use of them. D, the support company, was fortunate in finding good accommodation in a large cave.

The following day (the 12th) was fairly quiet, but the left company (A) was found to be cut off from communication with the rear in daylight, and the runners had several casualties in trying to get messages to them. The 1st Newfoundlands (29th Division) relieved us that night, and we marched back to the Ronville Caves by the Cambrai Road.

The immunity of this road from shell-fire was extraordinary. Here, on a main road running dead straight from Arras into the German lines, was a mass of traffic every night—infantry marching up to the line, interspersed with guns, ammunition columns, and all forms of transport, while in the other direction the troops which had been relieved were marching back. The resemblance to the Strand during a traffic block was emphasised by the frequent and irritating halts caused by two or three enormous trees which had been blown across the road, for the troops on foot had to climb over them, hampered as they were by equipment. Although the enemy continually shelled the tracks on each side of the road, it apparently never occurred to him that we should be so rash as to use the road itself; a few heavy shells on it would have transformed it into a shambles.

Captain Hind gives the following account of the adventures of our own Transport during these operations :—

"The Transport moved from Agnez-lez Duisans to the advanced line outside the Baudimont Gate, Arras, and remained there until after the advance, when they went into other lines in front of the Arras cemetery. Owing to the bad state of the ground —shell-holes, snow and slush—they were obliged to move back to the *Grande Place*, where troops were billeted in the cellars. The one and only main route to the ration dump was the Arras-Cambrai Road, which was worked to full capacity with heavy artillery and lorries. It was necessary to take rations up on pack animals, which further necessitated traversing unmarked tracks across country. The weather conditions also were so bad that it took from 6 p.m. to 1.30 a.m. to complete the return journey.

APRIL 1917

" Here is a joke against myself. As the pack-pony men had to walk I refused to ride and would not let my sergeant ride, neither did we take horses with us. I had clean forgotten that when the pack-pony men had dumped their loads they could, if tired, ride their ponies. The result was that on the homeward journey I had to walk, accompanied by a tired and peevish sergeant, while all the men rode in state."

The 13th was spent in cleaning up, the 14th in marching to Lattre-St. Quentin, and the 15th in reaching our rest billets at Mondicourt.

So ended for us the first phase of the battle, for our part in which we received congratulations from all the higher formations. We had captured two machine-guns and had passed 100 prisoners into the cages. The 12th Division had gained ground on its own front to a depth of over 4,000 yards, and the casualties, though severe, had been less than in previous important engagements— 568 killed and missing, and 1,430 wounded. After the action the following orders of the day were issued :—

" To the Officers, Warrant Officers, Non-commissioned Officers and Men of the 12th Division :—

" Lieutenant-General J. A. L. Haldane, C.B., D.S.O., commanding the VI Corps, desires me to express to all ranks his grateful appreciation of the brilliant work carried out by the 12th Division whilst under his command.

" A. B. SCOTT, *Major-General,*
" *Commanding 12th Division.*"

" To the Officers, Warrant Officers, Non-commissioned Officers and Men of the 12th Division :—

" I desire to express my warm appreciation of the excellent work you have done, and at times under very trying circumstances, in the preparations and training for the attack on the 9th April, 1917.

The Battle of Arras

"I also congratulate you on the brilliant and gallant manner in which you carried that attack through to such a successful conclusion. You have not only worthily upheld the reputation gained by the Division in its previous fighting, but added greatly thereto. APRIL 1917

"The mutual confidence which exists between the different arms has formed a powerful combination which, I feel sure, will lead to further successes when occasions arise.

"I thank you one and all.

"The march of the troops from the battlefield, where the conditions had been very severe, was worthy of the best traditions of the Army.

"The Division captured about 20 officers, 1,200 other ranks, prisoners; 41 field-guns and howitzers, 28 machine-guns, and 2 aerial torpedo throwers.

"A. B. SCOTT, *Major-General*,
"*Commanding 12th Division*."*

Our casualties for the four days in action were not light, and most of them had occurred on the first day, when 38 were killed.

	Officers	Other ranks
Killed and missing	—	45
Died of wounds	—	17
Wounded	4	90
Totals	4	152

Officers wounded: 2nd Lieutenants R. H. Fortescue (B), F. E. D. Hodges (A), A. H. Smart (D), and R. R. Surridge (C).

N.C.O.s killed: Sergeants H. J. Austin (C), A. W. Beale, M.M. (A), F. Mitchell (B), and E. Stoner (D).

A list of decorations awarded for this and the subsequent fighting is given at the end of this chapter.

Mondicourt was a drab village about five miles east of Doullens; it had been occupied previously by heavy gunners, whose tractors had churned all the roads and many of the fields into a muddy pulp. Billets were bad and tempers worse. Everyone suffered from ill-administered doses of "ginger," but an attempt to turn

---

* Quoted from *The History of the 12th Division*, p. 107.

The Battle of Arras

the men of the Quartermaster's and Transport departments into Military Tournament display troops failed miserably in the face of a " working-to-rule strike." A week of this gloom was quite enough, and a move forward again was welcome. There was a faint flicker of cheerfulness when certain officers, obeying a smartening-up order, appeared with monocles purchased in Doullens.

APRIL 1917

The 23rd April found us at Wanquetin again for a night; we had our old billets, and when the owners recognised us they gave us a warm welcome. On the 25th we relieved the 7th Suffolks in the Railway Triangle, after spending a night at Arras. Six officers and 90 men were left out as battle details under Captain G. Nagle, M.C., the Adjutant, for whom Lieutenant G. G. Stocks acted. We spent five days in this position and did much work on the construction of a new line of trenches on Orange Hill, on tidying up the battlefield and on the unusual task of filling in shell-holes. The newly captured dug-outs were more than usually lousy, and all suffered much discomfort. We moved forward to the newly-constructed Orange Line on the evening of the 30th, and on the afternoon of the 2nd May the Commanding Officer and company commanders reconnoitred the ground for the coming attack, which was to take place next morning.

The attack ordered for the 3rd May was on a large scale, and three Armies were taking part in it along a front of sixteen miles. It is unnecessary to give the exact objectives for this battle, since they were never attained. Roughly, the objective of the 36th Brigade was the capture, in three stages, of Pelves and the high ground to the east of it. But it was provided that the barrage would not lift away from in front of the objectives until they were actually captured, and that the zero hour for each successive objective would be determined by the progress of each stage. This was a wise provision, and it undoubtedly saved the battle from being an even worse failure than it was. In the event, not even the first stage was completed. It was, in fact, a most unpleasant battle, undertaken by the British Command, one understands, with the greatest reluctance and under the heaviest outside pressure.

MAY 1917

The advance of the 36th Brigade was led by the 9th Royal Fusiliers on the right and the 8th Royal Fusiliers on the left, with their left flank eventually to rest on the River Scarpe. We were to be in support, and the 11th Middlesex in reserve. As soon as

11. SCARPE

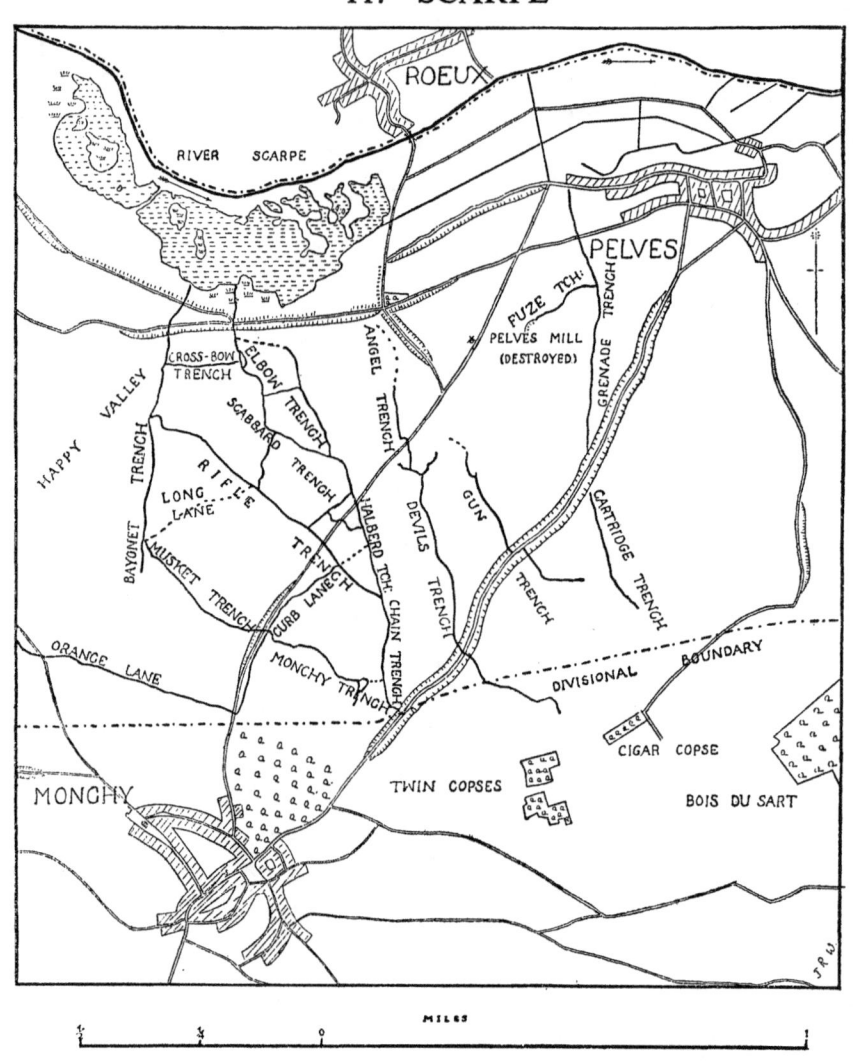

it was reported that the Royal Fusiliers had captured the first objective, we were to carry on the second stage of the attack upon Pelves itself.

The first objective, called the Brown Line, was roughly a line running southwards from the River Scarpe at Roeux, past Pelves Mill to Gun Trench. The two Fusilier battalions were attacking under conditions of great difficulty. Their numbers were small, about 450 for each battalion, and their rôle was to advance about 2,000 yards on a 900 yards front. Their starting-off positions were most involved, as only a portion of one of the trenches held by them—Rifle Trench—was in our hands. The Germans were well aware of our intentions, and they had massed an amount of artillery which was at least equal to our own.

MAY 1917

By 1.45 a.m. on the 3rd May the battalion had formed up in the network of old trenches to the west of Bayonet Trench, and at 3.45 a.m. advanced to occupy Bayonet and Rifle Trenches, which had been vacated by the Royal Fusiliers when they advanced. The order of companies, from right to left, was A, B, C and D, with Battalion H.Q. in an old German gun-pit in Happy Valley. After the leading battalions had gone forward it was found that Scabbard Trench, in front of us, had been re-occupied by the enemy. This was reported, and later on orders were received for B and C Companies to attack Scabbard Trench at 12.10 p.m., after ten minutes intense bombardment by 4.5 howitzers. The orders for this attack only reached the companies a few minutes before the bombardment opened.

All the time we were occupying Bayonet Trench the enemy artillery fire was extremely heavy. The shrapnel fire especially, bursting most accurately over the badly-damaged trench, inflicted a great many casualties. In front the situation was obscure. It was evident that the Royal Fusiliers had met with most determined opposition and that they had suffered very heavily. At several points it appeared that the enemy was counter-attacking. It was also disquieting to note that the attack against Roeux on the north side of the River Scarpe had not met with success, for this meant that the left flank of any advance by us would be enfiladed from that direction.

In spite of the short notice and all the other difficulties Captain Taylor led B and C Companies over at the appointed time, and, attacking with great dash, they successfully captured the whole of Scabbard Trench, taking 45 prisoners, including 3 officers and 3 machine-guns. Great credit was due to Captain Taylor for his leading part in this operation, of which Lieutenant W. H. Sainton gives the following personal account :—

"The trenches in which we formed up in the early hours of the 3rd May were only breast-high, or less. We were to wait here until green lights went up from Brigade H.Q. to show us that the chemical works on the other side of the Scarpe had been taken and further advance on our side was possible. These lights were never seen by us, although, owing to the extremely unpleasant position we were in, we kept a sharp and hopeful look out. Taylor went off on his own to our left front to find out what was happening, and on his return led us over to Rifle Trench. This trench was almost at right-angles to our front and was joined up with Scabbard Trench at the top, the two trenches in the rough form of a wishbone. At the join of these trenches the Fusiliers were trying to bomb the enemy out of Scabbard, and we passed all our bombs and spare bandoliers of S.A.A. up to them. Colonel Elliott-Cooper of the Fusiliers was somewhere up there too. When the order for our attack came through he sent runners to us saying he would get it stopped for fear of our barrage killing Fusiliers prisoners in Scabbard Trench. Taylor and I, and, I think, 2nd Lieutenant G. H. Atkinson, who had just joined the battalion, were left. As the men did not know the direction the attack would go, and since there was an element of doubt whether it would take place at all, we three passed up and down the trench saying to each man, 'If a barrage opens you will go over there; if it does not, you will stay where you are.' Taylor was sent for by Colonel Elliott-Cooper just before noon. The barrage of howitzers was not immediately recognised by the men, who no doubt expected something like that on the 9th, as it appeared like a succession of salvos. I suppose there were not enough heavy guns, and being heavies were slow to load. But directly they saw Atkinson and me and the men in our vicinity start they all followed along splendidly.

"The heavies were inaccurate and some fell amongst us while we were awaiting the lift. I remember getting half buried and thoroughly shaken up by one of them. Taylor joined us soon after the attack was launched. We took several prisoners and some machine-guns, which had had their feed-blocks removed; later, one or two of these feed-blocks were found by some men who went down to the Scarpe hoping to fill their water-bottles. We got one of the guns in working order. During our stay in this trench we used German rifles and ammunition to save our own. We got orders that in the evening we should find an enemy trench close by which appeared on an aeroplane photograph. Taylor and I found this, and it was only the start of a trench, about a foot deep, with a number of enemy dead therein. We heard the rumours of the enemy retiring, and Colonel Elliott-Cooper put out some groups in shell-holes on the hill opposite our trench. Later we heard that a British barrage would open on this hill, and I took a patrol across the valley in between and warned them of this. I remember the conflicting reports and orders regarding this attack, some from the Fusiliers and some from our own H.Q.

MAY 1917

" During our occupation of Scabbard Trench B and C can absolutely claim bringing down an enemy plane by rifle and machine-gun fire (Lewis and German guns). It fell into Pelves and was destroyed by our artillery fire, which opened on it a minute or two after it reached the ground. This plane was flying so low over us that A.A. guns could not have touched it."

Things were quieter after this attack. In the afternoon a patrol of D Company was sent out to reconnoitre and report upon the situation on the left front. Admirably led by Lance-Corporal H. Maughan, they did valuable work and released a number of Royal Fusiliers who were held as prisoners in dug-outs near the Roeux-Monchy Road. For this work Lance-Corporal Maughan, Private G. Bartholomew and another man (whose name is not on record) were awarded the Military Medal.

During the late afternoon rumours were received that the enemy was retiring, and warning orders were issued that the battalion would probably have to carry out a further attack that night in conjunction with the Royal Fusiliers. Realising the difficulties of communications, Colonel Sansom anticipated the attack orders which we would be given and issued his own orders to companies at 6 p.m. It was well that he did so.

At about 9.40 p.m. the two rear companies, A on the right and D on the left, received the definite order to advance on Pelves behind a barrage which was to start in front of the Brown Line at 9.45 p.m. The whole front line of the Division was supposed to be taking part. Thanks to the Colonel's anticipatory orders the companies were able to start at once, but it was obviously impossible for them to be at the assembly position in time, for they had well over 1,000 yards to go.

The companies advanced as ordered, and by 10 p.m. had reached a position level with Pelves Mill. Here a halt was made for touch to be obtained with the remainder of the attackers. B and C Companies remained in Scabbard Trench ready to move. It was a very dark night and the barrage had advanced a long way ahead. Patrols reported that they could find no trace of any other troops on or in front of the assembly position, so it was decided that the two companies should temporarily consolidate a position where they were. The fire from the direction of Roeux was heavy, and rifle-fire was also coming from the right rear. A patrol sent out to the left was captured by the enemy, who appeared to be manning a position strongly in front of the companies.

MAY 1917

Just before midnight, as the situation remained unchanged and no other troops could be located, Captain Reckitt decided to withdraw the two companies from their exposed position, which would obviously be untenable in daylight. He went back to Battalion H.Q. to inform the Commanding Officer of this movement, and while he was there orders were received from Brigade confirming the withdrawal, as the units on the right and left of the Brigade had been unable to advance. A and D Companies, therefore, returned to their positions in Bayonet Trench, while B and C were formed into one company under Captain Taylor, in occupation of Scabbard Trench.

D Company had received assistance in these operations from sections of the 36th Machine Gun Company and the 36th Trench Mortar Battery, each under an officer (whose names it has been impossible to identify); they had advanced in support of the company most faithfully throughout the day and night and had carried their heavy loads doggedly. Their presence was of the greatest value.

Our casualties on the 3rd May were as follows :—

	Officers	Other ranks
Killed	—	44
Died of wounds	1	11
Wounded	5	100*
Totals	6	155*

Officer died of wounds : 2nd Lieutenant W. Smith (C).
Officers wounded : Lieutenant E. C. Gorringe (C); 2nd Lieutenants J. Dunlevy (C) and A. J. Morris (B).†

* Approximate.
† And two others whom it has not been possible to identify, the War Diary being at fault here.

The Battle of Arras

The battalion continued to occupy its position for the next four days. Much work was done on consolidation and repairs to the trenches, which were continually being blown in. Two new communication trenches, Long Lane and Cross Bow, were dug, between Bayonet Trench and Rifle Trench, and Bayonet Trench and Scabbard Trench, respectively. An advanced post, later known as Elbow Trench, was also constructed. Advanced Battalion H.Q. was established in Bayonet Trench, near its junction with Long Lane, and signal communication to Brigade H.Q. was maintained. Rear Battalion H.Q. was moved to a deep dug-out on the eastern slopes of Orange Hill. To this the remaining nine officers of the battalion were sent in turn for a wash, a good meal and some sleep—a considerate and timely thought on the part of Colonel Sansom.

MAY 1917

The weather had now turned warm and there was an uncomfortable shortage of water, accentuated by the fact that the cans in which our water was brought up were badly tainted with petrol. The water of the Scarpe was undrinkable owing to the masses of dead fish. At dawn and dusk each day the enemy put an intense barrage on Bayonet Trench and Happy Valley, and the artillery fire for the rest of the day was also severe. Not many casualties were caused by this fire, since the frontage held by A and D Companies was so long that the men were widely spread out. The presence of a large number of unexploded Livens Projector gas-bombs around Bayonet Trench made the heavy shelling all the less welcome, and sentries were instructed to give immediate warning if any of the bombs were hit.

After a night of particularly heavy shell-fire we were relieved by the 6th Royal West Kents in the early morning of the 8th May and went back to the old Brown Line for a couple of nights. This was followed by one night in the support line in front of Monchy and two nights in the Orange Line, after which we took over the front line on the left of Twin Copses. A Company (now commanded by Captain W. H. C. Le Hardy, who had recently joined us from the 2nd Battalion) and D Company were in front, with B and C in support. Three days were spent in attempting to discover the exact German positions around Devil's Trench and to obtain touch with the unit on our right over the marshy and wooded ground. There was much artillery activity during the three days of our occupation of these trenches. On the 14th our guns carried out a "Chinese" bombardment of the German positions. The idea of this operation was that, by means of an intense bombardment by all calibres of our guns but without any infantry action, the enemy might be persuaded to disclose his system of S.O.S. signals and the line of his protective barrage, and possibly to unmask some of his silent batteries. The enemy retaliation on this occasion was extremely heavy, and more than 100 rounds a minute were fired on to our front lines.

As regards the Transport during these operations, Captain Hind writes as follows :—

"The transport lines were near the Quay at Arras. It was during the May battle that the Corps Ammunition Dump, situated at the Quay, blew up, most fortunately when we were away at the ration dump. Captain Clarke acted promptly and managed to clear the transport lines without any casualties. This was a very good piece of work, as shells of all kinds were hurtling through the air all round the camp. There were also many negroes employed at the shell dump, and when it went up they ran like hares for a few yards, then stopped and took off their boots to enable them to run quicker. Some were found twenty miles away."

MAY 1917

On the 15th May our long-expected relief came at last, and having handed over to the 6th Royal West Kents we left the line for billets near Arras Station. That was, for us, the end of these most unsatisfactory operations, during which the Division had lost 525 killed, 860 missing, and 2,129 wounded. The results gained had been negligible.

This chapter should not end without paying a tribute to Colonel Sansom's most inspiring leadership throughout the whole of these trying operations. His personal influence was very great during all the worst periods, and his anticipation of orders saved the battalion on more than one occasion. He was not awarded the decoration to which his exceptional conduct should have entitled him. The work of the battalion runners and signallers was also deserving of the highest praise, and the way in which communications were kept open under the severe and prolonged shelling was admirable.

After this operation the following letters were read out on parade :—

" From the Mayor of Arras to Field-Marshal Sir Douglas Haig, Commander-in-Chief, British Armies in France.

" 14th May, 1917.

" On the 9th April, after 30 months of constant battle at its gates, the town of Arras has seen the British Army break through the formidable enemy entrenchments which encroached upon it.

The Battle of Arras

"As Mayor of this poor Martyr-City I wish to express to you, and through you, to the splendid British Nation and to her heroic Army, the deep joy and gratitude of the inhabitants of Arras.

"This gratitude will endure for all time; as will that Peace, the foundations of which are being laid at this moment by the success of our Arms.

"There would be no need of any tangible objects to keep the memory of that success fresh in our minds, but we know that amongst the many batteries captured on the 9th, those of the Olga Group, to the North of Athies, to the East of Tilloy, and a heavy battery at Monchy le Preux had, as their special object, the bombardment of the town and its suburbs. Certain guns which are still serviceable have been removed to the rear. The remainder are still lying on the field of Battle.

MAY 1917

"We should be deeply grateful if, as a remembrance of our sufferings and of your victory, you would graciously allow to remain in the town of Arras some of these cannon which wrought its martyrdom and have made its greatness.

"Broken by the English Artillery and captured by your Infantry on the evening of the most glorious day of the War, these guns would remain to us symbols of the savage power which was smashed to pieces by British pluck on the 9th April, 1917.

"And in the future, after the final triumph, when the sons of England shall come to visit our ruins, how could they feel themselves strangers in this town, which was defended and saved by them, when they see before them the guns won by them at the price of blood which we shall venerate as we do the blood of France.

"With my undying gratitude, I have the honour to be, Sir,
"Your Obedient Servant,
(Signed) "E. ROHARD."

From Field-Marshal Sir Douglas Haig to the Mayor of Arras.
"Monsieur le Maire,

"In the name of all ranks of the Forces under my command, I thank you for your kind and generous letter.

"I deeply appreciate the warmth and sincerity of its terms, which will be regarded with gratitude by all my countrymen, and particularly the troops under my orders in France, who will value it as a full recompense and ample recognition of the sacrifices they have been privileged to make on the battlefield of Arras in the cause of liberty and civilization.

The Battle of Arras

"I can assure you that all Officers and men of the British Armies here are proud that it has fallen to their lot to be the instrument to drive the enemy from the gates of your noble city.

"It gives me great pleasure to be able to accede to your request to hand over to the town of Arras some of those guns with which a barbarous invader sought to work her ruin but wrought her glory. Set amid the evidence of her martyrdom, they will bear a witness for all time to the patient courage of her townsfolk and the triumph of our common cause and France.

May 1917

"Douglas Haig, Field-Marshal."

The battalion received the following decorations for the Arras and Scarpe operations :—

Military Cross :	Captain H. F. Taylor (C) ; Lieutenants C. W. Ballard (A), N. McCracken (B), and G. W. Prince (A).
Bar to Military Medal :	Sergeant A. Horne (A).
Military Medal :	Sergeants W. Baker (D), W. J. Osborne (D), and G. Preston (C) ; Lance-Corporal H. Maughan (D) ; Privates G. Bartholomew (D), T. H. Beale (B), P. W. Bridger (C), W. Carr (B), H. Clayton (B), C. Emery (C), E. Highgate (B), S. Isted (C), J. Penticost (A), P. Scott (A), and J. Smith (B).
Italian Bronze Medal for Military Valour :	Sergeant G. Hodges, D.C.M. (C).

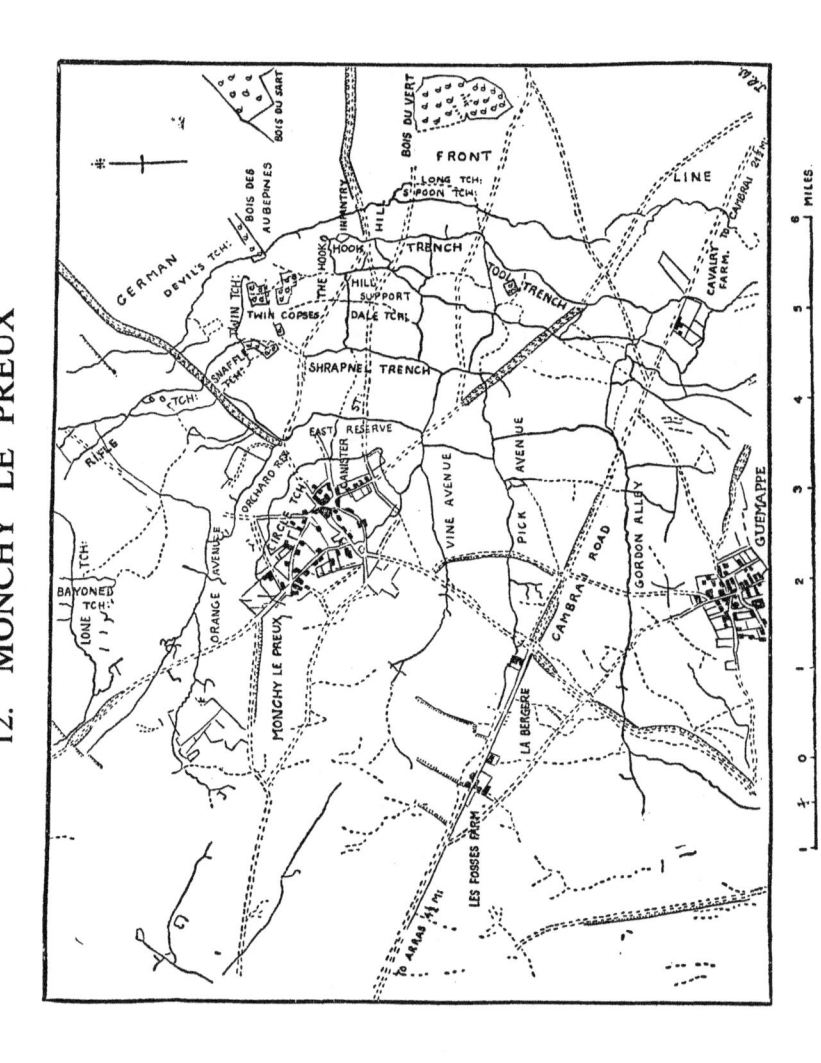

12. MONCHY LE PREUX

CHAPTER VIII

THE DEFENCE OF MONCHY

16TH MAY—16TH NOVEMBER, 1917
[Sketch Maps, Nos. 9 and 12]

After baths and a speedy reorganisation at Arras, we moved off on the 16th May at the uncomfortable hour of 3.45 a.m. and arrived at Agnez-lez Duisans just before midday, occupying a camp west of the village.

The next week was spent in general cleaning up and training, and on the 23rd the battalion, together with the 11th Middlesex, was inspected by Major-General Scott, who presented the ribbons of the decorations which had been awarded for the operations at Arras and the Scarpe. MAY 1917

On the 24th the Brigade marched to Grand-Rullecourt, where comfortable billets had been arranged. Our stay at this delightful spot lasted over three weeks, during which the excellent summer weather and the entertainments arranged by companies, battalion, brigade and division added much to our enjoyment. On the 1st June, the second anniversary of our arrival in France, the battalion sports were held. Brigadier-General Osborn, whose brigade was out at rest somewhere in the neighbourhood, delighted JUNE 1917
everybody by paying us a visit and presenting the prizes. The following day a brigade gymkhana was held, at which we won no less than eight first prizes, three seconds and one third. The following is a list of the events and the results* so far as they concerned the battalion :—

Competition	Result		
	1st	2nd	3rd
Pack Ponies	7/R.Sussex	—	—
Cookers	—	7/R.Sussex	—
Officers' Chargers ..	—	—	—
Limbers	7/R.Sussex	—	—
N.C.O.s Mounted ..	7/R.Sussex	—	—
Mess Carts	—	7/R.Sussex	—
Baggage Wagons ..	—	—	—
Water Carts	—	7/R.Sussex	—

* Quoted from *Letters from France* by A. J. Sansom, p. 365.

133

The Defence of Monchy

Competition	Result		
	1st	2nd	3rd
Driving Competition ..	7/R.Sussex	—	—
Officers' Jumping ..	—	—	7/R.Sussex
Bareback Wrestling ..	7/R.Sussex	—	—
Mule Race (Bareback)	7/R.Sussex	—	—
Mule Race (Officers) ..	7/R.Sussex	—	—
Mule Jumping.. ..	7/R.Sussex	—	—
Musical Chairs ..	—	—	—

The battalion corps of drums, under the able directorship of Sergeant-Drummer Aylmore, won the competitions held by brigade and division.

On the 18th June we returned to Agnez-lez Duisans, and on the following day moved up to positions in the Brown Line on the right of the Arras-Cambrai Road. This system of trenches had already been made habitable by a number of shelters, which had been built to provide sleeping accommodation for the men, and ample material was available for improving them. During its sojourn in the Brown Line each battalion added to the amenities, so that by the time the Division left the area it had become exceptionally comfortable.

JUNE 1917

Immediately west of the Brown Line, on the far side of the Feuchy Chapel cross-roads, the Germans had built a remarkable concrete house. To passers-by it appeared to be a large slab about the size of a tennis-court, but below the surface it consisted of three basement storeys, concreted throughout. The Padre was quick to recognise its possibilities and opened up a branch of the battalion canteen. It was particularly popular with passers-by, since it provided a safe shelter from the hostile artillery fire which was concentrated with annoying monotony on the cross-roads. The Division built some excellent baths on the opposite side of the road, just behind a large tank which had become derelict during the Battle of Arras.

In order that the activities of the battalion during the months of June to October may be appreciated, it is necessary to give a short description of Arras and of the defences of Monchy, which formed undoubtedly the key to the rehabilitation of that important city.

Of all places in France with which the 12th Division was connected perhaps Arras and Monchy hold more memories, both pleasant and unpleasant, than any other; and there can be few inhabitants who occupied the city during this period who do not recall the Ace of Spades.

The Defence of Monchy

Although Arras had suffered heavily during the first two and a half years of the war, life had been made possible by the numerous cellars under the houses. Above ground, shell-fire had severely damaged the area near the station and the cathedral, including the *Hôtel de Ville*, *Grande* and *Petite Places*. The Town Hall and the two *Places* had been built in the sixteenth and seventeenth centuries respectively and had been the pride of Arras. These buildings had been almost completely razed, but in the rest of the town the destruction, compared with what we afterwards learnt that word could mean, was trifling. When, therefore, the recent attack drove the Germans back about five miles from the most eastern part of the town, the inhabitants quickly returned—to find that their homes would still be habitable when the windows had been covered with canvas and the roofs patched with pieces of corrugated iron. Occasional " hates " interfered but momentarily with the life of the city, and the occupants were driven to the underworld, only to return as soon as comparative safety seemed assured.

JUNE 1917

By June more amenities had been established in the city than in any with which the battalion had been connected since the days of Armentières or Bethune. An Officers' Club was opened by the Expeditionary Force Canteen, the Divisional Concert Party, " The Spades," quickly seized the local theatre, and estaminets (of a most superior type) and hotels (of rather an inferior type) welcomed all ranks. Officers who were serving with the battalion at the time will not forget a dinner given to commemorate the birthday of two comrades at the Hôtel du Commerce, which compared favourably with a Mansion House feast.

Monchy le Preux, whose defence was the function of the Division, was not occupied at all. It was a small village which in pre-war days had been famous for its beauty and popular as a health resort. It stood on a hill, overlooking Cambrai or alternatively dominating Arras. It is said that, during the German occupation, " mixed " tennis-parties were seen there from our observation posts. After the original attack at Arras on the 9th April, heavy fighting had taken place around the Brown Line and Monchy, and our cavalry had suffered terrible casualties in the village. Although we had succeeded in capturing it, such was its prominence that the Germans were well able to deny us its occupation, and for months the ruined streets of Monchy remained strewn with the carcasses of horses. Except for one or two observation posts which

The Defence of Monchy

were built on its outskirts, Monchy could never be occupied, and the trench system skirted it in a semi-circle.

Immediately east of the village some natural springs made it impossible to dig trenches, and about two hundred yards of country had perforce to be left unoccupied. In this gap (between Twin Trench and Hill Support) lay two small copses, known as Twin Copses, which made connection over the marshy country between the dead ends of the two trench systems extremely difficult. It was essential that some communication should be established, but many weeks passed before it fell to the lot of Lieutenant I. D. Margary to gain touch with the trench system to the south and thus establish communication with the aid of a coil of wire.

JUNE 1917

According to the maps with which the British Army was supplied, the plateau known as Infantry Hill, to the east of Monchy, should have provided visibility almost to Cambrai, as from Bois du Vert the country fell sharply down to the valley of the River Cojeul. Unfortunately, however, the fall in the ground was so gradual before reaching the wood that no observation could be obtained beyond it from any trench system.

After the closing stages of the Battle of Arras the 3rd Division had taken over the Monchy defences, which at that time ran from Tool Trench to Hill Support, on to Twin Copses and then northward.

On the 14th June the 76th Brigade (3rd Division) was ordered to attack Hook and Long Trenches. The object was to develop an assault which would lead to the capture of Bois du Vert and so win the important visibility to Cambrai.

Since the principle of the attack was that it should be a surprise, no preliminary bombardment was to take place. The attack was carried out by the 1st Gordon Highlanders and the 2nd Suffolks at 7.20 a.m. At first it met with considerable success; Hook and Long Trenches were captured, while on the left, just north of Infantry Lane, elements appear to have penetrated into Devil's Trench.

At 5.25 p.m. the Germans counter-attacked in force and heavy fighting continued until the 18th June. The line, which was eventually consolidated, consisted of Tool Trench, Hook Trench, and a series of shell-holes, flattered by the names of Spoon and Long Trenches. Unfortunately no gain in observation had been secured, and actually Hill Support was a more suitable front line than the new one farther east; but with bulldog tenacity the British Army held on to the line captured by the 3rd Division.

The Defence of Monchy

Although in the initial attack the 3rd Division had suffered less than 50 casualties, by the end of the five days' fighting 28 officers and 870 other ranks had been put out of action. The occupation of the shell-holes that formed Long Trench was far from enviable, since their exact location was never mapped with great accuracy and their inhabitants were constantly exposed to "shorts" from our own artillery and trench-mortars.

JUNE 1917

This was the situation when the 12th Division moved up to relieve the 3rd Division on the 20th June.

The policy allotted to the Division was to be one of active defence in order to cause a doubt in the mind of the enemy as to whether the Battle of Arras was to be further developed; thus we should compel him to keep a strong force of men in the area and so relieve other sectors.

During this period life in the front line area was disturbed by raids, artillery and trench-mortar bombardments, the annoyance of low-flying enemy aeroplanes, and continuous working-parties when at rest. The raids will be more particularly described in due course. The artillery bombardments were unpleasant while they lasted, but, except in a few cases, innocuous. The trench-mortar bombardments were neither pleasant nor innocuous. The low-flying enemy planes were remarkable and extremely dispiriting. It needed a great deal to persuade the troops that the Press was correct in describing the British as "masters of the air." Every morning shortly after "stand-to" one or two planes would fly over so low that one felt a well-thrown bully-beef tin would hit them. The ingenuity of all ranks was brought to bear on the matter and the planes were heavily engaged with rifles, Lewis guns and even rifle-grenades, but they passed and repassed apparently unharmed. One ever-keen trench-mortar officer evolved a scheme for firing his Stokes gun at them, but was fortunately dissuaded.

The continual working-parties, although laborious, effected what must have been one of the most perfect systems of trenches on the British front. Deep dug-outs were constructed in the support line to provide safe shelter for officers and men; all trenches were duck-boarded, and a railway known as the "Monchy Express" was built in the back areas for bringing up rations and tools, and sometimes relieving troops.

The Defence of Monchy

Mention must here be made of a chalk-pit which existed south of Monchy and north of the Cambrai Road. The engineers had been ordered to build a system of dug-outs sufficiently large to accommodate the reserve company of the battalion in the front line, and shortly after drilling had been begun they had suddenly come on a vast cave, reputed to be of prehistoric antiquity. It was large enough to house a company with ease, but although it had two entrances the ventilation became horribly congested when occupied by about a hundred and fifty officers and men engaged in cooking by means of candles. In fact Pick Cave, as it was called, was as weird as it was unwholesome.

June 1917

The fighting during the period from June to October must be looked upon as a whole, and it is unnecessary to describe the general routine in any detail; it will suffice if the more outstanding incidents are recorded.

On the 4th July we were ordered to capture and consolidate the line of shell-holes running from Infantry Lane northwards towards Twin Copses. D Company was selected for this task. A short barrage of all arms, lasting a minute and a half, preceded the attack, which was timed for 2.30 a.m. Lieutenant A. E. Willard was temporarily commanding the company, but owing to Lieutenant F. W. Reading receiving a wound on the previous day, the only other officer in the company was 2nd Lieutenant C. Williams.

July 1917

The attack proved a costly failure, no progress whatever being possible against a well-prepared opposition. Lieutenant Willard, one of the most cheery and gallant officers in the battalion, and four of his men were never seen again, while 2 other men were killed, and 2nd Lieutenant Williams and 7 men wounded. Amongst those missing was an orderly, Private Benjamin Eggleton, an "Old Contemptible" belonging to the 2nd Battalion. He was one of the best men we had; no job was too big or too dangerous for him. He was a cheerful soul, and at reveille he would always start up Harry Lauder's famous chorus :—

> "It's far too early in the morning for to waken me;
> For such a thing as early rising I can't see.
> And I may say that with my health it never did agree—
> Rising early in the morning."

Everybody would join in and he would soon have the whole platoon in the best of spirits.

The Defence of Monchy

The battalion had scarcely recovered from this shock when the following evening it received more fatalities.

A "Chinese" bombardment had been arranged, and heavy gunfire was concentrated on Devil's Trench. All officers in the front line were warned to take particular note of the lights put up by the enemy during the bombardment. Colonel Sansom, and the Adjutant, Captain Nagle, whose headquarters was in Shrapnel Trench, decided to come out of their dug-out to see the display, and no sooner had they emerged than a shell burst between them. Both were killed instantaneously.

JULY 1917

Colonel Sansom had been in command of the battalion for nine most difficult months, and although older than the majority of battalion commanders in the Division he was perhaps the most vigorous and courageous. He was at all times a splendid example to the battalion. He was not a professional soldier—he had left his school, Devonshire House, Bexhill, to join the 5th Royal Sussex; and what added to the tragedy of his death was the fact that, on the very day he was killed, a letter reached Corps H.Q. from G.H.Q. saying that he was to be sent home to look after the affairs of his school. The pride he took in the battalion shines out in letters he wrote from the front to his wife—pride and a determination to do his best for those under him, even at the cost of popularity with his superiors.

"I *am* so proud of the Battalion," he wrote in one letter, "and I cannot imagine any more enviable position than to be in command of a Battalion that has done its duty well.... I cannot kow-tow to higher authority, or keep from expressing opinions on those who give orders which I consider cost, unnecessarily, the lives of men. But though I know my criticisms make me unpopular with higher authority, I again don't care a d—— if they have the least influence in making people thoughtful for others, and I believe I have succeeded in one or two instances. What is the value of a D.S.O. given to a gentleman sitting in an office in safety, compared to the thought that one may have saved lives of men under one's command?"*

Captain Nagle had joined the battalion as a subaltern in August, 1914, and had served continuously as a platoon and company commander, finally taking over the duties of Adjutant in July, 1916. In Colonel Sansom we lost a resolute but considerate leader, whose first thoughts had ever been for the efficiency of his battalion and for the comfort—such as it might

---

* Quoted from *Letters from France*, p. 341.

The Defence of Monchy

be—of his officers and men; in Captain Nagle we lost a good comrade and a dauntless brother officer who had proved his devotion to duty time and again.

Soon after this disaster we were relieved and spent a quiet time in billets at Achicourt and in the Brown Line. Major Osborne took over temporary command of the battalion and Captain Bowlby was appointed Adjutant. On the 22nd we took over Long, Spoon and Hook Trenches from the 8th Royal Fusiliers. During the subsequent days it was noted that enemy aircraft were even more active than usual, but there was no other indication of impending trouble.

JULY 1917

At 3 a.m. on the 25th a party of some 400 Germans from the *II Battalion* of the *162nd Regiment* (*17th Reserve Division*) attacked Long and Spoon Trenches and, by using *flammenwerfer*, gas trench-mortar bombs and a heavy artillery barrage, succeeded in capturing them. Small parties of the enemy penetrated as far as Hook Trench, but we counter-attacked at 11 a.m. and completely regained possession of it.

Two prisoners remained in our hands, while our total casualties were :—

	Officers	Other ranks
Killed	—	19
Missing	1	4
Died of wounds	—	6
Wounded	1	62
Totals	2	91

Officer missing: 2nd Lieutenant A. D. Bullock (D).
   „ wounded: 2nd Lieutenant H. C. Skingley (C).
N.C.O.s killed: Sergeants C. Adams (B) and A. Arnell (C).

The following decorations were awarded :—

Distinguished
  Conduct Medal: Lance-Sergeant F. Fairhall (B).
Military Medal: Private R. Coates (B).

A Company was in reserve in Pick Cave in the previously mentioned chalk-pit, and throughout what seemed one of the longest days of the war had to stand-to preparatory to launching a counter-attack to recover Spoon Trench and the lost ground. All who knew the locality as we did were bound to view such a project with misgiving, for it had long been realised that the tenure

The Defence of Monchy

of Long Trench, without the occupation of the high ground about Infantry Hill, was useless from the military point of view and extremely dangerous. The Germans were holding the recently captured ground in force and, according to statements made by the prisoners, were determined to resist attacks to the utmost.

July 1917

Strong representations were made to the Brigade by Battalion H.Q., and after a personal reconnaissance by Captain C. W. Haydon, of the Brigade Staff, these were passed on to the Division. Finally, at 6 p.m., it was learned, much to the relief of everybody, and especially of A Company, that the 8th Royal Fusiliers was to take over from us that night according to previous arrangements.

None who went through those hours in the asphyxiating atmosphere of that terrible cave, awaiting orders for what must have been almost certain death, is ever likely to forget them. The hours passed in complete silence, there being none of the cheery badinage or singing which usually enlivened such a situation. When at last Captain Le Hardy, the company commander, returned from Battalion H.Q. to announce that the attack was cancelled and that the relief would take place, fresh air seemed to permeate the whole place and songs flooded the catacomb-like cave. The reason for this sudden change was not that an unpleasant counter-attack had been abandoned, but that the Higher Command were allowing a perfectly useless piece of ground to stay in the hands of the enemy without wasting valuable lives in attempts to recover it.

After spending two days in the Brown Line and finding numerous working-parties, on the 28th we again relieved the 8th Royal Fusiliers in Hook and Tool Trenches. It was a stormy relief, as the enemy had put up a Verey light similar to our own S.O.S., with the result that our guns opened a fire which was quickly responded to by the Germans. Our casualties during this relief were 1 killed and 6 wounded. After this the following three days passed quietly, and on the 31st we were relieved by the 7th Norfolks, reaching Achicourt early the next morning.

On the 6th we relieved the 6th Buffs in the Monchy defences. On the following day a heavy bombardment of the enemy's trenches was begun at 6.15 a.m. in preparation for a raid on a large scale by the 35th and 37th Brigades, the Corps and Divisional Artillery being augmented by a special collection of heavy artillery, 15-, 12-, 9.2-, 8- and 6- inch howitzers, commonly known as " The Circus," which was kept in reserve for special occasions such as this. The raid, which started at 7.45 p.m., was very successful ; 89 prisoners were captured and heavy casualties were inflicted on the enemy.

On the 8th Lieutenant-Colonel G. H. Impey came back to us and took over command. He had left us some sixteen months previously to command the 12th Royal Sussex, and had received the D.S.O. for his fine work in leading it through its ill-fated attack on the Aubers Ridge on the 30th June, 1916, when he was badly wounded. All ranks welcomed his return.

AUGUST 1917

After a short spell in the Brown Line we relieved the 8th Royal Fusiliers on the 12th in the front sector north of Twin Copses, where, on the 18th, General Sir Julian Byng, G.O.C. Third Army, and Lieutenant-General Sir Charles Fergusson, G.O.C. XVIII Corps, paid us a visit and had a good look at the country from the excellent observation post we had near Battalion H.Q. in F Strong Point to the north of Monchy.

That evening we were relieved by the 1st Somerset Light Infantry (4th Division) and proceeded to billets in Achicourt. During this rest an unfortunate accident happened at a demonstration in the use of phosphorous bombs carried out by the 11th Middlesex in some practice trenches near Beaurains ; as the result of a premature explosion of a bomb the Bombing Officer of the 11th Middlesex was very badly burnt and 2nd Lieutenants D. T. Cohen and V. E. Rogers, of our battalion, together with 2 men, were wounded.

On the 2nd September we relieved the 11th Middlesex in the Monchy defences, after the 9th Royal Fusiliers had carried out a very successful raid, which resulted in 18 prisoners being captured and a new German division being identified.

SEPTEMBER 1917

After a further period of six days in the front line we went back to Achicourt, where we remained until the 17th, when we moved up to Bois des Bœufs, a small wood by the side of the Cambrai Road, about a mile short of the Feuchy Chapel cross-roads. Here we stayed for six days. During the next six days' tour in the Monchy defences the battalion received orders to carry out a raid, for which Lieutenant H. J. R. Farrow and 2nd Lieutenants E. C. Cutler and V. St. G.

Smith, all of D Company, and 80 other ranks from all companies were selected. It was unfortunate that this sector should have been chosen, since the 9th Royal Fusiliers and the 9th Essex had each recently made successful daylight raids there, and there was every reason to suppose that the enemy would be on the alert, as, indeed, he proved to be.

For the next few days enemy aeroplanes were very active, and the retaliation to a bombardment by our artillery on the 1st October was quick and severe. The raid was timed for 12.50 p.m. on the 3rd, and the raiding party actually assembled. But shortly before Zero reports were received from aeroplanes that the enemy had withdrawn from his front line and was occupying his support and reserve lines in considerable force, in evident expectation of an attack. In view of this information, and of the fact that the enemy had put out fresh wire over-night, the raid was cancelled and a heavy bombardment substituted, lasting from 2.30 to 6.30 p.m.

OCTOBER 1917

It was then arranged that two strong patrols from B Company, led by 2nd Lieutenants T. Clarke and G. H. Hill, should raid Spoon Trench under cover of a protective barrage at 8 p.m. The patrols found that Spoon Trench was strongly held, and although they killed four or five Germans it was impossible to secure any identifications. Our casualties amounted to 1 killed and 7 wounded.

It was most fortunate that the original raid did not take place, for there is little doubt that the raiding party would have fallen into a carefully conceived trap. The enemy would have allowed our troops to enter the front line, only to overwhelm and destroy them by counter-attacks from the flanks and from the support and reserve lines.

On the 5th we were relieved by the 9th Essex and proceeded by the " Monchy Express " to Achicourt, moving on the 8th into Schramm Barracks at Arras. These barracks belonged to the French Army and were situated near the main Arras-Doullens Road, in the Faubourg d'Amiens.

Our stay in Arras was somewhat disturbed by the Germans shelling the neighbourhood of the goods station with a long-range gun. Apparently information had reached them that French reinforcements were passing through Arras on that particular day (the 10th); if not, it was an extraordinary coincidence. This gun had previously shelled the newly constructed railway loop at Achicourt, with the result that our Transport, close at hand in the Faubourg de Ronville, sometimes got the " shorts " nearer to them than was pleasant; one shell, fortunately a dud, landed just outside the horse-lines and disclosed the fact that the gun was a 24-centimetre naval gun firing armour-piercing shell.

OCTOBER 1917

On the 11th we moved into the Brown Line, and on the 14th the 35th and 37th Brigades carried out another large raid, with the co-operation of "The Circus," and captured 64 prisoners. On the 23rd we were relieved by the 1st Rifle Brigade (4th Division) and returned to Schramm Barracks, where we spent one night.

The Division was now due for a long rest, having spent over four months in the Monchy sector, which had been a period of continuously active defensive operations of the most strenuous nature. The defence of Monchy, from the 20th June to the 23rd October, had cost the battalion a total of 178 casualties, of whom 4 officers and 58 men were killed, missing, or died of wounds.

Early on the 24th we left Arras and marched for Ambrines, spending a night at Hermaville on the way. While there we received the following message from the Divisional Commander:—

"The Division has been in the trenches for eighteen weeks and has held an important portion of the line.

"I desire to express my high appreciation of the manner in which all have performed their duties.

"The consolidation of the line and the improvement of communications have involved a great deal of hard work, and the results have been most satisfactory.

"You have had a considerable amount of fighting, repelled several attacks, and have carried out some highly successful raids.

"You have exhibited strong powers of endurance, and by your gallantry and determination have upheld the best traditions of the Army.

"I am glad to say that those important points of close co-operation and good feeling between the different arms are still well maintained in the Division.

"A. B. SCOTT, *Major-General*,
"25th October, 1917." "*Commanding 12th Division.*"

Our sojourn at Ambrines lasted only two days, for on the 28th we moved, not, as some had forecast, up to the Passchendaele battle, but for a rest in the Hesdin area. Battalion H.Q., C and

The Defence of Monchy

D Companies halted for the night at Framecourt, and A and B, with the Transport, at Ecoivres. Our final destination was Vieil Hesdin, a pretty little village situated on both banks of the River Canche, which was fordable in most places and had to be crossed by companies to reach the battalion parade-ground.

October 1917

Billets were comfortable but rather scattered, and Battalion H.Q. found an agreeable abode in the Château Forestel.

We were now far removed from the scenes of strife; in fact, we had never been so far from the front line since our landing in France. The usual reorganisation was started at once, but it was not very long before signs of greater events cast their shadows before them, and we started intensive training for operations with tanks.

The preparations for the coming attack were shrouded in the utmost secrecy. The most drastic precautions were taken to enforce this, and no details regarding the date or place of attack were allowed to penetrate beyond Division H.Q. Although clear details of the type of training required were issued to all units, no discussion of them was allowed when in billets. All necessary lectures, explanations and instructions in the course of training had to be delivered in the open air *outside* billets, to prevent the smallest chance of any eavesdropping on the part of the local inhabitants.

Most of us thought that the training we were undergoing was merely a new method of attack, and we did not realise that a military operation of the first order was about to be launched. The lateness of the season assisted in this illusion, for it seemed more probable that the Division, like Caesar's army, would shortly be going into winter quarters.

It was unfortunate that secrets which were so loyally kept by those who were to take part in the scheme were seldom, throughout the whole war, held so sacred by those on the Home Front far removed from actual contact with the enemy. The garrulity of people with access to confidential information was such that it seemed impossible for any military secret to be kept in England. So it was that, while the final details of the operation in question were unknown to Lieutenant-Colonel Impey or to any member of the battalion, 2nd Lieutenant G. H. Hill, the Lewis Gun Officer, was able, on returning from leave, to give the exact information which G.H.Q. had been at such pains to keep secret, even to the *time and place* of the operation. All this he had heard openly (and accurately) discussed in the Long Bar of the Trocadero.

The Defence of Monchy

The time passed very quickly and pleasantly at Vieil Hesdin and the men showed the utmost keenness in the new training, which augured well for its future success. At first it was impossible to get any practice with real tanks, and we had to resort to various expedients, such as two-wheeled stretchers and wheelbarrows, to represent these monsters, but it was a great day when (on the 10th) we marched by brigade to Eclimeux, where training with the real articles was carried out.

NOVEMBER 1917

It was demonstrated how efficiently the new tanks could surmount and crush down the most formidable wire entanglements, and the men were told that the nerve-racking preliminary bombardment would no longer be necessary, thereby adding assurance that the enemy would not be on the alert. All the necessary formations and the correct method of crossing the gaps in the wire crushed flat by the tanks were carefully practised. It was altogether a most interesting two days' training, which proved of the greatest value.

During our rest at Vieil Hesdin sports and games were not forgotten, and an exciting divisional football competition was held. On wet days lectures and general knowledge questions were usually given as part of the morning training. It was on one of these occasions that Captain Le Hardy asked a platoon of A Company the name of the Commanding Officer, and was quite astonished that complete silence greeted this question. At last one lad got up and with a nervous giggle said, " We don't know what his name is, but we know what we calls him—we calls him ' Impey ! ' "

It was significant that only two days before our departure was our actual destination disclosed to us and maps were issued. On the 15th November we marched to Sibiville, moving on the following morning to Frévent, where we entrained for Peronne.

Prior to the departure of the battalion from Vieil Hesdin, Major Osborne and some of the company commanders had proceeded to Gonnelieu to reconnoitre the area over which we were to attack.

13. CAMBRAI AREA, 1917

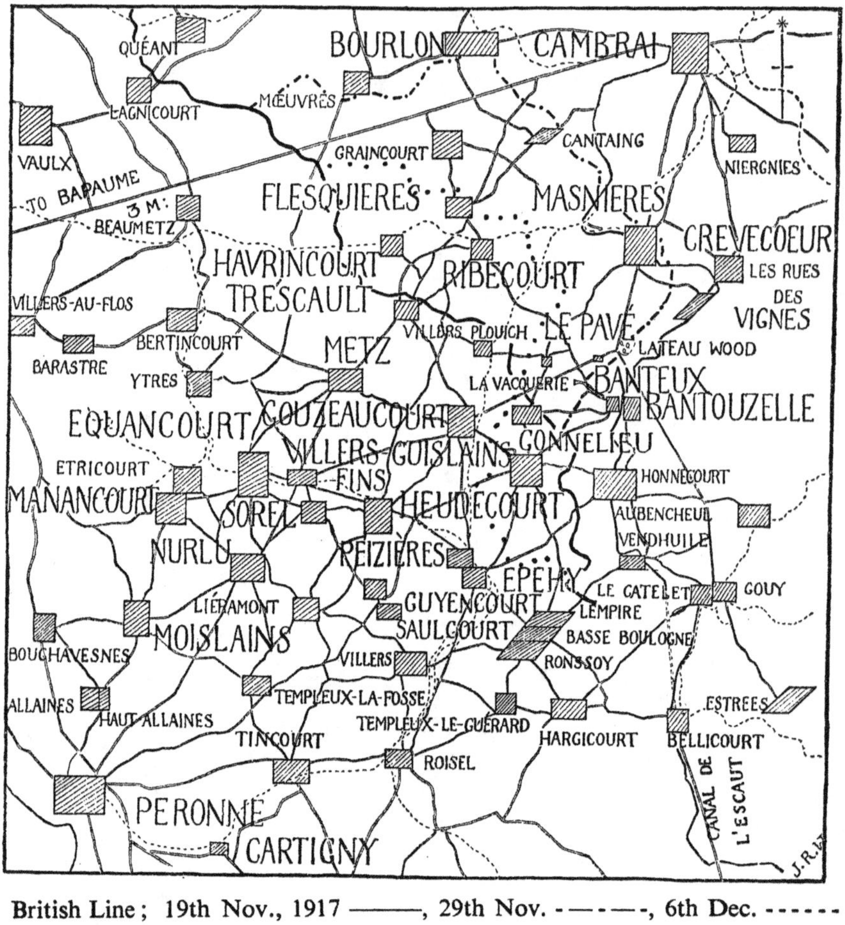

British Line; 19th Nov., 1917 ———, 29th Nov. —·—·—, 6th Dec. ······

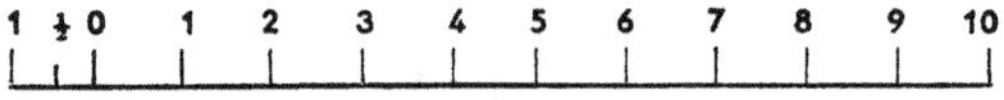

CHAPTER IX

THE BATTLE OF CAMBRAI

16TH NOVEMBER—3RD DECEMBER, 1917
[Sketch Maps, Nos. 13 and 14]

We reached Peronne at 11.30 a.m. on the 16th November after a long and roundabout journey. Now, for the first time, we saw country which had been laid waste by the enemy in the previous March during his retirement to the Hindenburg Line. Every village had been systematically destroyed with the usual German thoroughness, and although in most cases the outside walls were standing, the houses were roofless. During the previous six months, however, units in the area had done great work in erecting shelters and huts.

On arrival we at once proceeded to temporary billets in the town, since it was essential to prevent the enemy observing so large a concentration of troops, and strict orders had been issued for all ranks to keep under cover during daylight. Consequently we had no opportunity of visiting Peronne, a historic town which had been razed to the ground by the ravages of war for the second time within forty-seven years. That evening we marched by brigade to Moislains, a ruined village five miles distant, and remained there until dusk on the following day, when we moved to Equancourt, another ruined village, leaving the battle reserve under Major Thomson at Manancourt on the way.

The orders, which had been issued to ensure that evidence of an impending attack did not reach the enemy, included one that only the normal number of vehicles was to use the roads during daylight, and another that by night only fires proportionate to the usual small force of troops in the area were to be lighted. The former order caused inconvenience to Staff Officers, as they had to proceed in parties of three or four in one car; the latter caused the troops some discomfort, as the weather was cold and frosty at night.

The arrangements made by the III Corps, to which we now belonged, were excellent, and included the attachment to each battalion of a cyclist guide, who had previously reconnoitred the whole route and knew the actual billets to be occupied. All ranks had been warned on no account to answer questions by unknown officers while on the march. On one very dark and moonless night the Commanding Officer rode up to one of the companies and asked, " Who are you ? " The answer came back, " We're Kitchener's bloody Army ! " What a lesson for some of the garrison of the Home Front !

NOVEMBER 1917

Equancourt proved to be our last billeting place, and at 4.30 p.m. on the 18th we left for Vaucellette Farm, which we reached at 8 p.m. after an interesting march through Fins and Heudicourt. Any visions of further billets were quickly dispelled when it was discovered that Vaucellette Farm consisted merely of a cluster of ruined buildings on the east side of the main Peronne-Cambrai railway, the battalion being accommodated in some old trenches and dug-outs round about the railway embankment, about 200 yards short of the farm.

Later on in the evening a party consisting of the officers commanding companies and some platoon commanders went out to reconnoitre the assembly positions and the routes thereto, and while proceeding there came in for some gas-shelling in a sunken road between Villers-Guislain and Gonnelieu.

We spent the next day (the 19th) in completing our final preparations and had a chance to take stock of our position. Close at hand lay the ruined village of Epehy (which was to be the scene of a famous fight by the battalion ten months later), while farther off we could see the villages of Villers-Guislain, Gouzeaucourt and Gonnelieu, the last-named being only just behind our assembly position. The day passed very quietly, except for a few shells on Epehy, and the battalion left at 9.35 p.m. for the assembly position.

The origins of the Battle of Cambrai must now be considered, for in them can be seen the causes of failure and of the subsequent disasters. It is to-day well known that the employment of a large number of tanks in the Flanders swamps at the beginning of " Third Ypres " (the 31st July) had been contrary to the express warnings of the Tank Corps Headquarters.* When the opening

------

* For most of the details in this and the next two paragraphs the Compilers are indebted to Captain B. H. Liddell Hart's *The Real War*, p. 370 *et seq.*

The Battle of Cambrai

days of that attack conclusively proved the correctness of their unheeded advice, Tank Corps Headquarters, realising the need for restoring the confidence both of the General Staff and of the infantry in regard to the tanks, drew up a plan, on the 3rd August, for a large-scale tank raid against St. Quentin, where the ground was favourable to such an operation. When it was objected that this area would present the difficulty of collaboration with the French Army, another scheme was substituted for a raid against " the re-entrant formed by the Escaut-St. Quentin Canal between Ribecourt-Crevecœur-Banteux." The object of the raid was " to destroy the enemy's personnel and guns, to demoralise and disorganise him, and not to capture ground." The total force to be employed was to be three tank brigades and one or two divisions of infantry or cavalry, with augmented artillery, operating from a front of 8,000 yards and withdrawing within eight to ten hours.

NOVEMBER 1917

General Sir Julian Byng, whose Third Army occupied the sector in question, approved of the idea, although he wished to expand it into a set-piece attack to capture Cambrai, but the whole scheme was turned down by G.H.Q. Although Sir Douglas Haig was, on the whole, favourable, General Kiggell, the Chief of Staff, was not yet convinced that the Ypres attacks could not succeed, and pointed out that the British reserves were insufficient to allow us to fight two battles simultaneously.

However, the failure of repeated and costly attacks at Ypres, and continued pressure from General Byng and the Tank Corps, eventually led G.H.Q., in the middle of October, to sanction the project of an attack in the Cambrai area. But it was now a very different undertaking from that proposed in August. First, the Ypres offensive had weakened the British Army by nearly 275,000 men and 200 tanks, and of the 62 British infantry divisions then on the Western Front 54 had been involved in this " last word in human misery." Second, events were about to occur on the Italian Front which would cause five British divisions to be sent there as reinforcements. Lastly, and most important of all, the original notion of a raid had been fundamentally altered. Although General Kiggell pressed for a purely local attack, and Sir Douglas Haig put a provisional time-limit of forty-eight hours on the battle, the orders issued by the Third Army were for a large-scale operation, with provisions for extensive exploitation instead of for withdrawal. Two corps of infantry (III and IV), each of three divisions, the Cavalry Corps of two divisions,

The Battle of Cambrai

380 tanks, and 1,009 guns were to be employed. This force was to break through the heavily-entrenched Hindenburg Line between the Escaut-St. Quentin Canal and the Canal du Nord, capture Bourlon Ridge and Cambrai, and

NOVEMBER 1917

exploit this success in a northerly direction so as to cut off the German forces south of the Rivers Scarpe and Sensée. All the infantry divisions and the tanks were to be used in the initial attack, so that there would be no immediate reserves, except of cavalry, after the original impetus was spent. A French corps was, indeed, moved near to Peronne, but after the first day of the attack it was told that it would not be wanted.

It is difficult to imagine how the exploitation phase was to be effected, or how the resultant deep and dangerous salient was ever to be defended. There seems, in fact, to have been a lack of clarity in the intentions of the Third Army which was to react perilously upon the progress of the battle. In any case, it is obvious that the main interest was focussed upon the left flank, and especially upon the Flesquieres and Bourlon Ridges.

The task allotted to the 12th Division, in Lieutenant-General Sir William Pulteney's III Corps, lay on the extreme right of the attack, where it was to form a defensive flank in conjunction with the 55th Division (VII Corps) on its right, which was not to advance, but merely to make a demonstration with smoke and dummies.

The Division's first objective (the black line) consisted of the outpost line to the Hindenburg Front System, and, on our battalion front, stretched from the junction of Bleak and Quarry Trenches on the south to Sonnet Farm (exclusive) on the north. The second objective (the blue line) was the front and support lines of the Hindenburg Front System, and the third objective (the brown line) was a line drawn on the map about 2,000 yards in front of the blue line, and it included an area containing the Hindenburg Support System and the junction of the Cambrai-Peronne and the Cambrai-St. Quentin Roads.

After the capture of these objectives the Division had to form a defensive flank, facing roughly south-east, from Cheshire Street to Le Pavé, then along the Cambrai Road, skirting Lateau Wood on the east and joining on to the 20th Division some 500 yards to the north of the wood.

The 35th Brigade on the right and the 36th Brigade (less the 11th Middlesex) on the left had to capture the black and blue lines, while the 37th Brigade and the 11th Middlesex were to pass through and take the brown line.

The Battle of Cambrai

We were the right hand battalion of the Brigade, our boundary with the 9th Essex on the right being from a few yards south-east of Cheshire Street up to the junction of Breslau Support and Emden Support, about 400 yards south-east of the Cambrai Road. Our boundary with the 9th Royal Fusiliers on the left ran from where a sunken road crossed the British front line north-east of Gonnelieu to where the Hindenburg front line crossed the Cambrai Road, and from there along the road for about 500 yards to the blue line.

NOVEMBER 1917

C and B Companies formed, from right to left, the first wave, with the black line as their objective; A and D were to pass through to capture the blue line. The battalion was then to do a right turn and, by transforming German communication trenches into fire trenches, to form a somewhat weak defensive flank. Thus A and C would become the right and left front companies, and D and B the support companies. The company commanders were Captain W. H. C. Le Hardy, A; Lieutenant W. H. Sainton, B; Captain C. W. Ballard, C; and Lieutenant H. J. R. Farrow, D.

The approach march to our assembly position was accomplished with one slight mishap, two companies going temporarily astray at a forked road, but fortunately the mistake was quickly rectified and we reached our destination shortly after midnight without any further trouble. Great credit must be given to the Royal Engineers for the admirable way in which all assembly positions and routes thereto were marked out with white tape, an invaluable precaution, since there were no natural objects to guide us, and to all but the reconnoitring party the ground was unknown.

Our position of assembly was just north of Gonnelieu, between Sonnet Road and the road leading from the village to the Cambrai Road, a little behind Gun Support Trench, where Battalion H.Q. was established. The garrison of the front and support trenches, consisting of units of the 20th Division, had not been relieved, so that if by any chance a prisoner fell into the enemy's hands no new unit would be identified.

A long and weary wait now ensued and the men were encouraged to get all the rest they could, but it was very damp and cold and they were lying in the open. No smoking was allowed, which made the wait seem even longer. However, the hot tea and the rum that were served out helped to warm them and keep their spirits up. When not resting they beguiled the weary hours of waiting by observing the various secret

The Battle of Cambrai

preparations which gradually unfolded themselves, especially the enormous concentration of carefully concealed artillery, which, for obvious reasons, had carried out no registration. The Gunners had brought concealment to a fine art, and 2nd Lieutenant E. A. Bingen, of D Company, who was sleeping on a ground-sheet, suddenly found when it was removed that he was looking down the muzzle of an 18-pounder which was right out in the open.

NOVEMBER 1917

The question of the hour was, did the enemy know what was afoot? Had the *embusqués* and gossips done their worst? It certainly seemed that all was well. There was no unusual hostile shelling or machine-gun fire, although farther north, in the neighbourhood of Havrincourt Wood, we could hear the sound of guns. We afterwards heard that prisoners from a certain division in that sector had been captured two days previously in a raid by the Germans, who had learned from them that an attack was imminent there and that tanks might be employed, while on the 19th a German listening-set farther north at Bullecourt had picked up fragments of a telephone conversation in which the words "Tuesday Flanders" had occurred. This aroused suspicions, and although the size and scope of the attack were not realised certain counter-measures against a local enterprise at Havrincourt were taken. It was also fortunate that ten days' bad visibility had prevented any aeroplane reconnaissance, for it was learnt afterwards that the enemy ground-observers had noticed great activity behind our lines; nevertheless, the enemy did not anticipate a big attack so soon.

At length a distant rumbling heralded the approach of the tanks, but lest the noise of their engines should reach the enemy they halted 1,000 yards behind the front line; certainly to those waiting to go over the top it seemed as if the roar must be heard for miles. Our artillery sent over a few shells, just as they had made a point of doing on other days, so that suspicions should not be roused, and these helped to drown the noise. In reply, one or two hostile machine-guns opened fire for a short time and slightly wounded both of A Company's runners, Privates P. Scott, M.M., and E. J. Chatfield, who had been charged with the important duty of carrying the company's supply of whisky and rum; but Captain Le Hardy, with admirable presence of mind, was careful to relieve them of their precious burden before their departure for the dressing-station.

From now onwards a deathlike silence prevailed, and we became more and more confident that a surprise would be effected.

14. CAMBRAI, TRENCH MAP

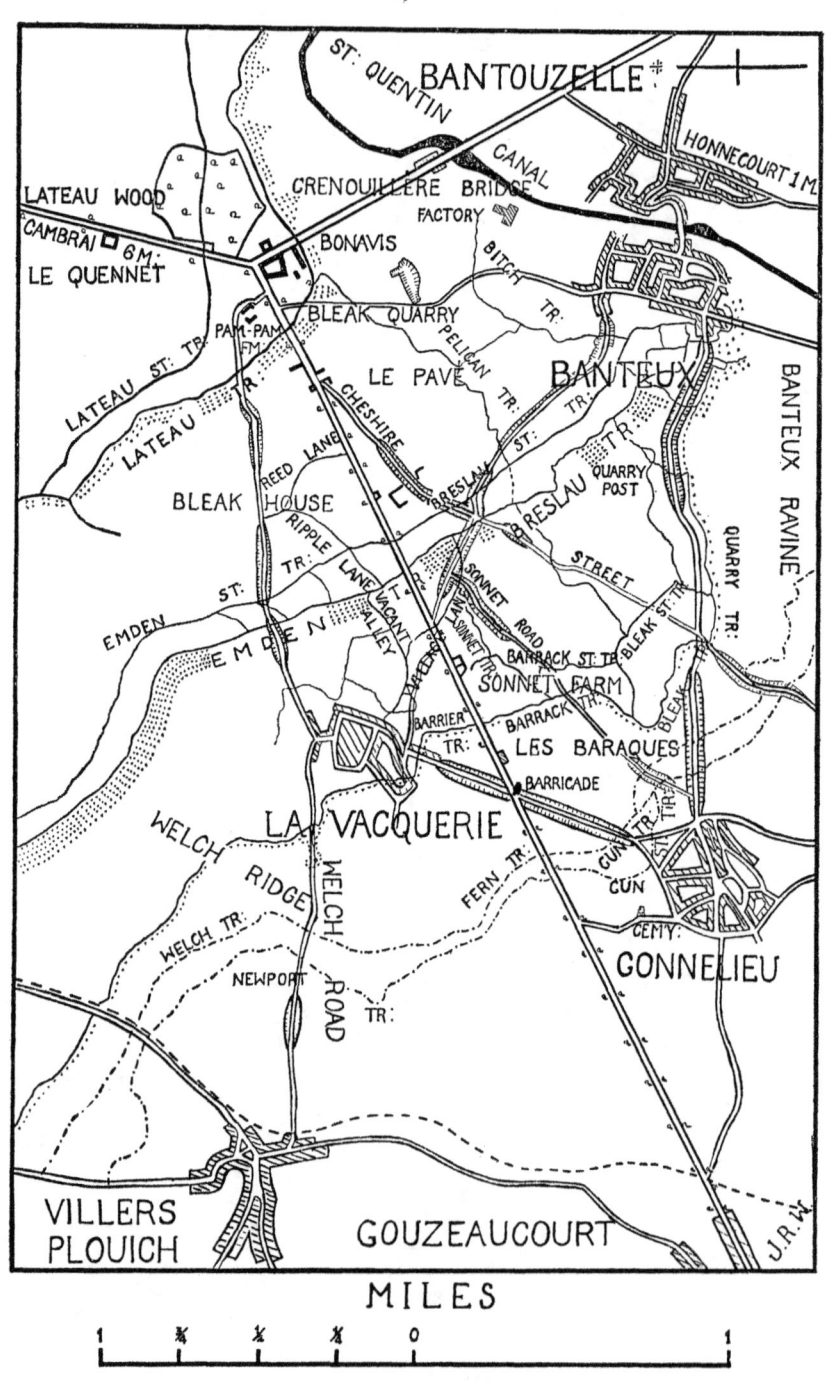

THE BATTLE OF CAMBRAI

Towards 6 a.m. the early streaks of dawn began to show themselves, disclosing for the first time the tanks, each bearing the Divisional Sign. They looked all the more fearsome for having huge fascines fixed on their tops, in order to negotiate the broad trenches of the Hindenburg Line. Twelve of them were operating on our battalion front.

NOVEMBER 1917

Zero hour had been fixed for 6.20 a.m. on Tuesday, the 20th November. From now onwards the minutes crawled. At length 6.10 came. Then 6.15. Still a dead silence. Could it continue? Would the enemy forestall us at the last moment? These were the questions in every mind. The suspense was terrible.

6.20 came at last. Instantly a hurricane barrage opened from guns of every calibre, to the accompaniment of showers of S.O.S. rockets of all colours from the German lines, which had become a mass of bursting shells. To add to the deafening noise, dozens of our planes, flying lower than most of us had hitherto experienced, appeared out of the mists of the dawn.

The advanced guard tanks started at Zero in order to make gaps in the broad and formidable belts of wire, and were followed ten minutes later by the main-guard tanks, accompanied by the infantry in special tank-formation, consisting of " blobs " of sections in file about fifty yards behind each tank.

There was no doubt that, from the opening of the attack, surprise was complete, owing to the omission of the usual lengthy barrage which on so many other occasions had given the enemy such timely warning, and retaliation was very feeble.

Our men, some with rifles slung, advanced leisurely across No Man's Land at the same speed as the tanks, as if at a rehearsal. A very curious impression was given to those watching the attack from the rear by numbers of men stopping to light cigarettes, a pleasure denied to them during the weary hours of waiting.

No Man's Land in our sector was 700 to 800 yards wide, and since there had been little or no shelling the going was very good. Everything went according to plan and the attack was the most successful the battalion had ever made. At the start a machine-gun, firing from a pill-box* at a point where the Hindenburg front line crosses the Cambrai Road, swept No Man's Land and caused a few casualties, including 2nd Lieutenant D. T. Cohen (D Company), who died of wounds, but on the whole the enemy was so taken by surprise and so paralysed with fear by the tanks that his resistance was negligible until we reached Sonnet Farm.

---

* Still in existence and a great landmark to this day.

The Battle of Cambrai

NOVEMBER 1917

Here a machine-gun gave us a certain amount of trouble and killed, amongst others, 2nd Lieutenant J. L. Knox (C Company). Large numbers of the enemy surrendered, one of our platoon commanders being smartly saluted and addressed in perfect English by a German sergeant-major. A large *minenwerfer*, the emplacement of which had been hit by a heavy shell which had killed the entire team, was captured in Barrack Support Trench.

We quickly gained the black line and passed on to the blue line, our final objective, where we established touch with the 9th Royal Fusiliers on our left and with the 35th Brigade on our right. The final positions of the battalion were:—B Company in Barrack Trench and Support, C in Sonnet Trench and Village Lane, D and A in the Hindenburg front line and support, A and C forming a defensive flank in the communication trenches facing east. Our total casualties for this attack were 2 officers killed and 1 wounded,* and 106 other ranks killed and wounded. Very few German casualties were observed.

The completeness with which the tanks carried out their task was magnificent. All the gaps in the wire were crushed flat, so that we had no difficulty in crossing them, and all machine-gun nests were quickly subdued. In fact, it is not too much to say that complete confidence in the tanks prevailed throughout the Brigade.

The regimental history of the *19th Regiment (9th Reserve Division)*, whose *I* and *II Battalions* were facing us, admits that the attack was a complete surprise and that the tanks struck terror into the hearts of the men, who cried: " What is the good of using rifles and bombs against armoured skins? " The tanks were described as black monsters moaning and panting. One group saw a tank coming under the barrage and started firing at the soldiers behind, but suddenly found themselves surrounded. They were greatly impressed at the way the tanks flattened the wire and mopped up the trenches. Another personal account says: " Amidst clouds of smoke, box-like shapes approaching everywhere, tanks appeared, surrounded by soldiers."

One German N.C.O. thought some of the British were drunk, since, while they were slowly advancing, some of them were seen to throw their steel helmets in the air and catch them again.

---

* 2nd Lieutenant F. Frewer (D) slightly wounded and remained at duty.

The Battle of Cambrai

Now comes an incident which was to prove of vital importance in the future. Captain Le Hardy, who was commanding A Company, could see quite clearly from his new headquarters the villages of Banteux and Bantouzelle in the valley of the St. Quentin Canal. He noticed with some surprise that although the houses appeared intact there was no sign of life in them. He accordingly detailed an officer's patrol under Lieutenant R. M. Howe to reconnoitre. This patrol had a curious experience. It penetrated into Banteux, crossed the canal by the bridge leading into Bantouzelle, walked right through that village (and some way up the hill beyond) without meeting or seeing a solitary German. In his initial panic the enemy had abandoned both villages, as well as the two covering trench lines (Pelican and Bitch Trenches) on the slope running down from the Cambrai Road.

NOVEMBER 1917

This information was reported to the Adjutant, who passed it on to the Brigade, but since the villages were out of our area nothing further could be done by us. We heard nothing more of the matter. The Higher Command here missed a golden opportunity of occupying unopposed what undoubtedly was the key to the canal-crossing on our front, the importance of which was evidently not unknown to them, for the following had appeared in Divisional Orders: " In order to render the flank more secure it is proposed to destroy the bridges at Les Rues des Vinges and Banteux and drive the enemy with tanks from the Western Bank," while the Divisional History states : " The weakness of the position was the inability to command the lower portions of the Canal Valley, either by fire or observation."* These statements render the inertia displayed even more inexplicable. No orders were given to the Royal Engineers as to demolitions, which the infantry could not have carried out without expert assistance. There can be no doubt that even if the question of occupying these important positions was ever thoroughly considered it had been entirely shelved, in spite of the fact that the buildings of the villages and the small woods and folds in the ground provided the enemy with admirable cover for hidden concentration.

Leading down to the villages from the Cambrai Road was a metalled road, sunken in parts ; the intervening ground, which in peace time had evidently been under cultivation, ran down in a gentle slope from the Cambrai Road towards the canal for a distance of about half a mile to where Pelican Trench, which was

---
* *Op. cit.*, p. 141.

a communication trench between the Hindenburg Front and Support Systems, zig-zagged in a north-easterly direction for about three-quarters of a mile, joining the Front System in Breslau Trench and the Support System just north of Bleak Quarry. From Pelican Trench the ground dropped a little more steeply to Bitch Trench, which in a rough semi-circle covered Banteux and the intervening ground up to a factory on the north, where it finally ended ; in the south it met the support trench of the Hindenburg Front System in a sunken part of the metalled road about 200 yards outside the village. It was a very useful position to the enemy, as it lay in dead ground, out of observation from our Cambrai Road positions but commanded by Pelican Trench, to which, connected in the middle by a communication trench, it formed an effective if somewhat distant support, possessing hidden facilities for concentration and good connection with the village by means of the sunken roads at each end. From our point of view the whole position was an admirable one for covering the crossing of the canal and denying the enemy numerous advantages for concentration, which it was essential for him to retain if he wished to threaten our flank.

The accuracy of these statements, only too evident at the time, has been fully confirmed by post-war reconnaissances. Although it was not possible to occupy the farther bank of the canal with the force available, no lack of reserves, nor any other excuse, can atone for the neglect on the 20th November both to destroy the bridge at Banteux and to occupy Pelican and Bitch Trenches. Had these precautions been taken there is not a shadow of doubt that the counter-attack on 30th November would have had a very different ending. There will, however, be more to say as to these trenches when the subsequent futile attacks on them come to be described.

The rest of the 20th was spent in consolidating the German trenches, in which ample accommodation was found in the capacious dug-outs of the Hindenburg Line. The elaborate construction of these indicated that the Germans had contemplated a long tenancy. The other units of the Brigade which had leap-frogged us had also reached their objectives. All ranks were elated by the success achieved, and after fire-trenches had been made to form the defensive flank the rest of the day was spent in

The Battle of Cambrai

a closer examination of the territory gained and in searching for souvenirs. Of these, cigars and mineral waters were most popular. A store of great-coats was used either for their legitimate use or in place of blankets.

The sight of the cavalry trotting up the Cambrai Road evoked loud cheers from the troops, NOVEMBER 1917 and a little later great interest was shown in a party of civilians who had been released from Masnieres by the 29th Division.

The next three days passed quietly enough and enabled our men to have a rest after the strenuous days through which they had passed. General work on the trenches was carried out, and since the enemy did not yet possess any observation we could move freely about above ground, but everyone realised well enough that this agreeable peace could not last much longer. Major Osborne's remark, "I wonder when the first 5.9 will arrive," aptly summed up our feelings. When we heard that joy bells had been pealed in London to celebrate our supposed victory we felt anything but encouraged, for it was unlikely that the enemy would tamely sit down under defeat.

Some reason must be found to account for the puzzling inertia on our front between the 20th and the 23rd November. Here was the 12th Division in a position where it could not properly perform its task of securing the right flank of the attack, although it had captured all the objectives allotted to it by the Higher Command. Its depleted battalions were strung out in converted communication trenches along a line of nearly 6,000 yards, with its headquarters and reserves of necessity badly placed, echeloned to its right rear. Its right boundary was the old No Man's Land, and this was also the boundary between the III and VII Corps. In front lay ideal assembly positions for the inevitable counter-attacks which were to come, positions which could have been denied to the enemy without opposition during the first three days of the attack had any reserves been provided. The tenure of these positions by our troops would decisively have prevented the enemy from striking at the base of the newly-created salient. But nothing was done.

The answer to the enigma is to be found in Sir Douglas Haig's despatch on the Cambrai Operations.* It is evident that only

---
* Vide *Sir Douglas Haig's Despatches*, edited by Lieutenant-Colonel J. H. Boraston, pp. 151-173.

the left flank of the attack was at this period exciting any interest. The enemy's defence of the Flesquieres Ridge had held up the left centre of the attack for a whole day, so that by the time the Commander-in-Chief's limit of forty-eight hours had elapsed the initial impetus was spent, and Bourlon Ridge, on the extreme left, was not entirely in British hands. Sir Douglas Haig had fixed this limit so that the advance could be stopped " unless the results then gained and the general situation justified its continuance."*

NOVEMBER 1917

Now Bourlon Ridge not only overlooked the positions north of Flesquieres, but " so great was the importance of the ridge to the enemy that its loss would probably cause the abandonment by the Germans of their carefully prepared defence systems for a considerable distance to the north of it."† This was a strange commentary from the Commander of the British forces, whose positions from Ypres to Cambrai were commanded by higher ground.

But the lure of high ground and the possibility of easily gaining the remaining Hindenburg defences (especially at Bullecourt, where so much blood had been vainly shed) proved too great a temptation to the Third Army Commander, so that when, on the morning of the 22nd, the order went out that the battle was to be continued, the few fresh reserve divisions now called up were thrown in on the Bourlon front. Sir Douglas Haig always assumed full responsibility for the actions of his subordinates, and, commenting upon this move, he remarks, " on the Cambrai side of the battlefield I had only aimed at securing a defensive flank to enable the advance to be pushed northwards and north-westwards, and this part of my task had been *to a large extent* achieved."‡

But General Byng was trying to establish a long suit before he had led out trumps. His trump lead was the security of his right flank by the domination of the crossings of the Escaut-St. Quentin Canal. The lead was not made, and the enemy, with the smaller trumps still in his hand, was able to " rough " and to defeat the contract.

It was not until the 23rd that General Pulteney, our Corps Commander, awoke to the importance of occupying Pelican Trench and thus of obtaining observation over the canal. It was now too late. The enemy had taken his opportunity and was

---

* *Op. cit.*, p. 152.
† *Op. cit.*, p. 159.
‡ *Op. cit.*, p. 160 (italics inserted by the Compilers).

strongly occupying the trench, so that an attack had to be prepared to advance our defensive flank to the line Quarry Post—Bleak Quarry, which included the whole of Pelican Trench. The task of capturing the trench was given to the 8th Royal Fusiliers, while units of the 35th Brigade were to collaborate farther south by capturing Quarry Post and the trenches in its vicinity. These attacks took place at 8 a.m. on the 24th and were entirely successful; but unfortunately the 8th Royal Fusiliers, having taken all its objectives, was driven out of the centre part of Pelican Trench, so that its gains were almost entirely nullified.

Hostile artillery activity increased after the attack, and—what was far worse—the weather broke; snow, sleet and rain set in and made the ground almost impassable. However, during the late afternoon we received orders to relieve the 8th Royal Fusiliers in the captured parts of Pelican Trench and to complete its capture the following morning.

On receipt of these orders the Commanding Officer held a hurried conference of company commanders at Battalion H.Q. in a dug-out near Sonnet Farm. The attack was a most complicated one. A Company on the right was to cross the sunken road which ran between Breslau Support and Pelican Trench and to bomb up the latter until they joined with B Company at the junction of the communication trench, which led from the centre of Pelican Trench to the centre of Bitch Trench, about 350 yards in front. B Company in the centre was to attack over the open from the northern portion of Pelican Trench and to capture the remainder of it and the whole of the communication trench. On the left, Bitch Trench was to be attacked frontally by C Company (on the right) and D (on the left), operating from the captured trenches north of Bleak Quarry.

The weather conditions were deplorable, and continuous rain or sleet had turned the trenches into rivers of clinging mud. We could not start moving into position until 1.30 a.m. on the 25th, and B, C and D Companies did not reach their assembly positions until 6 a.m. Battalion H.Q. moved into a concrete dug-out (still in existence) near Bleak House, which during the German occupation had combined the amenities of a soup kitchen with those of a quartermaster's store.

The attack, supported by a very feeble barrage, started at 7 a.m. In spite of some initial confusion as to direction, C and D Companies captured Bitch Trench without much opposition. Unfortunately C Company lost all its officers, and Captain

The Battle of Cambrai

Ballard, who had shown such admirable powers of leadership during his sixteen months with the battalion, was killed. Lieutenant Farrow, therefore, took command of both companies.

B Company from the start met with very heavy fire both from Pelican Trench and from the communication trench and was unable to make any progress, so that A Company, whose bombing attack had started so well that it had almost reached its objective, was exposed to the full weight of the German counter-bombing. To add to the difficulties of A Company the sunken road, which it was essential for everyone to cross, was swept continuously by machine-gun fire. The bomb-carrying parties, whose supplies were vital to the maintenance of the captured position, suffered a steady drain of casualties.

The German resistance to our thrust was most effective. By concentrating at first their main attention against B Company in the centre they were then able to turn and deal with the flanks of the attack. Taking advantage of the facilities for hidden concentration the enemy closed in around C and D Companies in their exposed position, and heavy bomb-fighting followed, during which 2nd Lieutenant E. A. Bingen (D) was wounded. When our bomb supply was exhausted, Lieutenant Farrow was forced to order both companies to retire over the open. This retirement was one of great difficulty, and the casualties, which had already been considerable, were sadly increased. However, the companies were most skilfully led back to their original line, from which a counter-attack by the enemy was successfully repelled.

The carrying of bombs over the exposed sunken road and through the awful mud put the unsupported A Company at a great disadvantage compared with the enemy, who had his supply at hand. It eventually became impossible for A Company to keep up such an unequal contest, and it was driven back, foot by foot, to its starting point.

Thus the attack ended. The greatest bravery and dash had been shown by all ranks, but the dreadful weather conditions, which caused rifles and Lewis guns to become clogged with mud, the difficulties of bomb supply, the lack of good communications, and the impossibility of previous reconnaissance were factors which made success highly improbable.

The men were thoroughly exhausted by this effort, but the Higher Command would not accept the inevitable. In spite of strong representations by the Brigade Commander a second attack was ordered, this time to secure only the central part of

The Battle of Cambrai

Pelican Trench. This involved a great deal of preparation for which numerous carrying-parties had to be found, and in this work invaluable assistance was given by the 11th Middlesex.

This second attack was timed for 10.50 p.m., when D Company was to start bombing from the northern end of Pelican Trench and A Company from the southern end. At first some slight progress was made from both ends, and in the hand-to-hand fighting which took place 2nd Lieutenant F. Frewer (D) distinguished himself before he was again wounded. It was evident, however, that the heavy exertions of the past twenty-four hours were telling on the men, and the Germans, with their better facilities for supply and reinforcement, were able to hold out. A Company again came in for heavy machine-gun fire down the sunken road and was eventually bombed out of the positions which it had captured.

NOVEMBER 1917

The net result of these two attacks was that the two blocks in Pelican Trench were slightly advanced and that we captured 11 prisoners (thus causing the identification of the *34th Division*, which had just been brought up from the French front). On the other hand, we suffered in casualties 1 officer killed and 4 wounded, together with 117 other ranks killed and wounded (including Company Sergeant-Major W. Robbins, formerly a drummer in the 2nd Battalion). It was a bitter thought that all this unnecessary slaughter might have been averted had Pelican and Bitch Trenches been occupied during the initial attack on the 20th November.

During these attacks we had been opposed by the *II Battalion* of the *67th Regiment (34th Division)*, from whose regimental history the following is a free translation :—

" On the morning of the 25th the *8th Company* had only been in position for a few hours when it got a very good proof of the dangerous nature of the position of its trenches. After a sudden burst of artillery fire the English advanced, but our *8th Company* and the *395th Regiment (9th Reserve Division)* to the north were on the alert, and a short but fierce rifle-grenade and bomb combat ensued. An N.C.O. of the *8th Company* distinguished himself by bringing his machine-gun into such a position that he could get a very fine field of fire ; a number of dead were left behind. They belonged to the Royal Sussex Regiment. A second attack was made the same night, when the position of the *8th Company* was in a salient which the English succeeded in occupying, but eventually were evicted out of most of it, leaving 3 dead and 1 wounded. They also belonged to the Royal Sussex Regiment.

The Battle of Cambrai

On our side one man was missing, probably taken prisoner by the English, and that was the reason why in papers captured on the 30th November we read that the identity of our Division was disclosed."

The next day (the 26th) passed quietly. In the evening the 11th Middlesex and the 9th Royal Fusiliers relieved us and we went into support, the battalion being distributed as follows :—
A Company in Village Lane, C in the trenches about La Vacquerie, B and D and Battalion H.Q. in Barrier and Barrack Trenches, the old German front line.

During the following three days large working-parties were found by day and night for work in the front line system, but the question of the moment was how much longer it would be before the enemy attempted to retrieve his losses.

NOVEMBER 1917 The fact that we were in a dangerous re-entrant without any reserves, coupled with the enemy's stubborn defence of Pelican Trench, pointed to a lull before a storm, and it was impossible not to feel uneasy. On the 28th and 29th vague reports reached us (attributed at the time to the usual trench gossip) of considerable hostile movements under smoke screens, together with other reports of general activity. There was also at times promiscuous hostile shelling which, had any suspicions been entertained, might have been attributed to registration, but no warning order of any impending counter-attack ever reached the battalion. Any fears which we might have had were allayed when details for training when in Brigade Support were given to us. Rifle exercises and platoon drill were included in the curriculum, and it had also been arranged that cookers should be sent up to the companies. It is a remarkable fact that no form of defence scheme was ever issued to us and that the duties of the battalion in the event of an attack were left entirely unexplained. The lack of any information is fully confirmed by the war diaries of all units of the 36th and 37th Brigades.

It is also significant that the battle surplus, consisting of Captains G. L. Reckitt and W. F. Campbell, Lieutenant E. C. Gorringe, and 2nd Lieutenants S. L. Burdett, V. E. Rogers, G. H. Atkinson and F. R. Paley, together with 109 other ranks, rejoined the battalion in the trenches on the evening of the 29th, for such action was not usually taken when a battle appeared imminent. As matters turned out their arrival was providential, for although casualties were comparatively light in the

The Battle of Cambrai

original attack on the 20th, the battalion strength had been greatly reduced by the futile attacks on Pelican and Bitch Trenches.

It would seem that the German defeat on the 20th November had caused the Higher Command to become over-confident, and all warnings of the coming storm appear to have been ridiculed.

Captain Liddell Hart* tells how General Snow, commanding the VII Corps on our right, " had forecast both the place and date of the counter-stroke nearly a week before," and how General Jeudwine, commanding the 55th Division on the left of the VII Corps, was " so convinced of the imminent menace " on the 29th November that he " asked that the neighbouring III Corps might put down a counter-preparation with 'heavies' on the Banteux Ravine just before daylight next morning, but his request was not met."

NOVEMBER 1917

The night of the 29th passed quietly, but at 7 a.m. on the 30th we were aroused by a violent barrage of high-explosive and gas shells. Everyone soon realised that an attack was coming. Captain Bowlby, who was Adjutant at the time, thus describes the situation at Battalion H.Q. :—

" I can vouch for the fact that no warning of a counter-attack ever reached the battalion. In fact, I can remember clearly that the first intimation at Battalion H.Q. of anything untoward was an unusual amount of shelling. I was then in the H.Q. dug-out eating my breakfast and went up into the trench with the Colonel and Major Osborne and found Regimental Sergeant-Major Joy on the top of the parapet looking through his glasses to the south. Some troops could be seen moving back across the open in a south-westerly direction between Battalion H.Q. and the outskirts of Gonnelieu. With the aid of glasses we could all see that they were British. It was the first time I had ever seen a rearward movement on so large a scale. We quickly finished breakfast—a wise precaution, as there was little to be had for the rest of the day."

In the meantime the Commanding Officer had issued warning orders for all companies to be ready to move at short notice, and H.Q. was hurriedly packed up. A strict look-out was kept for any enemy movements, and just before 8 a.m., to our consternation, German white position lights were seen to go up directly over Gonnelieu, which lay well to our right rear. It was then only too clear that our right flank was in the air and that the

---
* *The Real War*, pp. 378-9.

The Battle of Cambrai

35th Brigade, having been completely overwhelmed, had retired right back, north-west of the village.

Something had to be done at once. In view of the scattered position of the companies it was essential to get them into suitable positions to repel any attacks on our right flank. All telephone wires had long since been broken and messages were possible only by runner, consequently Battalion H.Q. moved up to a dug-out in the Hindenburg front line, finding en route that Captain Le Hardy, acting with great promptitude, had already anticipated orders by manning positions in Vacant Alley and Village Lane, facing the Cambrai Road.

NOVEMBER 1917

When H.Q. established touch with Lieutenant-Colonel W. V. L. Van Someren, M.C., commanding the 9th Royal Fusiliers, it was found that the 8th Royal Fusiliers (who, with the 9th, were left and right front battalions respectively) had been overwhelmed by an attack in the rear which had driven them back from Bonavis Ridge. A very gallant counter-attack by Lieutenant-Colonel N. B. Elliott-Cooper, D.S.O., M.C. (who, when mortally wounded, had been taken prisoner*), had practically restored the situation, and the remnants of the battalion, about 70 in number, under Major C. O. Skey, were now occupying their reserve line. Colonel Impey therefore decided to reinforce them with D Company, under Captain Reckitt.

There had also been heavy fighting on the front line held by the 9th Royal Fusiliers, and as early as 7.10 a.m. Germans in large numbers had been seen advancing up the spur from Banteux and had been fired on at about 800 yards range. Bomb fighting was going on in the Hindenburg front line, where, reinforced by some of the 7th Norfolks which had been driven back, the 9th Royal Fusiliers was holding some bomb-blocks and a support trench dug between it and the Cambrai Road; its right flank, as the result of the retirement of the 35th Brigade, was completely in the air. Unfortunately, in spite of the counter-attack by Colonel Elliott-Cooper, three strong-points just south of Bleak House (held by D Company of the 9th Royal Fusiliers) had been surrounded and captured.

Colonel Impey decided to reinforce the 9th Royal Fusiliers in the Hindenburg front line with B Company. This left C Company under Lieutenant Gorringe, in support about

---
* He was awarded the Victoria Cross, but died as a prisoner of war in Germany in February, 1918.

La Vacquerie, but owing to the serious situation this company had eventually to be sent up to the right of D Company.

These dispositions were complete by 10 a.m. The line now held by the battalion was approximately
A Company in Village Lane and Vacant Alley, which here formed the front line,
B Company in support to the 9th Royal Fusiliers in Emden Trench and Emden Support (Hindenburg Front System), and C and D Companies bridging the gap between the 9th and the 8th Royal Fusiliers by manning Ripple Lane between Emden Support and Reed Lane. Battalion H.Q. shared a dug-out with the 9th Royal Fusiliers in Emden Trench. Colonel Van Someren said that the first he knew of any attack had been, on emerging from his dug-out to see what was happening, to be confronted by an enormous German, whom he had promptly despatched with his revolver, which he was fortunate to have with him, as he had no idea that the battle had begun.

Severe bomb fighting continued on the farther side of the Cambrai Road. This quietened down by 2 p.m., but heavy shelling by the enemy, mostly with our captured guns, persisted. A deserted battery of our 6-inch howitzers, abandoned at Sonnet Farm (now occupied by the enemy), presented a pathetic sight.

Having described the general situation in which we found ourselves, it will be enlightening to add the following personal narrative by Captain Reckitt, who was commanding D Company :—

"On the 29th November I rejoined D Company in Barrier Trench. It was very quiet and everyone anticipated an easy tour. On the morning of the 30th I was awakened about 7 a.m. by a heavy barrage, and as this seemed on our immediate front the company stood-to and breakfasts were hurried on. Shortly afterwards I had a warning message from Battalion H.Q. ordering us to be ready to move at short notice. Then further orders came to move up to support the 8th Royal Fusiliers and to report to their H.Q. The company moved off via Village Lane and Vacant Alley, across Emden Trench and Emden Support to Ripple Lane, at the end of which lay the 8th Royal Fusiliers H.Q. We met with very little shelling or rifle-fire on the way, but low-flying aeroplanes were most troublesome, firing at us practically the whole time, though without causing any casualties. The remnants of the 8th Royal Fusiliers, consisting mostly of H.Q. personnel were commanded by Major C. O. Skey, who was, I think, their only surviving unwounded officer. We prolonged the line they were holding in Ripple Lane in a south-westerly direction as far as the sunken road behind Emden Support until Lieutenant Gorringe came up with C Company on our right and enabled us to close up towards the Fusiliers. The trench we occupied was a deep communication trench, and we made fire-steps on both sides of it. Owing to the slope of the ground we could see very little to the front; La Vacquerie lay about a thousand yards in rear, but we observed no enemy in that direction.

NOVEMBER 1917

"The company was not itself engaged in any active operations during this or the next day, but during the 30th low-flying aeroplanes were so persistent that I had to give orders forbidding any but sentries to fire at them for fear of exhausting ammunition. They caused no casualties. During both days light field-guns and howitzers (obviously English guns) shelled our position from the rear. Most of the shells were 'duds' and no casualties resulted. Reed Lane, the communication trench which the 8th Royal Fusiliers were holding in front of their position, was a constant source of trouble to them. During the morning of the 30th the enemy launched many attacks on the block which had been made fifty yards up, and more followed during the night. But the Fusiliers, magnificently led by Skey, repulsed them all. D Company acted as bomb-carriers from a reserve of bombs near our own Battalion H.Q. and also organised two bombing-parties to stand ready as a reserve when wanted, but they were not required. The conduct of the 8th Royal Fusiliers was admirable in these attacks. Although reduced to a mere remnant, they did not behave like one, and might well have been a fresh and fully organised unit instead of just a group of survivors. This was partly due to Skey's fine leadership, but the effect of Colonel Elliott-Cooper's counter-attack must be given all the credit it deserves, for after that the enemy made no further attempt to attack over the open on this front, but confined his assaults to bombing attacks along trenches.

"During the morning of the 30th the troops on the left of the 8th Royal Fusiliers sent a message stating they were going to retire. They did not immediately carry out their threat, although we constantly received from them other messages that masses of Germans were approaching; as these masses were never greeted with rifle-fire they presumably dispersed of their own accord."

The Battle of Cambrai

All this time A Company had been having a very anxious time in Vacant Alley. Its experiences are best described by its commander, Captain Le Hardy:—

"About 7 a.m. on the morning of the 30th, when the company was in reserve in Village Lane, I awoke to a violent bombardment, a large proportion of gas-shells falling in Vacant Alley and Village Lane. I immediately ordered the company to stand-to, but I had no information as to any attack nor, for the moment, any idea from what direction it was being launched. What seemed like a few minutes after this I found my trench full of men of various units of the 35th Brigade, without any officers and many without rifles. I put some of my officers and N.C.O.s in command of these men and told them to hold Vacant Alley. I then went and got my company into a line in front of La Vacquerie and afterwards went to report to Colonel Van Someren, near Bleak House. He ordered me to launch a counter-attack, but realising that I was, so far as I knew, the only reserve on that front, and seeing the Germans coming over Bonavis Ridge in large numbers on my left and over the Cambrai Road on my right, I declined to do this.

"On my way back I walked down Vacant Alley, when, to my horror, I discovered that the remnants of the 35th Brigade had departed. I at once went back to La Vacquerie and moved my company forward, two platoons occupying Vacant Alley as far as its junction with Village Lane, and two platoons in Village Lane as far as the point where it crossed the La Vacquerie Road.

"During the rest of that day and the whole of the next we were heavily shelled by German and British guns, and also fired on by machine-guns from both German and British aircraft. The trench was a wreck by nightfall on the 30th November, but fortunately we had very few casualties. By fixing a Lewis gun in the officers' latrine in Village Lane we were able to cover any attack by German troops crossing the filled-in trench over the Cambrai Road. After a few attempts no further attacks from this direction developed, and a number of German graves which I observed after the Armistice in the grass by the side of the Cambrai Road near this spot amply testified to our stubborn defence. During this attack the platoons in Village Lane were manning both the parapet and parados, as they were then able to fire on the Germans advancing over the Bonavis Ridge.

"My right flank had been very uncertain all this time, but during the afternoon of the 30th November an officer commanding a battalion of the 20th Division reported to me, and I asked him

November 1917

The Battle of Cambrai

to take over a continuation of my right running back towards Fern Trench, the old British front line. I also asked him to give instructions that if his men were obliged to retire they would give me warning. About half an hour later I went along to visit him and found that his men had been completely withdrawn, consequently my right flank was again left entirely in the air. Fortunately no attack developed from this direction.

"Of the messengers whom I sent to Battalion H.Q. during the early part of the day only one returned. This was a lance-corporal who rejoined several days afterwards, having spent two days behind the German lines; he was able to give some very interesting information.

"As soon as the attack developed on the 30th I sent Captain W. F. Campbell, who had come up to relieve me on the night of the 29th, to get touch with the 9th Royal Fusiliers, and Colonel Van Someren requested that he should remain with him for the time."

Captain Campbell adds his own experiences with the 9th Royal Fusiliers:—

"I was detailed to take a few men and try to get into touch with the Fusiliers on the left and got taken over by Colonel Van Someren and sent by him to take charge of his left flank, which mainly consisted of details of all units. Luckily we were never seriously attacked, although his right was pressed hard. If we had been, it would have been disastrous, for at that time there was no one on our left. I think I had about fifty men all told, from most units in the Brigade, and some machine-gunners without their machine-guns, so our prospects were not good. I lost nearly all the 7th Battalion men in the bombing attack the Germans made up the trench across the main road. I rejoined Le Hardy in the evening."

During all this fighting Battalion H.Q. had a most anxious time. There was no possibility of launching a counter-attack. Even if one had been launched it would only have resulted in disaster, owing to the superior numbers of the enemy. All communications had gone and there was no chance of any reinforcements. The only thing to do was to hang on like grim death and at all costs prevent the enemy from capturing La Vacquerie and Welch Ridge. The battalion gallantly responded to the call. The supply of ammunition and bombs was difficult to maintain, and a sanitary N.C.O. with a squad of men rendered valuable service in bringing supplies from the neighbourhood

The Battle of Cambrai

of La Vacquerie. Our anxieties were by no means lessened by the news of the intended withdrawal of the troops on our left.

Night came at last and some reorganisation was possible, for the shelling had died down. Then we received definite news that the troops on our left had retired. This caused renewed anxiety, and the situation created is thus described by Captain Reckitt :—

NOVEMBER 1917

"During the night of 30th November the line on our left became suspiciously quiet, and a patrol revealed the fact that the troops formerly holding it had, without further warning, adhered to their intention of the morning. Thus a large gap was created between the left of the 8th Royal Fusiliers and the right of the next unit, a battalion of the 20th Division. As it was impossible to hold this gap without reinforcements, which were obviously unobtainable, Skey decided to have it guarded by a small patrol, which was to go along it and fire rifles and Verey lights periodically. A strong-point was also formed on his left by the road from La Vacquerie to Pam Pam Farm, and our D Company was moved slightly to the left."

At the same time Colonel Impey ordered patrols from B Company to be sent along the Hindenburg front and support lines at frequent intervals to get into touch with the 20th Division. The remainder of the night passed comparatively quietly, but early next morning the enemy renewed his attacks on the bomb-blocks of the 9th Royal Fusiliers south of the Cambrai Road. Through a shortage of bombs the Fusiliers were forced to withdraw north of the Cambrai Road at 9.30 a.m. There blocks were made in the Hindenburg front and support lines; the intervening trenches between this line and the road were filled up with wire entanglements, B Company furnishing working-parties to assist. This slight withdrawal put the enemy at the disadvantage of having to cross the Cambrai Road in order to attack, and it is significant that, doubtless mindful of the heavy losses inflicted by A Company on the previous day, he made no further attempts to debouch into the open.

However, violent shelling of our positions continued throughout the day, and one of the entrances of the Battalion H.Q. dug-out, which, being a German one, faced the wrong way, was blown in and several casualties caused. Numerous low-flying hostile aircraft continued to attack us, sometimes flying barely fifty feet above the trench. Neither machine-guns, Lewis guns nor rifles could drive them off, and to prevent waste of ammunition orders had to be issued not to fire at them. Their aim was at times

The Battle of Cambrai

unpleasantly accurate, and one officer described the sight of bullets chipping off pieces all along the side of the trench as " one that was not easy to forget." The Hindenburg front and support lines were by no means ideal for defensive purposes when enfiladed. They were broad and shallow, and the troops occupying them felt naked before the low-flying planes.

NOVEMBER 1917

All this time it had been impossible to establish any communication with Brigade H.Q., which had moved to Villers-Plouich, and owing to the uncertainty of the position of units and headquarters a service of runners could not be maintained. This lack of information led the Higher Command to come to the unfortunate conclusion, which even appeared in an official *communiqué*, that La Vacquerie had been captured by the enemy at 10 a.m. on the 30th November. This caused the utmost peril to the luckless garrison and the troops (including ourselves) who were holding the line near by. The situation is described by Major Osborne :—

" La Vacquerie was officially reported as being in the enemy's hands early on 30th November. We were, of course, ignorant of this at the time, and having been harassed all day by the enemy's low-flying planes we were encouraged late in the afternoon to see one of our own coming over ; but to our annoyance and disgust the only notice he took of us was to drop bombs on La Vacquerie. In vain we shouted, and even placed tin hats on our bayonets and waved them in the air, but the bombs still continued to be showered on us. La Vacquerie was still in our hands when we were relieved."

The shelling continued, but the enemy made no further attempt to advance. At about 3 p.m. on the 1st December we received a most welcome visit from Captain N. H. H. Charles, the Staff Captain of the Brigade, who had come through the barrage to find out our position.

DECEMBER 1917

It was the first touch we had had with the Brigade for nearly thirty-six hours, and Captain Charles was very pleased to see us, for at Brigade H.Q. it was thought we had been exterminated. He brought us the good news that the 61st Division was waiting to relieve us as soon as he had located us.

Towards evening the enemy's bombardment lifted off our position and concentrated on Villers-Plouich, just about ration-dumping time, so that our Transport had a gruelling experience. Captain Hind afterwards described the conditions as the worst he had ever encountered.

The Battle of Cambrai

At length the shelling ceased, and about 9 p.m. our relief by a Territorial battalion of the Royal Warwicks (61st Division) began. Although the relief was naturally a welcome one, it was impossible not to feel uneasy at handing over our position in the state of confusion which prevailed. The incoming unit knew nothing whatsoever of the situation and was tired out on arrival. Some of the companies had no trench maps, only 1/100,000 maps of the district, and although we did our best to give them all the necessary information we could not repress a feeling of regret at leaving things as they were. All the S.O.S. rockets had been fired, and only a very scanty reserve of ammunition and bombs was left.

December 1917

The relief went off very quietly and was complete by 4 a.m. on the 2nd December. We took over Newport and Welch Trenches in the old British front line system in front of Villers-Plouich. Here we got into touch again with our Brigade H.Q. and also with the remnants of the 35th Brigade, who informed us that the Germans were certain to attack again at 9 a.m. This attack did not materialise, and the remainder of the day passed quietly except for some heavy shelling of Villers-Plouich.

At 4.30 p.m. the same day we set off for Heudicourt; fortunately the shelling had ceased, and we were able to pass through Villers-Plouich without any untoward accident. Our route lay through a sunken road, branching off in a south-westerly direction from the village; this road, a short distance up, was almost completely blocked by an abandoned 4.7 or 6-inch gun, a cause of considerable trouble and delay both to the 9th Royal Fusiliers and ourselves. After a difficult and tricky march across country tracks via Dead Man's Corner, Queen's Cross and the main road, we reached Heudicourt at 10.30 p.m. and took over some hutments near the brickworks.

The day after our relief (the 3rd December) was one of frequent alarms, and a state of tension prevailed. Early next morning a very heavy barrage from the direction of Villers-Guislain seemed to be a precursor of evil, but nothing happened, and orders were later received for the Brigade, which was now a mere skeleton, to move at 10.55 a.m. for Cartigny. On leaving Heudicourt the Brigade marched past General Scott, the G.O.C. Division, who called up each Commanding Officer in turn, and asked him to congratulate his battalion on its splendid performances during the recent operations, an attention which was deeply appreciated by all ranks.

THE BATTLE OF CAMBRAI

After the battle the following letter was received by the Divisional Commander from General Sir Julian Byng, the Army Commander :—

"I wish to express to you and your Division how much I have appreciated the work done by them whilst forming part of the Third Army. During their long period in the line, and in the attack on the Hindenburg Line, and finally in the successful repulse of the German counter-stroke, the Division has fully lived up to its splendid reputation."*

DECEMBER 1917

In publishing the above, Major-General Scott desired "to add his thanks to all concerned in maintaining this high record. The events of the 30th November, 1917, called for the highest soldier-like qualities under very trying circumstances. The counter-attack was carried out by a large number of the enemy, and although pushed back the Division can be justly proud of the fighting spirit it displayed."†

The casualties suffered by the Division on the 30th November alone were 164 officers and 3,362 other ranks, over half its fighting strength, compared with 66 officers and 1,144 other ranks killed, wounded and missing in the attack on the 20th. Our own casualties for the period from the 20th to the 30th November were :—

	Officers				Other ranks			
	20th	25th	30th	Total	20th	25th	30th	Total
Killed	2	1	—	3	17	27	9	53
Died of wounds	—	—	—	—	5	5	2	12
Wounded	1	4	—	5	84	85	12	181
Totals	3	5	—	8	106	117	23	246

Officers killed :	20th	2nd Lieutenants D. T. Cohen (D) and J. L. Knox (C).
	25th	Captain C. W. Ballard, M.C. (C).
,, wounded :	20th	2nd Lieutenant F. Frewer (D) (at duty).
	25th	2nd Lieutenants E. A. Bingen (D), F. Frewer (D), G. H. Hill (B), and T. W. Mills (C).
N.C.O.s killed	20th	Sergeant W. J. Osborne, M.M. (D) ; Corporal G. W. Preston, M.M. (B).
	25th	Acting Company Sergeant-Major W. Robbins (B) ; Sergeants F. C. Fairhall, D.C.M. (B), D. Funnell (C), and A. E. Paice (B) ; Corporal E. Alexander (C) ; Lance-Corporal H. Maughan, M.M. (D).
	30th	Corporal C. S. Sickelmore (A).

---

* Contrast these remarks with those quoted on p. 179.
† Quoted from *The History of the 12th Division*, pp. 159, 160.

The Battle of Cambrai

The following decorations were awarded :—

Military Cross :	Captain W. H. C. Le Hardy (A) ; Lieutenant H. J. R. Farrow (D).
Distinguished Conduct Medal :	Corporal E. W. Moss (A).
Military Medal :	Sergeants W. Golds (C), F. Ransom (B) ; Corporals S. Buckman (A), W. Dinnage (C), E. Porter (D) ; Lance-Corporal E. Cooper (A), E. Dendy (A) ; Private J. Evans (A).

Thus ended the most critical period we ever experienced in the whole war. The stubborn defence of the battalion, together with that of the remnants of the 8th and 9th Royal Fusiliers, who had fought so valiantly by our side in the earlier stages, completely frustrated the continual efforts of the enemy to occupy La Vacquerie and Welch Ridge, while the admirably placed Lewis gun and general defence of A Company under Captain Le Hardy in Village Lane and Vacant Alley saved the guns of the 169th Brigade, R.F.A. The whole action was a little epic of the war, and only further served to emphasise the stolid and imperturbable behaviour of the Sussex men under the most trying conditions.

NOVEMBER 1917

It would be impossible to give too much praise to the behaviour of all ranks in the Quartermaster's department and the Transport during those three terrible days. No matter how vile the conditions or how dangerous the dumps, we never at any time lacked a thing, and there is no doubt that the confidence the men felt in these two departments contributed in no small degree to the magnificent fight the battalion put up. Captain Hind gives the following account of his experiences :—

"The Transport was billeted at Guyencourt, near Saulcourt, up to the morning of the 30th November. I was Brigade Transport Officer and received instructions on the 28th to move the Brigade bomb dump during that night from The Barricade, in the old No Man's Land at the junction of the Cambrai and the Gonnelieu-La Vacquerie Roads, to a point south-west of La Vacquerie, where Village Road meets the tracks leading into the village. This undoubtedly accounts for the ample supply of bombs during the counter-attack. As the battle surplus had been ordered to rejoin the battalion, we expected that the battalion would be brought back into reserve ; in fact, orders were issued for cookers to rejoin their companies on the night of the 30th.

The Battle of Cambrai

"In the early hours of the 30th Lieutenant E. Penrose, the Transport Officer of the 36th Brigade Machine-Gun Company, returned from dumping rations and reported various 'trench rumours' of enemy concentrations and probable attacks. We did not take much notice, and actually the baths at Heudicourt had been allotted that morning to the Transport of the 36th Brigade, with the result that half our personnel was bathing when Major F. B. Sneyd, D.A.D.V.S., 12th Division, galloped into the camp with the news that the enemy had broken through and that we were to be ready to move at a moment's notice. The men were brought back at the double, dressing en route, and we moved the whole Brigade Transport within fifty minutes to a field south of Sorel-le-Grand. There was no news as to the whereabouts of Brigade H.Q. nor of any of the units, so we were faced with the pleasant job of finding them for ourselves.

NOVEMBER 1917

"Previous experience had taught us that limbered wagons were bad things to manoeuvre across trenches in the dark, so we indented for ninety sets of extra pack-saddles and were fortunate enough to get them by the evening, thanks to the efforts of Major W. R. Hughes, D.A.Q.M.G., 12th Division. Putting pack-saddlery together in a hurry during darkness is not an easy job, but we managed to accomplish it all in thirty-five minutes.

"We then moved off in the direction of Gouzeaucourt. On the way we heard from wounded men and from the Military Police that it was impossible to enter Gouzeaucourt and that we should try to reach Villers-Plouich by a cross-country route. When we got as far as an evacuated Field Ambulance we decided to park the wagons and to transfer their loads to the pack animals. While this was being done I went with Lieutenant J. F. Williams, the Transport Officer of the 8th Royal Fusiliers, to reconnoitre the neighbourhood, and at last, after many vain attempts, we found Brigade H.Q., who promised us guides. We had a rough journey back to our transport rendezvous to collect the pack animals, but rations were delivered safely about 3 a.m. on the 1st December, with the loss of one pack mule killed and 2 men wounded.

"On my return to camp I was sent for by Divisional H.Q., where I was able to give the map references of Brigade H.Q. Later in the day the Transport moved to the brick fields at Heudicourt. Our ration dump that night was at Welch Road in the support-line of the old British line, about 1,000 yards east of Villers-Plouich; it was quite as bad if not a worse dump than that of the previous night owing to the heavy shelling of the village, and we were well out of it with no casualties."

The drums and other details who could be spared from those who usually stayed out of the line at the transport lines were also drawn into this battle. Under Major A. L. Thomson, the Second-in-Command, they formed part of the mixed force which was collected by the Divisional Commander to defend Revelon Ridge on the right rear of the Division. From about noon on the 30th they occupied a position near Chapel Hill, in support to forward troops in Vaucellette Farm, until relieved on the night of the 3rd December.

DECEMBER 1917

The opponents of the 8th Royal Fusiliers had been the *40th Regiment* (*Hohenzollern Fusiliers*) of the *28th Division*, whose regimental history mentions that this unit captured Le Pavé and the Brickworks with 100 prisoners and many machine-guns and concentrated there owing to strong resistance. A heavy counter-attack is described (presumably Colonel Elliott-Cooper's) in which there were many English casualties, owing to their being caught by machine-gun fire in close formation. The German situation then became critical, for they were threatened from two directions and their right flank was now open. The *II Battalion* captured the high ground around Bleak House and Cambrai Road. Both the *I* and *II Battalions* admit terrible losses, many officers being killed. That the attack was a comparative failure is obvious from the remark of an officer of this regiment, who is quoted as saying, " This is the first day of a battle in which we were supposed to march on Trescault and Metz-en-Couture."

Their position on the evening of the 30th November was :— *II Battalion*, Brickworks and Bleak House ; *I Battalion* in support.

The *110th Regiment* (*Grenadiers*) was evidently against the 9th Royal Fusiliers. Its records state that the *I Battalion* captured two guns and 40 prisoners. An English counter-attack was repulsed. Bleak House was captured about 9 a.m.

The *II Battalion* crossed the canal bridge at Banteux at 9 a.m., advanced in the direction of Gonnelieu and captured a heavy battery (6-inch howitzer) near Sonnet Farm. The English put up a stiff resistance in the Hindenburg front and support lines, especially by means of machine-gun nests in destroyed tanks, and great difficulty also was experienced in clearing up trenches owing

The Battle of Cambrai

to heavy bomb fighting. Many casualties testified to the tenacity of the battle. They spent a very cold night in captured English trenches, but the great-coats and blankets left behind were very welcome. There was also plenty of food and drink and the trenches had been made very comfortable. The situation at night-fall (the 30th November) was :—*I Battalion*, Bleak House ; *II Battalion*, west of Gonnelieu.

DECEMBER 1917

There was a gap from the north of Gonnelieu to Les Baraques, and during the afternoon of the 1st December the *40th Regiment* was ordered to take La Vacquerie to protect the advance of the *110th Regiment* to Villers-Plouich. This order could not be carried out, as it was impossible to advance across the Cambrai Road owing to the stout resistance encountered.

The enemy's main attacks had been along Banteux Ravine, south of Banteux Spur, up the ravine to the metalled road leading up to the Cambrai Road, and also by the road leading from Banteux towards the western end of Bonavis Ridge. The canal had been crossed at Grenouillère Bridge in the north on the 37th Brigade front, and on our Brigade front by the bridge at Banteux. Several pontoon bridges had been used in other places. The enemy had also taken full advantage of the admirable facilities or hidden concentration afforded by the villages of Banteux and Bantouzelle, so gratuitously left open to him on the 20th November. The Divisional History states :—

"The possession of this valley enabled the Germans to concentrate troops unseen, while, owing to the contour of the ground, they were largely protected from shell fire. The terrain on the west of the canal was slightly commanding, and contained several woods suitable for the concealment of troops."*

Major-General the Rt. Hon. J. E. B. Seely, in his book *Adventures*, gives an interesting account of an interview he had with the Crown Prince Rupprecht of Bavaria, who commanded the group of German armies opposed to us.† The Prince admitted that the attack on the 20th November was a complete surprise and fell like a thunderbolt ; its effect was most demoralising, and there were the wildest rumours concerning the size, power and numbers of the tanks. Ludendorff was also much alarmed. The Prince said that he realised that the only thing to

* *Op. cit.*, pp. 147-8.
† *Op. cit.*, pp. 278-9, 286-7.

The Battle of Cambrai

restore confidence was to stage a counter-attack on the same spot. In addition to this, it was obvious to him that the British were in a most dangerous salient, only to be compared with that at St. Mihiel, and at the same time that the Crevecœur Spur afforded him perfect observation. The actual counter-attack was an entirely novel one, since the Germans, having been surprised by tanks, wanted to effect a surprise on us without them, and this entirely depended on finding men brave enough to creep right up to and under our hastily constructed defences and wire. The Prince also said that but for the arrival of the British cavalry the disaster would have been far greater.

DECEMBER 1917

The following information concerning the Guards Division, whose magnificent work on the right of our Division deserved all the publicity which it gained, will be of interest as an illustration of the general confusion existing during this attack. The Guards Division, the only available infantry division in reserve on our part of the front, was ordered to make two counter-attacks to regain Gouzeaucourt and Gonnelieu, one on the 30th November and the other on the 1st December. The final objective of its left brigade, which was moving up from Metz-en-Couture, was well to the north of La Vacquerie, so that this brigade, if its attack had fully succeeded, which it did not, would have bumped into the back of our troops in front of that village.

The official narrative of the Guards Division states that its patrols did not report that Villers-Plouich was occupied by British troops until 4.45 p.m. on the 30th. Throughout these operations the Guards appear to have been quite oblivious of the fact that we were holding a line over 2,000 yards to their left front. Had their patrols gained touch with A Company's right, which remained in the air during most of the battle, the subsequent defence of La Vacquerie might have been made considerably stronger.

The successful German counter-attack on the 30th November led to some trouble in Parliament, although the usual answer to all questions was given: that it was not in the public interest to discuss the matter nor to make any statement.

However, the following facts emerged from answers given in the House of Commons by Mr. Bonar Law (Chancellor of the

Exchequer) on the 15th and 21st January, 1918.* The War Cabinet sent instructions to Sir Douglas Haig to institute an inquiry into the circumstances leading to the disaster. They found that he had already, on his own initiative, instituted such an inquiry. A large number of documents relative to the inquiry, together with Sir Douglas Haig's own report, was examined by a committee of the Imperial General Staff, presided over by Sir William Robertson. All the relevant documents, together with the report of the Imperial General Staff, were examined by the War Cabinet, who requested General Smuts to go through all the documents and to report to them. His report was approved by the War Cabinet, but it was never published, nor were its conclusions made public, except that it was stated that it exonerated the General Staff at G.H.Q.

DECEMBER 1917

At the end of Government business on the 23rd January Major David Davies (Montgomeryshire) rose " to call attention to the inquiry into the military operations at Cambrai."

He was supported by Commodore H. D. King (Norfolk Northern) and Mr. Kennedy Jones (Hornsey). The nature of these remarks was mostly a violent attack on Sir Douglas Haig.

The Under Secretary of State for War (Mr. J. Ian Macpherson) replied for the Government.†

Mr. MACPHERSON (in the course of his speech) : . . . " This House is apt on all occasions—I do not know whether through prejudice or for what reason—but the moment a breakdown takes place it is always described as due to the Higher Command. There was never a greater mistake."

Mr. KENNEDY JONES : " Could you ascribe it to anyone ? "

Mr. MACPHERSON : " I am not going to ascribe it to anyone."

Mr. W. F. ROCH (Pembrokeshire) : " To the soldiers ? "

Mr. MACPHERSON : " There never was a more gallant lot in this world than our soldiers, but I can only say that, I for one, with the information I have got, will never ascribe that breakdown to the Higher Command. I can say no more."

Mr. ROCH : " Will the hon. gentleman say whether anyone at all, then, was to blame in any quarter ? "

Mr. MACPHERSON : " It is impossible to say in dealing with two or three Divisions who is responsible. . . ."‡

---

* *Vide The Times*, 16th January, p. 10, and 22nd January, p. 8.

† In the course of the debate the fact that no member of the War Cabinet was present was strongly commented on.

‡ *Vide Hansard*, Vol. 101, columns 1097, 1104, 1108, 1109.

The Battle of Cambrai

The debate was eventually " talked out " by Mr. Pringle, but Mr. Macpherson's implication was obvious. Certain highly-placed officers had in the end successfully whitewashed themselves —at the expense of the fighting troops. It was even alleged that the surprise was due to negligence on the part of those in the front line, and that no S.O.S. signals had been sent up, although records showed that in many cases warning of the coming danger had been given in vain to the Higher Command. There was, however, no mention of the lack of reserves, or of the missed opportunities at Banteux, while another fact which conveniently escaped notice was that all the troops had been fighting continuously for ten days, the only periods of rest being taken up with exhausting fatigue parties. Even General Byng, our own Army Commander, declared (to the disgust of all the fighting troops), " I attribute the reason for the local success on the part of the enemy to one cause and one alone, namely—the lack of training on the part of junior officers and N.C.O.s and men."*

December 1917

The account given in these pages of the way the 36th Brigade fought is the best answer to these allegations.

---

* Quoted from Captain B. H. Liddell Hart's *The Real War*, p. 380, where it is noted that Sir Douglas Haig, who had been kept in the dark as to the warnings, " in sending his report home generously assumed the whole responsibility—although he also sent home several of the subordinate commanders."

CHAPTER X

FLEURBAIX

3RD DECEMBER, 1917—21ST MARCH, 1918
[Sketch Map, No. 15]

Cartigny had been totally destroyed by the enemy during his retreat in the previous March, but good accommodation was found in the numerous huts and shelters. On the next day —the 4th December—we embussed at 7 a.m. and reached Dernancourt by 1 p.m. after an exhilarating and interesting drive in fine frosty weather through such well-known places as Peronne, Clery, Maricourt, Carnoy, Mametz, Becordel-Becourt, and Meault; with many of them the battalion was to renew its acquaintance in very different circumstances during August, 1918.

DECEMBER 1917

Dernancourt, a small village in the valley of the Ancre, two miles south of Albert, was still intact; but it was crammed with troops, and only with the greatest difficulty could we find accommodation. After two uneventful days we entrained on the night of the 7th, and a very cold and snowy journey brought us to Aire early next morning. Thence we marched to Quiestede and Cochendal and took over billets which, as at Vieil Hesdin, were very scattered. The Transport moved by road, brigaded under Captain Hind, now the Brigade Transport Officer. We now came under the orders of the XV Corps (First Army).

We were again far behind the line, and every form of training and reorganisation was carried out. A great deal of work had to be done to repair the heavy casualties of the recent battles, especially among the snipers, nearly all of whom had been lost. Additional interest was given to the training by a four days' liaison with the Royal Flying Corps; the officer who was attached to the battalion gave us many interesting lectures and demonstrations, while Major Osborne performed similar duties with the Royal Flying Corps units.

Everything went on peacefully and the battalion was getting into fine fettle again, while preparations for Christmas, which we hoped we should spend here, proceeded apace. But these hopes

15. FLEURBAIX AREA

"A"—CANTEEN FM: "B"—LE TROU POST "C"—PINNEYS AVENUE

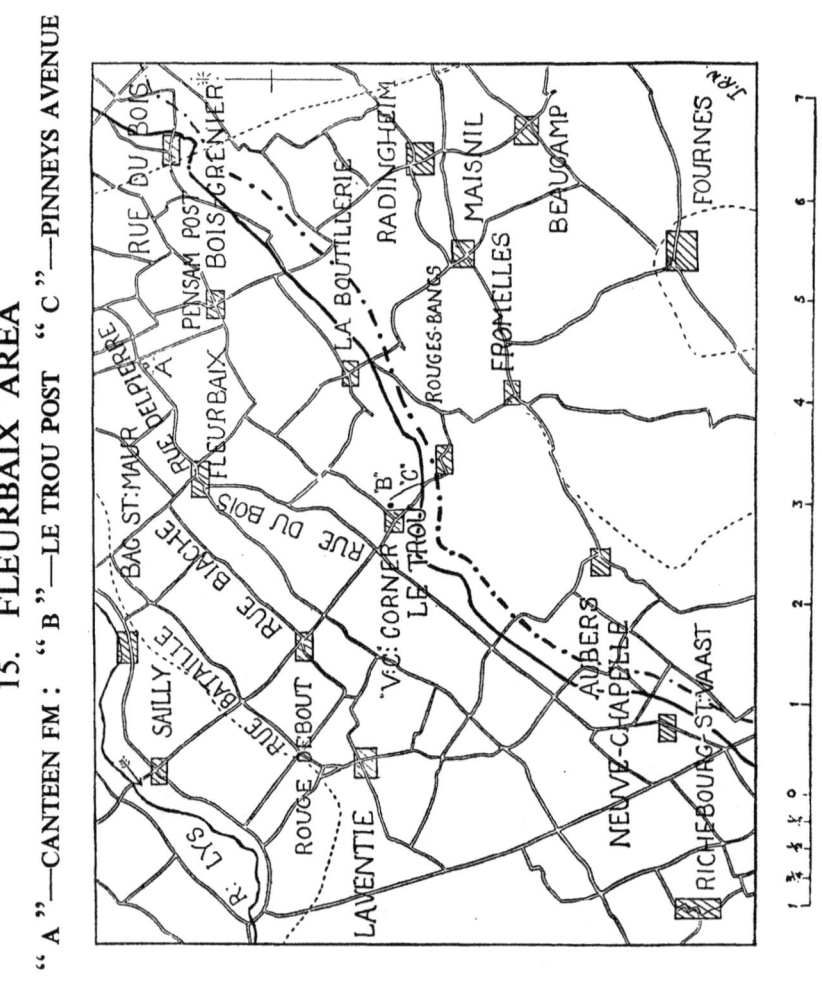

were not to be realised, for the whole Brigade moved on the 23rd by route march to an area around about Berguette. Brigade H.Q. and the battalion were in the village itself, and we once more occupied scattered billets, one company being in the adjoining village of Isbergues.

Berguette was a large and straggling village midway between Aire and Lillers. It was an important railway junction, where the single lines to St. Omer and Armentières branched off from the main Hazebrouck-Lillers-Bethune line. Close at hand in Isbergues some large steel works were working full time, in spite of being occasionally shelled by the German long-range guns.

DECEMBER 1917

The preparations for Christmas, which had already been well in hand at our previous billets, were now completed. All extras for Christmas dinners—pigs, turkeys, geese, beer, fruit, and so on—had been bought out of canteen funds, but prior to our move we had been ordered to dump them, since only regulation loads were to be carried by the transport. Needless to say, many of them, even including pigs, found their way into Lewis gun limbers. All the eatables were collected in due course, and the difficulty of finding suitable dining-room accommodation for the battalion was overcome by using the village school at Isbergues. We all spent a very happy Christmas, the last, as it happened, before the Armistice.

A slight drawback was that, owing to the scarcity of suitable accommodation, the various company dinners had to be held in relays. This was rather a strain on the Battalion H.Q. staff, who naturally visited all the companies to wish them the compliments of the season. As the Commanding Officer, Second-in-Command and the Adjutant, accompanied by Major Osborne, were walking towards the school along a road covered with snow and slush (and, like many other roads in France, flanked by deep ditches filled with water) they saw in front of them a distinguished member of the battalion who had evidently been keeping Christmas very successfully with his comrades in Berguette and was now tacking from one side of the road to the other like a racing yacht. Eventually the H.Q. party caught him up at the extreme limit of one of his tacks. Springing smartly to attention he saluted the Commanding Officer, but the effort proved too much for his equilibrium and he fell backwards into the ditch, to be rescued from drowning by the H.Q. party.

The next day, in order to work off the effects of the festivities, a route march was ordered, and on the 27th ordinary training was resumed. From then onwards until the 6th January the usual routine was continued, special attention being paid to musketry—fortunately a good range existed near Molinghem.

On the 2nd, Brigade H.Q. again benefited at the expense of A Company, for Captain Le Hardy left us to become Staff Captain, as Captain Evans had done in 1914. He remained in close touch with us until the end of the war, and his presence at Brigade was often of value to us.

JANUARY 1918

The Division had now been at rest for a month, so that no surprise was felt when orders came to relieve the 38th (Welsh) Division in the Fleurbaix sector. A preliminary move was made on the 6th January to Chapelle Duvelle, where training continued for another five days, and on the 13th the battalion took over the right sector at La Boutillerie from the 14th Welch Regiment.

After an interval of over two years we found we were again to experience conditions similar to those suffered at Festubert. The front and support lines of the new sector, being situated in low-lying ground, consisted entirely of sandbag parapets, mostly derelict and perished. The front line had to be held by isolated posts, and the support line was the line of resistance. The whole position was overlooked from the enemy's side by the sinister Aubers Ridge, which had already cost other battalions of the regiment so dearly in May, 1915, and June, 1916. This state of affairs on both sides entailed constant patrolling at night, a difficult operation owing to the numerous ditches, derelict trenches and wire entanglements, and often resulting in patrol affrays and small attacks on posts.

C and D Companies held the right and left front respectively; B was in support at Le Trou Post, and A in reserve near Battalion H.Q., which was in a ruined house in Rue du Bois, near V.C. Corner. In the front line we made the acquaintance of our oldest allies, the Portuguese, whose 2nd Division was on our immediate right. We established liaison with them by means of a combined post known as International Post.

Another feature of this sector, reminiscent of the old days at Le Touquet and Houplines, was the close proximity of civilians to the front line. An estaminet at Rouge de Bout did a roaring trade, while farms along Rue Biache were still occupied by their owners, who carried on as if nothing was happening. Things were very quiet and, as at Festubert, a kind of " live and let live " state of affairs seemed to prevail.

FLEURBAIX

On the 17th the first piece of excitement was provided when, during an inter-company relief, a hostile patrol of three men tried to enter our front line near the end of Pinney's Avenue; they were driven back, leaving a rifle behind.

The German artillery suddenly woke up on the 20th and shelled part of the back areas, including the neighbourhood of Rouge de Bout—to the great consternation of its occupants. It was significant that the day chosen was the one on which our Divisional Artillery took over from the 38th Division.   JANUARY 1918

The next day we were relieved by the 5th Royal Berks and proceeded to Doulieu. A great advantage of all sectors in this area was that reliefs were always possible in daylight, for the roads and approaches were well hidden from observation by trees. During our stay in these parts there was no occasion when a relief was shelled, but as a precaution it was customary to move in small parties at intervals. Doulieu was a village about three miles north-west of Sailly-sur-la-Lys. Except for the church, which had been destroyed by the Germans in 1914, it was quite untouched, and it provided good billets for us all.

On the 28th we relieved the 6th Royal West Kents as Brigade Reserve in the Bois Grenier sector and were billeted in Fleurbaix, a village 2,000 yards from the front line, still full of civilians and bearing many scars of war. It proved rather an unhealthy spot, owing to the close proximity of some 60-pounder batteries in Rue Delpierre, which attracted frequent shelling, but fortunately no casualties were sustained.

Working-parties from two to three hundred strong were provided daily for the next five days, and it is interesting to note that part of their labour was employed in converting Canteen Farm in Rue du Bois into a strong-point by the construction of a large pill-box, which was to prove invaluable during the great German attack the following April, when the 12th Suffolks (40th Division) made an heroic stand there and held up the enemy for a considerable time.   FEBRUARY 1918

We had heard much talk of certain units being reduced to conserve man-power, and it was during this period that these rumours materialised. Each infantry brigade was reduced by one battalion, and to our great regret we learnt that we were to lose our old comrades of many a battle, the 8th Royal Fusiliers (which was merged into its 9th Battalion) and the 11th Middlesex. The 5th Royal Berks was transferred to the 36th Brigade, and the 37th Brigade lost the 7th East Surreys.

FEBRUARY 1918 A month later the 7th Suffolks left the 35th Brigade, its place being taken by the 1/1st Cambridgeshires (T.F.). As an immediate result of these exchanges we received sudden orders late on the 2nd February to relieve the 8th Royal Fusiliers the next day in the left of the Bois Grenier sector. There was no time to make any previous reconnaissance, and this was soon to cost us dearly.

The relief was completed by noon of the 3rd, the distribution of the battalion being :—A and D Companies right and left front, with C and B in support. The trench system was exactly similar to that at La Boutillerie ; the posts in the front line and some of the communication trenches consisted entirely of sandbag breastworks, and the whole position was overlooked, as before, by Aubers Ridge. A strong-point in Bois Grenier had to be occupied by the right support company, and some of the cellars in the ruined houses were used as billets, but since the cross-roads served as a calibration point for the German artillery the neighbourhood did not encourage visitors.

During the day hostile heavy trench-mortars were active on the Brigade sector, especially on our own front in the neighbourhood of Tui Road, and at 5.30 a.m. on the 4th the enemy, after a short and fierce bombardment by heavy trench-mortars, raided Pensam Post on our right company front and succeeded in entering it, killing 3 of the garrison and taking 4 prisoners. It afterwards transpired from intelligence reports that for some time previously the enemy had rehearsed this raid, which had been carried out by a unit of storm troops especially imported for the occasion. The whole affair was most unfortunate, and the trouble was mainly due to the hurried relief of the 8th Royal Fusiliers without any previous reconnaissance. The incident gave the Higher Command, who were evidently not in possession of all the facts, an opportunity to shower a considerable amount of undeserved censure on the battalion.

On the 6th we took over part of the front of the 11th Middlesex in addition to our own, and the following evening a report was received that the enemy was massing in front of us. The artillery opened a harassing fire, but no attack materialised, and the rest of the tour passed quietly.

FLEURBAIX

On the 8th a draft reached us from the 12th Battalion, which was also being reduced. It was commanded by Captain W. C. S. Uppleby, who was unfortunately killed next day by a shell striking his billet in Rue Bataille.

The 7th Suffolks relieved us on the 14th FEBRUARY 1918
and we moved to tolerable billets in Sailly-
sur-la-Lys, a village on the main Armentières-Merville Road consisting of one long straggling street. The battalion returned to La Boutillerie on the 22nd, relieving the 6th Royal West Kents. It was on this day that Captain G. P. O'Malley, of the United States Army Medical Corps, was posted to us as our Medical Officer; he remained with us until the end of the war, a tower of strength in more ways than one. Captain Mills had left us, to our great regret, to become D.A.D.M.S., 12th Division.

We now received orders to carry out a raid, for identifications of the enemy divisions were urgently required. It was left to the Commanding Officer to select the spot to be raided, and he decided upon 200 yards of Necklace Trench,
just in front of Rouge Bancs in the MARCH 1918
German lines, and opposite to the end of
Pinney's Avenue in our lines. It was known that there was a hostile post where a communication trench, North Street, joined Necklace Trench, slightly to the right of the centre of the objective. Two smaller posts were suspected, one near each end of the front to be raided.

On the 2nd March the 9th Royal Fusiliers took over our line and we moved back to near Sailly railway station. The usual working-parties had to be found, but all else was concentrated on training for the raid. D Company was detailed for the operation. A model of the enemy trenches was marked out and the company spent much time in rehearsing its exact duties. The men showed the greatest keenness, and it was clear that they meant to give a good account of themselves. This chance of getting our own back on the enemy for the incident at Pensam Post gave great satisfaction to the whole battalion.

Included in the preparations was a great deal of patrol work, which was admirably organised by Lieutenant R. F. Clements. No Man's Land, which here varied from two to three hundred yards in width, was a swampy maze of abandoned trenches, old wire entanglements, and ditches full of mud and water. Each night before the raid Clements took out patrols and ensured that each leader knew his objective and that the route to it was clearly marked and free from obstacles. His forecast of the result was entirely accurate.

MARCH 1918

On the 6th the XV Corps Intelligence Officer lectured to the company in the Divisional Cinema and showed the latest air-photographs of the area by lantern slides. He again impressed upon all the urgency of obtaining identifications.

The raid was fixed for 4.30 a.m. on the 8th. There was to be no preliminary bombardment, and the opening of the barrage was to be the signal for the advance. The cutting of the wire had been begun some time previously by the artillery and had been continued by Clements's patrols; it was to be completed by the raiders themselves.

The pivot of the whole raid was the party which was to capture the main post near the junction of Necklace Trench and North Street. Two sections of 14 Platoon (Lieutenant Clements) would undertake this, while one section attacked the suspected post on the right and another section formed a defensive flank just beyond this post. On the left 15 Platoon (2nd Lieutenant V. St. G. Smith) would deal with the suspected post at this end of the objective and would secure Clements's left flank. 13 Platoon (2nd Lieutenant J. L. Soutter) on the right and 16 Platoon (2nd Lieutenant E. C. Cutler) on the left were to act as supports in case of need and, if possible, to pass over the front line and penetrate as far as the support line, about 200 yards ahead. A Company provided two Lewis guns in our front line on each flank of the raid. Captain Reckitt was to supervise the whole operation from a signal post in the British front line, where he would have the Artillery Liaison Officer with him. The raid was to last for ten minutes, after which the signal for withdrawal would be a series of short blasts on whistles.

The company spent the night of the 7th-8th in the support line and had formed up outside the British wire by 4 a.m. It was very quiet, and the enemy evidently had no inkling of what was going to happen. The men were wearing no equipment to hamper them, but were each carrying a rifle, with bayonet fixed, thirty rounds of ammunition, two bombs, and a pair of wire-cutters. The password, by which the raiders could identify each other in the darkness, was " Goodbye-ee," taken from a popular song of the day.

FLEURBAIX

The raid, supported by a most effective barrage of artillery, trench-mortars and machine-guns, went off without a hitch. The main post was captured with scarcely any opposition; of its occupants, 6 were killed and 2 brought back as prisoners. Our casualties amounted only to 2 men slightly wounded by our barrage, and the hostile retaliation was negligible. It was found that the main post was the only portion of the raided front which the enemy occupied. Indeed, the remainder of the front was so deep in mud and water that it proved impossible to penetrate beyond it or even, in most places, to enter it.

MARCH 1918

The following personal narrative is by 2nd Lieutenant V. St. G. Smith, who led 15 Platoon in the raid :—

" The morning was cold but dry and, as was usual in this part of the line, deadly still. At the end of Pinney's Avenue Captain Reckitt gave us his final instructions, telling us he would remain there during the raid. Colonel Impey visited us when we were formed up and wished us good luck. Punctually at 4.30 a.m. down came our supporting barrage. I had understood that the Portuguese gunners on our right were to support us as well, and I cursed them soundly for firing so short, for their shells seemed to be falling all round us and I remember being amused at the noise which stones, pieces of earth and metal were making on our tin hats.

" As we advanced the enemy was silent, and the men of my platoon were soon up to their knees in mud close to the straggling wire in front of their trenches, which were badly damaged and afforded little protection as we waited in readiness for any counter-attack which might be made. Between fitful flashes of light we could see several of Clements's men on the top of the pill-box. They found this pill-box shut up, with a few Germans inside; five were bayoneted and 3 taken prisoner; one of these tried to escape while being brought across No Man's Land by rushing his captors, who promptly gave chase and killed him. My platoon got back, after fulfilling a purely passive rôle, and found that of the 2 prisoners who had been brought back alive one was a small N.C.O. and the other a tall, magnificent man, who remained speechless and adamant."

The whole raid was an unqualified success, reflecting the greatest credit not only on all who took actual part in it, but also on Captain Reckitt for his careful organisation. The prisoners captured belonged to the *267th Infantry Regiment*, and the identification proved to be a valuable one. The prisoners eventually became communicative and said what our superiors wished to hear. It will be casting no reflection upon the excellence of D Company's performance to note that for this ten minutes' work (with 2 casualties) the company received nearly as many decorations as were awarded to the whole battalion for more than ten days' heavy fighting (and over 250 casualties) at Cambrai. Captain Reckitt and Lieutenant Clements received the Military Cross, Corporal E. Toney the Distinguished Conduct Medal, and Privates W. J. Eade, A. L. Groves, A. E. Josland, and D. R. Porteous the Military Medal. Congratulations poured in from the Army, Corps, Division and Brigade Commanders; it was all very agreeable after the abuse to which we had so recently been subjected, and the whole battalion preened itself accordingly.

After this we carried on for a fortnight with the usual routine of trench reliefs, but things began to liven up. The enemy's artillery showed considerable activity, especially with gas-shells. In the early morning of the 12th a violent bombardment of the Portuguese trenches caused the battalion to stand-to, but quietness prevailed by 8 a.m. The continual working-parties were not made easier by the heavy gas-shelling of the forward areas. Sailly itself came off lightly, but the civilians began to leave in large numbers. There was no doubt that the increased activity was the preliminary rumbling of the storm that was to break on the 21st March and that it was intended to divert the attention of the Higher Command from the actual locality to be attacked.

Orders were received for the Division to go into Corps rest, but there were few who imagined that this rest would prove either long or peaceful. Those who did were soon to be bitterly disillusioned.

16. AVELUY WOOD

CHAPTER XI

AVELUY WOOD

21st March—6th April, 1918
[Sketch Maps, Nos. 16 and 17]

On the 21st March the battalion was relieved by the 2/6th King's Regiment (57th Division) and marched to Caudescure and Arrewage, near the Nieppe Forest and about two miles north-east of Merville. On the way there we observed various signs—such as new railway lines and preparations for dumps—which seemed to indicate a coming offensive, but the same afternoon Battalion H.Q. received a visit from Colonel R. Burritt, the G.S.O.2 of the Division, who brought news that the great German attack had started that very morning on the front of the Third and Fifth Armies farther south. He gave us orders to move the next day to Steenbecque, where the battalion was to find large working-parties for the construction of an aerodrome.

MARCH 1918

Leaving our peaceful villages, which were fated to form part of the British front line less than a month later, we reached Steenbecque after a march through a part of the Nieppe Forest. Our stay there was not a long one, for at midday on the 23rd we received the ominous warning to dump all surplus stores and kit and to prepare for an immediate move. About midnight further orders came to proceed next day to Burbure, near Lillers, where the Brigade was to be concentrated, as it was then very scattered —in fact, some units were ten miles or more from one another.

On the morning of the 24th, before our start at 8 a.m., we learned that our probable destination was the Hermaville area, just behind Arras. We marched again through the forest to St. Venant, where we saw the damage done to the railway station by the recent shelling, and halted about a mile beyond the town on the Busnes Road. From a casualty clearing station near by we got the latest news of the battle, which was not at all encouraging. After a meal, we resumed our march and passed through Lillers, where many recollections of the past came back to the veterans of 1915 and 1916; after a fifteen miles' march Burbure was reached at 3.30 p.m.

Aveluy Wood

Our peace did not remain undisturbed for long. At 5.30 p.m. an order arrived warning us to be ready to embus immediately, and at 9 p.m. the Brigade started to assemble on the Lillers-Burbure Road, but owing to the late arrival of the 9th Royal Fusiliers, which had to make a long march from Lapugnoy, the bus column did not move off much before midnight. There was a full moon that night—a moon of extraordinary brilliance, which lit up every detail of the countryside, making conditions ideal for hostile aircraft. Several planes did come over and try to bomb the waiting column, but fortunately they dropped most of their " eggs " into the fields on either side of the road. One bomb, however, fell close to the quartermaster's stores lorry, on the box of which was seated our Quartermaster, who fortunately remained unscathed. None of these bombs caused us any casualties.

MARCH 1918

Our route southwards was by way of Pernes, St. Pol, Frévent, and Doullens, the column having to halt outside Pernes and St. Pol until the departure of hostile aircraft, which had given both places a bad bombing; but the column eventually reached Doullens without further incident and proceeded along the main Doullens-Albert Road. It was now clear that our destination was to be considerably south of Arras.

As soon as we entered this area we began to realise the appalling seriousness of the situation. This was indeed our first, and certainly our last, experience of meeting a defeated British Army, but there can be no denying that these back areas diffused a disheartening atmosphere of defeat.

It will be remembered that at day-break on the 21st March the Germans had launched an attack on a front of forty miles, from La Fère to Vimy. The attack had eventually succeeded almost everywhere, and by the evening of the 24th, when we reached the battle zone, the enemy was surging over the country which he himself had laid waste in 1917 and had reached the line of the old Somme battlefields of 1916.

The roads we were traversing towards this front were crowded like Fulham Road after a football match. The traffic, with the single exception of our column of buses, was all hurrying due west. Lorries filled with the luxurious furniture of a Corps Headquarters, to the exclusion of all necessities of war; troops without steel helmets or rifles; rumours of the most fantastic nature were lapping from mouth to mouth like flames of fire; these were the conditions through which we passed on our way to the battle.

AVELUY WOOD

The bus containing the officers, sergeant-major, and all the H.Q. staff of D Company broke down during the night, and the whole party was transferred to the repair lorry which was following the Brigade column. Later on this lorry also broke down. By the time it had been repaired it was far behind the rest of the Division, and nobody had any idea at all where the Division's rendezvous was to be, for no orders had been issued. None of the fugitives hurrying westward was likely to be of assistance. The driver had heard a rumour that the column was bound for Albert, so to Albert the lorry went, arriving about 11 a.m. on the 25th.

MARCH 1918

There the wildest scenes of disorder were witnessed. The party could find nobody in authority who knew anything of the situation or had ever heard of the 12th Division. The only Staff Officer encountered in the town brandished a revolver (luckily it proved to be unloaded) and tried to commandeer the whole lorry-load to lead a dejected group of stragglers in what he described as "a forlorn hope," though with no ascertainable objective. Shaking this gentleman off with some difficulty, D Company H.Q. decided to leave this unpromising area, which was being quite nastily shelled and bombed. Proceeding westward, many more fruitless enquiries were made until by chance a well-informed Staff Officer was met who directed the party to Lavieville. Here they found Captain Le Hardy, the Staff Captain, and their troubles were over. They rejoined the battalion at Henencourt during the afternoon.

The rest of the battalion reached Warloy about 9 a.m. on the 25th March and bivouacked temporarily in a field outside the village. Further rumours of the battle reached us, including the news that the enemy had been shelling Paris with a long-range gun.

While the battalion had been moving down by bus, the Transport had perforce to travel by road, brigaded under Captain Hind. It was not until the afternoon of the 26th that the Brigade Transport reached Senlis. Captain Hind thus describes the march :—

"Before starting we received orders to proceed with caution, owing to enemy cavalry having broken through. This proved to be a wild rumour. The only thing we encountered was a smoke barrage, which completely blotted out the view in one valley and seemed difficult to account for. However, on riding forward to investigate, I found several steam-rollers retreating at a speed which would have entitled them to the steam-roller world's record."

Aveluy Wood

During the morning of the 25th the battalion received orders to proceed to Lavieville and marched off at 3 p.m., only to be intercepted at Henencourt by Captain Le Hardy, the Staff Captain, who told us to stack packs and leave all surplus equipment. At the same time the Commanding Officer proceeded to Brigade H.Q. at Lavieville for instructions, as the Brigade had been ordered to take over a position in the line between Montauban and Bazentin-le-Grand. We later set off for Albert, with the 5th Royal Berks acting as advanced guard, and the 9th Royal Fusiliers as the leading battalion of the main body.

March 1918

We reached Albert about 9 p.m. and found it in a sorry state as the result of heavy bombing the previous night. The streets were choked up with broken transport vehicles, remains of buildings, dead men and horses. In spite of this a few of the inhabitants still remained. The Brigade marched through the town and halted just east of it on the Bray Road, when notification was received from a Staff Officer that as the halt would be a long one the troops were to get as much rest as they could.

The battalion had the good fortune to be close to some abandoned stables, and all ranks took advantage of this shelter to get a good rest. We noticed that the heavy guns in the neighbourhood were being pulled out, and were informed by a battery commander that he was withdrawing behind the Ancre, which seemed to indicate that a further advance was not intended.

We received orders about 2.45 p.m. on the 26th to retire across the River Ancre and occupy positions facing east to defend the crossings of that river in front of Aveluy Wood. Consequently the whole Brigade retraced its steps in that direction.

We were now in the V Corps, Third Army. The frontage allotted to the battalion—about 1,200 yards—extended from the south-east end of Aveluy Wood to Black Horse Bridge, in front of Authuille village. D and C Companies took the right and left front, with A and B in support. The company commanders were:—Lieutenant T. Clarke, A; 2nd Lieutenant G. H. Hill, B; Captain E. C. Gorringe, C; Captain G. L. Reckitt, D. Battalion H.Q. was first established in some huts belonging to an old prisoners of war camp, just outside the south-east edge of the wood, but as this was obviously an unsuitable place a move was soon made to a sandpit (afterwards known as Quarry Post) about 400 yards inside the wood, nearer the south-west corner. This new position, which was soon to prove of such momentous importance, was reconnoitred and selected by Major

Aveluy Wood

Osborne, the acting Second-in-Command, while the Colonel and Captain Bowlby, the Adjutant, were going round the front line.

The battalion was in position by 6.30 a.m. and touch was at once obtained with the 9th Royal Fusiliers on our right, and, later on, with the 6th Royal West Kents on our left. The arrival of the 35th and 37th Brigades, on the right and left of the Division, had been delayed, as they had been sent to reinforce other divisions in the neighbourhood of Maricourt and Pozières.

March 1918

Our positions in the valley of the Ancre were dominated by the hills on the east; even the river, which ran in front of our line, was not in itself a serious obstacle for the enemy, as the bridges were still intact and we had neither the time nor the means to destroy them. There were no trenches, the natural line of defence along the greater part of the front being the railway embankment. The front line companies were disposed in depth to deny the crossings, and the support companies were placed in similar positions inside the wood, in which at that time there was no obstruction to a hostile advance. Special dispositions were made to cover the various rides and tracks.

Every effort was now made to strengthen our position, and although the men were tired they worked magnificently. An amusing sight in D Company's position was a solitary arm-chair, richly upholstered in dark red, which had apparently been borrowed at some previous date from a neighbouring village and now served as a resting-place at intervals for weary workers. Our difficulties were intensified by the lack of picks and shovels, and we had no grenades, Verey lights, S.O.S. signals, telephones, and barbed wire. Communication was only possible by means of runners. It was remarkable how the Division had passed unsullied through the area of deep depression, and that the moral of our troops was extremely high.

Later on in the morning there was some slight hostile shelling and several enemy planes came over; one of them tried to fly very low over our position but was driven off by our fire. Small parties of the enemy were observed wandering aimlessly about the slopes on the other side of the Ancre, apparently occupied in looting the various huts, and we could see them paying particular attention to an abandoned canteen and coffee shop. We sniped them at long range and managed to disperse them with some casualties.

By the afternoon we had completed our defences as far as circumstances and appliances would permit, so that some rest

AVELUY WOOD

was possible. Throughout the afternoon countless rumours and reports poured into Battalion H.Q.

About 8.30 p.m. heavy firing was heard from the south, and a report was later received that the Germans had occupied Albert and that the 35th Brigade was in difficulties on its right flank. Darkness had now set in, and it was an awe-inspiring sight to see the whole of the old Somme battlefield a mass of blazing dumps, huts, and camps. The reflection of the flames in the moonlight caused a weird and ghostly glare to hang over the wood and increased the eerie effect.

MARCH 1918

Nothing further happened until 11 p.m., when some rifle shots, evidently at very long range, fell in the battalion area, but shortly afterwards it was reported that the enemy had broken through somewhere beyond the left of our sector. The left support company (B) was ordered to form a defensive flank facing north, and similar dispositions were made by the front companies. At the same time a tremendous uproar—bugles sounding, whistles blowing, and men cheering—arose on our left and lasted for about half an hour, but for some time it was impossible to get any definite news as to the cause of this. At length it transpired that the Germans had broken through and had been advancing up the Mesnil-Martinsart Road in force when they were counter-attacked by the Anson Battalion (63rd, Royal Naval, Division) and by units of the 37th Brigade and driven back with heavy loss. The Anson Battalion had just been relieved and was having its rum ration at the time of the break-through, so was doubtless in very good fettle.

Matters calmed down about midnight and the battalion resumed its normal dispositions. At 2 a.m. on the 27th the reserve battalion of our Brigade, the 5th Royal Berks, " beat " the greater part of the wood and found it entirely clear of the enemy.

In the meantime affairs had not been going any too well on the right of the 9th Royal Fusiliers. The 35th Brigade, owing to heavy enfilade machine-gun fire, was compelled to give ground in front of Albert about midnight, and this was shortly to involve the Royal Fusiliers, and also our own right flank, very seriously. We held our own, however, and the rest of the night passed quietly.

When daylight came we resumed our long-range sniping at parties of the enemy on the far side of the river until, later in the morning, the battle in front of Albert broke out again. The enemy reached the advanced posts of the Royal Fusiliers about 8 a.m., but his attempt to cross the river at Aveluy was repulsed.

Aveluy Wood

Half an hour later violent fighting broke out on the right flank of the Royal Fusiliers, which was compelled to fall back slightly owing to the retirement of the 35th Brigade, and a counter-attack to restore the position failed owing to withering machine-gun fire.

Between 10 and 11 a.m. another attack developed and the enemy began to press back the outpost company (A) of the Royal Fusiliers at Aveluy Bridge, eventually forcing its withdrawal; this was carried out with great skill by its commander, Captain G. la C. Baudains, and was effectively supported by our D Company with long-range fire. An extra platoon and all the Lewis guns of the company were moved up to the outpost line for this purpose and the enemy sustained a large number of casualties at the bridge, which was kept under heavy fire and rendered impassable for any formed bodies of troops. Our A Company was put into position on the right rear of our front, facing south to cover the threatened flank.

To our immediate front there was no sign of movement, and the left front company of the 9th Royal Fusiliers still held its original position. Fighting continued on our right, and the situation caused great anxiety, owing to the difficulty of obtaining accurate information. A personal note from Colonel Van Someren to Colonel Impey disclosed that he was much disquieted by the continual withdrawal of the 35th Brigade on his right. Consequently it was decided to strengthen the right flank still further by placing B Company into the gap between D and A.

The battalion thus formed two sides of a square, with C and D Companies facing east and A and B facing south, and Battalion H.Q. behind the junction of the sides. The right front company of the Royal Fusiliers was later obliged to retire behind its support line as its outer flank was in the air, but the battalion, together with the left front company of the Royal Fusiliers, still held its original positions. The battle dragged on with a slight lull until 5 p.m., when the climax came and the attack spread to our own front.

The enemy soon began to show increased activity by sniping from the farther side of the river and also from a south-easterly direction, for by that time he had dribbled men across the river at Aveluy. At 6 p.m., after a short but intense bombardment by light artillery and trench-mortars, assisted by low-flying planes, the enemy attacked in force from the south and south-east, making clever use of the railway cutting from Aveluy village and of the various sunken roads leading towards the wood. The left

AVELUY WOOD

front company of the 9th Royal Fusiliers was forced back, and the brunt of the attack then fell on our A and B Companies on the southern fringe of the wood. A Company was out-flanked from its right and compelled to give ground, making the enemy pay very dearly for his advance. In the preliminary bombardment B Company lost 2 officers (2nd Lieutenant Manley killed and 2nd Lieutenant Paley wounded) and a number of other ranks, but succeeded in holding up the attack on its left flank, only to find its right flank pressed back owing to A Company's withdrawal.

MARCH 1918

The Germans thus succeeded in driving in a wedge between the two companies and in surrounding Battalion H.Q. in Quarry Post, where a terrific fight took place. Every member of the H.Q. staff manned the position and used a rifle, except the Commanding Officer, who directed operations and distributed ammunition, and the Adjutant, who hastily burnt official papers lest they should fall into the enemy's hands.

Time after time the enemy tried to rush the position, only to be forced back by a steady and well-directed fire from that small but determined garrison, whose resolution was such that at length the Germans were compelled to retire with heavy losses, leaving one prisoner behind. After this intensive little action several of the enemy, including the remnants of a machine-gun team, were found dead at the rear of Battalion H.Q., having penetrated there through the wood. The defenders of the Post did not escape unscathed, and among the casualties were the Sanitary Corporal and an Orderly Room clerk, both of whom were killed, while Private T. H. Beale, M.M., one of the Commanding Officer's orderlies, was killed about the same time by a bullet from an aeroplane. He had been with the battalion throughout the war and had held the post of orderly to each successive Commanding Officer. For this action Colonel Impey was awarded a bar to the Distinguished Service Order which he had already received.

There is no doubt that this stubborn resistance on the part of Battalion H.Q. was largely responsible for saving the situation in that part of the line, a fact to which due prominence has been given in the various diaries and histories.*

In the meantime D Company had posted two of its platoons facing south on the southern edge of the wood to repel an attack from that direction, and, when the bombardment started, a third

---

* *E.g.*, Sir Arthur Conan Doyle in *The British Campaign in France and Flanders*, Vol. V., p. 68, " The battle raged for a time round the battalion headquarters of the Sussex, where Colonel Impey, revolver in hand, turned the tide of the fight like some leader of old."

AVELUY WOOD

platoon had been sent there to keep touch with B. There were no trenches nor cover of any description and, owing to the nature of the ground to the immediate front, it was very difficult to see what was happening.

The result was that the company became involved in the retirement, owing to B Company's withdrawal, and was forced back to positions near Battalion H.Q., which it held with B and A Companies.

MARCH 1918

Although C Company had not yet been drawn into the fighting to any great extent, there now existed a gap of about 1,000 yards between its position and the other three companies now around Quarry Post, and the enemy had obtained a footing in the south-east corner of the wood. Therefore, when the attack died down and the general situation on the Brigade front had been ascertained, plans were made for a readjustment of our line.

The manoeuvre was a most difficult one to organise with inadequate maps in the darkness and thick undergrowth. The main idea was that, with B Company occupying Quarry Post and positions in the vicinity, and C Company remaining where it was, the intervening ground should be occupied by A and D. The line would then face south-east, still in touch with the 9th Royal Fusiliers on the right and the 6th Royal West Kents on the left.

In the early hours of the 28th, A Company was sent off to establish itself at the junction of two rides, about 400 yards to the north-east of Quarry Post, which, judging by the map, should have been a commanding position; B Company was to put out posts to keep in touch with it. D Company was to manoeuvre into the gap between A and C and to occupy a position as far forward as possible. Battalion H.Q. and D, therefore, proceeded round the southern and western outskirts of the wood as far as the track leading into it from Martinsart; here Battalion H.Q. was established. On the way it was a consolation to see ample evidence of the losses sustained by the enemy, for piles of his dead lay around, especially near Quarry Post.

After dropping the H.Q. staff the Commanding Officer led D Company along the track in the direction of Black Horse Bridge and halted it behind a bank by the side of the track (facing south over a large clearing), while he and Captain Reckitt went forward to C Company's position, which lay about 400 yards to the south-east. After he had explained the new dispositions to Captain Gorringe and had ordered D Company to find suitable positions, Colonel Impey returned to H.Q.

AVELUY WOOD

When Captain Reckitt came to reconnoitre with his platoon commanders, he discovered that the small-scale map issued for these operations was most inaccurate. The marking of rides and contours on the map bore no relation to their actual positions on the ground, and in the dense wood it proved impossible to find A Company's new position, which had been selected from the map. Another reason for this will be seen later. However, as dawn was approaching and the enemy snipers were becoming active, he decided to abandon the search and to set his company to prepare a series of posts facing south-east, towards the supposed position of A on the right and in sight of C on the left.

MARCH 1918

Dawn broke while the company was starting to dig in laboriously with light entrenching tools, and some German aeroplanes came over and dropped flares over all the new positions. Captain Reckitt went back to Battalion H.Q. to report the situation, leaving Company H.Q. behind the bank where the company had been halted by the Commanding Officer.

At 9 a.m., while he was at Battalion H.Q., a general attack developed. 2nd Lieutenant Hill, with his platoons in their prepared positions in Quarry Post, beat off the enemy with heavy loss, and once again proved the worth of this strong-point. But the centre companies did not fare well.

Lieutenant Clarke had found that A Company's selected position was not as the maps had shown it, but that it was untenable owing to the thickness of the wood and the slope of the ground. He had not had time to choose and strengthen a new position before the enemy was upon him and the company was forced back, almost to Battalion H.Q. D Company also was caught digging in the open. Its covering parties were driven in by heavy rifle fire and a withering trench-mortar bombardment was opened on the company, which had no cover. Lieutenant A. H. Smart and several men were badly wounded and taken prisoner, but 2nd Lieutenant E. C. Cutler, although seriously wounded in the eye, assembled most of the remainder of the company and led them back over the clearing to where their H.Q. had been placed behind the bank, from which position they effectively stopped the enemy from advancing any farther. He was awarded the Military Cross for this action.

But there was again a dangerous gap; the right flank of C Company (whose fortunes will be described later) was exposed and B Company's platoons in Quarry Post were isolated.

Aveluy Wood

Major Osborne, therefore, hastily collected A Company, and elements of B and D who had become detached from their companies, and taking Captain Reckitt with him led them up three parallel rides running east until he reached the high ground in the centre of the wood. In making this advance it was difficult to distinguish friend from foe, for many of the enemy wore British steel helmets taken from our casualties. Captain Reckitt was put in charge of the composite company so formed and a line was dug facing east just behind a ride, with advanced posts pushed out.

MARCH 1918

The left of this new line rested on the south-western edge of the clearing along whose northern end, some 300 yards away, lay the bank where portions of D Company were holding off the enemy. The line extended southwards for about 400 yards down the ride, where groups of the enemy were encountered. It was not until the evening that it was found that the ride eventually ran down almost to Quarry Post, which B Company still held, about 400 yards away. Later in the morning a company of the 6th Royal West Kents came up between the composite company and D Company. The enemy was now held at bay, but C Company and most of B were still isolated.

The fate of C Company was causing much anxiety, and the story of its adventures is best told by 2nd Lieutenant V. E. Rogers, one of its subalterns :—

" On the morning of the 28th March, about 9 a.m., C Company was being badly enfiladed from its right flank and parties of the enemy were seen advancing from that direction to cut us off. We kept up a heavy fire with our rifles and Lewis guns, and certainly gave as good as we received, but the Germans appeared to be determined to advance at all costs. We were having a very anxious time, as we discovered that our right flank was entirely in the air. However, our left flank was secure on the railway, and an enemy advance from that direction would have been difficult. In order to get in touch with both flanks, the other companies having apparently withdrawn, Captain Gorringe decided to take up a position farther back, and, as it was necessary to find a covering party for this withdrawal, I was detailed with eight men for the duty.

" I decided to keep one Lewis gun on the right, together with two men firing rifles, the remainder being spaced out along the front, with the second Lewis gun in the centre. The right gun fired down a track and caused the enemy many casualties.

AVELUY WOOD

Unfortunately two of my party were hit by ricochets, but being only slightly wounded were able to carry on. A runner managed to get through to me during this fighting to tell me that the company had got back safely and that my party was to retire on them as soon as possible, but this was not easy, for we were very short of ammunition and one of the Lewis guns was out of action; also the Germans appeared to be in great force and were using smoke-bombs, which at times made observation almost impossible.

MARCH 1918

"At last there was a lull in the fighting and, the firing having almost ceased, we took the opportunity to crawl back a few yards under cover of the smoke, and were going to attempt further withdrawal when we were alarmed to hear a voice order us in very good English to put our hands up. I then saw, to my dismay, that there was a large party of Germans covering us with a light machine-gun, on our right, about thirty yards away, cleverly concealed in some bushes.

"There was nothing for it but to obey, and a few minutes later we found ourselves trudging along into the denser parts of the wood, strongly escorted by Germans armed with revolvers. The German officer walked in front with me, and with a sort of ironic kindness gave me a Gold Flake cigarette, doubtless looted a short time previously from one of our canteens; I was, however, very glad to get it. We proceeded on a little farther, and, having previously been able to explore the wood thoroughly in 1916, I happened to know it very well, so when the officer asked me numerous questions regarding the direction of our positions, I was able to give him information which led us into the left front company of the 6th Royal West Kents on the railway line.

"When we got to within about a hundred yards of their position, walking along the railway line and being heavily shelled, the German officer, seeing the men stretched out between the rails, immediately tried to save himself by pointing his revolver at me, but was shot in the stomach by one of the Royal West Kent snipers—incidentally the revolver went off as he fell and the shot just missed me, and I should like to pay my humble tribute to the sniper concerned.

"The Royal West Kents shouted to us to stand to the side of the railway, which we did with all speed, and they then opened a withering fire on the Germans, who hurriedly retired into the wood. We then joined up with the Royal West Kents and finally found our way back to the company after going through a heavy

Aveluy Wood

bombardment. All the eight men of my party got back safely, the two wounded ones sticking it out splendidly."

This account shows how completely isolated the company was and how confused was the nature of the fighting. Captain Gorringe received the Military Cross for his stubborn defence.

During all this fighting Battalion H.Q. had had a harrowing time, for, owing to the bad communications and the general confusion, it was almost impossible to obtain any definite reports. There was nothing to be done but watch the white position lights which the enemy fired at intervals to denote his progress.

MARCH 1918

In the course of the afternoon the situation became quiet. The enemy's attack was spent. But it was found necessary to clear out some small hostile parties who still remained in the upper part of the wood.

After dark several adjustments took place. The 2nd Oxford and Bucks Light Infantry (2nd Division) relieved the 6th Royal West Kents and our D Company; the latter were then put on the left of our line along the ride, with A Company on its right. Patrols established touch again with the victorious B Company in Quarry Post, and C Company was withdrawn from its awkward position which it had defended so gallantly. The composite company was split up and the men rejoined their proper companies, and when Quarry Post was handed over to the 9th Royal Fusiliers later the same night C Company came up on the right of A, and B was placed between C and the Royal Fusiliers.

The 29th passed quietly enough, but rain set in and made things even more uncomfortable. It was satisfactory to observe, however, that the plight of the enemy on the old Somme battlefield was undoubtedly far worse than our own, and it seemed likely that his advance would be hampered.

The movements of the Transport during these strenuous times are described by Captain Hind as follows:—

" The transport lines were continually being moved from one place to another, Englebelmer, Bouzincourt, Warloy and Senlis all being used in rapid succession. On the night of the 27th we were instructed by Brigade H.Q. to pick up the Brigade runners outside Martinsart and were told that they would inform us of

Aveluy Wood

the latest movements and positions of the battalions. The ration dump was alongside a rough track running from Martinsart to a point north-west of Aveluy Wood. We picked up rations there and proceeded to the wood, and on arrival were informed that the battalion had ceased to exist, having been surrounded and annihilated, and that everyone was either killed or taken prisoner. I did not believe this alarmist report, and after a long search I found the battalion safe and sound, and duly delivered rations."

MARCH 1918

Up to the night of the 27th rations had been drawn and delivered by the transport of the 63rd (Royal Naval) Division.

In the evening of the 29th we handed over to the 24th Londons (47th Division) and marched to Warloy. The march was not without its incidents; it took place in bright moonlight, the weather having cleared up. The route followed was by the sunken road from Martinsart to Bouzincourt, which had been heavily shelled and was partly in flames, and then through Senlis, which the enemy was shelling with a solitary gun, pronounced by experts to be one of our own captured 6-inch howitzers, but no casualties were caused. The Commanding Officer and the Adjutant had a narrow escape while taking a short cut across the fields west of the village to the Warloy Road, when they walked right on to the muzzles of a battery of our own 6-inch howitzers which was about to fire a salvo, and only just saved themselves from becoming the targets. Warloy, a large and pleasant village situated in a valley seven miles west of Albert, had been abandoned by its inhabitants, and billets were easy to obtain, so that we had all settled down by 4 a.m. on the 30th.

Thus ended, so far as we were concerned, the first phase of the great German attack, in which our losses had been:—

	Officers	Other ranks
Killed	1	30
Died of wounds ..	—	8
Wounded and prisoner	1	10
Wounded	4	68
Totals ..	6	116

Officer killed : 2nd Lieutenant H. D. Manley (B).
 „ wounded & prisoner : Lieutenant A. H. Smart (D).
Officers wounded : Lieutenant G. H. Atkinson (B); 2nd Lieutenants E. C. Cutler (D), S. Lotham (C), and F. R. Paley (B).
N.C.O.s killed : Sergeants A. J. Heydon (B), H. Lambert (D), and E. G. Minall (B).

Aveluy Wood

The following decorations were awarded for the action (and for that of the 5th April described in the following pages) :—

Bar to Distinguished Service Order :	Lieutenant-Colonel G. H. Impey (H.Q.).
Military Cross :	Major G. F. Osborne (H.Q.), Captain E. C. Gorringe (C), and 2nd Lieutenant E. C. Cutler (D).
Military Medal :	Sergeant A. Trevor (D); Corporal T. Burch (A); Lance-Corporal T. Phillips (D); Privates P. Griston (A), B. Holder (A), O. C. Morris (A), J. Randall (D), W. Smith (B), and A. Taylor (C).
Belgian Croix de Guerre :	Sergeant C. Griffiths (A).

MARCH 1918

In the defence of Aveluy Wood the battalion had been through one of the most critical periods of its existence, and its stout resistance, in conjunction with the other units of the Brigade, contributed greatly to the holding up of the attack. Sir Arthur Conan Doyle, referring to the 12th Division (whose casualties amounted to 1,634 in all), says that " they withdrew from their line in glory, for it is no exaggeration to say that they had fought the Germans to an absolute standstill."*

Had the Germans succeeded in occupying Senlis, Hédauville, Englebelmer and the adjoining ridges, which were afterwards found to be their actual objectives, a very serious, if not fatal, situation would have been created. It is of interest to record that an officer of the Division, writing home after this battle, remarked, " I believe we are nearer winning the war than ever before."

All this fighting had been carried out in most disadvantageous conditions—continuous travelling, no hot meals or proper sleep for six nights, the absence of tools, proper maps, Verey lights and means of communication, and, lastly (a very important point), it was the battalion's—indeed, the Division's—first experience of wood fighting.

Our opponents in Aveluy Wood had been the *54th Reserve Division (Württemburg)*, consisting of the *246th, 247th* and *248th Regiments*, while farther on their left, in front of Albert, was the *3rd Marine Division*. During the night of the 26th the *II Battalion* of the *247th Regiment* was to cross the river at Authuille and push straight through the wood, while the *I Battalion* of the *248th Regiment* advanced through Aveluy. The Germans had expected that our side

---

* *The British Campaign in France and Flanders*, Vol. V., p. 50.

of the Ancre would be only weakly held, and orders for a pursuit as far as Hédauville and Senlis had been issued.

After the capture of Aveluy village at 1.10 p.m. on the 27th a regiment of field artillery was brought up, MARCH 1918 and further orders were issued to push forward to the high ground west of the village and the cross-roads between there and Bouzincourt. The troops on our actual battalion front were the *III Battalion* of the *248th Regiment*, whose records state that after penetrating into the south-eastern corner of the wood they ran into many machine or Lewis gun posts and claimed 70 prisoners and 5 Lewis guns from our Division. It is also stated that they thought at first that they were only being opposed by weak rear-guards; however, " considerable " casualties are admitted.

The attack on the 28th was carried out by the same two regiments, which hoped to effect a surprise, as their patrols were not very strongly opposed at the start. But on penetrating farther into the wood they found that " our opponents had obviously strengthened their lines and soon gained a superiority in numbers, and since casualties were mounting up at an alarming rate it was necessary to retire." The total losses of the *247th Regiment* were 26 officers and 600 other ranks killed, wounded and missing. Another extract from the *54th Reserve Division* diary says that the *3rd Marine Division* and *9th Reserve Division* " got very drunk in Albert and were consequently useless for further fighting, and this was probably the reason why no progress was made on our left."

These German histories reveal that the first signs of disaffection in the German Army appeared at this time. The diary states: " Troops when remonstrated with by their officers for smoking gave impertinent replies, saying that their working day was only six hours. This is a spirit totally foreign to our Army, and is also very repulsive."

In addition to these histories, Rudolf Binding, the German novelist, who was an officer on the staff of a division during this offensive, gives a most vivid description in *A Fatalist at War** of what was going on behind the German lines:—

" March 28, 1918.—To-day the advance of our infantry suddenly stopped near Albert. Nobody could understand why. Our airmen had reported no battle between Albert and Amiens. The enemy's guns were only firing now and again on the very edge of affairs. Our way seemed entirely clear. I jumped into a car

---

* *Op. cit.* (Translated 1928), pp. 209-210, 218-219.

with orders to find out what was causing the stoppage in front. Our division was right in front of the advance and could not possibly be tired out. It was quite fresh. When I asked the Brigade Commander on the far side of Meaux why there was no movement forward he shrugged his shoulders and said he did not know either; for some reason the divisions which had been pushed on through Albert on our right flank were not advancing, and he supposed that this was what had caused the check. I turned round at once and took a sharp turn with the car into Albert.

MARCH 1918

" As soon as I got near the town I began to see curious sights. Strange figures, which looked very little like soldiers, and certainly showed no sign of advancing, were making their way back out of the town. There were men driving cows before them on a line; others who carried a hen under one arm and a box of notepaper under the other. Men carrying a bottle of wine under their arm and another one open in their hand. Men who had torn a silk drawing-room curtain from off its rod and were dragging it to the rear as a useful bit of loot. . . . Men dressed up in comic disguise. Men with top-hats on their heads. Men staggering. Men who could hardly walk.

" They were mostly troops of the Marine divisions. When I got into the town the streets were running with wine. Out of a cellar came a lieutenant of the Second Marine Division, helpless and in despair. I asked him, ' What is going to happen?' It was essential for them to go forward immediately. He replied, solemnly and emphatically, ' I cannot get my men out of this cellar without bloodshed.' When I insisted . . . he invited me to try my hand, but it was no business of mine, and I saw, too, that I could have done no more than he. . . ."

" . . . April 19, 1918.—It is practically certain that the reason why we did not reach Amiens was the looting of Albert and Moreuil. The same thing happened in both places; in Albert I saw it myself. The two places, which were captured fairly easily, contained so much wine that the divisions, which ought properly to have marched through them, lay about unfit to fight in the rooms and cellars."

Our time at Warloy was spent in rest and reorganisation, and also in the inevitable working-parties, but it was gratifying for the battalion to be complimented by the Divisional

AVELUY WOOD

and Brigade Commanders on its work during the recent operations. On 1st April, owing to some heavy firing farther south, the battalion had to stand-to at 6 a.m., but nothing further transpired, and the following evening we marched to Senlis and then along a track across country, past Senlis Mill, to relieve the 10th Sherwood Foresters (17th Division).

APRIL 1918

Our new position was in Brigade Reserve on the forward slopes of the ridge south of Bouzincourt, overlooking a valley running down towards Albert. Battalion H.Q., with C and D Companies, were in some old trenches near a track leading from Bouzincourt to Millencourt and had very good observation, while A and B were in a sunken road parallel to the main Albert Road.

The first day passed very quietly, but this state of affairs was not to continue, for after considerable hostile artillery activity at 1 p.m. next day (the 4th) the enemy attacked the 35th Brigade on our right, but made little or no progress. However, our turn was to come, and during the night of the 4th we received warning that another heavy attack was expected next day along the whole front from Amiens northward.

This certainly proved no idle rumour, for next morning the enemy attacked strongly on a twelve mile front from Dernancourt to Bucquoy—the last throw in the great gamble of his Somme offensive. At 7 a.m. an intense bombardment opened along the whole front, the valley in front of our position being heavily gassed. Two hours later the enemy tried to attack over Bouzincourt Ridge against the 5th Royal Berks and the 9th Royal Fusiliers, but was driven off and the attack died down. Undeterred by this reverse the enemy opened another heavy barrage on the Royal Berks about noon, and a serious attack developed. After heavy losses through frequent advances in close formation the enemy obtained a footing in the front line trench held by the centre and left Berkshire companies. A counter-attack by the reserve company failed to restore the position, while three platoons of the reserve company of the Royal Fusiliers who bombed down the front line in an attempt to restore the line were stopped by a bomb-block.

Then followed one of the most exasperating experiences which can befall a battalion in action: the splitting up and scattering of its companies. At 1 p.m. we received orders from Brigade to send a company (C) to the 9th Royal Fusiliers to replace their reserve company which had just carried out the bombing attack, and shortly afterwards A and B Companies were placed at the

Aveluy Wood

disposal of Major T. V. Bartley-Denniss, commanding the 5th Royal Berks, with the result that Colonel Impey was left with only D Company.

Between 3 and 4 p.m. Bouzincourt and its approaches were very heavily shelled. The situation remained obscure and there was no definite news. Altogether there was a gap of about 600 yards (including the Orchard) in the Berkshires' front line, but it could not be accurately ascertained whether parts of this gap were not still held by isolated posts of the Berkshires. Consequently, in the late afternoon, Major Bartley-Denniss decided to use our companies to regain the lost ground. He and the two company commanders, Lieutenants J. S. Collins (A) and R. M. Howe (B), reconnoitred the front as soon as possible. They were heavily fired on the whole time, which indicated that the enemy was holding the trench in force and that nothing could be done before dark. This reconnaissance probably only helped to put the enemy on the alert; very little could be seen, and the portions of the line to be attacked were only very vaguely indicated to our company commanders. The whole outlook was most unpromising, but it was obvious that the Division considered an attack to be imperative, and that no representations of the situation would alter that opinion.

April 1918

This ill-starred venture started without artillery support at 8.45 p.m., with B Company on the right and A on the left, each advancing in two waves. Owing to the pitch darkness the waves had to keep very close together, and there was still much uncertainty whether any part of the objective was occupied by men of the Royal Berks; in fact, orders had actually been issued to refrain from firing on that account. The usual fighting order was worn, with the mess-tins hanging loose on the haversack, and the rattle of these gave the enemy further warning of our approach, for the night was exceedingly quiet.

The advance was extremely slow; there were no signs of trenches nor any other guide as to where resistance might be encountered. When the leading wave had just passed a sunken road about two feet deep, the enemy fired a shower of Verey lights and opened a shattering rifle and machine-gun fire from the front. This fire was so intense that very heavy casualties occurred in the first few moments, and the only way of saving complete annihilation was for the leading wave to charge directly towards the enemy in order to obtain slight cover in some excavations ahead. The second wave, which succeeded in getting into the sunken road, suffered rather less. At length, no further advance being possible, the two companies were compelled to retire to their original position. Their total casualties were 1 officer (Lieutenant J. S. Collins) and 37 other ranks killed; 1 officer (2nd Lieutenant G. P. Mossop, B Company) and 90 other ranks wounded, of whom five died of wounds.*

APRIL 1918

It was bitterly mortifying for the battalion to have its two companies almost blotted out under such conditions, and the action only bore out the invariable experience that when an immediate counter-attack has failed (in this instance two had failed) any further attempt must be properly organised, with effective artillery and machine-gun co-operation, before it can have any hope of success. Haphazard attacks such as this, delivered after a long interval, are not only futile but also very costly.

Our opponents were the *II Battalion* of the *3rd Marine Division*, who, in their attack during the morning, only claimed a gain of 100 metres and admitted casualties amounting to 10 officers and 150 other ranks killed and wounded.

At 11 p.m. that evening (the 5th) orders were received to relieve the 5th Royal Berks in the front line and also to take over the other positions belonging to that battalion but held by the 9th Royal Fusiliers. This relief was complete by 4 a.m. on the 6th April. D and C Companies occupied the right and left front, while the remnants of A and B were amalgamated into one company in support and a composite company of the Royal Berks was placed at our disposal in reserve. The 6th Queen's was lent as a Brigade Reserve and took over our old position; our Battalion H.Q. was moved to a small excavation in a sunken road farther down the valley towards Albert. At 10 a.m. S.O.S. signals went up on the 35th Brigade front to our right, and also beyond, causing a very heavy hostile barrage, which extended to our right, D Company suffering particularly. Later on the shelling died down and all was quiet until about 5 p.m., when, probably as the result of some shelling of traffic on the Albert-Amiens Road by our own artillery, the enemy put up an S.O.S. and opened a barrage on the whole front, to which our artillery promptly retaliated. At one time it seemed as if an hostile attack

* For decorations awarded see p. 203.

was imminent, but nothing further happened, and all was quiet by 7 p.m.

Communication was very difficult owing to the shelling, but Battalion H.Q. managed to get a message by lamp back to the H.Q. of the 6th Queen's, for transmission to Brigade H.Q., that there was no sign of any hostile advance. The same night we were relieved by the 6th Queen's and moved back behind the slopes overlooking Senlis.

CHAPTER XII

MAILLY AND BOUZINCOURT

7TH APRIL—30TH JULY, 1918

[Sketch Map, No. 17]

APRIL 1918

The only accommodation available on the Senlis slopes was a line of burrows in the side of the hill, so that the battalion had to bivouac, except Battalion H.Q., which secured a small hut. The enemy bombarded Senlis with gas and other shells, most of which fortunately went over our bivouacs, but some men at the aid-post were gassed when the mustard-gas vaporised with the rise of the sun. No blankets or comforts of any description were available, and we were quite glad to take over from the 5th Northants* in the left sector of the right Brigade front on the night of the 9th April.

Our new position was some distance to the right of Aveluy Wood, on the farther side of the Albert-Bouzincourt Road. The front line consisted of a series of isolated posts, which were completely cut off except during the hours of darkness. All the front line companies shared a communal H.Q. in a hut within full view of the enemy, but luckily it was never shelled.

Nothing of note occurred during this two days' tour, but the Transport had a disagreeable experience on the Bouzincourt-Albert Road, which is described by Captain Hind and Sergeant-Major Hanlon :—

" The battalion was holding the line in front of Bouzincourt and one night, no guides having turned up, we were trying to find its position in order to deliver rations. The Transport had pulled up on the right side of the road when a salvo of whizzbangs burst almost on top of us. This caused a temporary stampede amongst the horses, which was fortunately checked, except that two of the horses (Jerry and Jumbo by name) in one of the field-kitchens bolted down the road in the direction of the enemy's line. The field-kitchen was completely wrecked, but, thanks to a splendid piece of work on the part of Private Laker, the driver, the horses

---

* The pioneer battalion of the Division, which was constantly being called upon in an emergency to appear in the front line as a fighting unit, and always carried out this rôle as capably as its ordinary duties—which is saying a great deal, for our popular " maid of all work " was highly efficient.

17. MAILLY AND BOUZINCOURT

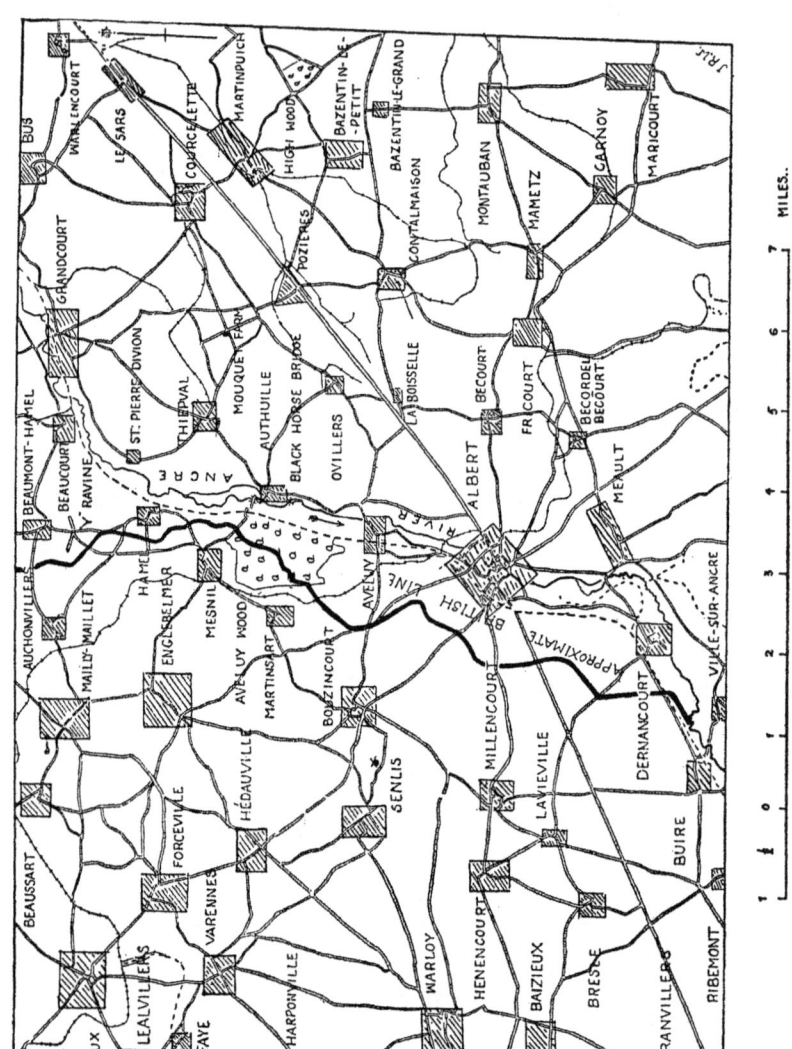

were rescued almost on the enemy's wire. We eventually received orders to return to Bouzincourt, where we remained until, in the early hours of the morning, the ration parties at last arrived."

A draft of 204 other ranks had recently reached the Transport at Contay, this being the first we had received for some time. It preceded many others which were sent out in a great hurry when at last the home Government realised that France was the principal theatre of war, and released troops in England which they had hitherto carefully preserved for operations in other theatres or for " the defence of England." The extreme youth of this draft was most noticeable.

APRIL 1918

On the night of the 11th we were relieved by the 14th Welch Regiment (38th Division). The relief was not complete until 3 a.m., and we did not reach Warloy until 4.45 a.m. the next morning. We rested there until 2 p.m., when a move was made for Contay, where all the companies had baths and a change of clothes. Later in the afternoon we continued our journey to Mirvaux, and the battalion was settled in billets by 9.30 p.m.

Mirvaux was a pretty little village tucked away in a hollow about midway between Contay and the main Doullens-Amiens Road, and far removed from all forms of strife except air raids. Here we spent a period of welcome peace and rest, coupled with range practices and other training, until the 16th, when a general post was suddenly ordered and we moved to Pierregot, another village close by. Our stay there was even more brief, for the following morning the advanced party of a French regiment arrived to arrange billets in the village for their men. This regiment was part of a division which was proceeding north to reinforce the line in the Kemmel sector, for the German attacks on the Lys had broken out on the 9th. It appeared that we had been allotted this village (which was in the French Army billeting area) through a mistake by the Q Staff of the Corps. However, matters were amicably arranged with the French authorities, and hurried orders were issued from Corps H.Q. for us to resume our former billets in Mirvaux.

On the 19th another move took place, this time to Harponville, a small village situated in a valley between Toutencourt and Senlis. The whole Brigade was billeted in the village, so that accommodation was none too plentiful. Training during our stay here was considerably curtailed owing to the large working-parties required each day for the construction of the rear defensive lines, of which no organised system yet existed, so that their rapid completion was most important.

Our time at Harponville came to an end on the 22nd, when we moved to Acheux, and next day relieved the 2nd and 3rd Battalions of the New Zealand Rifle Brigade in the front line. This sector consisted of the old British trenches which had been held at the time of the Battle of the Somme, and we found ourselves facing such well-known places as Beaumont Hamel and Y Ravine. The trenches had long been unoccupied and were in a deplorable state, so that a great deal of work had to be done on them. We remained in this sector for eight days.

APRIL 1918

On the 26th the Division sustained a very severe loss, when Major-General A. B. Scott left to take command of the Lucknow Division in India. He had been our Divisional Commander since the 2nd October, 1915, and had guided the Division through all its most critical periods and hardest fighting. His invariable kindness and courtesy, together with his fine soldierly qualities, had endeared him to all ranks, who all felt that it was indeed a case of "dropping the pilot." He was succeeded by Major-General H. W. Higginson, who for two years had commanded the 53rd Brigade (18th Division), from which appointment he was transferred.

Before leaving the Division General Scott issued the following order:—

"In relinquishing command of the 12th (Eastern) Division I once more desire to express my high appreciation of the fighting qualities of the Division. I also wish to thank all those who, by carrying out their duties efficiently, have aided the Division in reaching the high standard it has attained. The mutual confidence between all branches has greatly assisted to this end, and made the task of commanding an easy one. To my staff and all those in command I express my deepest gratitude for their assistance.

"There is no better command than that of a division in the field, and I thoroughly appreciate the honour I have had in commanding the 12th Division for over two and a half years. To leave it is a great wrench and I feel it very much, but, you may be assured, my thoughts will always be with you, and I shall continue to watch carefully for your doings. Under all circumstances be as you always have been, cheerful and confident. To you all good-bye and the best of luck."

MAILLY AND BOUZINCOURT

On the 1st May we were relieved by the 9th Royal Fusiliers and moved back to Acheux. The battalion was now in Divisional Reserve, and the five days' rest was mainly occupied in finding large working-parties for the Purple Line, a new reserve line running through Mailly-Maillet. Many rumours were rife as to impending enemy attacks, one of them being that Field-Marshal von Mackensen, the only German commander who had never yet met with a reverse and had won great victories over the Russians and Roumanians, was being sent to capture the Channel Ports. It was a consolation to know that, even if this were true, this formidable leader had yet to make his first acquaintance with the Western Front, where his proud record might well be broken.

MAY 1918

Acheux came in for a certain amount of shelling, usually at night, the neighbourhood of the château in which Battalion H.Q. was billeted being the chief target. On the night of the 2nd 3 men were wounded there and a large splinter of shell penetrated the Commanding Officer's bedroom during his absence, wrecking a large locked cupboard full of documents, which were scattered in all directions.

On the 6th we relieved the 5th Royal Berks as Brigade Reserve in the Purple Line, which was still by no means complete, and working-parties had to be found every day to assist the Royal Engineers and the other reserve units. The village of Mailly-Maillet was actually in this line, and being almost intact it provided a certain number of billets, but it received considerable attention from the German guns. The enemy had lately invented a new infliction, known as artillery " crashes," which consisted of two-minute concentrations at irregular intervals on the various tender spots; two of these were the road junction at the church and the cross-roads, about 800 yards south-west of the village. These crashes proved both disconcerting and expensive in casualties, but it was a game at which two could play, as no doubt the Germans found to their cost.

Mailly-Maillet became very unhealthy for the Transport, and its lines in Acheux Wood were frequently bombed. One bomb registered a direct hit on the lines of the 37th Brigade and killed over 20 animals. Our Brigade Transport had three Lewis gun anti-aircraft sections, and since the battalion could not spare gunners from the companies, the transport drivers were taught the use of the guns. During this instruction one driver, on being told to practise an aim without touching the trigger (as the gun was loaded with live ammunition), promptly fired, with the result that two men in an observation balloon close by, thinking the shots came from hostile aircraft, jumped for their lives and made a hurried descent by parachute.

We returned to the front line on the 12th, relieving the 5th Royal Berks in our old position. During the evening of the 14th the 9th Royal Fusiliers on our left carried out a silent raid, but were unable to secure any identification. This was followed on the 16th by another raid on the 37th Brigade front, opposite Beaumont Hamel, which woke the enemy up, and hostile aircraft became active, while between the 15th and the 19th Mailly-Maillet was frequently shelled, mostly with gas-shells, particularly during the evening and early morning. The Transport and ration-parties were thus compelled to wear box-respirators continually, which greatly hampered them in their work.

MAY 1918

We were relieved by the 6th Buffs on the 20th, when another hostile attack was reported to be imminent, with the result that we manned the Purple Line all night instead of proceeding to Acheux; but again nothing happened, and the battalion arrived at Acheux at 10.30 a.m. next morning, less A Company, which had been left as a garrison in the Purple Line.

These constant alarms were most unsettling. Before the counter-attack at Cambrai, as we have complained in a previous chapter, no official warnings reached us; but now the cries of "wolf" were almost deafening. These, resounding generally in a censorious tone, were most disheartening, and gave us at the time the impression that the new brooms at Division were bent on sweeping clean imaginary evils. In fact, they had not yet gained confidence in their command, which was not easy to understand in view of the Division's fine fighting record, so recently exemplified in and around Aveluy Wood. It is only fair to say, however, that this hypercritical atmosphere evaporated when we went into action again.

On the evening of the 24th a raid on a large scale was carried out by the 5th Royal Berks in co-operation with the Anson Battalion (63rd Division) on our right, in which 8 prisoners were taken. We assisted by lending eight stretcher-bearers, two of whom were missing. The next day the long expected divisional relief took place, and the battalion was relieved by the 7th Border Regiment (17th Division).

On relief we marched back to Beauquesne, a large village typical of the Somme area, pleasantly situated and with good accommodation. About a mile outside the village, in the direction of Acheux, was the picturesque château of Val Vion, standing amidst lovely surroundings; it had been advanced G.H.Q. during the battle of the Somme and was now used by the H.Q. of our Division.

MAY 1918

During this rest the battalion, under directions from the V Corps, experimented with a new organisation whereby Lewis gun platoons were formed for each company and for Battalion H.Q. The idea was not considered a success and was quickly dropped. In our area two ranges were available, of which one was used for field firing. Thus for the first time for many months we were able to carry out this essential form of training. A spell of fine weather now set in, and with all the flowers and orchards in bloom the countryside was looking its best.

On the 1st June the Division was transferred to G.H.Q. Reserve and was put on one hour's notice to move between 6 a.m. and 10 a.m., and three hours' notice at other times. As we were not called upon to move, it was possible to hold the battalion sports during the afternoon of the 1st. This was the third anniversary of the battalion's arrival in France, and it had been hoped that General Osborn would be able to attend and distribute the prizes. Unfortunately he was not able to leave the 5th Brigade (2nd Division), which he was now commanding.

On the 4th Lieutenant-General C. D. Shute, G.O.C. V Corps, inspected the Brigade and expressed his satisfaction. The next day the Division was transferred to the XXII Corps, which was in reserve to the First French Army, south of Amiens, but remained in its present location.

JUNE 1918

As the result of this transfer orders were received for a party of officers, consisting of brigade and battalion commanders, to reconnoitre the French front in the neighbourhood of Boves, Cottenchy and Guyencourt, and some very interesting days were spent examining the dispositions and methods of the French Army. During this period we took full advantage of the opportunities the country offered for training in open warfare, which was to prove invaluable to the battalion during its final advance. The time was not entirely occupied by training, and on the 11th June the brigade sports were held, the great feature of which was a drum competition between our drummers and those of the 9th Royal Fusiliers for a special prize presented by the Brigadier, which the Fusiliers won by a narrow margin.

Mailly and Bouzincourt

A battalion tactical exercise, which General Owen attended, was carried out on the 14th in the divisional training area; the scheme, which included advanced guard, attack and outpost operations, lasted the whole day, and proved a fitting and instructive termination to the training.

Our stay at Beauquesne lasted nearly a month, and was our longest rest since the previous Christmas. It was a great relief not to have to find the usual working-parties so invariably associated with these periods, and the result was that the battalion was able to reap the full benefit of the various forms of training, and to rest and play as well.

JUNE 1918

The Division's transfer back to the V Corps indicated that a move was imminent, and on the 17th we moved from Beauquesne at 10 a.m., the battle reserve of 11 officers and 124 other ranks having left for Domqueur under Major Osborne the previous day. We marched to a valley north-east of Warloy adjoining the road to Hédauville, not far from the spot where we had debussed the previous March. There we bivouacked until 9.30 p.m., when we relieved the 18th Lancashire Fusiliers (35th Division) in Brigade Reserve near Senlis. The position we occupied was on the slopes where we had bivouacked the previous April, and in some trenches on either side of the main Hédauville-Bouzincourt Road.

After three quiet days we relieved the 9th Royal Fusiliers on the Bouzincourt Spur, of which the enemy held the highest point. Our trenches were only just to the left of the place from which the disastrous counter-attack of the 5th April had been made, and they required much repair. Another task which had to be done was the cutting of the long grass in No Man's Land, a reminder of the old days at Houplines. The Germans had a habit of wandering about in the open behind the support line, presumably under the delusion, speedily removed by our snipers and Lewis guns, that they would not be seen. A considerable amount of dead ground existed between our support line and Bouzincourt which was convenient for the Transport when dumping rations, as the village itself was a most unhealthy spot and was out of bounds for all ranks during the daytime. On the 23rd Lieutenant S. C. Boys was killed by machine-gun fire when superintending a working-party.

Mailly and Bouzincourt

It was about this time that the terrible wave of Spanish influenza swept over not only many units in the Division, but also both the Expeditionary Force generally and the German Army; on the whole we escaped very lightly.

On the 25th we were told that the 37th Brigade was preparing for an attack in conjunction with the 18th Division on our right, in order to capture the remaining high ground of the Bouzincourt Spur, so that during the last three days of the tour our artillery and trench-mortars were very active, though they provoked only slight retaliation. *JUNE 1918* On the 29th we were relieved by the 6th Queen's and 6th Royal West Kents and proceeded to our old bivouacs in the valley north-east of Warloy as Divisional Reserve, not arriving until 4.30 a.m. on the 30th. At 9.35 p.m. the attack of the 37th Brigade took place and proved very successful, but the battalion had to stand-to from 2.30 to 3 a.m. in case of emergencies during the withdrawal of the advanced troops. At 8 p.m. that evening (the 1st July) a violent enemy bombardment was heard from the direction of Bouzincourt Spur and *JULY 1918* our S.O.S. signal was seen to go up. An hour later we were ordered to move to the Purple Line, east of Senlis, but there was no need for this alarm as the enemy attack did not develop.

At 9.30 p.m. on the 2nd the Germans again counter-attacked under cover of an intense bombardment and completely re-occupied the greater part of the positions which they had lost on the 30th, including the part which had been taken by the 18th Division.

The battalion, though still in Divisional Reserve, now had the misfortune to be taken from its own brigade and placed at the disposal of the G.O.C. 37th Brigade, from whom, at 1.35 a.m. on the 3rd, sudden orders were received to counter-attack at 3 a.m. and recover all the lost positions on the brigade front. At such short notice this was an almost impossible task, but the companies were hurried as soon as possible on the way to their assembly positions, with little time for directions to be given. They were heavily shelled on the way, and one platoon of D Company was almost wiped out by a direct hit from an 8-inch shell. Then, at 2.45 a.m., orders were received cancelling this counter-attack.

Mailly and Bouzincourt

It appeared that the G.O.C. 18th Division, which was also to have taken part, grasping the peril of the operation, had cancelled the orders for his units to attack, and at the same time was responsible for saving us from the possibility of even greater slaughter than we suffered on the 5th April.

On receipt of orders that the attack was cancelled, the companies returned to their positions in the Purple Line, arriving at 5 a.m., and on the same day (the 4th) the battalion relieved the 6th Buffs in the right of Aveluy Wood, where it remained uneventfully in the front line until the 10th. We were then relieved by the 12th Manchesters (17th Division) and moved back to Toutencourt Wood.

JULY 1918

On the 13th, after inspecting the battalion, Colonel Impey bade farewell to it and left for England. We all parted from him with deep regret. He had been one of the original officers with the battalion on its formation and had left us in April, 1916, to command the 12th Royal Sussex. Since his return to command us in August, 1917, he had led us through some of our most stirring times, notably at Cambrai and Aveluy Wood. Major A. L. Thomson took his place as Commanding Officer.

On the 14th the battalion embussed west of Herissart and proceeded to billets in Fremontiers and Uzenneville. The following evening the bus journey was continued until we reached Oresmaux, a large village eight miles south of Amiens and midway between the Rivers Noye and Celle. The Transport, which had left Toutencourt Wood by route march on the 13th, arrived about the same time.

The whole Division was now well south of the front held by British troops and was in the XXII Corps in support of the IX and XXXI French Corps. A well-earned rest followed, and the three Brigades remained in this district until the 30th July.

On several occasions Battalion H.Q. officers and company commanders had to reconnoitre the fronts of the 3rd, 15th and 66th French Divisions, and those who went were impressed with the attention the French paid to the use of camouflage and with the lack of any movement in the vicinity of the front line compared with what we were accustomed to see behind our own front. There were no fires visible, and all transport was camped in woods or copses, or, where this was impossible, was camouflaged with branches in the fields or along the roads.

On one of these reconnaissances the party, which included General Owen, was strongly remonstrated with for riding horses as far as the H.Q. of a French regiment (which would correspond

Mailly and Bouzincourt

to that of our brigade), while the lorry in which the officers of the Division made their first reconnaissance was stopped by sentries four miles behind the line.

This period of rest passed off without any untoward event. The weather was gloriously hot and its enjoyment was marred only by the swarms of irritating flies arising from the mass of filth to be found in the garden of every house.

The one outstanding incident during our stay at Oresmaux was that the Transport had an increase in the family. This was a filly foal named Somme, which afterwards accompanied the battalion to victory and eventually reached England, where she was sold, in Chichester Market, for £45 to Captain H. Sadler, whose deeds at Ovillers have already been related. Of the amount received £25 went towards Harold's board and lodging when in quarantine at the Blue Cross Kennels, Blackheath, and the balance was given to the Regimental Widows and Orphans Fund.

July 1918

At the end of July Captain Bowlby, the Adjutant, was promoted to Major, and his place was taken by Captain E. S. Ellis, M.C., who had joined us in April and had been commanding A Company.

CHAPTER XIII

THE BATTLE OF AMIENS

30TH JULY—30TH AUGUST, 1918

[Sketch Map, No. 18]

JULY 1918 Our long rest at Oresmaux came to an end on the 30th July, for on that day we left by train for Vignacourt, where we found excellent billets and a first-rate canteen.

On the evening of the 3rd we embussed for Round Wood, east of Behencourt, and there took over a camp of huts and tents from the 6th Royal West Kents. Most of our time here was spent in digging down the tents in case of air raids. We were now in the III Corps, Fourth Army.

A large number of guns in the neighbourhood gave us our first hint that an attack was maturing, and as a great battle began two days later and we were one of the AUGUST 1918 battalions to lead it, our ignorance was an excellent example of the secrecy with which the preparations were made. Sir George Aston, in his book *Secret Service*, describes the attack as one of the best kept secrets of the war, and states that the reason for this undoubtedly was because no previous mention of it had been made either to the War Office, the War Cabinet, or to any other authorities in England, so that the gossips on the home front for once did not have an opportunity to give the soldier away.

On the 6th August it was evident from the sounds heard by us in Round Wood that there was some activity going on in front, and it was no surprise when we moved closer to the line that night and took over part of the Lahoussoye Switch in front of Franvillers from the 8th Royal Berks (18th Division).

Early next morning the company commanders* went with Colonel Thomson to reconnoitre the line held by the 54th Brigade (18th Division) south-west of Morlancourt, but the object of the reconnaissance was not made clear until they had reported to the

---

* A Company, Lieutenant G. W. Prince; B, Captain R. M. Howe; C, Lieutenant C. Clayton; D, Captain G. L. Reckitt.

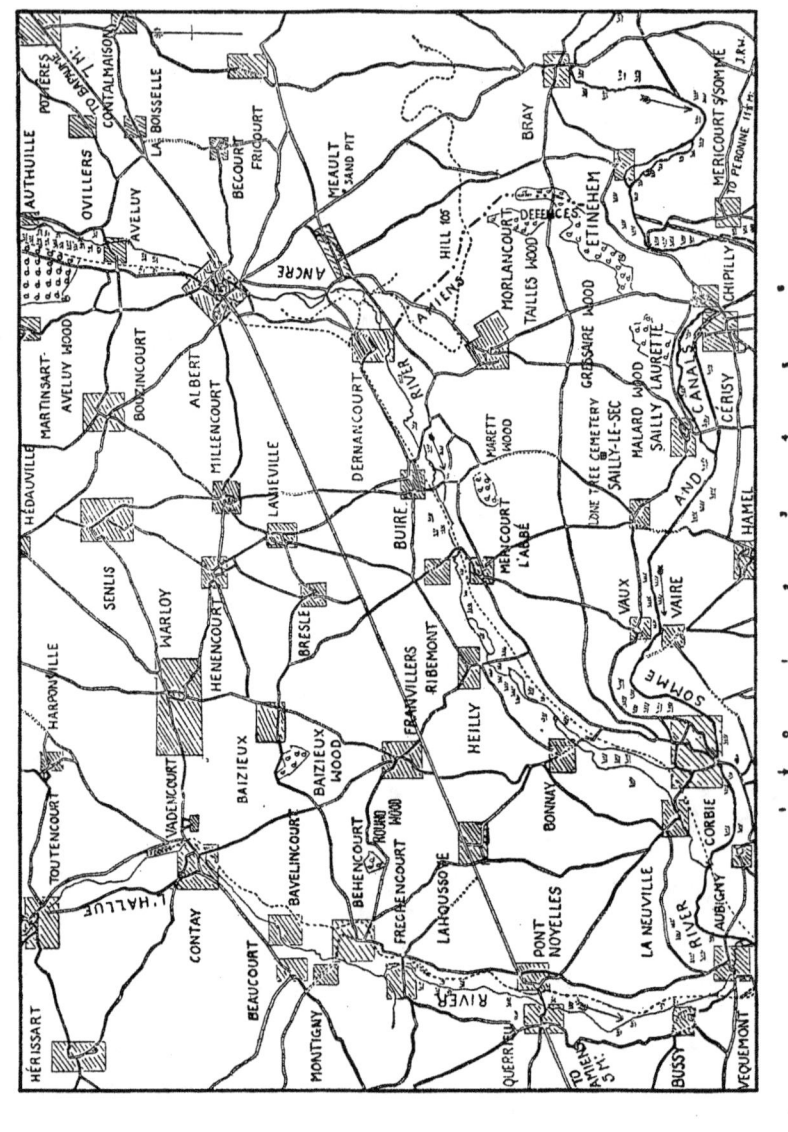

18. SOMME—SOUTHERN AREA

THE BATTLE OF AMIENS

G.O.C. 54th Brigade, Brigadier-General L. W. de V. Sadleir-Jackson, C.M.G., D.S.O. From him they gathered that a large attack was to start at dawn next day, and that the 36th Brigade was to take the place of his brigade in the 18th Division, for his troops had been badly knocked about in stopping a heavy German attack by the *27th Württemburg Division* on the 6th. This attack, which had taken place during an inter-brigade relief, had succeeded in penetrating for 800 yards and in capturing 200 prisoners, including some artillerymen who were establishing a forward dump of shells. None of the prisoners disclosed any information, but the enemy must have suspected that something serious was about to happen on this front.

AUGUST 1918

The battle was still going on when our officers arrived and they were obviously rather in the way, but the Brigadier, who was winning, and much enjoying, his battle, put them out of the way in a trench from which they could see something of the front. When the situation had been more clearly ascertained they started up for the front line, but the reconnaissance was of very little value, for no one knew where the assembly trenches would actually be or the objectives in the attack. After what seemed hours of weary struggling through battered trenches, Colonel Thomson decided that they could gain no useful information and that they would do better to rejoin the battalion as soon as possible. They got back about 5 p.m.

By that time the orders for the battle had reached the battalion. From them we learnt that the Fourth Army, assisted by the First French Army on its right, was attacking early next morning on an eleven mile front between the Rivers Luce and Ancre. The initial objective was to gain the outer lines of the old Amiens defences and thus to render the town and the Paris-Amiens railway safe from bombardment. If this object was attained the advance would be continued eastwards and south-eastwards so as to threaten the communications of the German forces in the Montdidier salient, which had been created by the March offensive.

The task of the III Corps was to capture the Amiens defences between the Somme and the Ancre as a defensive flank to the main attack by the Canadian and Australian Corps south of the Somme. Owing to the difficulties of the ground, which was very steep and rough, the objectives of the first day were limited to capturing the Chipilly Spur and the high ground south and north of Morlancourt.

The Battle of Amiens

The 18th Division, to which our Brigade was now attached, was in the centre of the Corps advance, with the 58th Division on its right and the remainder of the 12th Division on its left. The 36th Brigade was to lead the attack and secure the first objective, the green line, after which the 53rd Brigade would pass through to the second objective, the red line. On our brigade front the green line ran in a semi-circle (facing east and north-east) from the spur 500 yards north-east of Malard Wood to the British front line in front of Morlancourt; for there was to be a gap of 500 yards in the attack from that point up to the positions north of Morlancourt, from which the 12th Division was to attack. The red line on the 18th Division front faced north, from Tailles Wood to the green line south of Morlancourt.

August 1918

The battalion was attacking on an 800 yard frontage on the right of the Brigade, with the 174th Brigade (58th Division) on our right and the 9th Royal Fusiliers on our left. Our starting line could not be given definitely owing to the uncertainty as to the exact position of the front line, but it would be somewhere in front of Lone Tree Cemetery, which was a mile north-east of Sailly-le-Sec. D and C Companies, from right to left, were to form the first wave and to advance for about 1,000 yards until they came to the top of the rise overlooking the Sailly-Laurette-Morlancourt Road, when B and A Companies would pass through them and advance another 1,200 yards to the green line, which was just beyond the track leading from the east of Malard Wood to Morlancourt. These objectives were, of course, imaginary lines on the map and did not correspond to the enemy's lines of defence, which were only vaguely indicated. There was to be no preliminary bombardment, and it was doubtful whether any tanks would be able to operate on our front owing to the roughness of the ground.

There was a great deal to be done before marching off at 8.30 p.m. It was difficult for the company commanders to explain much to their subordinates, for the battalion's assembly positions could not be given and its objectives were obscure even to those who had seen something of the ground. Zero hour was not to be disclosed until after the march had begun.

D Company led, followed by C, B, and A Companies. During the march our own guns were quiet, but the enemy artillery was shelling both front and back areas considerably. When passing through Heilly, C Company H.Q. and its leading platoon received a direct hit from a shell of large calibre. Lieutenant P. S. Dixon was killed, and Lieutenants C. Clayton and V. E. Rogers seriously wounded, while several other ranks were also killed and wounded. The 8th Royal Sussex, the pioneer battalion of the 18th Division, which was in billets close by, attended to our wounded. Later on, half way up the Corbie-Bray Road, another shell landed in front of 15 Platoon and killed 2nd Lieutenant A. Murray ; several others in this platoon were killed and wounded.

AUGUST 1918

The night was extremely dark and the going very rough after we picked up our guides and turned off the road. However, we managed to reach our assembly positions by 2.45 a.m. without further casualties. D and C Companies were in the right and left front, B and A in the right and left support positions ; Battalion H.Q. was established near Lone Tree Cemetery. There were no troops in the line taken over, but some wounded men in a dug-out were of assistance in giving roughly the lie of the land. They did not, however, know of the position of any other troops, although they said that they thought there were some isolated posts still remaining in front. Our patrols could not find any of these posts, so that orders had to be given to all ranks to look out for them as they advanced. Not much more time remained and patrols were not able to gain touch with the 58th Division, which was said to be on our right. C Company was in touch with the 9th Royal Fusiliers on the left.

When going along to find the Royal Fusiliers Captain Reckitt discovered that 2nd Lieutenants S. Lotham and W. T. Trowell were the only surviving officers of C Company, and that Lieutenant Clayton had not been able to let them know the time of zero hour before he was wounded. Zero had been fixed for 4.20 a.m., an hour before sunrise.

The enemy shelling was heavy and most of it fell on the support line, where A and B Companies suffered severely both during this waiting period and when they started to advance. Shortly before Zero the noise of tanks could be heard distinctly, but this was soon drowned, according to plan, by the arrival of several low-flying aeroplanes. Our Brigade began the operations without any tanks. About an hour before Zero a heavy mist came down, and this, by the time we went over, limited visibility to about a dozen yards.

From the moment of starting it was obvious that the attack would have to be taken slowly. The heavy mist, the uncertainty as to the presence of any troops in front, the exposed flank on the right, and the lack of knowledge of the ground or of the enemy's defences all made caution necessary. In spite of a dense barrage by our artillery, the enemy rifle and machine-gun fire was at first heavy, though mostly over our heads; enemy shell-fire, once the advance started, was negligible. As soon as we had covered the wide No Man's Land we found that the enemy was manning short lengths of deep trenches, mutually supporting each other, and that there was little or no wire. The trenches were very difficult to locate in the echoing mist, even from a few yards' distance, and the attack became a mixture of hide-and-seek with blind-man's-buff. Any attempts at orderly progress were made more difficult by the appearance of units from other formations which had lost their way in the fog, and casualties became heavy during this period.

AUGUST 1918

When it appeared to Captain Reckitt, from slackening in the enemy's fire and from a feeling that he was looking downhill, that he had reached his objective, he halted as many of D and C Companies as he could find and discovered that he was in touch with the 9th Royal Fusiliers on his left. The right was still open. Touch was later obtained with A and B Companies, a complete reorganisation was made, and patrols were pushed out, preparatory to a further advance when the mist should lift. The company runners experienced much difficulty in finding Battalion H.Q. over strange ground in the fog. Many men, temporarily reported missing, had got carried on with other units and rejoined later. Lieutenant R. F. Clements, for instance, with 14 Platoon, had got involved with the 58th Division and took part in the assault on Malard Wood, only rejoining late in the afternoon.

The position at this juncture is thus described in *The Story of the Fourth Army**: " As was to be anticipated, uncertainty of the position on the front of the 18th Division at Zero made the advance of the 36th Brigade more difficult, and, at the moment when it should have been on the first objective, the situation was obscure and caused some anxiety. By 9 a.m., however, the position had been made good, partly by the troops originally detailed for the task, and partly by the 53rd Brigade moving up on its way to the second objective."

About 10 a.m. the mist lifted and revealed the fact that the battalion was short, and rather to the right, of its objectives. A and B Companies, therefore, prepared to move forward to the green line, but as there was still a gap between us and the 58th Division, and as the 53rd Brigade had just been

---

* By General Sir A. Montgomery-Massingberd, at p. 48.

forced back by a strong counter-attack from Gressaire Wood, they were ordered to occupy a line, short of their objective, in the valley beyond the Sailly-Laurette-Morlancourt Road, and the reserve battalion of the Brigade, the 5th Royal Berks, passed through us to occupy the green line. Meanwhile, C and D Companies were distributed in depth as a reserve in the short lengths of captured trenches.

AUGUST 1918

The day passed quietly after this, and at 9.30 p.m. A and B Companies relieved the 5th Royal Berks in the front line, while C and D Companies took over the positions vacated by A and B.

The morning of the 9th was uneventful, and in the late afternoon units of the 58th Division, with cavalry and tanks, passed through us to renew the attack. There was slight shelling, during which 2nd Lieutenant S. Lotham was wounded, and Company Sergeant-Major E. N. Venn, of C Company, one of the battalion's original N.C.O.s, was killed. We then moved back to shelters in Marett Wood near Méricourt, where we arrived about 10 p.m. We expected, and needed, a good night's rest, but at midnight we were on the move again to occupy positions in the old British and German lines just west of Morlancourt. We were now in reserve to (and under the orders of) the 37th Brigade, and so were back with our own Division again.

The 10th was spent quietly in rest and reorganisation after our considerable casualties, until sudden orders were received that we were to relieve elements of the 9th Essex (also attached to the 37th Brigade) and 6th Buffs in the front line of the old Amiens defences beyond Morlancourt and west of Hill 105.

The situation was difficult, because no one seemed to have much idea where the line actually was, but eventually we were led to a point near the front line by Lieutenant-Colonel A. S. Smeltzer, the Commanding Officer of the Buffs.

The conditions in which this relief took place were most unnerving. The companies were forced to stand about in the open for long periods during an intense bombardment, while those responsible for leading them were trying to get information where to go. Uncertainty is the mother of apprehension, and it says much for the men that they endured those nightmare hours of confusion with that stolid courage which had already brought them through so much. To make matters worse, there seemed at one time every chance that the battalion would be caught in the open in daylight; as it was, the relief was not complete until 5.30 a.m., so that the last companies were not in position until day was breaking, while some posts of the units we relieved could not venture out of the line until the following evening.

AUGUST 1918

There had been no time for a proper handing over of the positions, so much of the next day (the 11th) was spent in finding out where the enemy and neighbouring troops were. The enemy was located in trenches on the east side of Hill 105. The 5th Royal Berks was on our right and the 9th Royal Fusiliers on our left, and we extended our front so as to gain touch with these battalions.

The III Corps was anxious that the enemy's position on Hill 105 should be captured as soon as possible, as it was a hindrance to the preparations for a further advance. The officers of the Corps Staff were, as always during the whole advance, most helpful and reasonable, and some of them were daily up in the front line, prepared to listen to suggestions as well as to make them. We suggested that the position could be taken by strong patrols, without a set-piece attack, and two attempts were made, one by day and one by night. These attempts failed, however, for the day patrol was spotted at once from some distance away on the left flank, and the night patrol was seen as soon as it got over the crest of the hill.

Accordingly an attack was arranged for the morning of the 13th at 4.55 a.m., the orders for which were given orally to company commanders. It was made by one platoon of A Company on the right, operating along a trench which led into the enemy position; D and C Companies, from right to left, attacked over the open in two lines each, with the 9th Royal Fusiliers on their left. The remaining three platoons of A Company, and the whole of B Company, moved up to the vacated front line and acted as a reserve. Captain Reckitt was in charge of the attack, Lieutenant B. H. C. Clark led A Company; Captain R. M. Howe, 2nd Lieutenant W. T. Trowell, and Lieutenant R. F. Clements were the only officers left with B, C and D Companies respectively. The attacking troops assembled in front of the trenches before Zero, and advanced as soon as the barrage started.

Owing to the impossibility of any proper registration by the artillery the barrage was very uneven, and as soon as the men rose to their feet C Company was overwhelmed by a rain of our own shells. Its only officer, 2nd Lieutenant Trowell, was wounded,

The Battle of Amiens

and the company was for a time seriously disorganised. On the right of the attack Lieutenant Clark led his platoon with a rush and quickly overcame the opposition for about 300 yards, capturing 12 prisoners and two machine-guns. The right of D Company reached the enemy's trench, but the other troops could not subdue the enemy's resistance after the barrage had passed ahead. The Germans were probably expecting the attack, for in a short time a counter-attack in considerable force was launched against the elements of A and D Companies in the captured trench, who were forced to retire to the original lines.

AUGUST 1918

The battalion was relieved that night by the 5th Royal Berks and went back to the old British lines west of Morlancourt, but not before Lieutenant Clements, who had shown great gallantry in all these operations, had been killed by a stray bullet.

The first phase of the Battle of Amiens was now over. In spite of our heavy casualties there was a general feeling of elation, for we realised that a great victory, moral and material, had been won. Our Corps had captured all its objectives from a determined and prepared enemy, Amiens was freed from bombardment, and the sensational rumours which had reached us of the exploits of the Australian and Canadian Corps were established as facts. The change since the harrowing days of March and April was striking, and it was obvious that the initiative now lay with the Allied forces.

From the 7th to the 13th August our casualties had been :—

	Officers	Other ranks
Killed	6	45
Died of wounds	—	12
Wounded	8	178
Totals	14	235

Officers killed : Lieutenants R. F. Clements (D) and P. S. Dixon (C); 2nd Lieutenants C. P. Burley (B), A. Murray (D), H. J. Palmer (A), and W. S. Roussell (B).

„ wounded : Lieutenants C. Clayton (O.C. C Company), S. J. Davis (B), and G. W. Prince, M.C. (O.C. A Company); 2nd Lieutenants S. Lotham (C), V. E. Rogers (C), J. L. Soutter (D), A. W. Swift (B), and W. T. Trowell (C).

N.C.O.s killed : Company Sergeant-Major E. N. Venn (C); Sergeants A. Ashenden (A), L. Dawson (A), H. T. Sayers (C), and A. E. Selby, M.M. (A); Corporals A. Mountstephens (A), T. W. Philcox (C), and E. Wise (D).

The Battle of Amiens

The officers who came through these operations were :—

Battalion H.Q. : Lieutenant-Colonel A. Thomson (awarded D.S.O.), Captain E. S. Ellis, Adjutant, and Lieutenant G. H. Hill, Assistant Adjutant.
A Company : Lieutenant B. H. C. Clark (awarded M.C.) and 2nd Lieutenant T. Forster.
B Company : Captain R. M. Howe (awarded M.C.).
C Company : Nil. (2nd Lieutenant S. Lotham awarded M.C.)
D Company : Captain G. L. Reckitt (awarded bar to M.C.),

Sergeants F. Ransom, M.M. (B), and A. Trevor, M.M. (D), were awarded the Distinguished Conduct Medal.*

The captures of the battalion during this period were one 77 m.m. gun, 11 machine-guns, 2 trench-mortars, and about 120 prisoners.

AUGUST 1918

On the 16th we were relieved by the 9th Essex and moved back to Méricourt. Reorganisation was difficult, for no drafts were received to replace our casualties. We took the opportunity of organising several very pleasant bathing-parties in the small stream which ran near the village. This caused some concern to the authorities and bathing was forbidden, but after urgent representations small parties were allowed to go down, much to everybody's joy, despite the risk of an occasional shell.

On the evening of the 20th we relieved the 6th Buffs on the outskirts of Morlancourt, and shortly afterwards received orders that the attack was to be renewed two days later, so as to conform to the movements of the Third Army, which was joining in with the advance north of Albert on the 21st.

The morning of the 21st was spent in reconnoitring our assembly positions, to which we began to move at 11 p.m. There was heavy gas-shelling from midnight onwards, and the battalion had to wear masks for a long time.

The objective of the 12th Division was the high ground east of the Bray-Albert Road. The 9th Royal Fusiliers led the attack

---

* For a variety of reasons the other honours awarded to the men of the battalion for these and the subsequent operations were not gazetted until 1919, mainly in two long lists. As the Battalion Recommendation Book has been destroyed, it has not been found possible, as hitherto, to apportion these honours to the various battles described in this and the following chapters. All awards, and the dates of their gazette, are to be found in Appendix D. See also pp. 267-8.

of our Brigade as far as the hill west of the Bray-Meault Road, after which we were to pass through and secure the ridge immediately east of the Bray-Albert Road, a total advance of nearly 5,000 yards. The 5th Royal Berks was detailed to capture Meault, and the 35th Brigade was operating on our right.
On the left, the 18th Division was attacking farther to the north.

As on the 8th August, there was to be no preliminary bombardment before zero hour at 4.45 a.m. Three heavy tanks were to co-operate with the battalion and a contact plane was to fly over three and a half hours after Zero. There was to be an especially heavy concentration of 6-inch howitzers on Meault and Becordel-Becourt.

The battalion advanced in two waves; B and D Companies, from right to left, were in front, with A and C Companies following. In spite of the earlier hostile bombardment, there was very little shelling when the attack actually started and not much resistance was encountered, although the advance was rendered difficult owing to the mist, which was made thicker by the smoke from the barrage. The thermite shells, which were being used by the artillery for direction purposes, were most valuable.

The 9th Royal Fusiliers advanced successfully according to plan, and we passed through to gain our objectives by 10 a.m. with slight casualties.

While we were waiting for the barrage to move forward before advancing to the final objectives one of our tanks actually passed through the standing barrage before its commander realised that he had gone too far. However, it returned quite safely and the commander descended from his chariot and proceeded to offer liquid refreshment to some of the officers. C Company then formed up in echelon, with the tank in the centre, and completed the advance quite comfortably, its escort occasionally firing off a three-pounder from pure light-heartedness.

This advance of nearly three miles was the nearest approach to open warfare we had so far experienced. Lieutenant A. J. Morris was the only officer casualty, although Battalion H.Q. had a very narrow escape, being sniped by a whizzbang battery when exposing themselves on the skyline, with the result that the Adjutant, Captain Ellis, was slightly wounded in the head by a splinter, but remained at duty.

Of the 60 prisoners captured by D Company, Sergeant Trevor secured 30 from a large dug-out in the sandpit by the side of the

Bray-Albert Road, which had evidently been a regimental headquarters. It was equipped with medical stores, clothing, wine and live pigeons, and the table was ready laid for somebody's breakfast. Fourteen prisoners and 2 machine-guns were also captured by C Company farther to the left.

AUGUST 1918

At 7 p.m. on the 23rd we received orders to continue the advance at 1 a.m. the next morning. From our battalion only B and D Companies were to take part, with the 37th Brigade on their right. They were to attack from the ridge south of Becordel-Becourt and to capture this village and the hill west of, and overlooking, the Fricourt cross-roads; touch was to be obtained with the 18th Division on the left.

From their assembly positions on the ridge the attacking companies had behind them a wonderful view of the guns firing the supporting barrage, while ahead could be seen burning dumps and villages and all sorts of enemy units on the move.

All objectives were attained with very little resistance; 26 prisoners and a night-signalling apparatus were captured. The 18th Division came up on the left, and patrols were pushed out to the valley in front.

At 2.30 a.m. on the 25th the 9th Royal Fusiliers, with our A Company in support, passed through our line and, without encountering any opposition, reached the ridge on the farther side of the Bray-Fricourt Road, a key position which dominated Fricourt, Mametz and the main Peronne Road, and was an essential stepping-stone to further operations. At 3.15 a.m. the remainder of the battalion moved forward to the neighbourhood of Fricourt, where A Company rejoined. The advance was now continued by the 35th Brigade against the Carnoy Ridge.

While we were at Fricourt we received sudden notice at 1 a.m. on the 26th that the Brigade would attack again that morning at 4.30. The G.O.C. Brigade arrived at 2 a.m., and shortly afterwards a conference of Commanding Officers was held at our Battalion H.Q., when oral orders were given that the attack was to be carried out through the positions reached by the 35th Brigade; the 5th Royal Berks was to be the right battalion and ourselves the left. There were three objectives: first, the ridge between Pommiers Redoubt and Carnoy; second, the Maricourt-Briqueterie Road; and third, Maltz Horn Farm Knoll, north of Hardecourt. Thus a change of direction in our advance was to be made from north-east to almost due east, which involved some rapid movement at short notice, especially as the front line was then about 2,000 yards beyond Fricourt. The battalion moved off at 3 a.m. to positions just east of Mametz.

Almost from the first strong opposition was encountered, and we were held up in the valley in front of the ridge by numbers of well-handled machine-guns. Remarkable examples of the Germans' ingenuity in siting their machine-guns were to be seen; on one slope two German machine-gunners in light order were later found dead beside their guns, and although they had a fine field of fire they themselves were invisible at 150 yards.

AUGUST 1918

As soon as daylight came it was almost impossible to make any movement without drawing furious machine-gun fire, which poured in from both flanks and held the advance up altogether at 9 a.m. Later on we made slow progress; portions of front trenches were captured and the men pushed along the communication trenches, but a nest of machine-guns on the Albert-Peronne light railway to our left front caused considerable trouble. On our right the 5th Royal Berks was held up in front of Carnoy.

The enemy started to withdraw from his forward positions at 3 p.m. and strong patrols followed him up until, by 5 p.m., we had occupied the first objective. The 9th Royal Fusiliers then passed through us to the second objective, coming under heavy machine-gun fire from the direction of Briqueterie. At nightfall the battalion advanced its position to a valley and ridge about 500 yards west of the Maricourt-Montauban Road.

Captain Howe writes:—" This was a most unpleasant day, and although I do not know whom we were up against I am sure they were some of the very best troops of the German Army. I never saw any of them, but their presence was most obvious until they withdrew."*

Captain S. A. Andrews, who had joined the battalion a fortnight before and was leading A Company in this attack, gives the following account of the day's operations:—

" Presumably this attack was decided on by the Higher Command at very short notice, and I think it illustrates how difficult it is for success to be obtained at such a stage in the operations when the units concerned have no clear knowledge of their objectives nor of the type of ground over which they are to advance, no opportunities of explaining anything to the men, and no proper artillery preparation or support.

---

* These troops were later identified as belonging to the *2nd Guard Division*, which had recently reinforced this part of the front.

The Battle of Amiens

August 1918

"Personally I had no real idea of our objective nor the slightest knowledge of the ground over which we were to advance, as the orders were received in the very early hours of the morning just as a thunderstorm was dying away. We were told that only a loose barrage would be employed, and our final objectives were given as about 3,500 yards from the starting positions. The company commanders had no time to explain matters to the platoon leaders, even if they had known anything themselves, for almost at once the battalion found itself moving along the road towards Mametz. Presently the column turned off to the right on to grass land and the companies were informed that the jumping-off place had been reached. Platoons were hastily strung out in battle order, and after a short wait the advance began. Our way led down into a valley and then rose sharply, and it was when we began the ascent that the trouble started. Machine-guns from front and flank opened up, and it was at this stage that the worst casualties occurred, including Lavender, who was killed immediately.

"We reached the crest and dislodged the occupants from the first line of a trench system which we discovered there, and then tried to carry the next line, but the machine-gun fire was deadly. Honeyman, who was in charge of one of the leading platoons, tried to take them on but was shot through the stomach, and several of his men also fell, so we had to take what cover we could and endeavour to work up the communication trenches. We succeeded in entering the next line and captured a machine-gun, but immediately became embroiled in a bombing affair, and owing to our own supply running short we had to get out again.

"We had nobody on either flank, and for a time the situation was very nasty, as the enemy endeavoured to work up from both sides, and on one occasion two sergeants and myself, who were exploring on our own, found ourselves faced across a low traverse by four Germans equipped with automatics and plenty of stick-bombs. As one of the sergeants had a German automatic which jammed, and the other a rifle which he had forgotten to reload, the situation was decidedly unpleasant, and after three or four hasty rounds from a very shaky Webley the party quickly retired under a hail of bombs, which by a miracle failed to do more than slightly wound one member of the party in the foot. Shortly afterwards we succeeded in disposing of several of our troublesome assailants, and when we had pushed forward a little farther the enemy retired."

The Battle of Amiens

During the action Captain O'Malley, the Medical Officer, gallantly attended several wounded who were lying out in the open under heavy machine-gun fire. He was afterwards awarded the Distinguished Service Order for his gallantry.

Casualties in this engagement were heavy, and the totals from the 22nd to the 26th August were as follows:—

	Officers	Other ranks
Killed	1	25
Died of wounds	—	10
Wounded	5	75
Totals	6	110

Officer killed : 2nd Lieutenant H. R. Lavender (A).

Officers wounded : Lieutenant-Colonel A. L. Thomson; Lieutenants A. J. Morris (B) and G. A. Phipps (D); 2nd Lieutenants G. G. Honeyman (A) and T. S. Rowsell (D).

N.C.O.s killed : Sergeants E. V. Billing (A), A. Chevalier (A), H. J. Cruttenden (A), and F. J. Tooms, M.M. (A).

The following decorations were awarded* :—

Distinguished
Service Order : Captain G. P. O'Malley (United States Army Medical Corps, attached).

Bar to
Military Cross : Captain S. A. Andrews, M.C. (A).

Military Cross : Lieutenant V. C. Branson (A).

In the evening Major Bowlby took over the command of the battalion from Colonel Thomson, who had been slightly wounded and proceeded to the transport lines for two days.

The next day (the 27th) the 37th Brigade continued the advance and the battalion remained in its position in support. In the evening orders were issued for us to support the 9th Royal Fusiliers in an attack next morning. At 3.30 a.m. on the 28th the companies moved forward to trenches near the Maricourt-Briqueterie Road, and at 4.55 a.m. the Royal Fusiliers attacked, with the 35th Brigade on its left, the objective being a line from Hardecourt to Maltz Horn Farm. All objectives were gained with many prisoners, and we moved up in close support to the west of Favière Wood. The Royal Fusiliers continued to advance successfully, our A Company being attached to that battalion to help in the consolidation of the line east of the wood.

AUGUST 1918

---

* For other decorations awarded during this period see pp. 228 (note) and 267-8.

The Battle of Amiens

During the night the enemy fire slackened down, and at dawn it was found that he had withdrawn. The other brigades were sent in pursuit, while the 36th Brigade was relieved by a brigade of the 47th Division, and at 6 p.m. the battalion moved to the valley west of the Carnoy-Montauban Road, near where it had attacked on the 26th. Here the Transport rejoined us.

August 1918

The next two days were spent in rest and reorganisation, and some very happy " sing-songs " were arranged in the evenings as a result of the introduction of a concertina acquired by one of the cooks. By this time the battalion was badly in need of reinforcements, and on the 30th a draft of 13 officers and 253 other ranks arrived.

August had been a month of almost continuous movement and attack, during which the Division had advanced 15,000 yards, from Morlancourt to Leforest. After the attack on the 8th the battalion had become very weak both in officers and other ranks, but had never failed, except in the small local operation on the 13th, to carry out the task that had been allotted to it. The achievements of the past month are all the more notable when it is remembered that most of these operations took place over the old Somme battlefield, which had been churned up by two years' shelling and was a maze of abandoned trenches, craters and derelict belts of wire.

19. NURLU

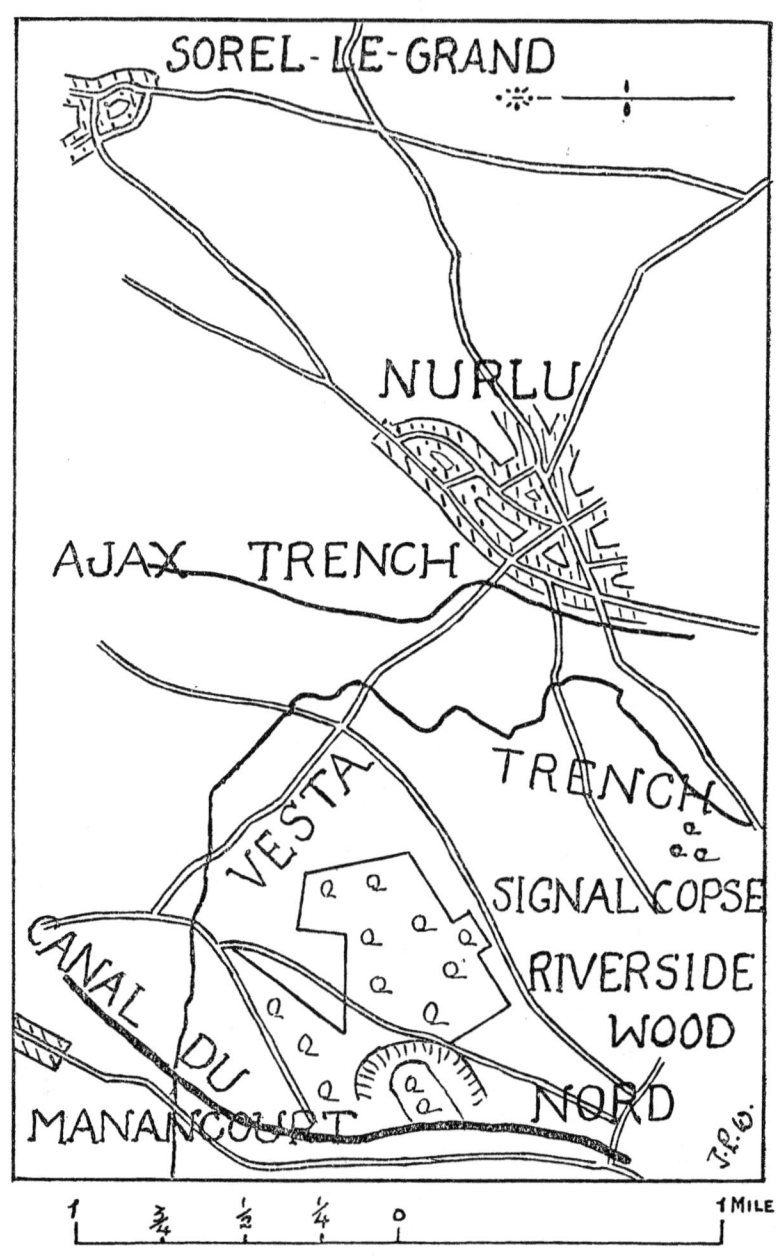

CHAPTER XIV
THE BREAKING OF THE HINDENBURG LINE.
1st September—30th September, 1918
[Sketch Maps, Nos. 19 and 20]

September opened with a warning for a fresh move forward in pursuit of the enemy, who was now withdrawing to his strong positions in the Hindenburg Line, and at 4 a.m. on the 2nd we set off and occupied some old trenches 2,000 yards east of Leforest.

Here we remained until the afternoon of the 4th, when we went forward to a position south-east of St. Pierre-Vaast Wood to relieve the 7th Queen's (18th Division). The wood was littered with dead horses, mostly gun teams. One team of six lay in their harness on their right sides, as if they had deliberately lain down in that position. The heavy shelling of the wood with gas forced us to make the latter part of our advance in masks, and it was not until 5.30 a.m. on the 5th that we were able to take over our new front line, which ran along the bank of the Canal du Nord, north of Moislains. While we were moving forward we received orders (at 3 a.m.) for an attack on Nurlu at 6.45 a.m., so that there was little or no time for previous reconnaissance. Indeed, to quote our Commanding Officer, " It was one of those hastily-organised operations for an early morning attack which had become so fashionable at this time."

The battalion was ordered to capture the Nurlu trench system, consisting of Ajax and Vesta trenches, and then to occupy the village. The 47th Division was on our right and the 35th Brigade on our left, and once Nurlu had been taken the 36th Brigade would be advanced guard with two troops of the Corps Cavalry.

A and B were the assaulting companies, with C in support and D in reserve. Very little progress could be made owing to incessant machine-gun fire. By 11 a.m. the 35th Brigade on our left was held up in front of Ajax Trench, while we had reached a line just east of Signal Copse, in touch with the 7th Norfolks on the left and the 141st Brigade (47th Division) on the right; but no further advance was possible. However, by 5 p.m. some of our men managed to filter through a gap and occupied parts of Vesta Trench in front of the brick works just west of the village, in touch with the 1/1st Cambridgeshires on the left. Here our progress was arrested by uncut wire and heavy machine-gun fire from the ridge. Nurlu was defended by the newly-arrived *6th Cavalry Division*, which put up a stout resistance.

[Marginal note: SEPTEMBER 1918]

Captain Andrews gives the following description of this attack :—

" As a preliminary the battalion had to cross the canal by a number of foot bridges which were under long range machine-gun fire. At the same time the Germans shelled the line of the canal with H.E., in which they had mixed some type of sneezing-gas that proved most unpleasant, especially as one had no warning of it until one had taken a good mouthful. Just prior to zero hour figures were observed moving on the crest to our right front and fire was opened by several of our Lewis guns. Later it was learnt that, owing to bad Staff work, the 47th Division had been ordered to attack at 5.45 a.m.—one hour before us—but we had received no notification of this and had actually fired on some of them ; fortunately, I believe, with no results, as it was at very long range.

" After crossing the canal we had to advance up a long grass-covered slope, quite devoid of cover as far as the crest, where a small copse marked our right flank ; it was here that we got in touch with the London Division and learnt about the difference in zero hour. All the way up the slope machine-gun bullets could be seen kicking up little dust clouds, but not a sign of the enemy until the first line reached the crest; then a perfect hail of bullets came from all along the front and the advance was completely held up.

" The Lewis guns in the front line engaged several German machine-guns, which were spotted by the faint smoke made by the guns in action, but there seemed dozens of them, very skilfully hidden from the front but with a splendid field of fire in enfilade."

As the result of pressure from Corps, orders were received for a further attack to be made at 7 p.m. the same evening, with a view to capturing Nurlu and occupying the trenches east of it, in conjunction with the 35th Brigade on the left and the 47th Division on the right. This second attack is thus described by Captain G. E. Thornton, who was then commanding a platoon of B Company :—

" At about 7 p.m. the attack was begun again. It was then pouring in torrents and orders were only received a very short time before Zero. The troops were strung out along the ridge and it was difficult to get things moving in time; it was also hard to keep direction and touch in the pouring rain and pitch darkness. We got to the outskirts of Nurlu, but were again held up by persistent machine-gun fire, and no further progress could be made."

2nd Lieutenant H. H. Mylius, who was with C Company in this attack, contributes the following details:—

"C Company advanced up the slope and lay in an extended line on the left of A and B, Captain Gorringe being on the extreme right of the company and myself in the centre, with two platoons on each side. After advancing over the ridge we proceeded some distance and were just beginning to hope the enemy had retired when machine-gun fire opened from the front and from the left flank, causing Gorringe and myself to dive into shell-holes and scattering the men, some of whom retired in haste to the safety of a bank where we had been earlier in the day. Luckily it was now dark and the machine-gun fire was rather high and wild, so we were able to advance by crawling through the mud. I was joined in my shell-hole by Private Pratt, whom I promoted to company runner, and with his assistance we proceeded to round up the company.

SEPTEMBER 1918

"Having got through the wire, we eventually gained the trenches, and after exploring some distance to right and left without finding any signs of occupation I decided the best thing to do was to collect the remainder of the company. This was done after two more trips back through the wire and by peering into shell-holes in the ground we had recently crossed. On the last trip we were nearly shot at by a very efficient sentry. We eventually got in touch with the Cambridgeshires on our left flank and to the rear.

"Before leaving we had a very welcome breakfast at about 2 a.m., and although it was a hasty meal it sent Pratt and myself back to the company much refreshed. Later we got in touch with B Company on our right, and the 5th Royal Berks, taking off from these trenches, completed the capture of Nurlu village.

"C Company was now withdrawn to occupy a small copse on the top of a ridge to the rear, and in this isolated position the company was commanded by myself, with Sergeant Richardson as the next in rank, and corporals or lance-corporals acting as platoon commanders."

The Breaking of the Hindenburg Line

During these two attacks on the 5th September the casualties had been :—

	Officers	Other ranks
Killed	2	7
Died of wounds	—	4
Wounded	3	60
Totals	5	71

Officers killed : Captain E. C. Gorringe, M.C. (O.C. C Company), and 2nd Lieutenant T. P. Ashby (C).
„ wounded : Lieutenants V. C. Branson, M.C. (A) and G. P. Mossop (C); 2nd Lieutenants H. R. Bennett (B) and W. E. Price (C).
N.C.O.s killed : Sergeants C. G. Burroughs (C) and W. L. Morley (C).

At 9.20 p.m. on the 5th, when it became evident that the battalion could make no further progress, the Divisional Commander ordered the attack to be resumed by the 5th Royal Berks, which relieved us early next morning, and occupied Nurlu soon after 10 a.m.

SEPTEMBER 1918

Later in the day the Brigade took up a line from the cemetery at Lieramont to Sorel Wood, with the 5th Royal Berks in the front line, the 9th Royal Fusiliers in support, and ourselves in reserve in trenches round Nurlu.

On the 8th the Division was relieved by the 58th Division, when Major-General Higginson issued the following order :—

" I wish to convey to all ranks of the 12th Division my high appreciation of the great services they have rendered during the past month, and of the gallantry and soldierly qualities they have shown in the many actions in which the Division has taken part. In the initial attack on the 8th August, as well as on several other occasions, the Division went into action at very short notice.

" The energy and determination shown by officers, warrant officers, N.C.O.s and men have on many occasions enabled us to overcome great difficulties and to gain a great victory over the enemy.

" Since the 8th August the Division has delivered no less than seventeen attacks and advanced a distance of seventeen miles.

" The captures amount to :—

Prisoners : Officers, 17 ; Other ranks, 1,010

who have passed through the divisional cage.

" In addition a large number captured by the Division have proceeded through other cages.

Guns, 17 ; Machine-guns, 194 ; Trench-mortars, 102.

20. EPEHY

The Breaking of the Hindenburg Line

"The present lull in operations is only temporary, and I have the utmost confidence that the Division will continue to show the same splendid fighting qualities in the future which it has done in the past. We have many hard battles still before us, but final victory is already assured. I request that commanding officers will ensure that my personal thanks are conveyed to all ranks under their command for the great services that they have rendered to our King and Empire."

SEPTEMBER 1918

We remained in the neighbourhood of Nurlu, spending our time in reorganisation and general training, for it was known that the Brigade would be wanted in the near future for another big attack. During this period we were reinforced by a large draft of officers and other ranks.

Since the beginning of the battle on the 8th August the Transport, as usual, had been doing magnificent work; it was continuously on the move, dumping by night, moving camp and horse lines by day, while great care had to be taken owing to the lack of water and the poisoned wells. A dummy camp, lit up at night, was erected about two miles behind the transport lines, and acted excellently as a decoy for the enemy aeroplanes, which were very active at this time.

The Germans were now, although not actually on the run, engaged in a deliberate strategic retirement; nevertheless, they were capable of putting up a tough fight when necessary, and having been gradually forced back from all their key positions in the old Somme battlefield to the line of the St. Quentin Canal, there was no doubt that they would offer a stubborn resistance of that line and of the bridge-heads that covered it. One of the strongest positions on this line was the village of Epehy, which the enemy had transformed into a miniature fortress with a number of keeps and strong-points, of which Fisher's Keep was perhaps the most formidable, covering all approaches. The surrounding country down to the line of the canal lent itself to defence, consisting as it did of various ridges protected by a network of trenches and strong-points, and intersected by valleys enfiladed by cunningly-placed machine-gun nests.

The capture of this outpost of the Hindenburg Line was to be our next task. Great secrecy was observed in the preparations for this operation, and special orders had been issued against patrols exposing themselves. The attack was ordered for the early morning of the 18th September, and at 10 p.m. on the 17th the battalion moved up to its assembly positions, about 1,000 yards south-west of Epehy, preparatory to an attack at dawn.

The task allotted to the Division was the capture of Epehy and the ridge running south-east of it, followed by a further advance of two miles. The first objective (the green line), which included Epehy and the ridge, started from Ridge Reserve, where touch would be obtained with the 18th Division on the right, and ran just east of Malassise Farm and Tétard Wood to Chestnut Avenue; this line was thus about 1,000 yards east of Epehy. The second objective (the red line) lay about 2,500 yards farther on and included Little Priel Farm and Kildare Post. The green line was to be taken by the 36th Brigade on the right (less the 5th Royal Berks, which was in reserve with the 37th Brigade) and the 35th Brigade on the left, after which the reserve troops of the Division would pass through to secure the red line.

SEPTEMBER 1918

In order that the 36th Brigade should not be enfiladed from Epehy when it advanced, the 35th Brigade, operating with two tanks and with the 58th Division on its left, was ordered to assault Epehy and Peizière at zero hour (5.20 a.m.), while the 36th Brigade stood fast. But, simultaneously with the advance of the 35th Brigade, each of the assaulting battalions of our Brigade —the 9th Royal Fusiliers on the right and ourselves on the left— was to send forward a company to clear the forward area as far as the main Cambrai-Epehy-Peronne Railway (to be called in future the C.E.P. Railway). The battalions would slowly follow up their forward companies so as to be formed up along the C.E.P. Railway ready to advance to the assault of the green line at 6.50 a.m., by which time it was thought that Epehy would have been cleared. This was, as it sounds, a complicated manoeuvre, for the preliminary movement of the 35th Brigade was in a north-easterly direction, while our Brigade was attacking south-eastwards.

The battalion was attacking on a frontage of 800 yards. About 300 yards beyond the C.E.P. Railway lay another railway line, the Vélu-Epehy-St. Quentin branch line (to be called in future the V.E.St.Q. Railway), with Prince Reserve Trench just behind it; east of that position a network of trenches formed the outer defences of Malassise Farm. A Company was to be our forward company and, after it had performed its first rôle, it was to continue as advanced guard as far as Prince Reserve, when the other companies were to go through to the green line.

The Breaking of the Hindenburg Line

We reached our assembly positions, some 800 yards behind the British front line, between 3 and 4 a.m., through a considerable amount of harassing fire, mainly from gas-shells. It was afterwards discovered from the interrogation of a prisoner that the enemy expected an attack on Epehy that morning and that he was deliberately keeping the forward areas under a concentrated gas bombardment. Heavy rain was falling, which continued during the morning and made the going very bad for infantry and tanks. The darkness of the drenching night was succeeded at early dawn by a thick mist, which made it impossible to pick up the few known landmarks and to keep direction at the beginning of our complicated evolutions.

A Company (whose movements will be described in more detail later) started off at zero hour from the right of the battalion's assembly positions and successfully cleared the area as far as the C.E.P. Railway without meeting much opposition. Reports were sent back and the company waited for the rest of the battalion to assemble.

But the other companies had not fared so well. A heavy smoke barrage put down by our artillery had added to the obscurity of the mist and the half-light of the pelting dawn, with the result that the three companies lost their direction during the long approach-march and bore too much to the left. At first all went well; the assaulting waves were close together and the enemy's fire was not troublesome. Suddenly the advance was stopped by thick belts of wire and it was obvious that something must be wrong, for no such obstacles had been shown on the map. At this moment intense machine-gun fire was opened from Epehy. The 35th Brigade had met with very strong resistance and had not yet been able to clear the village towards which our companies, owing to their loss of direction, were now approaching.

In spite of very heavy casualties from this enfilade fire the advance was restarted in the proper direction, but another mishap occurred almost at once. For one of the British tanks, which should have been operating in Epehy, had also lost its way and, appearing suddenly out of the mist, opened fire on our men. The crew soon realised the mistake and ceased fire, showing a tricolour flag to proclaim their identity. But much confusion had been caused, and it was some time before the battalion could be reformed.

However, the V.E.St.Q. Railway was reached by 8 a.m., although the harassing enfilade fire still persisted from the machine-guns in Epehy. By this time C and D Companies had no officers left and B Company only one, but the battalion established itself in Prince Reserve by 8.30 a.m. Our advance was continued to North Lane, north-west of Malassise Farm, and on our right the 9th Royal Fusiliers succeeded in capturing Deelish Post and part of Ridge Reserve, as well as the western outskirts of the farm. The farm itself was strongly defended, and the mass of wire-entanglements, old and new, which surrounded it made its capture extremely difficult, especially as any advance had to be made through the continuous flanking fire of the enemy machine-guns as well as against the defenders of the position. Epehy was still untaken and the enemy was also holding positions east of the village, such as those in Tétard Wood, which enfiladed our advance.

September 1918

Further progress was impossible to our shattered battalion, which had suffered over 200 casualties, including all the company officers except Captain Andrews (A) and 2nd Lieutenant Coxhead (B). So we decided to consolidate our gains on the objectives already attained, and as our left flank and left rear were open, a defensive flank was formed by the support company near the railway-crossing south of the village.

Epehy was finally cleared of the enemy at 7.45 p.m., when we at last had a respite from the deadly fire which had been causing so disastrous an execution in our ranks all day. At nightfall the battalion was holding, with two companies (A and D), a line from just south of South Lane to the point where Prince Reserve joined the V.E.St.Q. Railway, with posts in North Lane towards Malassise Farm. The other two companies (B and C) were in support near the level-crossing of the C.E.P. Railway.

The positions in and around Epehy had been stoutly defended by the German *Alpine Corps*, an unusually fine unit, organised as a division. Its infantry consisted of two *Jäger* regiments and one regiment of the *Royal Bavarian Infantry Body Guard* (*Das Königliche Bayerische Infanterie Leibregiment*), each with a machine-gun company. The *2nd Guard Division* was on its left, so that the opposition we encountered was as strong as it could be.

From the records of the *Alpine Corps* it would appear that the *1st Jäger Regiment* was in position about Epehy when the attack started and that the *Bavarian Body Guard Regiment* came into action east of the village during the afternoon. It is claimed that the corpses (of the British) were " piled so high that they had to be moved to allow a field of fire," but it is admitted that, by 8 a.m., " our defence was at a standstill and the English Command had not realised our defeat."

The *Jägers* were so badly cut up by the September 1918 attacks that they had to be withdrawn.

Captain Andrews gives the following account of A Company's fortunes that day :—

" A Company was detailed to move off at zero hour on the left of the 9th Royal Fusiliers and clear up as far as the railway crossing along the line of the C.E.P. Railway, where it was to halt until the remainder of the battalion arrived, and then, at Zero plus ninety minutes, the attack would be continued from this point, A Company continuing for about 400 yards, after which the other companies were to pass through and continue to the green line. The battalion assembly positions lay just outside Epehy, well to the left of A Company ; Epehy was to be dealt with by the 35th Brigade, which was attacking more or less across the line of our advance, nor was it expected that we should meet with any resistance until after the 35th Brigade had reached the railway crossing.

" We were guided to our assembly positions and waited in the rain and mist for the ' off,' while the officers and N.C.O.s checked up the various details of the advance. With the company were two splendid fellows, Lieutenant J. A. Wright (whose brother had just joined the battalion) and 2nd Lieutenant S. G. Huggett, and I believe that there was a third subaltern, but of this I am not certain.

" We started off at Zero with Wright in charge of the left leading platoon, and soon afterwards they ran into a German post. I was told by the N.C.O. who brought the platoon on that some of the enemy held up their hands and Wright took his men towards them without firing. Suddenly a number of shots were fired from the post at very close range, killing Wright and killing or wounding several of his men, but the remainder dealt with all the occupants there before the arrival of our supports.

" Beyond this, very little resistance was encountered, and in due course the company found itself at the railway crossing and squatted down to await the arrival of the rest of the battalion. At this time it was still rather misty and visibility was restricted to a fairly short distance, but Huggett and I realised that something had gone wrong, as heavy machine-gun fire could be heard on our left and slightly to the rear, while as Zero plus ninety minutes approached there was no sign of the rest of the battalion.

"What actually happened to the other companies I never clearly understood, but a sergeant who joined me later on in the day said that at the beginning everything went quite normally, and, in fact, the men were keeping rather close together in order to maintain touch. Suddenly a belt of wire was reached and the first wave had started to get through when a heavy fire was opened on them from the direction of the village, and the utter unexpectedness of this caused considerable disorder. All the company officers except one in the three companies were killed or wounded before they reached the railway.

SEPTEMBER 1918

"To the left the railway ran through a cutting, so we walked up that way in order to try and make touch with the 35th Brigade, which by that time should have met us there. Suddenly we encountered quite a number of them without any officers, running down the cutting and followed by sharp machine-gun fire. They were unable to give us any real information and appeared lost; we gathered that, owing to the mist, they had got too far north and had passed behind Epehy instead of through it. They also stated that they had suffered heavily from machine-gun fire. Shortly afterwards they returned up the cutting and the machine-gun fire sounded closer.

"By then it was time for our second advance, and as the battalion was still missing we decided that the only thing to do was to get on. Accordingly Huggett took over the leading platoon and I followed with the remainder, our idea being to get to our objectives, and we hoped by that time that the others would turn up. We left a small post at the crossing to explain and guide the battalion to our new position, which could just be seen.

"The mist was clearing by this time, and on our way from the railway line we were suddenly greeted with enfilade machine-gun fire and then a burst from the left rear. At the same time the leading platoon, which was just nearing its objectives, met a heavy fire from front and flank, but succeeded in reaching some trenches, while the supports took cover immediately in rear in a sunken track lined on one side with low bushes. Here we established ourselves and soon found it necessary to form a defensive flank, as we were fired on from both front, flank, and left rear, and our two Lewis guns found plenty of work to do. Poor Huggett was shot through the head while endeavouring to work his way through the rough trench system in front of Malassise Farm, but our other casualties were very light in view of our position.

"Some hours later a burst of firing heralded the arrival of Burdett, who, unaccompanied, had succeeded in mak'ng the journey from the railway to our position and gave us news of the terrible time which the battalion had gone through.

"It may be of interest to give the actual strength of the companies the day after the attack, copied from an official report rendered to Battalion H.Q., which shows how badly we had suffered.

SEPTEMBER 1918

	Officers	Other ranks
A Company	1 (Andrews)	87
B Company	1 (Coxhead)	37
C Company	0	23
D Company	1 (? Hill, sent up later from B.H.Q.)	50 "

Lieutenant H. J. R. Farrow, who was commanding C Company in these operations, gives the following account of the day :—

"The start on the morning of the 18th was far from encouraging, as we were shelled heavily while taking up our positions, which must have been nearly 800 yards behind our own front line. During this period we had about 6 casualties, including my Sergeant-Major ; we also had to put up with a very heavy downpour of rain throughout the night. We started off at Zero and were supposed to leave Epehy on our left, but unfortunately, owing to our smoke barrage and also to the mist, we made over rather too much to our left, and it was then that the enemy in Epehy spotted us. We were then easing over slowly to the right, so as to leave Epehy on our left, when suddenly a German tank (as we imagined) came along and for a few seconds gave us hell. I am afraid we scattered. However, almost immediately, those on the tank gave us the signal 'All O.K.,' but the damage had already been done, and Reading, who was commanding D Company, and myself did our best to collect our men together again ; it was just then I got a machine-gun bullet through my leg, and when reporting at Battalion H.Q. I remember Reading being carried in on a stretcher with a similar wound in his knee.

"I consider that it was a mistake for our assembly positions to have been so far behind our own front line. The misty morning and our own smoke barrage were our first enemies, and then being strafed for those few seconds by our own tank fairly put the lid on things. The weather conditions were appalling; I was absolutely soaked through when I reached the dressing-station, and, I must also say, really not sorry to have stopped that bullet."

Lieutenant J. H. B. Kenderdine, of C Company, adds the following narrative :—

"As regards the incident of our being fired on by one of our own tanks, I should say this occurred before 8 a.m., as the mist was very heavy at that time, and the tank in question had spotted a German machine-gun post in one of our old Nissen huts which had been left standing since the March retreat. The tank advanced on this hut, taking the complete hut away on the top of its caterpillars, and in the mist it then presented a most grotesque appearance and caused considerable consternation among our troops, who began to shout 'German Tank,' and were about to scatter when the hut toppled off the tank and then we could see it was one of our own.

"Lieutenant A. C. W. Uloth, who was commanding B Company, was wounded three times that morning before he finally gave in. I know this for a fact, as I personally bandaged him up the second time."

Captain E. S. Ellis gives the following details concerning the battle :—

"The reconnaissance work by Lieutenant S. L. Burdett (Assistant Adjutant) was an outstanding piece of work. Accompanied by a runner he worked along the railway in broad daylight and obtained a very good idea of our own and the enemy's dispositions. He was sniped at by machine-gunners and riflemen while going out and coming back, about a mile in all.

"One sometimes heard stories of German artillery observers remaining behind and keeping in touch with their batteries from within our lines, and I rather think this actually happened at Epehy, since our Transport was continually shelled with great accuracy after the Germans had lost the ridge, and search parties were sent out from two or three battalions to comb out the cellars of the village. A report was received that an artillery post had been found, and, whether or not this was true, the shelling of transport in dead ground ceased."

Captain Ellis also comments upon the excellence of the captured warrant officers of the *Alpine Corps* with whom he talked. They were old regular soldiers, fine big bearded men whose moral was untouched. Their influence among the young German private soldiers was most marked, and they showed none of the glad-to-be-out-of-it-at-any-price attitude which we had noted with other prisoners recently.

The following note by our Commanding Officer illustrates the wastage of officers at this time. "Practically all the officers were new to the battalion," he says, " and just after Nurlu we had a whole batch of officers, most of whom had been in the 11th, 12th and 13th Battalions; almost all of them became casualties by the end of the Epehy period. I remember that either the night after Epehy (18th September), or the next night, we got some more officer reinforcements, one officer, whose name I cannot remember, coming fresh from Sandhurst. I never saw him, for I was asleep when the rations came up, and the Adjutant sent him to a company at once. By daylight he had been killed. There was, I know, a certain amount of difficulty in identifying him, as no one was quite sure what he looked like."

SEPTEMBER 1918

We reorganised as well as we could during the night, and early next morning (the 19th) found that the enemy had retired some distance beyond Malassise Farm. This was reported to Brigade H.Q., and orders were received to hold the general line of Ridge Reserve Trench. Shortly before 11 a.m. the 37th Brigade passed through us and attacked towards Old Copse and Horse Post, while we continued to occupy Ridge Reserve Trench between Malassise Farm and Tétard Wood, being heavily shelled during the day. Room Trench, to our immediate front, was held by the enemy.

During the afternoon the 9th Royal Fusiliers was withdrawn for an attack on Kildare Post, but on a warning being received that a hostile counter-attack was imminent this operation was cancelled. The night passed quietly, however, and during the next day (the 20th) the battalion was reorganised as a two-company unit, A and D forming one company, B and C the other. In addition to the Colonel and Adjutant there were only 4 officers and about 200 other ranks.

About 9.30 p.m. the same evening orders were received for an attack, in conjunction with the 37th Brigade on the right and the 58th Division on the left, on the line Bird Trench-Mule Trench and then through this line to the final objective, Little Priel Farm-Cruciform Post-Cottesmore Trench.

These positions were very strongly held, and as Bird and Mule Trenches were situated near the farther end of the main ridge running north-west from Malassise Farm they completely commanded all frontal approaches, while on the left a valley ran parallel to the whole length of the ridge, finally branching north-west behind the position, which it separated from the next ridge, where Cottesmore Trench and the two strong-points, Cruciform Post and Little Priel Farm, stood. The whole valley was dominated by machine-guns, and the position was as formidable as any we had yet encountered.

SEPTEMBER 1918

The 9th Royal Fusiliers was to be the right battalion and ourselves the left. Zero hour was fixed at 5.40 a.m. on the 21st, and we reached our assembly positions in Ockenden Trench in good time. The enemy was putting down a crashing barrage, and the machine-gun fire was incessant; nevertheless, the advance progressed favourably enough at first. Towards 8 a.m., however, we were held up along Little Priel Cutting, just in front of Mule Trench, but small parties succeeded in working up this cutting towards Cruciform Post. Mule Trench had already been occupied both by the 9th Royal Fusiliers and ourselves, but the Fusiliers could not advance owing to machine-gun fire from Heythorp Post, although they attempted to do so at terrible cost. Owing to the configuration of the ground we got off far lighter.

By 3 p.m. the attack had died down without the farther objective being gained, our final position being along the line of Mule Trench, with parties still in Ockenden Trench and the trenches in front of it.

In this attack we lost 1 officer killed and 1 wounded (2nd Lieutenant B. Daunt and Lieutenant N. McCracken), and 40 other ranks killed and wounded.

At midnight the 5th Royal Berks passed through and continued the attack, eventually capturing Heythorp Post and Trench, as well as Little Priel Farm. During the next day (the 22nd) the battalion withdrew to Deelish Avenue, Ockenden and Room Trenches, and re-formed. The battalion remained in the same area all the 23rd as Brigade Support, and at nightfall a readjustment of the line took place, when two of our companies relieved the Royal Berks in the right front sector, which comprised Little Priel Farm, Cruciform Post and Cottesmore Trench as far as Catelet Copse.

At 11.30 a.m. on the 24th the enemy opened an intensive barrage on the whole front and under its cover counter-attacked with six or more companies, supported by low-flying planes. The attack was repulsed everywhere on the battalion front with heavy casualties, but the enemy succeeded in getting a footing in Dados Loop on our left, held by the 9th Royal Fusiliers, which made repeated attempts to regain the position, but in vain.

Little Priel Farm was first defended by one of the *Jäger* battalions of the *Alpine Corps*, and when it retired the *10th Company* of the *Bavarian Body Guard Regiment* took over the area. Early in the morning the *10th Company* reported that it could no longer hold on owing to the retirement of the *Jägers*; all its communications were under heavy fire and the whole of the *Alpine Corps* had to go back.

Two battalions of the *445th Regiment* SEPTEMBER 1918 (*232nd Division*), which had been sent up as reinforcements, tried to recapture Little Priel Farm. The *5th, 10th, 11th* and *12th Companies* and the machine-gun company of the *Bavarian Body Guard Regiment* also took part in this attack and managed to get into Dados Loop.

On the 25th the situation on our front was fairly quiet, and welcome news came through that we were to be relieved at nightfall by the 5th Northants. This relief was complete by 1.30 a.m. on the 26th, when the battalion took over some reserve trenches about Chestnut Avenue and Fir Support. On the evening of the 27th we took over again from the Northants in the front line, but, except for slight shelling, the next day passed without much incident, except the following, which is related by 2nd Lieutenant Mylius :—

"In the early hours of the morning of the 28th September the *Alpine Corps* made a determined raid on the 9th Essex (on our right flank) and drove some of them along our trench almost to C Company H.Q. dug-out. I was in the dug-out with Lieutenant G. A. Phipps at the time, when a body flung itself down into our presence with the information, 'The Jerries are coming along the trench.' We took no notice, thinking it was some form of 'wind-up,' but the news came again, this time reporting that the Germans were only two fire-bays away, so we went up to see, and discovered the report to be only too true. We had only a few batmen and runners, and by then a few of the Essex, to help stop them, but after some hectic bombing with Mills bombs, which were replied to with German ' eggs,' they were beaten back ; a sergeant in the Essex put in some extraordinary good work, and the enemy, I believe, left 16 dead and a machine-gun. Everyone then returned to their former posts and I visited the main portion of the company in the outpost trenches, to find that they had no idea that they had been almost surrounded."

SEPTEMBER 1918

On the 29th the 37th Brigade passed through us and renewed the attacks on Dados Loop, Swallow and Catelet Trenches, in conjunction with another big attack on our right by Australian and American Divisions, with the result that we came in for some heavy shelling, and several casualties were sustained.

Mylius recollects that " one crew of a stranded American tank caused a moment of excitement by appearing through the mist behind the left flank of one of my two platoons. These enthusiasts thought they had reached the German trenches, and my men thought the Germans had got behind them. The only thing that really saved a serious mishap was that neither could account for their opponents' uniforms. They had several wounded among them and I was able to send these back with some of my own men who were also bound for the dressing-station, and the tank was directed on its way."

Our casualties for this period (18th-24th September) were as follows :—

	Officers	Other ranks
Killed	6	56
Died of wounds	2	10
Wounded	10	184
Totals	18	250

Officers killed : Lieutenant J. A. Wright, M.C. (A) ; 2nd Lieutenants B. Daunt (D),* E. C. Ericson, M.M. (C), W. Howett (B), S. G. Huggett (A), and J. Mennie (B).

„ died of wounds : Lieutenant A. C. W. Uloth, M.C. (O.C. B Company) ; 2nd Lieutenant T. E. Lawrence (C).†

„ wounded : Lieutenants H. J. R. Farrow, M.C. (O.C. C Company), N. McCracken, M.C. (B)*, and F. W. Reading (O.C. D Company) ; 2nd Lieutenants W. T. Axell (D), H. Clemetts (D),‡ H. C. Goodwin (D), J. H. B. Kenderdine (C), A. J. Lyons (D), R. Stephen (B), and F. L. Wright (C).

* On the 21st, † on the 24th, ‡ on the 22nd ; the remaining officer casualties occurred on the 18th.

The Breaking of the Hindenburg Line

N.C.O.s killed : Sergeants G. Hardham (C) and H. P. Hygate (B); Corporal F. Newton (C).

„ died of wounds : Sergeant F. J. Ransom, D.C.M., M.M., Croix de Guerre (B) (one of the original 7th Battalion).

The following decorations were awarded* :—

Distinguished Service Order : Captain S. A. Andrews, M.C. (Officer Commanding, A).

Military Cross : Lieutenant S. L. Burdett (Assistant Adjutant) and 2nd Lieutenant L. G. Coxhead (B).

Bar to Distinguished Conduct Medal : Sergeant A. Trevor, D.C.M., M.M. (D).

Distinguished Conduct Medal : Sergeants E. J. Head (C) and C. West, M.M. (B).

We had now been through seven weeks of practically incessant fighting, and the original battalion that had gone into action on the 8th August had almost ceased to exist. More than 40 officers and 800 other ranks had become casualties —nearly twice its fighting strength. There was not a unit in the Division but had suffered equally. Since the 8th August the Division had advanced twenty-six miles and captured many prisoners, together with 22 guns, 320 machine-guns, and 72 trench-mortars ; but it had lost nearly 300 officers and 6,000 other ranks, so that if ever troops had earned a rest we had. Relief came on the 30th September, when we handed over to troops of the 18th Division and moved back to bivouacs near Guyencourt and Lieramont.

SEPTEMBER 1918

On leaving the III Corps and the Fourth Army the following messages were received :—

" It is with the greatest regret that I bid *au revoir* to the 12th Division.

" During the brief period the Division has been with the IIIrd Corps it has not only fought with gallantry and determination, but also with that spirit of mutual co-operation and comradeship which ensures success.

" I wish also to convey my personal thanks to General Higginson, the Staff, and all ranks of the 12th Division for their loyal support and for the manner in which they have always

---

* For other honours awarded, see pp. 228 (note) and 267-8.

'played up.' I trust that it may be my good fortune, at no distant date, to have the Division in my command again in further victorious operations.

(Signed) " R. BUTLER, *Lieutenant-General,*
" Commanding IIIrd Corps.

" 30th September, 1918."

" Orders have been received for the transfer of the 12th Division to another part of the battle front, and before it leaves the Fourth Army I desire to express to all ranks my appreciation of the prominent part it has played during the recent fighting and my admiration of its gallantry and fighting spirit.

SEPTEMBER 1918

" After two and a half months' strenuous operations and a great deal of heavy fighting the Division has maintained a really high standard of discipline and efficiency, of which all ranks may justly feel proud.

" Throughout the advance, and in spite of hard marching with few opportunities of rest, all ranks have invariably responded to the call of duty and have exhibited a degree of endurance and tenacity which has been admirable.

" A long list of successes, including Morlancourt, Carnoy, Maricourt, Hardecourt, Maurepas and Nurlu, culminating in the capture of the strongly-fortified village of Epehy, constitutes a record which has seldom been equalled, and I wish to convey to every officer, N.C.O. and man of the 12th Division my gratitude for the magnificent example they have set, and my warmest thanks for the invaluable services they have rendered.

" I wish all ranks every good fortune in the future, and trust that at some future time I may again find the 12th Division under my command.

(Signed) " H. RAWLINSON, *General,*
" Commanding Fourth Army.

" 2nd October, 1918."*

---

* Quoted from *The History of the 12th Division*, pp. 213-14.

CHAPTER XV

THE FINAL ADVANCE

1st October—11th November, 1918
[Sketch Maps, Nos. 21 and 22]

On the 1st October we embussed at Saulcourt, and passing through Peronne bivouacked in dug-outs for the night in Proyart Wood. The whole battalion having enjoyed baths next morning, we entrained at Chuignolles at 10 p.m. and reached Acq, near Mont St. Eloi, at midday on the 3rd. The village lay just behind the Vimy Ridge, and we were now in the VIII Corps of the First Army, operating in the Vimy sector. From Acq we marched to a camp at Bois de la Haie, and on the 4th reconnoitred the line in front of Vimy.

OCTOBER 1918

At 4 p.m. next day we moved by bus to the cross-roads west of Thélus, and marched from there to take over the line south-west of Méricourt from the 6th Shropshire Light Infantry (20th Division).

The Shropshires told us that the enemy was expected to retire at any moment. They had been trying to drive the German rearguards out of their positions and had succeeded in establishing a footing in the German outpost line at one point, but further progress had been stopped by machine-gun fire from concrete emplacements.

The forward position in the German line was held for twenty-four hours by each of our companies in rotation, starting with C and followed by B, A, and D. This trench lay some 500 yards in front of the British line and could be approached only at night along a route marked by a telephone wire. On the right a narrow block, near a concrete pill-box which served as Company H.Q., separated it from the line still held by the enemy, while on the left, towards Méricourt, the trench gradually died away. If the enemy had been aggressive it would have been a most difficult position to defend, but although he actively opposed any movement by our patrols he luckily showed no sign of taking any offensive action.

The Final Advance

On the 8th October, when D Company was in the forward trench, the persistent rumours of the German retirement crystallised into a definite report from the 8th Division on our right that the enemy had gone from his positions on that front. This information was received at 7.30 p.m., but it was not until 9 p.m. that the enemy evacuated his side of the block in the forward trench. Lieutenant R. S. Browning, who had been awaiting this movement, at once led a patrol of half-a-dozen men over the block and along the German front line for some seven or eight hundred yards on the heels of the departing enemy. Here the trench faded away, near the outskirts of Acheville, and a communication trench about 500 yards long led back to the German second line, Acheville Trench; another communication trench led into this trench from a point near the block.

OCTOBER 1918

Reports were sent back to Battalion H.Q. and D Company moved forward up the two communication trenches to occupy Acheville Trench without opposition. B Company was sent up from support and took over the left of the line, while D Company moved to the right, but attempts to advance farther down the communication trenches towards the German positions near the railway line north-west of Rouvroy were met by accurate fire from machine-guns and trench-mortars. As it was now daylight and the mass of wire-entanglements made an attack over the open impossible without proper preparation, the companies were ordered to consolidate a series of strong-points and to wait for other troops to come up on their flanks.

Although Acheville Trench had been occupied without fighting, it is probable that the enemy had not expected to be followed up so closely as he had been by Lieutenant Browning's daring patrol. Many large deep dug-outs were found in Acheville Trench, and two or three pill-boxes in the front line, already prepared for demolition with charges laid and fuses fixed; the removal of the latter was quickly performed by some of 16 Platoon's miners, whose experience of shot-firing was of great help. As the charges were not contact or delayed-action ones, it is most likely that the enemy had hoped to be able to destroy these dug-outs at his leisure after he had taken up his new position, but was prevented from doing so by the quick action of Lieutenant Browning and his men.

It was obvious that the enemy was withdrawing his guns, for there was no shell-fire during the 9th except in the evening, when some gas-shells fell on Acheville Trench just before the 5th Royal

21. COURCELLES

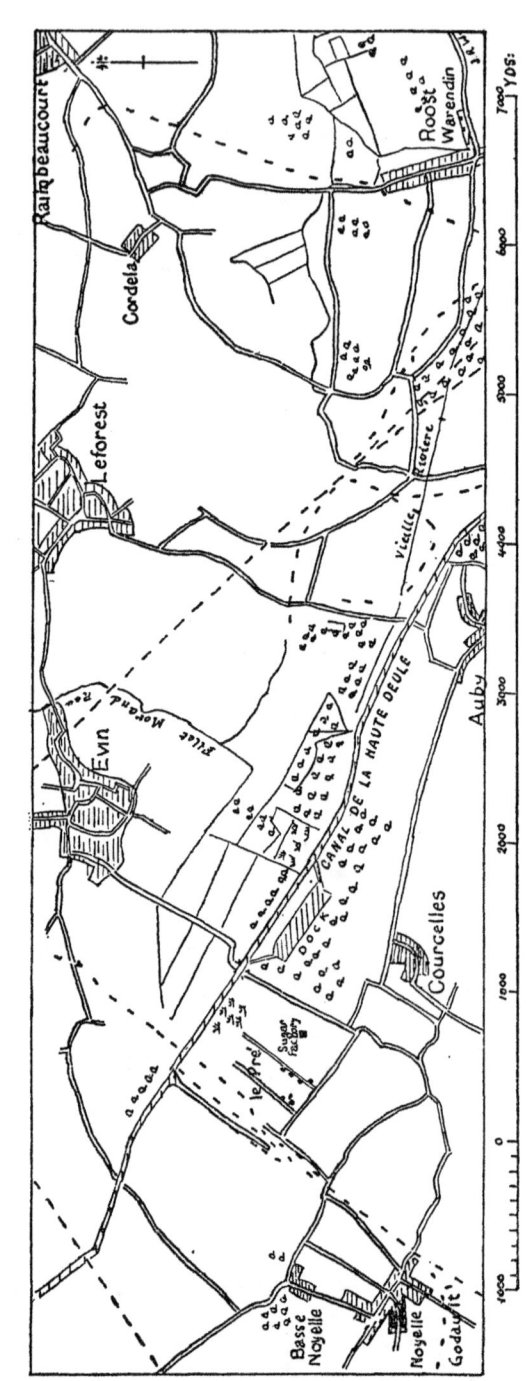

The Final Advance

Berks came up to relieve the forward companies. The battalion then concentrated in the old British front line as Brigade reserve.

The enemy continued his retirement, followed up by the 9th Royal Fusiliers and the 5th Royal Berks, who occupied the Drocourt-Queant line on the 11th, with patrols pushed forward into Henin-Liétard. The enemy was now withdrawing rapidly, and on the 12th we moved up, still in reserve, into the Drocourt-Queant line and Billy-Montigny. The whole countryside was littered with booby-traps, and perhaps the most ingenious of them was a knob at the top of a staircase in one of the billets which anyone would be likely to grasp as he turned on to the landing, the knob being connected to a mine. Probably the whole house would have been blown up had not the Royal Engineers visited the house and short-circuited this contrivance. As a precaution against such traps all ranks were warned against touching or tripping over telegraph wires; every house and every fitting had to be treated with suspicion.

OCTOBER 1918

The Royal Fusiliers continued the advance towards the Haute Deule Canal, where the enemy had destroyed all the bridges and held the farther bank in force, so that further progress was temporarily arrested. On the 13th the battalion came up from reserve and took over the front line from the Royal Fusiliers, with orders to force the crossing of the canal and to establish bridge-heads on the farther side.

The forward position taken over was right on the bank of the canal north-east of Courcelles and astride the road from this village to Evin. C Company held the right of our line with the 7th Norfolks on its right and B Company the left, in touch with the 58th Division, amongst the mine buildings and railway sidings of Le Pré. The support companies, D and A, were in trenches and cellars on the outskirts of Courcelles and Le Pré, with a joint Company H.Q. in Noyelle-Godault; Battalion H.Q. was in Basse Noyelle.

The Germans were in strong field positions on the other side of the wide canal and were obviously prepared to resist any attempt at crossing. The front line was generally quiet, but any movement in daylight was met with heavy machine-gun and

The Final Advance

trench-mortar fire from ingeniously concealed emplacements; this greatly hindered the reconnaissance of the forward positions with a view to effecting a crossing. The shelling of the villages behind was violent and persistent.

On the evening of the 15th D and A Companies relieved C and B, and on the following day we received orders to cross the canal early in the morning of the 17th.

A floating bridge, consisting of trench-boards lashed to slabs of cork, had been constructed behind the line by the 69th Field Company, Royal Engineers. This bridge was to be brought up by a carrying-party from C Company during the night to the right of D Company's position, where a dock standing back from the main canal provided a suitable place for the bridge to be put together by the Royal Engineers, preparatory to it being pushed into position near the broken bridge on the Courcelles-Evin Road. As soon as it had been adjusted to reach across the canal, D Company was to cross and establish a bridge-head with two platoons, pushing the other two platoons on ahead to the main Douai-Lille Railway 2,000 yards away. A Company, now commanded by Lieutenant Browning, was to be in close support and ready to move when D reported all clear or required assistance. A and D Company H.Q.s were moved up to the Sugar Factory just behind the front line. The other two companies would be in reserve, while the 58th Division on our left was also attempting a crossing. D Company arranged for covering fire from houses in flanking positions on the canal bank, but only in case the enemy opened fire. The operation, timed for 1 a.m., was to be a silent one with no artillery support, and the element of surprise was to be relied upon for success.

OCTOBER 1918

The night was one of impenetrable blackness and, since movement in daylight had to be restricted, no one knew the ground very well. During the early part of the evening there had been unusual hostile rifle and machine-gun activity, and it was perhaps fortunate that several unforeseen incidents caused a postponement. The first was that C Company's carrying-party lost its way and reached the front line some time after the hour fixed for the operation. The second was that the bridge, when it had finally been put together and launched across the canal, was found to be far too short, for it failed to reach the opposite bank by several yards.

Just before this the Germans had blown up some dumps close behind their line, and it seemed that they might be contemplating

THE FINAL ADVANCE

a retirement. Their front line was completely quiet, but it was not possible to tell whether they had evacuated their positions.

Some bad moments followed. Dawn was almost breaking and the platoons were all ready for the crossing; in the dead stillness even the smallest noise could be heard, so that at any minute we expected the enemy's machine-guns to open fire. There was therefore nothing for it but to haul the bridge back, lengthen it, and launch it again. By the time this was done it was apparent that either the enemy was nowhere in the vicinity or else he had prepared an elaborate trap. It was not long before we discovered that he had definitely gone, and about 6.30 a.m. D Company crossed without opposition and pushed on patrols towards the Douai-Lille Railway without a shot being fired. A slight diversion in the serious task of pursuing the enemy was caused by D Company H.Q. staff hilariously pushing along the officers' kit and mess stores in a broken-down bassinet, which provoked a red-tabbed rebuke.

OCTOBER 1918

A Company soon followed over the canal, and the two companies, advancing in a north-easterly direction, had made good the line of the railway by 9 a.m. There they halted and sent out patrols, which went long distances without gaining contact with the enemy. The 58th Division came up on the left, but on the right the 35th Brigade remained in its original position.

About midday orders were received that the battalion was to occupy Raimbeaucourt, which lay to the east of the line already gained. D Company, therefore, acting as advanced guard, with A and C as main body, turned half-right along the railway line and, after passing through the southern outskirts of Leforest, crossed a large open plain dominated by two slag-heaps without encountering any opposition.

When the company reached Cordela, a hamlet on the western outskirts of Raimbeaucourt, it at first appeared entirely deserted, but presently one bold head appeared, followed by others, until all the inhabitants, convincing themselves at last that we were British troops (whom they had never seen before), proceeded to make enthusiastic demonstrations of welcome. The troops of the leading sections soon found themselves decked with flowers and embraced by all and sundry. The Officer Commanding D Company in particular seemed to come in for a heavy and accurate fire of kisses from by no means attractive females.

The inhabitants of Raimbeaucourt reported the village clear of the enemy, but said that he was not far away, so D Company established an outpost line, which was later on relieved by C and B Companies. Other troops soon filled the village and the people gave them a cheery reception, which the arrival of a few enemy shells did not damp. Thus ended a highly satisfactory day's work, the chief factor of which had been luck.

On the 18th we were relieved by the 9th Royal Fusiliers and passed into Brigade Reserve, remaining at Raimbeaucourt for another night, after which we moved to Le Bourgage. On the 20th we marched to Orchies, where another and even more affectionate demonstration awaited us. This comparatively large town had received very severe treatment from the Germans in 1914 and had been almost completely destroyed, so the story went, as a punishment for refusing to supply the Germans with what they demanded.

OCTOBER 1918

The Colonel and the Adjutant, who were riding in front of the column, received a message from a member of the Divisional Staff saying that since we were among the first troops to enter the town the G.O.C. thought we should play " The Marseillaise " as we marched in. This we did, and the results were more moving than any one could have imagined.

There was an immense *Place* in the town, and as we approached it the band struck up the inspiring air. In a few moments an enormous crowd had surrounded the band and ourselves, and the children (who in spite of the German occupation had been taught their national anthem) joined in, but most of the older people were too overcome with emotion to do more than wave.

No one who was there that day is likely to forget the scene: the great square, gay with flags (the Union Jack as well as the French Tricolour) which had been hung in welcome; the church bells pealing; the marching troops, merry and elated by their victorious advance; the throng of civilians crowding to greet the soldiers and pressing coffee upon them—more coffee than they could ever drink; and, above all other sounds, the rousing strains of "The Marseillaise," which to those good people heralded the end of four years' German domination. That day meant even more to them than it meant to us. They were free again. It was no wonder that they wept for joy.

As Major Osborne, Captain Eliis and Captain O'Malley dismounted they were surrounded by damsels and soundly

22. CHÂTEAU L'ABBAYE

The Final Advance

embraced, and that evening, as the Commanding Officer was sitting down to dinner, the owner of the house appeared and made a ceremonious speech of welcome.

On the 21st we marched to Landas, which we left at midnight, when the 36th Brigade was ordered to lead the attack. The advance had now become an open warfare operation as practised on Laffan's Plain or other training grounds.

The leading battalion of the Brigade, the 9th Royal Fusiliers, advanced with the recognised vanguards and main guards, while our battalion and the Berkshires moved forward in column of route with drums beating. A sharp look-out had always to be kept by the leading troops for the screen of very efficient machine-gunners left behind by the enemy. Our march took us through Rumegies, which was on the borders of Belgium, and afterwards the road passed for about a mile through that country which, strangely enough, we had not revisited since leaving Le Touquet in July, 1915.

OCTOBER 1918

During this advance we saw much evidence of the attempts made by the enemy to delay the pursuit. Bridges had been blown up and roads in many places destroyed by mines, some of which had delayed-action, so that all cross-roads (where such traps were most commonly found) were treated with great suspicion. Hostile resistance was now stiffening, and during the morning (the 22nd) the Royal Fusiliers was held up in front of Fort de Maulde. The battalion still remained in support and moved to Rue Lasson, near Lecelles.

The next day Mont de la Justice and Fort de Maulde were reported to be held by the enemy, and the battalion was ordered to move to Nivelle and to send a company across the canal. B Company accordingly crossed, followed by C, and a line was established north of Mairie de Nivelle, whilst A and D Companies remained in billets west of the canal, with Battalion H.Q. at Mont du Proy. Much machine-gun fire was encountered from the direction of Mont du Moulin, and Battalion H.Q. was heavily shelled and forced to move. During the night further posts were established across the canal, while Mont du Moulin and Locron and La Motte Farms were barraged by our artillery. We obtained touch with the 6th Buffs on the right, but any further advance was held up by machine-gun fire from the north end of Buridon, the enemy's main position being apparently along the Château l'Abbaye-Buridon Road. About 2 p.m. on the 24th some of our men occupied Mont du Moulin, and later on in the evening an attempt

The Final Advance

to make good a line above Château l'Abbaye was frustrated by the enemy, who held the houses there with machine-guns.

OCTOBER 1918

It was evidently the intention of the enemy to hold up our advance on this line, and he had taken the precaution of flooding the surrounding country (a task made easy by the number of canals and streams which intersected the neighbourhood), so that all movement was confined to the roads, which he covered by machine-gun fire.

The next morning (the 25th) the enemy was still holding Mont de la Justice, and we again received orders to clear Château l'Abbaye. An attempt was made at 5.10 p.m., when B and C Companies reached La Motte Farm, but could make no further progress. There were, however, certain indications that the enemy would continue his rearward movement, and at length Mont de la Justice was found unoccupied by the 9th Royal Fusiliers and garrisoned with a platoon on the morning of the 26th. Thus a formidable position fell into our hands, but further progress on the battalion front was held up by the machine-guns in Château l'Abbaye. In spite of this the Higher Command impatiently advocated a continuation of the advance, which was impossible unless severe casualties were to be suffered.

Captain Ellis thus describes the situation as it was on the morning of the 26th :—

" It was one of those typical shows one came in for so often just before the Armistice. Divisional H.Q. insisted that the Germans had retired on our front; we knew they had not, and reported accordingly, saying that to press on haphazard would involve heavy and unnecessary casualties. We were then told we must be more alive in establishing touch. Accordingly I, Lieutenant Browning (commanding A Company) and another officer started off in the fog about 7 a.m. and walked along the road which ran from our line in the direction of the village. We got half-way and were beginning to think that Divisional H.Q. might be right after all, when the fog started to lift, and almost at once a machine-gun opened up on us from a position to the side and a little behind us. The gunners must have failed to see us in the fog as we approached their line. Unfortunately both sides of the road were flooded, so we could only run straight past the machine-gun, which, luckily for us, was as much as 200 yards away. The shots (of which about the first went through the fleshy part of my leg, but only added to my speed) splashed up the water all around us. We had about 80 yards to go to gain cover and about 250 yards to our line, but had no further casualties. Before being evacuated I reported that an advance was undesirable owing to the flooded nature of the country."

A and C Companies made further attempts to advance during the day, but owing to unlocated machine-guns sweeping the only two approaches which had not been flooded, they were not successful. At 7.15 p.m. we received further orders that the Château l'Abbaye area must be definitely cleared by the battalion at 2.30 a.m. next morning.

OCTOBER 1918

These orders were not very cheering after the unfortunate experiences of the other companies, but this small operation, which was entrusted to D Company, proved to be the last attack in which the battalion was involved, and it luckily ended successfully. D Company was given exactly the same task as A and C Companies had had, but was promised the assistance of a barrage and darkness. There was not a great amount of supporting artillery behind us, and the enemy machine-guns remained unlocated. The approaches to the village consisted solely of two exposed tracks which ran to either end of the village; all else was flooded and intersected by deep ditches, concealed by the water.

Captain Reckitt ordered Lieutenant S. C. Thomas to lead 14 and 15 Platoons, in file with sections at intervals, along the right-hand road, and 2nd Lieutenant A. C. Shilston to proceed in the same manner along the left-hand road with 13 Platoon. 2nd Lieutenant H. H. Mylius, with 16 Platoon, was to try to find a way along on the extreme left, between the Scarpe and the Traitoire Rivers, where the map and the ground suggested that the banks of some dykes might possibly bring him out in a position to outflank the village from the north-west. Company H.Q. was to remain at La Motte Farm, which was the starting point of the attack.

An hour or two before Zero explosions were heard behind the German lines, and we began to hope that the enemy had again saved us much trouble by retiring from a position which was impregnable from the direction of our attack, as he had done from the Haute Deule Canal ten days previously.

These hopes were soon realised. At 2.30 a.m. the platoons set off while a thin field-gun barrage played on Château l'Abbaye, to which not a shot was fired in reply. By 3.30 a.m. messages came back that the village had been reached without opposition. There was a very thick mist after dawn, and so it took some time

The Final Advance

OCTOBER 1918

to put 14 and 15 Platoons in position as garrison for the village, to send 13 off to the left to try and capture the bridge over the River Escaut at Le Fort, and to collect 16 Platoon (whose route had not proved practicable) to assist 13 Platoon. By 7 a.m. all the ground west of the River Escaut was clear of the enemy, who blew up the bridge on the approach of our troops. Touch was obtained with the 9th Royal Fusiliers in the Zinc Works and with the 37th Brigade on the right. The line finally ran through Château l'Abbaye and Château de Mortagne to Le Fort. The company sustained no casualties, but 2 prisoners were captured —not very thrilling captives these, for they were unarmed men who had been sent back for some stores which the Germans had forgotten when they retired.

The battalion was relieved at 10 p.m. by the 5th Royal Berks, by which time the flooded water was up to the main road, leaving only a narrow passage of retreat. This was the last occasion on which the battalion was in action.

Of the Transport's activities throughout this period Captain Hind writes :—

" Since coming north the Transport had been on the move the whole time and was badly handicapped by mined roads and felled trees, not to mention the booby-traps; all water had to be tested before we could allow the animals to drink or before we could use it for cooking purposes. We had several narrow escapes through cross-roads going up shortly after the ration column had passed over, and these demolitions made the return journeys very difficult in the dark."

Our casualties between the 23rd and 27th October had been 1 officer killed (2nd Lieutenant R. H. Bourne, A Company), 1 died of wounds (2nd Lieutenant J. Bradley, B Company). 2 officers wounded (Captain E. S. Ellis, Adjutant, and 2nd Lieutenant G. E. Thornton, B Company), and 30 other ranks killed and wounded.

On the 28th the whole Brigade was relieved by the 156th Brigade (52nd Division), the 7th Cameronians taking over from us, and we went to Vieux Condé, near St. Amand. On the following day we marched back to Montreuil, near Flines, and remained there until the 10th November.

The Final Advance

During this time there were rumours of an early Armistice and there was much speculation as to whether we should be sent into the line again before it came about, but on the 10th we moved back to Landas, and about 9 a.m. on the 11th came that fateful telegram:—

" Hostilities will cease at 11 hours."

The full entry in the Battalion War Diary for the 11th November, 1918, runs as follows :—

" Wire received that Armistice would commence 11 a.m. 11 a.m. Church Parade."

Other War Diaries may have been more eloquent, but that entry says really all that could be said at the time.

The Armistice was not unexpected, and after the long and expensive attacks since the 8th August it was more than welcome. The physique of the battalion was by no means good at this time. Our already much reduced rations had been still further lessened during the past month owing to the necessity which had arisen for feeding the French population in the regained territories. The inundations which the enemy had effected during his retreat had considerably increased our discomfort, and epidemics of influenza and bronchitis were becoming serious in the battalion.

NOVEMBER 1918

Stress must also be laid upon the difficulties with which we had to contend at this period, difficulties which, if the Armistice had not come when it did, would have necessitated a halt somewhere near the line then reached by the forward troops. There was no water transport and all railways and roads had to traverse an area about twenty miles wide which had been devastated by four years of war. The rapid repairs made were naturally not of a permanent nature, and no lorry of any considerable weight could cross the devastated area. Railway lines had been blown up and large dug-outs undermined the embankments. Constant breakdowns occurred. In fact, it is true to say that at no period during the whole war were rations and other necessities more scarce. If the war-correspondents of some of the more bloodthirsty newspapers had been living with us in those times we should not perhaps have heard so much about fighting our way to Berlin, nor should we have been told that the Armistice was premature.

" So far as I remember," writes Captain Reckitt, " a very feeble cheer greeted the news of the Armistice. The normal method of celebration of great events was denied us, for the battalion was, owing to the long and difficult lines of communications, entirely without any form of alcoholic refreshment except, I believe, for a small rum ration which was issued in the evening."

The whole Brigade attended the thanksgiving parade service, conducted by our Padre, the Reverend W. J. Williams, M.C. This was an impressive sight. The Brigade paraded at almost full strength and an old warrior of the campaign of 1870 stood strictly to attention in the centre of the square, holding aloft a large Tricolour. The parade was dismissed on the ground and the officers marched in close formation behind the old man to the mess of the 36th Field Ambulance, where " medical comforts " were provided and the toasts of the victorious Allies were drunk with great enthusiasm.

The men went back to billets, where the company commanders subsequently read out the preliminary scheme for demobilisation, planned some time previously. The basis of this scheme was, roughly, on the principle of " first in, first out," with a provision for the early release of " key " men.

The rest of the day was devoted to general rejoicing; but it was a calm rejoicing; its quality more that of relief than of hilarity, and in the field there were none of those extravagant festivities that were held in London, Paris, and New York. The war was over. Those who had won it were profoundly glad. But they accepted the Armistice as they had accepted the fortunes of battle, without undue excitement. They were just thankful to be finished with war, and that was all.

H.R.H. The Prince of Wales Presenting the King's Colour to the Battalion at Erre on the 4th February, 1919

CHAPTER XVI
AFTER THE ARMISTICE
11TH NOVEMBER, 1918—17TH JUNE, 1919

The days of training which followed the Armistice naturally seemed an anti-climax after all we had been through; but even though the war was won, idleness in the Army was still a crime, and it was necessary to find the men something to do.

Three platoons of B Company were sent on the 12th November to guard the mined area of Orchies and Flines, and did not return to us for some days, but the rest of the battalion remained at Landas until the 25th, when it moved to Hornaing, between Douai and Valenciennes, and this was destined to be its resting-place until the 12th March, 1919.

NOVEMBER 1918

The area being a mining one which had suffered during the German occupation, the billets were rather poor, but after various improvements had been made all ranks were soon fairly comfortable.

The officers took over an excellent mess which had been used for the same purpose by the enemy, and this was the first battalion mess we had enjoyed since March, 1917, when out of the line behind Arras.

Demobilisation was put in force almost immediately, and the first persons to leave us belonged entirely to such privileged classes as miners and students, while those less fortunate remained to spend their time in salvaging the surrounding country. The constant changes in the methods of demobilisation, all theoretically based upon the demands of industry and not at all upon the length of service of the individual man, led to much dissatisfaction amongst those who were left behind in France.

Employers apparently forgot the extravagant promises they had made to the men who had joined the army in 1914, and demanded the release of those who had only recently come to us. Many of the men of the original battalion, and many of those who had come to us from other Royal Sussex battalions, were employed in agriculture, which appeared to be disregarded by the Government, and very few allotments were given.

After the Armistice

NOVEMBER 1918

The vote-catching ruse of demobilising men when on leave during the period prior to the election of December, 1918, and the subsequent total stoppage of demobilisation, added to the general dissatisfaction. The mass of Coalition election literature showered upon the battalion, both newspapers and candidates' addresses, was staggering. The lack of similar Opposition literature was equally curious. One officer, for example, voted for an Opposition candidate, only to find about a fortnight later, on receiving his election address, that he was a " Pussyfoot " !

It cannot be said that the period after the Armistice was a happy one, nor that it was a fitting climax to the fine work done by the battalion since 1914. Parades dragged on in a perfunctory way, but it was hard to make them seem realistic to men who were not professional soldiers. For most of the early period the severe weather made games very uncomfortable, and the educational training which had been instituted was made almost inoperative by the lack of teachers, text-books, and materials.

In place of the dream of the 7th Royal Sussex marching home behind its drums and colours after its work was done, a triumphant array of happy comrades, there was the ugly reality of the gradual break up of the 7th Battalion and of all that it had meant to us. The dream was perhaps impossible of fulfilment, but it need not and should not have been beyond the imagination of our governors to devise some method of disbandment of the great citizen armies other than the disastrously erratic and unidealistic schemes which were employed. In those days England lost much that had been gained from dire tribulation ; much that can never be regained.

We spent a cheerful Christmas, however, and throughout this period a large part of each day was devoted to sport and to inter-company, battalion, and divisional competitions. Second Lieutenant Mylius was appointed Battalion Sports Officer and applied his energies especially to teaching the men to play Rugby football. His keenness brought him a reproof from the Higher Command, " not to touch any of the standing timber," but as he and his fellow-enthusiasts had already cut down the few trees needed for goal-posts no one was seriously alarmed.

Two excellent race meetings were held on a first-class race-course laid out by the 5th Northants, which the Officers' Mess attended in great style in a regimental drag, consisting of a field ambulance without a roof and a four-in-hand, to the accompaniment of Captain Reckitt blowing an improvised post-horn.

After the Armistice

On the 13th January, 1919, the King's Colour for the battalion was drawn from Somain by Lieutenant J. H. B. Kenderdine. The Colour was consecrated on the 4th February by the Rev. H. P. Berkeley, M.C., the Senior Chaplain of the Division, and was presented to the battalion by His Royal Highness the Prince of Wales, who addressed the battalions of the Brigade in these words :—

FEBRUARY 1919

" It gives me very great pleasure to be here to-day and to have the honour to present the King's Colours to the battalions before me.

" You were raised in August, 1914, and came out to France in the 12th Division in May, 1915.

" Since that date, in addition to much hard fighting in minor engagements and long periods of strenuous work in the trenches, you have taken a conspicuous part in the following battles :—

" Loos, Hohenzollern Craters, Somme 1916, Arras, Cambrai, Somme 1918, Epehy, and the German retreat to the Scheldt, which culminated in the final victory of our arms.

" I know full well that these Colours will always be honoured and cherished by you and that you will worthily uphold in the future, as you have always done in the past, the glorious traditions of the regiments to which you belong.

" These Colours are emblems of the heroic deeds which have been performed by your battalions. I now entrust them to you, confident that you will guard them as worthy successors of those gallant soldiers who have so gloriously fallen in the service of their King and Country."

During February and March the Gazettes were at last published which gave the names of those who had been awarded decorations during the heavy fighting from August onwards. These Gazettes announced the awards of 1 Distinguished Conduct Medal, besides those already given above, and 30 Military Medals, with 6 bars and 1 second bar. A subsequent Gazette in July contained a further 18 Military Medals and 1 bar.

MARCH 1919

These honours are all set out in Appendix D, where it will be seen that the name which appears most frequently is that of Private E. Highgate, one of B Company's stretcher-bearers, who in these Gazettes received the Distinguished Conduct Medal and 2 bars to the Military Medal he had won at the Battle of Arras.

After the Armistice

Too little has been said in our history of the amazing work of the battalion's stretcher-bearers, who distinguished themselves in every battle. There is no doubt that the consistent gallantry and efficiency of these men inspired and reassured all ranks of the battalion when in action. The lists contained the names of several other stretcher-bearers, of whom Private C. Emery, of A Company, received a bar to his Military Medal.

MARCH 1919

Bars to the Military Medal were also awarded to Sergeants P. W. Cornwell (C), J. Simmonds (B), and S. Buckman (A); and Privates P. Griston (A) and A. L. Groves (D).

On the 2nd March we sent a draft of 4 officers and 115 other ranks to the 1/4th Battalion, which formed part of the Army of Occupation on the Rhine. Other smaller drafts followed this one, and the remainder of the battalion was formed into one composite company.

Another sign of the ruins to which the battalion was being reduced was the removal of that veritable corner-stone of the whole fabric, Captain Clarke, who had been our Quartermaster continuously from the formation of the unit, except for a short period when he was wounded. He was awarded an O.B.E. for his invaluable services and left us to go to the 2nd Battalion, Captain Hind now combined the duties of Quartermaster with those of Transport Officer.

On the 12th a move was made to Villers-Campeau, where the battalion remained until it set out for England on the 7th June. On the 16th Major-General H. W. Higginson, C.B., D.S.O., left the Division to take up an appointment in the Army of Occupation. His farewell order of the day ran as follows:—

" On relinquishing command of the 12th Division I wish to express to all ranks of every unit and department my deep sense of gratitude for their unfailing support, loyalty and comradeship during the past eleven months, during which it has been my privilege to have the proud honour of being its commander.

" The months of May, June, and July, 1918, were ones of constant vigilance and hard work in the trenches owing to the expected renewal of the German offensive. During this period the Division distinguished itself in several successful raids which were on a considerable scale.

" On the 8th August, 1918, you attacked with the rest of the Fourth Army, and during a period of constant hard fighting and

After the Armistice

attacking almost daily you drove the enemy from position to position to Vendhuile, which you reached on the 30th September, a distance of twenty-six miles from your position on the 8th August.

"You were then transferred to the First Army and went into the line near Lens on the 6th October.

"The following day the enemy was in retreat in front of you, and you drove him back in daily encounters until you reached the line of the River Escaut, a distance of thirty-two miles from your starting line, on the 27th October, and were relieved there on the 29th.

"This is the record of the six months preceding the Armistice.

"Previous to this the Division played a prominent part in many famous battles. Its achievements at Loos, the Somme, Arras, and Cambrai were worthy of its best traditions.

MARCH 1919

"Between May, 1915, when the Division first landed in France, and the 11th November, 1918, the Division lost 2,105 officers and 46,038 other ranks in action. This testifies that your laurels have not been lightly earned and to the gallantry and devotion to duty shown by you who have survived the great ordeal, and by those brave comrades who have given their lives for our King and Country, and who by their sacrifice have won immortal fame.

"In a few weeks the Division will have ceased to exist, but wherever our fortunes may lead us in the future we shall all remember with pride the days when we fought in the 12th Division, and will retain the spirit of comradeship and loyalty to each other which has carried us to victory in this Great War.

"I wish you all good luck and God-speed."

The composite company, which had now shrunk into the Cadre of the battalion, left for England on the 7th June and embarked at Dunkirk on the 16th.

The officers who returned with it were:— JUNE 1919
Major G. F. Osborne, M.C., Commanding;
Captain G. H. Hill, Adjutant; Captain G. A. Phipps, Machine-Gun Officer; Captain R. C. D. Hind, M.C., Quartermaster.

On arrival at Chichester it was met by Lieutenant-Colonel F. W. B. Willett, D.S.O., the Officer Commanding the Depot, his Adjutant, the Mayor of Chichester and the Depot Band, and, after receiving a speech of welcome from the Mayor, to which Major Osborne responded, marched to the barracks, where it received a warm welcome.

After the Armistice

Thus, after nearly five years of life, the 7th (Service) Battalion of the Royal Sussex Regiment ceased to exist. Those who had served with it had seen war in all its phases; they had known its boredom, its excitements and its alarms; its stupidity; its filthiness; and (upon occasion) its compensating glory. They had found billets in scores of French and Flemish villages; they had laid down in bivouacs under the stars; they had been tenants of dug-outs—flimsy or bomb-proof, waterlogged or snug. They had marched and fought in blizzards and blazing sunshine; they had wallowed in mud; they had dug innumerable trenches; they had blessed the light of the full moon when holding the line, and cursed it when out with wiring-parties or patrols. They had written letters home by the thousand for others to censor; they had known that eager anticipation for the mail and the thrill of opening parcels; and had become familiar with the tragedy of the mince-pie that arrived crushed in the embrace of a melted cheese.

JUNE 1919

They had listened to the leisurely rustle of the 5.9 with its shattering crash, the sudden swiftness of the whizzbang, the whistle of the rifle-grenade, and the clamour of great bombardments. They had heard the dreaded gas-signal and had groped in masks; they had cowered in shell-holes and had given thanks for duds; and had looked out of their dug-outs a hundred times to ask the question, " Where did that one go ? "

They had laughed in the front line and grumbled in their work-filled rests; they had crossed No Man's Land in darkness together and together had advanced across open country in high daylight. They had known the bitterness of failure and the exaltation of success. And they had known, too often, what it meant to see their comrades crumple into huddled heaps of khaki by their side.

Flanders had seen their star and plume, and the Somme, and Arras, and Cambrai, and the Somme again. They had played their part in the great advance.

Throughout those years they had been something more than a mere unit in an Expeditionary Force, for together they had created a fellowship of their own which disbandment, and change, and the passing years cannot sweep away; since that which has been well and truly created can never wholly die. Something remains, and this record is its substance : for those who are here to read it, a remembrance of other days; and a tribute, in some measure, to the selfless courage of those who died.

APPENDICES

NOTE TO APPENDICES.

Memories are short and the surviving records of the battalion are scanty, so that it has been difficult to collect the details for these appendices.

The Compilers apologise for any omissions or inaccuracies, and hope that the general interest of the whole will be their justification for presenting the appendices in their necessarily imperfect form.

In order to save space certain abbreviations have been used throughout : k. in a., for killed in action ; d. of w., for died of wounds ; d., for died from natural causes, &c. ; w., for wounded ; acc., for accidentally ; attd., for attached ; demob., for demobilised, &c. Ranks have also been abbreviated : thus Col., Capt., Lt., Sgt., Cpl., and Pte. stand for Colonel, Captain, Lieutenant, Sergeant, Corporal, and Private.

The date given against any honour or promotion is the date of publication in the *London Gazette*, whenever that is known.

APPENDIX A.

DIARY OF MOVEMENTS IN FRANCE, 1915-1919.

1915

May	30th	Transport and M.G. Sections left Aldershot for France; embarked Southampton for Havre.
,,	31st	Remainder of Battalion left Aldershot for France; embarked Folkestone.
June	1st	Arrived Boulogne 1 a.m.; camp at Ostrohove.
,,	2nd	Entrained Pont de Briques, where Transport and M.G. Sections rejoined.
,,	3rd and 4th	Billets, Blendecques.
,,	5th	Bivouacs, Les Cinq Rues, near Hazebrouck.
,,	6th-9th	Billets, Steenwerck.
,,	10th-14th	Billets, Armentières; and instructional tours in trenches under 82nd Brigade.
,,	15th-24th	Billets, Steenwerck.
,,	25th and 26th	Billets, Pont de Nieppe.
,, / July	27th to 1st	Trenches, Le Touquet.
,,	2nd-5th	Billets, Le Bizet.
,,	6th-9th	Trenches, Le Touquet.
,,	10th-14th	Billets, Pont de Nieppe.
,, / Sept.	15th to 25th	Billets and trenches, Houplines. (Six days in and six days out, in rotation.)
,,	26th-27th	Billets, Armentières.
,,	28th	Billets, Busnettes.
,,	29th	Billets, Verquigneul.
,, / Oct.	30th to 6th	Trenches, Hulluch. (*Battle of Loos.*)
,,	7th-11th	Billets, Verquin.
,,	12-13th	Billets, Noyelles and Philosophe.
,,	14th-20th	Trenches, N. and S. of Hulluch Road. (*Action of Hohenzollern Redoubt.*)
,,	21st-24th	Billets, Fouquereuil.
,,	25th-27th	Billets, Annequin.
,,	28th-31st	Billets and reserve trenches between Vermelles and Noyelles.
Nov.	1st-11th	Front and reserve trenches, Hohenzollern Redoubt.
,,	12th-15th	Billets, Sailly Labourse.
,,	16th-17th	Billets, Bethune.
,, / Dec.	18th to 2nd	Rest, St. Hilaire.

Appendix A

1915

Dec.	3rd-9th	Billets, Hingette.
,,	10th-18th	Village line and trenches, Festubert.
,,	19th-22nd	Billets, Hingette.
,,	23rd-28th	Trenches and keeps, Givenchy.
,,	29th-30th	Billets, Le Quesnoy.
,,	31st to	
	1916	Billets, Hingette.
Jan.	3rd	
,,	4th-12th	Trenches and village line, Festubert.
,,	13th-15th	Billets, Bethune.
,,	16th to	Rest, Ham-en-Artois. (One night, 30th/31st Jan.;
Feb.	4th	manoeuvres at Blessy.)
,,	5th-10th	Rest, L'Ecleme.
,,	11th	Billets, Sailly Labourse.
,,	12th-20th	Trenches, Hohenzollern Redoubt.
,,	21st-27th	Billets, Fouquereuil.
,,	28th	Billets, Annequin.
,,	29th to	Trenches, Hohenzollern Redoubt. (*Battle of the*
March	4th	*Craters*.)
,,	5th	Billets, Annequin.
,,	6th	Billets, Fouquereuil.
,,	7th-10th	Billets, Sailly Labourse.
,,	11th-13th	Trenches, Quarries Sector.
,,	14th-16th	Billets, Noyelles and Vermelles.
,,	17th-26th	Front and support trenches, Quarries Sector.
,,	27th-29th	Billets, Annequin.
,,	30th to	Billets, Bethune.
April	2nd	
,,	3rd-16th	Front and reserve trenches, Hohenzollern Redoubt.
,,	17th-19th	Billets, Annequin.
,,	20th-21st	Billets, Bethune.
,,	22nd-23rd	Billets, Noyelles and Vermelles.
,,	24th and 25th	Trenches, Quarries Sector.
,,	26th	Billets, Annequin.
,,	27th to	Rest, Lapugnoy.
May	21st	
,,	22nd-26th	Manoeuvres, Estrée Blanche.
,,	27th-28th	Manoeuvres, Floringhem.
,,	29th to	Rest, Lapugnoy.
June	7th	
,,	8th-12th	Billets, Bully Grenay and Maroc.
,,	13th-15th	Billets, Drouvin and Vaudricourt.
,,	16th-26th	Billets, Vignacourt.
,,	27th-29th	Billets, Flesselles.
,,	30th	Billets, Fréchencourt.
July	1st-2nd	Bivouacs, Baizieux Wood; and Albert-Bouzincourt reserve line. (*Battle of the Somme, 1916; Albert*.)
,,	3rd	Trenches, Albert Railway Cutting. (*Ditto*)
,,	4th-6th	Reserve trenches, Albert-Bouzincourt line. (*Ditto*)

Appendix A

	1916	
July	7th-8th	Trenches, Ovillers. (*Battle of the Somme, 1916; Albert.*)
,,	8th	Bivouacs, near Albert. (*Ditto*)
,,	9th	Billets, Senlis. (*Ditto*)
,,	10th	Billets, Forceville. (*Ditto*)
,,	11th-13th	Billets, Bus-les-Artois.
,,	14th-15th	Bivouacs, Sailly-au-Bois. (*Reserve for Battle of the Somme, 1916, Bazentin Ridge.*)
,,	16th-19th	Camp, Bus Wood.
,,	20th-23rd	Billets, Mailly-Maillet.
,,	24th-25th	Camp, Bois du Warnimont.
,,	26th	Billets, Hédauville.
,,	27th-29th	Support trenches, La Boisselle. (*Battle of the Somme, 1916; Pozières Ridge.*)
July Aug.	30th to 5th	Trenches, Pozières. (*Battle of the Somme, 1916; Pozières Ridge.*)
,,	6th-7th	Reserve trenches, Albert.
,,	8th-10th	Reserve trenches, Bouzincourt.
,,	11th	Billets, Varennes.
,,	12th-14th	Billets, Puchevillers.
,,	15th	Billets, Sarton.
,,	16th	Billets, Sus-St. Léger.
,,	17th-18th	Billets, Izel-lez-Hameau.
,,	19th	Billets, Berneville.
,,	20th-25th	Trenches, Agny.
,,	26th-31st	Billets, Dainville.
Sept.	1st-18th	Front and reserve trenches, Agny.
,,	19th-23rd	Billets, Dainville.
,,	24th-25th	Trenches, Agny.
,,	26th	Billets, Berneville.
,,	27th-28th	Billets, Bouquemaison.
,,	29th-30th	Bivouacs, Pommiers Redoubt.
Oct.	1st-10th	Trenches, Gueudecourt. (*Battle of the Somme, 1916; Le Transloy.*)
,,	11th-16th	Camp, Bernafay Wood. (*Ditto*)
,,	17th and 18th	Trenches, Gueudecourt. (*Ditto*)
,,	19th-21st	Camps, Mametz Wood, Fricourt, and Buire.
,,	22nd-25th	Camp, Gouy-en-Artois.
,, Dec.	26th to 15th	Billets, Dainville; and front and reserve trenches, Agny. (Six days in and six days out, in rotation.)
,,	16th	Billets, Ambrines.
,, 1917 Jan.	17th to 17th	Rest, Sibiville.
,,	18th-22nd	Billets, Wanquetin.
,, March	23rd to 1st	Billets and trenches, Arras. (Four days in and four days out, in rotation.)
,,	2nd	Billets, Montenescourt.
,,	3rd-20th	Rest, Lignereuil.
,, April	21st to 2nd	Billets, Lattre-St. Quentin.

Appendix A

1917		
April	3rd	Cellars and Caves, Arras.
,,	4th-12th	Trenches, Arras, Feuchy Chapel, and Monchy le Preux. (*Battle of Arras*; *1st Scarpe*.)
,,	13th	Bivouacs, Ronville Caves, Arras. (*Ditto*)
,,	14th	Billets, Lattre-St. Quentin.
,,	15th-22nd	Rest, Mondicourt.
,,	23rd	Billets, Wanquetin.
,,	24th	Billets, Arras. (*Battle of Arras*; *2nd Scarpe*.)
,, May	25th to 15th	Trenches, Arras and Monchy le Preux. (*Battle of Arras*; *3rd Scarpe and Arleux*.)
,,	16th	Billets, Arras. (*Ditto*)
,,	17th-23rd	Billets, Agnez-lez Duisans.
,, June	24th to 16th	Rest, Grand-Rullecourt.
,,	17th	Billets, Agnez-lez Duisans.
,,	18th	Billets, Arras.
,, Oct.	19th to 7th	Front and reserve trenches, Monchy, and billets Achicourt, &c.
,,	8th-10th	Billets, Arras.
,,	11th-22nd	Reserve trenches, Monchy.
,,	23rd	Billets, Arras.
,,	24th	Billets, Hermaville.
,,	25th-27th	Billets, Ambrines.
,,	28th	Billets, Framecourt and Ecoivres.
,, Nov.	29th to 14th	Rest, Vieil Hesdin.
,,	15th	Billets, Sibiville.
,,	16th	Bivouacs, Moislains.
,,	17th	Bivouacs, Equancourt.
,,	18th	Bivouacs, Vaucellette Farm.
,, Dec.	20th to 1st	Trenches, Gonnelieu, La Vacquerie, and Villers-Plouich. (*Battle of Cambrai, 1917*.)
,,	2nd-3rd	Bivouacs, Heudicourt. (*Ditto*)
,,	4th	Bivouacs, Cartigny.
,,	5th-7th	Billets, Dernancourt.
,,	8th-22nd	Rest, Quiestede.
,, 1918 Jan.	23rd to 5th	Rest, Berguette and Isbergues.
,,	6th-12th	Billets, Chapelle Duvelle.
,,	13th-20th	Trenches, La Boutillerie.
,,	21st-27th	Billets, Doulieu.
,, Feb.	28th to 13th	Billets and trenches, Fleurbaix.
,,	14th-21st	Billets, Sailly-sur-la-Lys.
,, March	22nd to 1st	Trenches, La Boutillerie.
,,	2nd-20th	Reserve line and billets, Sailly-sur-la-Lys.
,,	21st	Billets, Caudescure and Arrewage.
,,	22nd-23rd	Billets, Steenbecque.
,,	24th	En route to Warloy.

Appendix A

1918

March	25th-29th	Trenches, Aveluy Wood. (*1st Battle of the Somme, 1918; 1st Bapaume*.)
,, April	30th to 1st	Billets, Warloy.
,,	2nd-11th	Trenches and bivouacs, Albert and Senlis. (*1st Battle of the Somme, 1918; The Ancre*.)
,,	12th-21st	Rest, Mirvaux, Pierregot, and Harponville.
,,	22nd	Billets, Acheux.
,,	23rd-30th	Trenches, Beaumont Hamel.
May	1st-5th	Billets, Acheux.
,,	6th-20th	Trenches, Mailly-Maillet and Beaumont Hamel.
,,	21st-24th	Billets, Acheux.
,, June	25th to 16th	Rest, Beauquesne.
,, July	17th to 10th	Trenches, Senlis and Bouzincourt.
,,	11th-13th	Camp, Toutencourt Wood.
,,	14th	Billets, Fremontiers and Uzenneville.
,,	15th-29th	Rest, Oresmaux.
,, Aug.	30th to 2nd	Billets, Vignacourt.
,,	3rd-5th	Camp, Round Wood, near Behencourt.
,,	6th-7th	Reserve trenches, Lahoussoye Switch, near Franvillers.
,,	8th-9th	Trenches S.W. of Morlancourt. (*Battle of Amiens*.)
,,	10th	Bivouacs, Méricourt-l'Abbé, and reserve trenches. (*Ditto*)
,,	11th-15th	Trenches, E. of Morlancourt. (*Ditto*)
,,	16th-19th	Bivouacs, Méricourt-l'Abbé.
,,	20th-28th	Trenches, Morlancourt, Fricourt, and Mametz. (*2nd Battle of the Somme, 1918; Albert*.)
,, Sept.	29th to 1st	Bivouacs, Valley W. of Carnoy-Montauban Road. (*2nd Battle of the Somme, 1918; Bapaume*.)
,,	2nd-7th	Trenches, Leforest and Nurlu. (*Ditto*)
,,	8th-16th	Bivouacs, Nurlu.
,,	17th-29th	Trenches, Epehy. (*Battles of the Hindenburg Line, Epehy, and St. Quentin Canal*.)
,,	30th	Bivouacs, Guyencourt and Lieramont.
Oct.	1st-2nd	Bivouacs, Proyart Wood.
,,	3rd-4th	Camp, Bois de la Haie.
,,	5th-7th	Trenches, Méricourt. (*The Final Advance, Artois*.)
,,	8th-12th	Reserve trenches, Acheville and Drocourt-Queant Line. (*Ditto*)
,,	13th-16th	Trenches, Haute Deule Canal, near Noyelle-Godault. (*Ditto*)
,,	17th-18th	Billets, Raimbeaucourt. (*Ditto*)
,,	19th	Billets, Le Bourgage. (*Ditto*)
,,	20th	Billets, Orchies. (*Ditto*)
,,	21st	Billets, Landas. (*Ditto*)
,,	22nd	Advancing; Rumegies and Rue Lasson. (*Ditto*)
,,	23rd-26th	Open Fighting; Nivelle to La Morte. (*Ditto*)

APPENDIX A

	1918		
Oct.	27th		Capture of Château l'Abbaye. (*The Final Advance*, Artois.)
,,	28th		Billets, Vieux Condé, near St. Amand.
,, Nov.	29th to 9th	}	Billets, Montreuil, near Flines.
,,	10th-24th		Billets, Landas.
,, 1919 March	25th to 11th	}	Billets, Hornaing, during which time the battalion was reduced to Cadre strength. (29th-31st December, salvage work at Bouchain.)
,, June	12th to 7th	}	Cadre in billets at Villers-Campeau.
,,	8th		Cadre entrained for Dunkirk.
,,	9th-15th		Cadre in camp in Dunkirk.
,,	16th		Cadre embarked for England.

SUMMARY

1st June, 1915—11th November, 1918

Number of days spent :	1915	1916	1917	1918	Totals
In Rest areas	19 (9%)	86 (23%)	105 (29%)	42 (14%)	252 (20%)
In Billeting areas	105 (49%)	150 (41%)	110 (30%)	110 (35%)	475 (38%)
In Trenches	90 (42%)	130 (36%)	150 (41%)	163 (51%)	533 (42%)
Totals	214	366	365	315	1260

APPENDIX B.

(i)

SUMMARY OF CASUALTIES, KILLED AND DIED, 1915-1919.

	OFFICERS			OTHER RANKS			TOTALS	
	K. in A.	D. of W.	Died	K. in A.	D. of W.	Died	Offrs.	O.R.
1915 ..	3	—	—	53	23	7	3	83
1916 ..	19	2	—	254	60	3	21	317
1917 ..	6	2	2	200	61	6	10	267
1918 ..	19	4	—	248	81	15	23	344
1919 ..	—	—	—	—	—	1	—	1
Totals ..	47	8	2	755	225	32	57	1012

NOTE.—The total number of wounded amounted, approximately, to 90 Officers and 2,500 Other Ranks.

Appendix B

(ii)
SUMMARY OF CASUALTIES, KILLED AND WOUNDED, IN MAIN ENGAGEMENTS.

Note.—The numbers given are generally approximate.

Engagements	Dates	Officers		Other Ranks		Totals	
		Killed, d. of w. and missing	Wounded	Killed, d. of w. and missing	Wounded	Officers.	Other ranks.
Hohenzollern Craters	3rd-4th March, 1916	4	5	35	175	9	210
Ovillers	7th-8th July, 1916	8	13	134	306	21	440
Pozières	30th July-5th Aug., 1916	5	5	63	151	10	214
Gueudecourt	1st-8th Oct., 1916	2	5	41	134	7	175
Arras	5th-13th April, 1917	—	4	62	90	4	152
Scarpe	3rd-4th May, 1917	1	5	55	100	6	155
Spoon Trench, Monchy	25th July, 1917	1	1	29	62	2	91
Cambrai	20th-30th Nov., 1917	3	5	65	181	8	246
Aveluy Wood	26th-28th March, 1918	2	4	48	68	6	116
Bouzincourt Ridge	5th-6th April, 1918	1	1	42	85	2	127
Morlancourt	7th-13th Aug., 1918	6	8	57	178	14	235
Fricourt, Mametz, &c.	22nd-26th Aug., 1918	1	5	35	75	6	110
Nurlu	5th Sept., 1918	2	3	11	60	5	71
Epehy, &c.	18th-24th Sept., 1918	8	10	66	184	18	250

Note.—Apart from the above main engagements, therefore, trench routine, &c., cost the battalion the following casualties :—
  Died .. 13 officers and 269 other ranks.
  Wounded .. 16 officers and 650 other ranks.

APPENDIX C.

ROLL OF HONOUR.

(i)

OFFICERS.

[1]ASHBY, Thomas Philip, 2/Lt. (C), k. in a., 5/9/18.
BALLARD, Charles William, Capt., M.C. (C), k. in a., 25/11/17.
BEALE, Clifford William, Lt. (C), k. in a., 3/3/16.
[2]BOURNE, Rowland Hurst, 2/Lt. (A), k. in a., 24/10/18.
BOYS, Sidney Charles, Lt. (A), k. in a., 23/6/18.
BRADLEY, James, 2/Lt. (B), d. of w., 26/10/18.
[1]BURLEY, Cyril Percival, 2/Lt. (B), k. in a., 9/8/18.
BUSSELL, John Garrett, Capt. (A), k. in a., 28/6/15.
CASS, Leonard Francis, Capt. (A), k. in a., 13/12/15.
CLEMENTS, Reginald Francis, Lt., M.C. (D), k. in a., 14/8/18.
[3]COHEN, Dudley Trevor, 2/Lt. (D), d. of w., 20/11/17.
[4]COLLINS, John Stratford, Lt. (A), k. in a., 5/4/18.
COOKE, Henry Frederick, 2/Lt. (B), k. in a., 4/8/16.
COX, Norman John, Lt. (B), k. in a., 23/8/15.
DADSWELL, Clifford Irwin, 2/Lt. (D), k. in a., 7/7/16.
DAUNT, Barry, 2/Lt. (D), k. in a., 22/9/18.
DIXON, Peter Sydenham, Lt. (C), k. in a., 7/8/18.
ERICSON, Eric Charles, 2/Lt., M.M. (C), k. in a., 18/9/18.
FIELD, John Morton, 2/Lt. (A), k. in a., 13/4/16.
[5]FITZSIMONS, Terence, 2/Lt. (C), k. in a., 4/8/16.
FOSTER, Percy George, 2/Lt. (C), d. of w., 2/4/16.
[6]FRANKLIN, William Joseph, 2/Lt. (D), k. in a., 5/10/16.
GODWIN, John Charles Raymond, 2/Lt. (B), k. in a., 7/7/16.
[6]GOLDS, Frank, 2/Lt. (A), k. in a., 5/10/16.
GORDON, Henry Bernard, Lt. (Bombing Officer), k. in a., 7/7/16.
GORRINGE, Edward Clifton, Capt., M.C. (C), k. in a., 5/9/18.
HOWETT, William, 2/Lt. (B), k. in a., 18/9/18.
HUGGETT, Sidney George, 2/Lt. (A), k. in a., 18/9/18.
[7]KENWARD, Robert, 2/Lt. (A), k. in a., 7/7/16.
KNOX, John Lawrence, 2/Lt. (C), k. in a., 20/11/17.
[8]LAVENDER, Harry Richard, 2/Lt. (A), k. in a., 28/8/18.
[9]LAWRENCE, Thomas Edward, 2/Lt. (C), d. of w., 24/9/18.
LEDGER, Robert John, 2/Lt. (D), d. of w., 11/3/17.
LE DOUX VEITCH, Dallas Gerard, 2/Lt. (D), k. in a., 4/8/16.
MANLEY, Hamilton Douglas, 2/Lt. (B), k. in a., 27/3/18.
[10]MATTHEWS, J. L., 2/Lt. (A), d., 28/12/17.
MAY, Richard Trelawney, Capt. (A), k. in a., 7/7/16.

Appendix C

MENNIE, James, 2/Lt. (B), k. in a., 18/9/18.
MONTESOLE, Eric Alfred, 2/Lt. (L.G. Officer), k. in a., 4/3/16.
MURRAY, Arthur, 2/Lt. (D), k. in a., 8/8/18.
NAGLE, Gilbert, Capt., M.C. (Adjutant), k. in a., 5/7/17.
PALMER, Horace John, 2/Lt. (A), k. in a., 8/8/18.
[10]REES, A. A., Capt., R.A.M.C. (M.O.), d. 4/2/17.
ROUSELL, William Stephen, 2/Lt. (B), k. in a., 8/8/18.
[8]SANSOM, Alfred John, Lt./Col. (C.O.), k. in a., 5/7/17.
SING, Charles Millington, 2/Lt. (B), d. of w., 7/7/16.
[11]SMITH, Wilfred, 2/Lt. (C), d. of w., 9/5/17.
SUTTON, Eric Guy, Lt., M.C. (B), k. in a., 8/4/16.
[12]THOMSON, Alfred Maurice, Capt., R.A.M.C. (M.O), k. in a., 7/7/16.
[13]ULOTH, Arthur Curtis Wilmot, Lt., M.C. (B), d. of w., 19/9/18.
[4]UPPLEBY, Wyvil Charles Spinola, Capt. (B), d. of w., 9/2/18.
WARING, Frederick Royden, 2/Lt. (A), k. in a., 7/7/16.
WELLS, Ronald Graham, Lt. (D), k. in a., 4/3/16.
WILLARD, Albert Ellis, Lt. (D), k. in a., 4/7/17.
WOOD, Thomas Victor, 2/Lt. (A), k. in a., 4/8/16.
WOODHAMS, Geoffrey, Capt. (B), k. in a., 19/3/16.
WRIGHT, John Armer, Lt., M.C. (A), k. in a., 18/9/18.

NOTE.—The foregoing list, compiled from various sources, has been checked with the Royal Sussex Regiment Memorial Panels in St. George's Chapel, Chichester Cathedral, and with the Official List—" Officers died in the Great War 1914-1919."

Certain errors have been noted. On the Panels and in the Official List, Arkcoll, Frederick Thomas, 2/Lt., appears as k. in a., 30/6/16, with the 7th Battalion, whereas he was serving with the 12th or 13th Battalion; the Official List gives Flowers, John Arthur, 2/Lt., k. in a., 1/9/16, with the 7th Battalion, whereas he was serving with the 9th Battalion; Gale, Harold William, 2/Lt., k. in a., 8/8/18, with the 5th Royal Berks, given in the Official List as posted to the 7th Battalion, never served with us.

The following numbers, given in the foregoing list, refer to other corrections :—

1. No battalion given in Official List.
2. Attached from R.A.S.C.; omitted from Panels; under R.A.S.C. in Official List.
3. Under 4th Battalion on Panels and in Official List.
4. Under 12th Battalion on Panels and in Official List.
5. Date given as 4/4/16 in Official List.
6. Attached from 11th East Surreys; omitted from Panels; under East Surreys in Official List.
7. Under 2nd Battalion on Panels and in Official List.
8. Under 5th Battalion on Panels and in Official List.
9. Date given as 22/9/18 in Official List.
10. Omitted from Panels and Official List.
11. Under 6th Battalion on Panels and in Official List.
12. Attached from R.A.M.C.; omitted from Panels; under R.A.M.C. in Official List.
13. Under 11th Battalion on Panels and in Official List.

Appendix C

(ii)
OTHER RANKS.

PREFATORY NOTE.—The authorities from which this list has been compiled are :—

A. Part II Orders of the 7th Battalion The Royal Sussex Regiment.
B. The Official List—" Soldiers died in the Great War 1914-19; Part 40, The Royal Sussex Regiment," pp. 27-36.
C. The Royal Sussex Regiment Memorial Panels in St. George's Chapel, Chichester Cathedral.

In the list given below

‡ denotes that the name is found in A and B but not in C,
§   ,, ,, ,,   A and C   ,,   B,
*   ,, ,, ,,   B and C   ,,   A,
†   ,, ,, ,,   A only ;

otherwise the name is found in all three authorities.

Further notes, giving corrections to B and C, are numbered and given at the end of the list.

ABEAR, Charles, Pte. (A), d. of w., 2/10/16.
ABRAMS, Herbert, Pte. (D), k. in a., 18/9/18.
ADAMS, Albert, Pte. (A), d. of w., 15/10/15.
ADAMS, Charles, Sgt. (B), k. in a., 25/7/17.
ADAMS, Charles Emanuel, Pte. (D), k. in a., 4/7/18.
ADES, Bernard Henry, Pte. (A), k. in a., 3/5/17.
ADKIN, Stanley, Pte. (B), k. in a., 2/8/16.
ADSETT, Arthur, Pte. (D), k. in a., 31/7/16.
AHERN, John, Pte. (B), k. in a., 7/7/16.
AITKIN, James, Pte. (C), k. in a., 3/5/17.
ALDERTON, James Alfred, L/Cpl. (D), k. in a., 27/3/18.
ALDRIDGE, William Nathaniel, Pte. (A), k. in a., 7/7/16.
ALEXANDER, Edwin Albert, Pte. (C), k. in a., 25/11/17.
ALLCORN, Alan, Pte. (C), d. of w., 18/10/16.*
ALLEN, Reginald Gordon, Pte. (A), k. in a., 5/4/18.
ALLEN, William, Pte. (B), k. in a., 5/10/16.
AMES, Harman Herbert, L/Cpl. (D), k. in a., 3/5/17.
ANDRESS, Arthur William, Pte. (A), k. in a., 5/10/16.
ANSELL, Basil, L/Sgt. (B), d. of w., 26/7/16.
ANSELL, John William, Pte. (D), k. in a., 26/3/18.
APPLEBY, Arthur Fenwick, Pte. (A), k. in a., 5/4/18.*
ARNELL, Albert, Sgt. (C), k. in a., 25/7/17.
ARNELL, Sidney, Pte. (B), d., 26/5/15.

Appendix C

Arnott, Frederick, Pte. (A), d. of w., 19/2/17.
Arrowsmith, Samuel, Pte. (D), k. in a., 16/4/16.
Ashdown, Thomas Charles, Pte. (C), k. in a., 16/10/18.
Ashenden, Archibald, Sgt. (C), k. in a., 8/8/18.
Ashman, George, L/Cpl. (A), d. of w., 27/3/18.
[1]Aslett, Albert Edward, Pte. (A), d. of w., 5/7/17.
Atkinson, William Henry, L/Cpl. (A), k. in a., 17/4/16.
Attwood, William, Pte. (A), k. in a., 11/9/15.
Auberton, Gilbert William, Cpl. (D), k. in a., 24/12/15.
Aukett, Albert Edward, Pte. (B), d. of w., 9/4/17.
Aukett, Joseph Frederick, Pte. (B), k. in a., 3/5/17.
Austin, Harry James, Sgt. (C), k. in a., 9/4/17.
Austin, J., Pte. (A), k. in a., 22/8/18.§
Avey, Thomas, Pte. (A), k. in a., 19/5/18.
Avis, Edward Arthur, Pte. (D), k. in a., 8/8/15.
Avis, George Henry, Pte. (C), d. of w., 11/4/17.
Ayling, Alec Oliver, Pte. (B), k. in a., 7/7/16.
Back, John Albert, Pte. (A), k. in a., 7/7/16.
Bacon, Edward, Pte. (A), k. in a., 3/3/16.
Bacon, Samuel, Pte. (C), d. of w., 26/3/16.
Baggett, Edwin Victor, Pte. (C), d. of w., 28/3/18.
Bailey, Arthur Frederick, L/Cpl. (A), k. in a., 7/7/16.*
Bailey, Arthur George, Pte. (D), k. in a., 13/8/18.
Baker, Albert William, Pte. (C), k. in a., 30/6/18.
Baker, Cecil, Pte. (C), k. in a., 27/9/15.
Baker, Charles, Pte. (D), d. of w., 30/3/18.
Baker, George, Pte. (A), k. in a., 7/7/16.
Baker, Louis James Henry, Cpl. (A), k. in a., 25/9/17.*
Baker, Matthias, Pte. (D), k. in a., 3/7/18.
Baker, Ralph Dudley, Pte. (A), k. in a., 20/5/18.
Balcombe, George William, Pte. (A), k. in a., 3/5/17.
Baldwin, John, Sgt. (A), drowned, 17/11/15.*
Banger, Charles, Pte. (A), k. in a., 5/4/18.
Barber, Edward, Pte. (B), k. in a., 3/5/17.
Barker, Leslie Morris, L/Cpl. (D), d. of w., 10/4/17.
Barnes, Edwin Richard, Pte. (D), k. in a., 3/5/17.
Barnes, Ernest, A/Cpl. (D), k. in a., 3/5/17.
Barnes, George, Pte. (D), k. in a., 7/7/16.
Barnes, Gilbert James, Pte. (B), k. in a., 2/9/18.
Barnes, Hubert William, Pte. (B), d. of w., 10/10/16.
Barron, Harry, L/Cpl. (C), d. of w., 5/8/15.
Barrs, Alec Richard, Pte. (C), d., 19/4/18.*
Bartholomew, Harold, Pte. (B), k. in a., 25/7/17.
Bartup, George Albert, Pte. (B), k. in a., 26/9/16.
Barwick, William Rufus, L/Cpl., M.M. (D), k. in a., 26/8/18.
Basson, Albert, Sgt. (B), k. in a., 27/9/15.
Batchelor, John Thomas, Pte. (A), k. in a., 31/3/17.
Bateman, Sidney George, Pte. (D), k. in a., 25/7/17.
Bateman, William James, Pte. (A), k. in a., 5/4/18.
Battensby, Harry John Charles, L/Cpl. (A), d. of w., 9/8/18.
Baxter, Walter, Pte. (C), d., 24/11/18.

Appendix C

BEALE, Alfred William, A/Sgt., M.M. (A), k. in a., 9/4/17.
BEALE, Thomas Henman, Pte., M.M. (B), k. in a., 27/3/18.
BECK, Percy George John, Pte. (D), d. of w., 24/9/17.
BECKETT, Arthur Samuel, Pte. (C), k. in a., 25/11/17.
BEDFORD, William Henry, Pte. (C), d. of w., 10/8/18.
BEECHING, James Wallace, Pte. (B), k. in a., 9/4/17.
BELFIELD, Percy, Pte. (C), k. in a., 13/8/18.
BELL, Percy, Pte. (A), k. in a., 7/7/16.
BELLAMY, David, Pte. (C), k. in a., 4/8/16.
BENNETT, Albert Armand, Pte. (D), d., 17/10/18.
BENNETT, Frederick, Pte. (C), k. in a., 26/2/17.
BERRY, Alfred, Pte. (B), d. of w., 22/4/18.
BERRYMAN, Sidney, Pte. (A), k. in a., 28/8/15.
BIANCHI, Percy John, Pte. (A), d. of w., 27/8/18.
BIGGS, Sydney, Pte. (D), d. of w., 4/3/16.
BILLING, Cuthbert Stanley, Pte. (A), d. of w., 21/4/18.
BILLING, Edward Victor, A/Sgt. (A), d. of w., 22/8/18.
BINSTEAD, Charles, Pte. (B), k. in a., 7/7/16.
BIRD, Arthur, Pte. (C), k. in a., 9/4/17.
BIRD, James, Pte., M.M. (D), k. in a., 7/7/16.
BISHOP, Sidney George Edmund, L/Cpl. (D), k. in a., 7/10/16.
BISHOPP, George, Pte. (B), k. in a., 25/7/17.
BISSMIRE, Harry, Pte. (D), k. in a., 7/7/16.
BLACKHURST, Cecil, Sgt. (D), k. in a., 7/7/16.
BLAKE, Arthur William, L/Cpl. (A), k. in a., 24/10/18.
BOAKES, Frederick George, Pte. (C), k. in a., 7/7/16.
BOATER, James, Pte. (D), k. in a., 27/3/18.
BONAS, George Frederick, Pte. (D), d. of w., 10/4/17.
BONE, Frederick John, Pte. (D), k. in a., 25/7/17.
BONIFACE, George, Pte. (B), k. in a., 5/4/18.
BONIFACE, Martin John, Pte. (A), d. of w., 27/4/17.
BOORMAN, Albert, Pte. (C), k. in a., 18/9/18.
BORROW, Arthur, L/Cpl. (D), k. in a., 24/12/15.
BOTTING, Jasper, Pte. (B), k. in a., 31/7/15.
BOWLEY, Charles, Pte. (C), d., 18/5/15.
BOWLEY, Charles James, Pte. (A), k. in a., 3/3/16.
BOWRA, Percy John, Pte. (C), k. in a., 7/7/16.
BOXALL, John, Pte. (A), k. in a., 7/7/16.
BOYDE, Arthur, Pte. (B), k. in a., 7/7/16.
BRABAN, George Thomas, Pte. (B), k. in a., 20/11/17.
BRACE, Frank William, Pte. (C), k. in a., 8/8/18.
BRACKSTONE, Albert Henry, Pte. (A), k. in a., 3/5/17.
BRAIN, Harry, L/Cpl. (C), k. in a., 7/7/16.
BRAY, Frank, Pte. (C), k. in a., 24/3/16.
BRAZIER, Sidney, Pte. (A), k. in a., 30/11/17.
[2]BREED, Elija, Pte. (C), k. in a., 30/10/16.
BREWSTER, Richard, Sgt. (B), k. in a., 3/3/16.
BRIDGLAND, William Thomas, L/Cpl. (A), k. in a., 13/8/18.
BRIDGER, James, Pte. (C), k. in a., 5/10/16.
BRIDGER, Percy William, Pte., M.M. (C), k. in a., 3/5/17.
BRIDGSTOCK, Ralph, Pte. (D), k. in a., 4/5/17.

Appendix C

Bridle, Walter Frank, Pte. (D), d., 13/4/18.
Bright, Henry James, Pte. (B), k. in a., 5/4/18.
Brind, Albert George, Pte. (D), k. in a., 24/8/18.
Bristow, Frederick, Pte. (B), k. in a., 29/6/18.
Britt, Harry William, Pte. (C), d. of w., 23/3/16.
Brooks, Jesse, Pte. (B), k. in a., 7/7/16.
Brooks, Samuel, Pte. (A), k. in a., 4/3/16.
Brooks, William, Pte. (C), d., 8/2/17.
Broomfield, Edward William, L/Cpl. (D), k. in a., 20/11/17.
Brown, Frederick, Pte. (C), k. in a., 3/5/17.
[3]Brown, Frederick, Pte. (B), k. in a., 3/3/16.
Brown, John, Pte. (C), k. in a., 30/9/15.
Brown, John Francis, Pte. (D), d. of w., 24/8/18.
Brown, Leonard Marshall, Pte. (B), k. in a., 9/4/17.
Brown, Samuel John, Pte. (A), d. of w., 4/2/18.
Browne, Alfred John, L/Cpl. (B), k. in a., 5/4/18.
[4]Browne, Edward Miller, Pte. (C), k. in a., 8/8/18.
Bryant, James George, Pte. (C), k. in a., 7/7/16.
Bryder, William, Pte. (C), k. in a., 27/3/18.
Buckman, E., Pte. (B), d. of w., 20/11/17.†
Buckwalter, Harry, Pte. (A), k. in a., 5/9/18.
Budd, Thomas William, L/Cpl. (B), k. in a., 1/10/17.
Budgen, George, Pte. (B), d. of w., 14/1/16.
Bumstead, Frank Henry, Pte. (D), k. in a., 7/7/16.
Bumstead, George, Pte. (B), k. in a., 25/11/17.
Bunker, Jesse, Pte. (B), k. in a., 19/5/18.
Bunning, Robert Charles, Pte. (C), k. in a., 7/7/16.
Burden, Alfred, Pte. (C), k. in a., 7/7/16.
Burgess, A., Pte. (C), k. in a., 8/8/18.†
Burgess, Albert Henry, Pte. (D), k. in a., 24/12/15.
Burgess, John, Pte. (D), k. in a., 28/3/18.
Burgins, Leonard Bertram, Pte. (C), d. of w., 26/4/17.
Burrough, Cyril George, Sgt. (C), k. in a., 5/9/18.
Burt, James, Pte. (B), k. in a., 7/7/16.
Bushell, Daniel, Pte. (C), k. in a., 25/4/18.
Buss, Jesse, Pte. (C), k. in a., 2/3/16.
Buswell, Percy Bates, Pte. (C), k. in a., 5/10/16.
Butcher, Thomas Horeland, Pte. (D), k. in a., 13/8/18.
Caddow, Robert, Pte. (C), k. in a., 18/9/16.
Callaghan, Daniel, Pte. (D), k. in a., 7/7/16.
Cane, Thomas Harry, L/Cpl. (D), k. in a., 20/11/17.
Cannon, Arthur, L/Cpl. (D), d. of w., 2/12/17.
Cannons, George Harry, Pte. (C), k. in a., 22/8/18.
Canton, George, L/Cpl. (A), k. in a., 27/3/18.
Carn, Charles Percy, Pte. (C), d. of w., 14/3/16.
Carson, William James, Pte. (A), d., 6/11/18.*
Carstairs, Philip Gordon, Pte. (D), d. of w., 9/8/18.
Carver, Alfred William, Pte. (A), d. of w., 7/9/18.
Carver, J., Pte. (C), k. in a., 3/10/16.†
Cassidy, Albert, Pte. (A), d. of w., 29/11/17.
Cate, John, Pte. (B), k. in a., 9/4/17.

Appendix C

CATT, William Nathan, Pte. (B), k. in a., 7/7/16.
CAVE, Herbert Stanley, L/Cpl. (C), k. in a., 26/3/18.
CHAFFEY, George, Pte. (C), k. in a., 7/7/16.
CHALK, William Edwin, Sgt. (A), k. in a., 10/8/16.
CHAMBERS, Albert Edward, Pte. (D), k. in a., 9/4/17.
CHAPMAN, Ernest, Pte. (D), k. in a., 13/8/18.
CHAPMAN, Reginald George, Pte. (A), d. of w., 28/9/15.
CHAPPELL, Ernest, Pte. (B), d. of w., 27/7/17.
CHAPPLE, George Richard, Pte. (B), k. in a., 7/7/16.*
CHARMAN, Arthur, Pte. (A), d. of w., 6/3/16.
CHATFIELD, Frederick George, Pte. (A), k. in a., 5/9/18.
CHEESMAN, Reginald, Cpl., D.C.M. (C), d. of w., 5/10/16.
CHEESMAN, William, Cpl. (B), k. in a., 7/7/16.
CHEESMORE, Alfred, Pte. (D), d. of w., 27/12/17.
CHEERIMAN, Joseph Edward, Pte. (D), k. in a., 26/7/15.
CHERRYMAN, Alfred, Pte. (C), k. in a., 24/9/18.
CHEVALIER, Albert, L/Sgt. (A), d. of w., 26/9/18.
CHEVIS, George Edward, Cpl. (B), d. of w., 12/7/16.
CHEVIS, James Henry, Cpl. (D), k. in a., 31/7/16.
CHILD, William Henry, L/Cpl. (B), k. in a., 5/4/18.
CHILDREN, Richard William, Pte. (B), k. in a., 8/8/18.
CHIPPERFIELD, Stanley, Pte. (D), d. of w., 21/5/18.
CHUNN, Erling Victor, L/Cpl. (D), k. in a., 3/5/17.
5CLARK, Edwin Arthur, Pte. (C), k. in a., 26/8/18.
CLARK, Lionel, Pte. (B), d. of w., 3/11/15.
CLARK, William, Pte. (B), k. in a., 15/3/16.
CLARK, William Frank, Pte. (B), k. in a., 26/8/18.
CLARKSON, Charles Athelstan, Pte. (A), k. in a., 18/9/18.
CLARKSON, William George Dunbar, Pte. (D), k. in a., 31/3/17.
CLUFF, George, Pte. (D), k. in a., 18/9/18.
COBB, George Edward, Pte. (B), k. in a., 31/7/16.
COBBY, Benjamin James, Pte. (B), k. in a., 25/7/17.
CODY, Alfred, Pte. (A), d. of w., 27/3/18.
COE, Arthur George, Pte. (A), d. of w., 14/7/16.
COLBURN, George, Cpl. (C), d. of w., 16/4/18.
6COLBURN, William, Pte. (D), d. of w., 8/2/18.
COLEMAN, Bertram, Pte. (B), k. in a., 27/3/18.
COLEMAN, Percy, L/Cpl. (B), d. of w., 5/3/16.
COLES, Albert Edward, Pte. (C), k. in a., 18/9/18.
COLES, Ernest Walter, Pte. (C), k. in a., 18/9/18.
COLES, Reginald Joseph, Pte. (B), k. in a., 9/8/18.
COLLIER, Walter Samuel, Pte. (B), k. in a., 27/3/18.
COLLINGS, James William, Pte. (C), k. in a., 7/7/16.
COLTMAN, Victor Joseph, Pte. (D), k. in a., 3/5/17.
COMBER, Bernard, Pte. (A), d. of w., 10/4/17.
COMPER, Thomas James, Pte. (B), k. in a., 7/7/16.
CONVOY, Bertie George, Pte. (B), k. in a., 5/9/18.
COOK, Fred, Pte. (B), k. in a., 5/4/18.
COOK, Henry John Lewis, Pte. (D), k. in a., 23/9/18.
COOKSEY, Leonard, Pte. (C), k. in a., 17/8/17.
COOMBER, Percy George, Pte. (D), k. in a., 25/7/17.

Appendix C

Coombes, Warren, Pte. (D), d. of w., 8/10/16.
Cooper, Ashey James, Pte. (C), d., 4/11/15.
Cooper, George, Pte. (D), d. of w., 11/8/16.
Cooper, Joseph, L/Cpl. (A), k. in a., 27/3/18.
Coote, Charles, Pte. (D), d. of w., 10/4/17.
Copping, Thomas Kenneth, Pte. (B), k. in a., 20/11/17.
Corbett, Harold, Pte. (B), k. in a., 8/8/18.
Corder, Charles, Pte. (A), k. in a., 5/4/18.
Corke, William, Pte. (C), k. in a., 20/11/17.
Cornford, Charles Samuel Joseph, L/Cpl. (B), k. in a., 25/7/17.
Cornish, Graham, Pte. (A), k. in a., 28/3/16.
Cotterill, Frederick, Pte. (D), d. of w., 27/9/15.*
Court, Frederick William, Pte. (B), k. in a., 8/8/18.
Court, Septimus, Pte. (A), k. in a., 25/9/15.
Covell, Alfred John, Pte. (B), k. in a., 9/4/17.
Cowdrey, Harry, Pte. (D), k. in a., 26/8/18.
Cowtan, Sydney Francis, Pte. (A), d. of w., 7/11/18.*
Cox, George, Pte. (C), k. in a., 2/3/16.
Cox, Sidney, Pte. (C), k. in a., 13/8/18.
Crabb, Albert, Pte. (A), d. of w., 17/5/17.
Cracknell, Arthur, Pte. (B), d. of w., 27/4/17.
Cramphorn, Thomas Howard, Pte. (A), k. in a., 4/8/16.
Crawley, James, A/Cpl. (B), k. in a., 7/7/16.
Creighton, William Thomas, Pte. (B), k. in a., 8/8/18.
Cripps, John Henry, Pte. (A), k. in a., 31/3/17.
Crittenden, Henry Albert, Pte. (D), k. in a., 7/7/16.
Croft, Ernest Frank, Pte. (B), k. in a., 7/7/16.
Croft, Horace Guy, Pte. (C), k. in a., 8/8/18.
Crooke, Moses John, Pte. (B), k. in a., 7/7/16.
Crouch, Douglas, Pte. (B), k. in a., 31/7/15.
Crouch, William Charles, Pte. (D), k. in a., 4/7/17.
Croucher, James Frederick, Pte. (D), d. of w., 26/6/17.*
Cruttenden, Henry John, A/Sgt. (A), k. in a., 26/8/18.
Cundell, Arthur, Pte. (A), k. in a., 4/8/16.
Curd, Henry, L/Cpl. (D), k. in a., 18/9/18.
Curtis, Percy, Pte. (A), d. of w., 6/2/18.
Cusack, John, Pte. (B), d. of w., 13/8/16.*
Daborn, William Henry, Pte. (A), k. in a., 7/7/16.
Dadswell, Charles, Pte. (A), k. in a., 24/3/16.
Daniels, Joe, Pte. (D), d. of w., 29/7/16.*
Dann, John, Pte. (B), d. of w., 5/11/15.
Davidson, Thomas, Pte. (C), k. in a., 15/10/15.
Davis, Ernest, Pte. (D), k. in a., 4/8/15.*
Davis, Thomas Stephen, Pte. (B), k. in a., 25/7/17.
Dawes, Bert, Pte. (C), d. of w., 18/8/17.
Dawson, Leonard, L/Sgt. (A), d. of w., 9/8/18.
Day, Frank Gilbert, Pte. (D), d. of w., 14/8/18.
Day, George, Cpl. (B), k. in a., 2/9/18.
Deadman, James, Pte. (A), k. in a., 3/5/17.
Deadman, Sidney Herbert, Pte. (C), k. in a., 3/5/17.
[7]Deadman, William Walter, Pte. (A), k. in a., 22/8/18.

Appendix C

DEAN, Arthur Castle Gordon, Pte. (A), d. of w., 3/5/17.
DEAN, Joseph, Pte. (A), k. in a., 13/2/16.
DEAN, Wesley William, Pte. (C), k. in a., 4/8/16.
DEANE, Thomas, Pte. (C), d. of w., 5/5/17.
DEARLING, Alonzo Robert, Pte. (D), k. in a., 5/4/18.
DEBENHAM, Herbert, Pte. (C), k. in a., 13/8/18.
DE GRUCHY, George Henry, Pte. (B), d. of w., 18/7/16.
DELL, Henry, L/Cpl. (D), k. in a., 7/10/16.
DENNIS, Alfred Orton, Pte. (A), d. of w., 3/5/16.
DENTON, Walter, Pte. (C), k. in a., 28/3/18.
DENYER, Charles George, L/Cpl. (C), k. in a., 25/7/17.
DENYER, George Charles, Pte. (A), k. in a., 7/7/16.
DE ST. CROIX, Arthur Nicholas, Cpl. (D), k. in a., 23/10/15.
DEWAR, George Nash, Pte. (C), d. of w., 2/10/18.
DEWLEY, William George, Pte. (B), k. in a., 9/5/17.
DICKENSON, J., Pte. (A), k. in a., 7/7/16.†
DINMORE, John James, Pte. (D), k. in a., 8/8/18.
DIXON, Albert Ernest, Pte. (A), d. of w., 11/7/16.
DOLLERY, Sidney Thomas, L/Cpl. (C), d. of w., 2/10/15.
DORSET, Albert, Pte. (C), k. in a., 4/8/16.
DOWN, James Frederick, Pte. (A), k. in a., 9/4/16.
DOWNHAM, Leonard James, Pte. (C), k. in a., 8/8/18.*
DOYLE, Alexander William, Pte. (D), k. in a., 21/9/18.
DRAKE, Samuel, L/Cpl. (D), d. of w., 4/12/17.
DRISCOLL, Jerry, Pte. (C), d. of w., 19/3/16.
DUFFIELD, Oscar Sidney, L/Cpl. (B), k. in a., 3/5/17.
DUKE, Alfred William, Pte. (D), k. in a., 7/7/16.
DUMSDAY, Frederick, Pte. (A), k. in a., 5/4/18.
DUNN, S., L/Cpl. (A), k. in a., 7/7/16.†
DYKES, William Albert, Pte. (D), k. in a., 10/7/16.
EADE, William John, Pte., M.M. (D), k. in a., 20/5/18.
EALDEN, John, Pte. (D), k. in a., 23/10/18.
8EASON, Henry, Pte. (C), d. of w., 6/10/15.
EAST, Frank Bernard, Pte. (A), d. of w., 24/9/18.
EATON, John, Pte. (A), d. of w., 5/12/18.*
EDMUNDS, George Thomas, L/Cpl. (C), k. in a., 13/4/17.
EDWARDS, Albert William, Pte. (B), k. in a., 25/11/17.
EELLS, Richard Walter Robert, Pte. (B), k. in a., 9/4/17.
EGGLETON, Benjamin, Pte. (D), k. in a., 4/7/17.
ELLIOT, S., Pte. (C), k. in a., 25/11/17.†
ELLIOT, Stanley John, Pte. (D), k. in a., 25/11/17.
ELLIS, Percy, Pte. (A), k. in a., 6/8/15.
ELLIS, Richard, Pte. (B), k. in a., 5/4/18.
ELMS, Gordon William, Pte. (B), k. in a., 7/7/16.
ELPHICK, Walter, Pte. (C), k. in a., 18/9/18.
ELSEY, Frederick James, Pte. (C), d. of w., 23/3/16.
EMBLEN, Albert, Pte. (D), k. in a., 25/11/17.
EMERY, Walter, Pte. (B), d. of w., 24/8/18.
EVANS, Arthur James, Sgt., M.M. (A), k. in a., 7/7/16.
EVANS, Cecil James, Pte. (A), k. in a., 2/11/15.
EVANS, Owen, L/Cpl. (B), k. in a., 7/7/16.

Appendix C

Evans, Sidney Charles, Pte. (C), k. in a., 18/9/18.
Evenden, George, Pte. (A), d. of w., 25/4/17.*
Everett, Ernest William, L/Cpl. (A), k. in a., 1/8/16.
Eyles, Charles, Pte. (A), d. of w., 10/4/17.
[9]Faircloth, Henry Latham, C.Q.M.S. (B), k. in a., 28/12/15.
Fairhall, Frederick Charles, Sgt., D.C.M. (B), k. in a., 25/11/17.
Faulkner, Thomas Edward, Pte. (C), k. in a., 14/5/17.
Fearnley, Joseph Henry, L/Cpl. (A), d. of w., 24/11/17.
Feist, John Thomas, L/Cpl. (A), d. of w., 3/5/17.
Fickling, Walter, Pte. (A), k. in a., 27/3/18.
Filtness, Frank, Pte. (C), k. in a., 6/4/18.
Finch, Leonard, Pte. (A), k. in a., 30/11/17.
Fish, Frederick Charles, Pte. (C), k. in a., 18/9/18.
Fisher, Ernest, Pte. (A), k. in a., 24/9/18.
Fitch, Frederick William, Pte. (C), k. in a., 7/7/16.
Fitt, Thomas, Pte. (D), k. in a., 9/4/17.
Fitzell, Herbert, Pte. (D), k. in a., 27/3/18.
Fitzpatrick, Lawrence, L/Cpl. (B), d. of w., 30/6/18.
Flecknoe, Frederick George, L/Cpl. (C), k. in a., 3/5/17.
Foord, George, L/Cpl. (A), d. of w., 19/7/16.
Foster, Alfred, Pte. (B), k. in a., 8/4/16.
Foster, William Henry, Pte. (B), k. in a., 24/9/18.*
Framp, Eric William John, Pte. (D), k. in a., 9/2/17.
Franks, Frank William, Pte. (A), k. in a., 2/1/16.
Freeland, William Charles, Cpl. (A), k. in a., 4/2/18.
French, Ernest William, Cpl. (C), k. in a., 3/5/17.
Frost, Archibald, Pte. (C), k. in a., 7/7/16.
Frost, Joseph Alfred, Pte. (C), k. in a., 25/4/18.
Fuller, Charles, Pte. (A), k. in a., 9/8/18.
Funnell, Albert, Pte. (D), k. in a., 3/5/17.
Funnell, Douglas, L/Sgt. (C), k. in a., 25/11/17.
Furner, Charlie, Pte. (D), d. of w., 18/7/18.
Gale, George, Pte. (A), d. of w., 25/12/16.
Gale, Joseph, Pte. (A), d., 31/3/16.
Gallard, Henry, Pte. (A), k. in a., 5/4/18.
Gander, Thomas, Pte. (B), d. of w., 6/4/18.
Gates, George, Pte. (D), k. in a., 10/4/17.
Gaunt, William, Pte. (B), k. in a., 18/9/18.
Geall, Samuel George, L/Cpl. (D), d. of w., 26/8/18.
Gearing, John Ambrose, Pte. (A), k. in a., 4/3/16.
Gearing, Sidney, Pte. (C), k. in a., 18/9/18.
Geer, Frederick, L/Cpl. (C), k. in a., 30/6/18.
[10]Gell, Walter Henry, Pte. (B), k. in a., 3/5/17.
George, Albert William, Pte. (D), d., 28/1/15.
George, Edward, Pte. (B), k. in a., 6/11/15.
George, William, Pte. (C), k. in a., 3/5/17.
[11]Gibbs, Charles Arthur, Pte. (C), k. in a., 14/5/17.
Gibby, Albert William, Pte. (D), k. in a., 24/9/18.
Gibson, Sidney James, L/Cpl. (B), k. in a., 18/9/18.
Gibson-Lee, William Charles, Pte. (C), k. in a., 18/9/18.
Gillham, Frederick Stephen Michael, Sgt. (C), d. of w., 4/3/16.

Appendix C

Gladwish, William, L/Cpl. (A), k. in a., 4/8/16.
Glue, Charles Richard, Pte. (A), d., 22/3/15.
Goble, George William, Cpl. (B), k. in a., 3/7/17.
Goble, John, Pte. (A), k. in a., 4/8/16.
Gocher, Aubrey Cyril, Pte. (A), k. in a., 7/7/16.
Goddard, John, Pte. (D), d. of w., 29/7/17.
Goddard, Percy William, Pte. (D), k. in a., 7/7/16.
Godden, Charles Tower Rayson, Pte. (A), k. in a., 14/5/17.
Godden, George, Pte. (A), k. in a., 4/3/16.
Godden, George Henry, Pte. (A), k. in a., 3/5/17.
Godfree, Henry, Pte. (B), k. in a., 15/4/16.
Godfree, Richard, Pte. (B), k. in a., 7/7/16.
Goldsmith, George Thomas, Pte. (C), k. in a., 9/4/17.
[12]Gooderson, Harry, Pte. (B), k. in a., 8/8/16.
Gough, John, Pte. (A), d., 8/3/18.
Gould, James, Pte. (D), d. of w., 10/8/18.
Gower, Charles Henry, Pte. (B), d. of w., 25/7/17.
Graham, Harry, Pte. (A), d. of w., 10/4/17.
Grant, Charles, Pte. (D), k. in a., 4/8/16.
Grant, William Christian George, Pte. (A), k. in a., 9/4/17.
Gratwicke, Frederick, Pte., M.M. (D), k. in a., 9/4/17.
Gray, Henry, L/Cpl. (B), d. of w., 25/7/17.
Greenfield, Harry, Pte. (A), k. in a., 7/7/16.
Greenway, William James, Pte. (B), d. of w., 10/4/17.
Gregory, Harry, Pte. (A), d. of w., 28/8/18.
Grender, Sidney, Pte. (B), d. of w., 4/3/16.
Griffiths, Victor, Pte. (D), k. in a., 26/8/18.
Grover, Albert Henry, Pte. (B), k. in a., 6/8/15.
Grover, Reginald, Pte. (B), k. in a., 5/9/18.
Grover, Walter John, Pte. (B), k. in a., 15/2/16.
Gunton, Harry Victor, L/Cpl. (B), d. of w., 15/5/18.
Gutsell, George, Pte. (A), k. in a., 5/4/18.
Hack, Roland, Pte. (A), k. in a., 19/10/16.
Hale, George James, L/Cpl. (C), k. in a., 24/6/18.
Hall, Harry Francis, Cpl. (D), d. of w., 24/5/18.
Hall, J., Pte. (B), k. in a., 9/4/17.†
Hall, Robert, L/Cpl. (C), k. in a., 25/11/17.
Hall, William John, L/Cpl. (A), k. in a., 31/3/17.
Hallam, William, Pte. (D), k. in a., 21/10/16.
Hammocks, Frederick Francis, Pte. (D), d. of w., 29/10/18.
Hampton, William Montague, Pte. (A), k. in a., 12/4/17.
Hamson, Thomas, Pte. (A), k. in a., 8/8/18.
Hand, Fred, Pte. (C), k. in a., 24/8/16.
Harbour, Harry, Pte. (C), k. in a., 16/5/18.
Harbour, Thomas, Pte. (B), k. in a., 4/3/16.
Hardham, George, Sgt. (C), k. in a., 18/9/18.
[13]Harding, Victor Bertram, Pte. (D), d. of w., 20/10/16.
Hardy, William Albert, Pte. (D), k. in a., 13/10/18.
Hare, Percy Herbert, Pte. (A), k. in a., 3/5/17.
Harper, Thomas William, Pte. (A), k. in a., 5/4/18.
Harris, Ernest Albert, Pte. (D), d., 9/11/18.

Appendix C

Harris, Ernest Alfred Cecil, Pte. (B), k. in a., 27/9/15.
Harris, John, Pte. (B), k. in a., 14/11/16.
Harrison, Harry Oscar, Pte. (B), k. in a., 7/7/16.
Harvey, Alec, Pte., D.C.M. (D), k. in a., 18/9/18.
Harwood, George, Pte. (C), k. in a., 22/8/18.
Hassall, James, L/Cpl. (B), k. in a., 29/3/16.
Hawkins, Thomas Frederick, Pte. (B), k. in a., 3/5/17.
[14]Haworth, William, Pte. (D), k. in a., 24/8/18.
Haydock, Frederick Bernard, Pte. (B), k. in a., 25/11/17.
Hayes, Harry, Pte. (B), k. in a., 3/7/18.
Haylor, Allan, Pte. (B), k. in a., 8/4/16.
Hazeldine, Frederick, Pte. (A), k. in a., 7/7/16.
Head, Arthur Henry, Cpl. (D), k. in a., 7/10/16.
Hearsay, William, Pte. (B), k. in a., 4/3/16.
Heasman, James, Pte. (B), k. in a., 25/11/17.
Heasman, William George, Pte. (A), k. in a., 5/4/18.
Heasmer, Edgar, Pte. (D), k. in a., 9/4/17.
Heath, James George, Pte. (B), k. in a., 18/9/18.
Hedger, William James, Pte. (B), d. of w., 6/5/17.‡
Hemsley, Robert, Pte. (B), d. of w., 28/4/18.
Hendry, William, L/Cpl., M.M. (B), k. in a., 2/11/16.
Henson, James, L/Cpl. (B), k. in a., 20/11/17.
Heydon, Archibald John, L/Sgt. (B), k. in a., 27/3/18.
Hill, Harry, L/Cpl. (D), k. in a., 25/11/17.
Hill, Herbert Henry, Pte. (D), k. in a., 20/11/17.
Hill, John, Pte. (C), d., 1/2/17.
Hill, R., Pte. (B), k. in a., 8/4/16.†
Hilton, Fred, L/Cpl. (C), k. in a., 24/3/16.
Hiscock, Harry Albert, Pte. (A), k. in a., 1/12/17.
Hoadley, William Lewis, L/Cpl. (A), k. in a., 19/10/15.
Hodges, Frederick George, L/Cpl. (A), k. in a., 29/8/18.
Hodgkinson, James Bradley, L/Cpl. (A), k. in a., 4/3/16.
Hogan, James Henry, Pte. (B), k. in a., 11/9/15.
Holden, Charles, A/Cpl. (A), k. in a., 5/10/16.
Holden, Frank William, Pte. (B), k. in a., 7/7/16.
Holland, Henry, Pte. (D), k. in a., 30/6/15.
Hollingdale, Leslie Herbert, Pte. (B), k. in a., 7/7/16.
Hollingdale, R., Pte. (D), d., 23/3/15.†
Hollingsworth, George, Pte. (B), k. in a., 19/3/16.
Holliss, Harry Lee, Pte. (A), k. in a., 20/11/17.
Hollman, Thomas, Pte. (C), d. of w., 18/3/16.
Holloway, Percy Leonard, L/Cpl. (B), k. in a., 8/9/15.
Holmes, George, Pte. (D), k. in a., 7/7/16.
Hook, Ernest, Pte. (D), k. in a., 9/4/17.
Hook, Frederick Charles, L/Cpl. (A), k. in a., 8/11/15.
Hopkins, Alfred George, Pte., k. in a., 5/9/17.*
Hopkins, Percy, Pte. (A), k. in a., 25/9/15.
Hopkins, William Charles, Pte. (C), k. in a., 25/11/17.
Hopper, Sydney Mark, Pte. (A), k. in a., 5/3/16.
Horn, John Felix, Pte. (B), d. of w., 11/7/18.
Horney, Robert, L/Sgt. (C), k. in a., 6/4/18.

Appendix C

Hosier, Christopher Arthur, Pte. (C), k. in a., 20/11/17.
Houghton, Frank, Pte. (B), d., 10/5/17.
Howard, Alfred William, Pte. (D), d. of w., 8/10/16.
Howard, John, Pte. (C), k. in a., 7/7/16.
Howden, Samuel, Pte. (A), k. in a., 5/4/18.
Howell, Wilfred, Pte. (D), k. in a., 25/11/17.
Hubbold, John Thomas, Pte. (B), k. in a., 7/7/16.
Hudson, George Ernest, L/Cpl. (D), k. in a., 13/8/18.
Huggett, George, Pte. (D), k. in a., 5/4/18.
Hughes, Charlie, Pte. (A), d. of w., 28/8/18.
Hulkes, E., Sgt. (B), k. in a., 4/8/16.†
Hulme, Joseph Arthur, A/Cpl. (B), k. in a., 3/10/16.
Humberstone, Edward Owen Bray, Pte. (A), k. in a., 3/5/17.
Humphrey, James Thomas, Pte. (D), k. in a., 28/3/18.
Humphreys, George Frederick, Pte. (A), k. in a., 27/3/18.
Humphreys, Harry, Pte. (A), d. of w., 9/2/17.
Hutchison, William Sylvester, Pte. (D), k. in a., 18/9/18.
Huteson, Thomas Edward, Pte. (A), k. in a., 6/7/16.
Hyde, George, Pte. (B), k. in a., 3/5/17.
Hygate, Harold Philip, L/Sgt. (B), d. of w., 23/9/18.
Hyland, George, Pte. (B), k. in a., 25/11/17.
Hylands, Albert, Pte. (D), k. in a., 29/9/18.
Ireson, Alfred, Pte. (C), d. of w., 1/12/17.
Isted, Daniel Frederick, L/Sgt. (C), k. in a., 9/4/16.
Ives, Albert Edward, Pte. (D), d. of w., 21/8/18.
Jackman, Hubert George, Pte. (A), d., 17/11/18.
Jackson, Frederick William, Pte. (B), k. in a., 7/7/16.
Jackson, Richard James, Pte. (C), k. in a., 16/10/18.
Jacobs, Charles Edmund, Pte. (A), k. in a., 1/8/16.
James, Ernest Alfred, Pte. (A), d. of w., 10/5/18.
James, George, Pte. (A), k. in a., 27/3/18.
Jarman, Thomas, Sgt. (B), k. in a., 7/7/16.
Jarrett, William, Pte. (A), k. in a., 27/3/18.
Jarvis, Charles, Pte. (C), d. of w., 21/1/17.
Jeffery, Frank, L/Cpl. (D), k. in a., 9/4/17.
Jeffrey, Eardley Robert Preston, Pte. (C), k. in a., 30/11/17.
Jenner, Douglas, Pte. (C), k. in a., 4/10/15.
Jenner, Edward, L/Cpl. (D), d. of w., 28/3/18.
Jenner, George, Pte. (D), d. of w., 18/7/16.
Jenner, Gordon William Alfred John, Pte. (A), k. in a., 9/8/18.
Jerome, Reginald Frederick, Pte. (B), k. in a., 7/7/16.
Jinks, Charles, Pte. (D), k. in a., 7/10/16.
Johnson, George, Pte. (A), k. in a., 29/12/15.
Johnson, Walter James, Pte. (A), k. in a., 25/7/15.
Johnstone, Edward, Pte. (B), k. in a., 5/11/15.
Jones, Alfred John Joseph, Pte. (A), k. in a., 5/4/18.
Jones, Henry Cornelius, Pte. (B), k. in a., 24/8/18.
Joy, Benjamin Henry, L/Cpl. (A), k. in a., 18/10/15.
Jukes, Louis, Pte. (A), d. of w., 5/5/17.
Jupp, George William, Pte. (C), k. in a., 18/9/18.
Kay, Andrew, Pte. (D), k. in a., 8/8/18.

Appendix C

KAYE, William Faislie, Pte. (B), k. in a., 20/11/17.
KEATING, Joseph, Pte. (B), k. in a., 27/3/18.
KEHLBACHER, George, Pte. (D), k. in a., 25/7/17.
KEIGWIN, Sydney, L/Cpl. (A), d. of w., 17/8/18.
KELLY, Albert Alfred, Pte. (A), k. in a., 27/3/18.
KEMPTON, Jabez, Pte. (A), k. in a., 17/8/17.
KENNABY, James Charles, Pte. (C), k. in a., 13/8/18.
KENNARD, Robert, Cpl. (C), d. of w., 21/10/16.*
KENNEDY, Herbert, Pte. (C), k. in a., 18/9/18.
KENSETT, George, Pte. (C), d. of w., 8/10/15.
KENT, George Alfred John, Pte. (C), k. in a., 5/8/16.
KENT, Herbert, Pte. (B), k. in a., 25/11/17.
KENT, Joseph Charles, Sgt. (B), k. in a., 7/7/16.
KERSWILL, Alfred Leslie, Pte. (A), k. in a., 9/8/18.
KEWELL, Harry, Pte. (C), k. in a., 7/7/16.
KEWELL, Walter, Cpl. (A), k. in a., 4/2/18.
KING, Charles James, Pte. (A), k. in a., 9/8/18.
KING, George, Pte. (C), k. in a., 13/6/15.
KING, James, Sgt., D.C.M. (A), k. in a., 4/3/16.
KINGSHOTT, Frederick, Pte. (D), k. in a., 24/3/16.
KINGSLAND, Albert, Pte. (A), d. of w., 3/5/17.
KIRBY, Alfred Harold, Pte. (A), k. in a., 9/4/17.
KIRK, George Stanley, Pte. (B), k. in a., 25/11/17.
KNIGHT, Archibald, Pte. (A), k. in a., 6/3/16.
KNIGHT, Thomas, Pte. (B), k. in a., 5/4/18.
KNIGHT, Thomas James, Pte. (C), d. of w., 9/11/16.
KNIGHT, William Harold, Pte. (A), k. in a., 8/8/18.
KNOWLES, Arthur Herbert, Pte. (A), d. of w., 4/9/16.
KNOWLES, Charles, Pte. (B), d. of w., 15/10/16.
KNOWLES, Herbert, Pte. (C), d. of w., 8/4/18.
KOHLER, Roland, Pte. (A), k. in a., 5/10/16.
LAKE, John Henry, Pte. (D), d., 18/3/18.
LAKE, Percy Albert, Pte. (D), k. in a., 30/11/17.
LAMBERT, Harry, Sgt. (D), k. in a., 27/3/18.
LATHAM, William, Pte. (A), k. in a., 7/7/16.
LAWES, Ernest Alexander, Pte. (C), d. of w., 29/3/18.
LAWES, James Percy, Cpl. (A), k. in a., 5/4/18.
LAWSON, Frank, Pte. (A), k. in a., 4/8/16.
LAWSON, Thomas Arthur, Pte. (A), k. in a., 13/8/18.
LEA, Henry Thomas, Cpl. (C), d. of w., 23/7/15.
LEE, Percy, Pte. (A), k. in a., 10/2/17.
LEE, Thomas George, Pte. (D), k. in a., 24/8/18.
LEVETT, Jesse, Pte. (A), k. in a., 9/4/18.
LEWCOCK, Horace, Pte. (C), k. in a., 5/10/16.
LEWINGTON, Ernest Victor, Pte. (C), k. in a., 18/9/18.
LEWIS, Arthur, Pte. (A), k. in a., 1/7/17.
LEWIS, George Frederick, Pte. (A), d. of w., 22/10/17.*
LEWIS, James, Pte. (C), k. in a., 7/7/16.
LEWIS, William, Pte. (C), k. in a., 7/7/16.
LIGHT, William John, L/Cpl. (C), k. in a., 7/7/16.
LILLYWHITE, Edwin, L/Cpl. (A), k. in a., 7/7/16.

Appendix C

LINDEN, Walter, Cpl. (B), k. in a., 1/8/16.
LINFIELD, William Denn, Pte. (B), k. in a., 5/4/18.
LITTLE, John Robert, Pte. (A), k. in a., 29/12/15.
LITTLECHILD, George Edward, Pte. (C), k. in a., 30/11/17.
LLOYD, Gerald Burton, Pte. (A), k. in a., 18/9/18.
LLOYD, William, Pte. (A), k. in a., 9/4/17.
LONG, Clarence Sidney, Pte. (C), k. in a., 25/11/17.
LONGBOTTOM, John, L/Cpl. (B), k. in a., 24/8/18.
LONGHURST, William John, Pte (A), d. of w., 10/7/16.
LUCAS, Albert James, Pte. (C), k. in a., 18/9/18.
LUCAS, Frederick George, Pte. (B), k. in a., 3/5/17.
LUCK, Herbert Edward, Pte. (A), k. in a., 31/3/17.
LUXFORD, Arthur Ernest, Cpl. (D), d. of w., 6/5/17.
LUXFORD, Percy, Pte. (D), k. in a., 7/7/16.
LYDDALL, Herbert Percy Sydney, L/Cpl. (B), k. in a., 25/11/17.
MACE, Robert Sidney, Pte. (D), k. in a., 5/10/16.
MACKEY, Arthur, Pte. (A), k. in a., 12/4/17.
MACKEY, John, Pte. (C), k. in a., 5/10/16.
MADGE, William, Sgt. (A), k. in a., 7/7/16.
MAHER, Frank, Pte. (D), k. in a., 7/10/16.
MAIN, Thomas George, Pte. (A), k. in a., 7/7/16.
MALCHER, James Dennis, Pte. (D), k. in a., 1/8/16.
MAN, Reginald Herbert Richard, Pte. (C), k. in a., 5/10/16.
MANKTELOW, George William, Pte. (A), k. in a., 4/8/16.
MANSBRIDGE, William, Pte. (B), k. in a., 20/11/17.
MARCH, Charles William, Pte. (C), d., 7/4/18.
MARCHANT, Frederick, Pte. (A), k. in a., 5/4/18.
MARCHANT, James Henry, Pte. (D), k. in a., 9/4/17.
MARCHANT, Phillip Henry, Pte. (C), k. in a., 9/4/18.
MARDLE, Ernest, Pte. (A), k. in a., 4/2/18.
MARE, Cyril R. C. J., Pte. (A), k. in a., 6/10/18.
MARKS, Harry, Pte. (D), k. in a., 7/7/16.
MARSH, Robert Samuel, Pte. (B), k. in a., 1/10/15.
MARSH, Tom, Pte. (A), k. in a., 5/4/18.
MARTIN, Amos, L/Cpl. (D), d. of w., 5/11/18.*
MARTIN, Harold Sales, Pte. (A), k. in a., 4/3/16.
MARTIN, John, Pte. (D), d. of w., 10/4/17.
MARTIN, Joseph, L/Cpl. (A), k. in a., 3/3/16.
MASCALL, Victor Edward, Pte. (B), d. of w., 13/9/18.
MASKELL, Frederick Charles, Pte. (A), k. in a., 26/8/18.
MASKELL, Harry, Pte. (B), k. in a., 1/8/16.
MASLIN, George, L/Cpl. (D), d. of w., 26/11/17.
MATTHEWS, Frederick George Alexander, Pte. (C), k. in a., 5/10/16.
MAUGHAN, Henry, L/Cpl., M.M. (D), k. in a., 25/11/17.
MAXWELL, George Ernest, Pte. (B), d. of w., 6/4/18.
MAY, Harry, Pte. (C), k. in a., 11/8/18.
MAYNARD, Samuel Charles, Pte. (B), k. in a., 25/11/17.
MCCAUL, Lawrence, Pte. (A), k. in a., 7/7/16.
[15]MEASOR, Frederick, Pte. (A), d. of w., 12/4/16.
MEEKINGS, Horace Jacob, Pte. (B), k. in a., 18/9/18.
MEETEN, George, Pte. (C), k. in a., 17/10/15.

Appendix C

MEETEN, Harry, L/Cpl. (A), d. of w., 10/7/16.
MEIN, William James, Pte. (B), k. in a., 25/7/17.
MERCER, Harry, Pte. (B), k. in a., 21/9/18.
MERRITT, George Thomas, Pte. (D), d. of w., 3/7/15.
MERRITT, Samuel George, L/Cpl., k. in a., 28/8/18.*
MERTON, Charles Frederick, Pte., k. in a., 30/12/16.*
MIDDLETON, Walter, Pte. (D), k. in a., 20/11/17.
MIDMORE, Alfred Ernest, Pte. (A), k. in a., 7/7/16.
MILES, Alfred Edward, Pte. (A), k. in a., 5/10/16.
MILES, Arthur John, Pte. (A), k. in a., 4/8/16.
MILLARD, Frederick William, Pte. (B), k. in a., 7/7/16.
MILLER, Alfred, Pte. (C), k. in a., 13/3/16.
MILLER, Arthur John, Pte. (C), k. in a., 13/8/18.
MILLS, Ernest Richard, Pte. (B), k. in a., 25/7/17.
MILLS, Frank, Pte. (B), k. in a., 9/4/17.
MILLS, George, Pte. (B), d. of w., 31/12/15.
MILLS, John Robert, Pte. (D), d. of w., 4/10/15.
MILSTED, William Walter, L/Cpl. (C), k. in a., 3/5/17.
MINALL, Edward George, Sgt. (B), k. in a., 27/3/18.
MINNIS, James, Pte. (D), k. in a., 3/7/18.
MISSELBROOK, Stephen, Pte. (B), k. in a., 18/9/18.
MITCHELL, Frank, Pte. (A), k. in a., 18/9/18.
MITCHELL, Frederick, Sgt. (B), k. in a., 9/4/17.
MITCHELL, Frederick George, Pte. (A), k. in a., 19/10/15.
MITCHELL, James Frederick, Pte. (A), k. in a., 5/4/18.
MOCKFORD, N., Pte. (A), k. in a., 31/3/17.†
MOORE, Arthur, Pte. (B), d. of w., 3/9/18.
MOORE, Sidney, Pte. (C), k. in a., 3/5/17.
MOORE, Wilfred, L/Cpl. (A), k. in a., 29/7/17.
MORGAN, Aubrey Lloyd, Pte. (B), k. in a., 21/10/15.
MORGAN, Alfred Thomas, Pte. (B), k. in a., 20/11/17.
MORLEY, William Leonard, Sgt. (C), k. in a., 5/9/18.
MORRIS, Andrew George Warder, Pte. (C), d., 15/3/17.
MORRIS, Edward Frederick, Pte. (C), k. in a., 4/8/16.
MORRIS, Owen Corby, Pte., M.M. (A), k. in a., 26/8/18.
MOUNTSTEPHENS, Arthur, Cpl. (A), d. of w., 15/8/18.
MUIR, Charles, Pte. (A), k. in a., 8/4/16.
MUIRHEAD, William Charles Read, Pte. (A), k. in a., 4/8/16.
MUNNS, William, Pte. (D), d. of w., 27/9/18.
MURRAY, John George, Pte. (D), k. in a., 7/7/16.
MURRELL, William Edward, Pte. (A), k. in a., 3/5/17.
NAISBITT, John, Pte. (D), d. of w., 5/10/15.
NAPPER, Maurice, Pte. (B), k. in a., 17/3/16.
NEW, Ernest Reginald, Pte. (A), d. of w., 30/3/18.
NEW, John Edward, L/Cpl. (C), k. in a., 7/7/16.
NEWINGTON, Percy, Pte. (C), k. in a., 23/2/17.
NEWMAN, William Joshua, Pte. (D), k. in a., 25/9/15.*
NEWTON, Frank, Cpl. (C), k. in a., 18/9/18.
NEWTON, William, Pte. (C), k. in a., 22/7/15.
NICHOLLS, Charles Herbert, Pte. (B), k. in a., 3/5/17.
NICHOLS, Frank Victor, Pte., M.M. (B), k. in a., 4/8/16.

Appendix C

Nicholson, Samuel, Pte. (A), d. of w., 13/7/16.
Nickless, Thomas, Pte. (D), k. in a., 8/8/18.
Niederauer, Albert, Pte. (B), d. of w., 27/9/15.
Nightingale, Leonard, Pte. (D), k. in a., 9/4/17.
Noble, James, Pte. (B), k. in a., 3/5/17.
Norman, H., Pte. (A), d., 6/1/19.†
Norman, John Cecil, A/Cpl. (A), k. in a., 5/10/16.
Norris, William Edward, Pte. (A), k. in a., 9/4/17.
North, George, Pte. (D), k. in a., 24/3/16.
Norton, Alfred, Pte. (D), k. in a., 28/2/17.
Nurden, Charles, Pte. (A), k. in a., 9/4/17.
Oakley, William Edwin, Pte. (A), k. in a., 1/8/16.
Olley, John George, Pte. (B), d. of w., 6/9/18.
Onslow, Albert George William, Pte. (C), k. in a., 9/4/18.
Oram, Leonard, Pte. (A), k. in a., 7/7/16.
Osborn, Harry Cecil, Pte. (C), k. in a., 9/4/18.
Osborne, Harry, Pte. (D), k. in a., 25/9/15.
Osborne, Walter Jesse, Sgt., M.M. (D), d. of w., 24/11/17.
Osborne, William James, Pte. (B), k. in a., 13/10/16.
Owen, Thomas, Pte. (B), d., 30/5/15.*
Pack, George Robert, Pte. (D), k. in a., 7/7/16.
Packham, Reuben, Pte. (C), k. in a., 8/8/18.
Padfield, Herbert George, Pte. (B), k. in a., 4/8/16.
[16]Page, Albert, Pte. (A), k. in a., 1/10/17.
Page-Mitchell, Sidney William, Pte. (D), k. in a., 26/8/18.
Paice, Arthur Edward, Sgt. (B), k. in a., 25/11/17.
Paice, Edgar William, L/Cpl. (C), k. in a., 5/10/16.
Pain, George Montague, Pte. (B), d. of w., 10/4/17.
Palmer, Maurice William, L/Cpl. (B), k. in a., 7/7/16.
Palmer, Percy Alexander, L/Cpl. (B), k. in a., 3/5/17.
Palmer, Sydney, Pte. (A), d. of w., 2/10/18.*
Pannell, Frederick Lawrence, L/Sgt. (A), k. in a., 1/10/17.
Papworth, Frederick, Pte. (D), k. in a., 8/8/18.
Papworth, Leonard, Pte. (D), k. in a., 3/7/18.
Park, Colin Archibald, L/Cpl. (C), k. in a., 25/10/18.
Parkinson, William James Frederick, Pte. (A), k. in a., 20/5/18.
Patten, Maurice, L/Cpl. (B), d. of w., 13/1/16.
Payne, Frank Harry, Pte. (D), d., 12/12/16.
Pearson, Herbert, Pte. (D), d. of w., 25/9/15.
Peart, T., Pte. (C), d. of w., 15/4/17.†
Peckham, Charles William, Pte. (B), d. of w., 11/7/18.*
Peen, John Robert, Pte. (C), k. in a., 20/11/17.
Pegram, Edgar George, Pte. (A), k. in a., 5/9/18.
Pelling, Ernest Alfred, Pte. (D), k. in a., 25/7/17.
Penfold, Henry Leonard James, Pte. (A), k. in a., 9/11/15.
Penfold, J., Pte. (B), k. in a., 18/9/18.†
Pennell, Charles, Pte. (C), d. of w., 7/5/17.
Penrith, James, Pte. (C), k. in a., 13/4/17.
Pepper, Leonard Lionel, Pte. (C), k. in a., 7/7/16.
Perry, Ernest, Pte. (B), d. of w., 9/10/15.
Peters, Henry William, Pte. (C), k. in a., 18/9/18.

Appendix C

Philcox, Thomas William, Cpl. (C), k. in a., 8/8/18.
Phillips, Arthur, Pte. (A), k. in a., 31/7/16.
Phillips, Richard Charles, Pte., k. in a., 9/9/16.*
Phillips, Steven, Pte. (C), k. in a., 2/10/15.
Pink, William, Pte. (B), k. in a., 18/9/18.
Pirie, Ernest, Pte. (B), k. in a., 7/7/16.
Playford, Harry, Pte. (C), k. in a., 7/7/16.
Plummer, Frank, Pte. (B), d. of w., 27/5/18.
Plummer, John Robert, Pte. (C), k. in a., 18/9/18.
Pockney, Ernest James, Pte. (B), d. of w., 7/10/15.
Pocock, Amos, Pte. (D), k. in a., 9/4/17.
Poole, Henry George, Pte. (C), k. in a., 5/8/16.
Pope, Edward George, L/Cpl. (B), k. in a., 7/7/16.
Porteous, Dennis Reid, Pte., M.M. (D), k. in a., 28/3/18.
Portington, Edward Horace, Pte. (B), d. of w., 3/8/17.
Potter, Frederick, Pte. (C), d. of w., 7/9/18.
Powell, Arthur, Pte. (B), d. of w., 3/5/18.
Pratt, Joseph Walter, Pte. (C), d. of w., 8/8/18.
Pratt, William, Pte. (D), d. of w., 13/3/16.
Pratt, William George, Pte. (A), k. in a., 3/5/17.
Preater, George Montague, Pte. (C), k. in a., 4/8/16.
Preece, Stanley, Pte. (B), k. in a., 5/4/18.
Preston, George William, Cpl., M.M. (B), k. in a., 20/11/17.
Prevett, Robert, Sgt., D.C.M. (B), d. of w., 6/10/16.
Prevost, Arthur George, Pte. (C), k. in a., 18/9/18.
Prior, William James, Pte. (B), k. in a., 7/7/16.
Pullen, Gerald Cliff, L/Cpl. (D), k. in a., 7/7/16.
Pullen, William Robert, Pte. (A), k. in a., 1/10/16.
Pumphrey, George, Pte. (D), k. in a., 3/5/17.
Purchase, Charles, Pte. (B), d., 26/4/18.
Quaife, George Henry, L/Cpl. (D), k. in a., 7/10/16.
Quelch, Arthur Leslie, Pte. (B), k. in a., 7/7/16.
Quested, Alec William, Pte. (A), k. in a., 24/9/18.
Quinn, John, L/Cpl. (A), k. in a., 5/4/18.
Ralph, Albert Edward, Pte. (B), k. in a., 7/7/16.
Rand, James, Pte. (B), k. in a., 8/8/18.
Randall, Leonard Victor, Pte. (C), k. in a., 27/3/18.
Ransom, Edward Alfred, Pte. (C), k. in a., 3/3/16.
Ransom, Frederick James, Sgt., D.C.M., M.M., Croix de Guerre (B), d. of w., 8/10/18.
Ratcliffe, Albert, Pte. (C), k. in a., 3/5/17.
Raven, William, Pte. (A), k. in a., 7/7/16.
Rawling, Leonard John, Pte. (A), k. in a., 12/4/17.
Ray, Joseph, L/Cpl. (D), k. in a., 6/4/18.
Rayment, John William, Pte. (B), d. of w., 19/9/18.
Reed, Richard, Pte. (C), d. of w., 23/9/18.
Reed, Thomas John, Pte. (D), k. in a., 9/4/17.
Reed, William George, L/Cpl. (A), k. in a., 4/8/16.
Reeve, Frederick Joseph, Pte. (B), k. in a., 24/8/18.
Reickie, William Herbert, Pte. (A), k. in a., 9/8/18.
Relf, Henry, Pte. (D), k. in a., 25/7/17.

Appendix C

Relfe, Percival Edward, Pte. (C), k. in a., 21/9/18.
Rich, Frederick Arthur, Pte. (B), k. in a., 18/9/18.
Richardson, Charles, Pte. (C), k. in a., 7/7/16.
Richardson, Harold Thomas Burchett, L/Cpl. (A), k. in a., 7/7/16.
Richardson, William Henry, L/Cpl. (C), k. in a., 3/5/17.
Ridley, James Frank, Pte. (A), k. in a., 9/4/17.
Robbins, William, C.Q.M.S. (B), k. in a., 25/11/17.
Roberts, Roy Alfred, L/Cpl. (B), k. in a., 26/8/18.
Roberts, William Alfred, Pte. (D), k. in a., 18/12/15.
Robins, Ernest, Pte. (C), d. of w., 8/10/16.
Robinson, Alfred, Pte. (C), k. in a., 7/7/16.
Rodgers, William, Pte. (B), k. in a., 4/3/16.
Rogers, Edward Thomas, L/Cpl. (B), k. in a., 4/3/16.
Rogers, James Vincent, Pte. (D), d. of w., 9/7/16.
Rogers, John, Pte. (D), k. in a., 20/11/17.
Routledge, Ernest Gordon, Pte. (C), k. in a., 30/11/17.
Rowe, George, Pte. (B), k. in a., 7/7/16.
Roxbee, Charles Frederick, Pte. (B), d. of w., 6/10/16.
Russell, Alfred, Pte. (C), k. in a., 25/10/18.
Russell, Frederick John, Sgt. (B), k. in a., 3/10/16.
Russell, Frederick William, Pte. (A), k. in a., 27/3/18.
Russell, William, Pte. (D), k. in a., 5/7/17.
Rutland, George William, Pte. (A), k. in a., 27/3/18.
Sadler, Alfred James, Pte. (B), k. in a., 3/3/16.
Sadler, Stanley Victor, L/Cpl. (C), d. of w., 28/8/18.
[17]Sales, Frederick Charles, Pte. (A), k. in a., 3/5/17.
Salvage, Harry, Pte. (C), d., 14/7/18.
Salvage, John Albert, Pte. (D), d. of w., 9/4/17.
Sambrook, George Frederick, Pte. (D), d. of w., 29/7/17.
Sammonds, John Edward, L/Cpl. (A), k. in a., 5/4/18.
Sanders, Albert George, Pte. (A), k. in a., 22/8/18.
Sands, John, Pte. (C), d. of w., 26/11/17.
Sands, Walter, Cpl. (A), k. in a., 29/8/18.
Sands, William, Pte. (D), k. in a., 29/9/18.
Savage, Charles, Robert, L/Cpl. (C), k. in a., 3/5/17.
Sawyer, Arthur, Pte. (C), d. of w., 30/4/18.
Sawyer, George Harry, Pte. (B), k. in a., 5/4/18.
Sayers, Harold Theodore, Pte. (A), d. of w., 11/7/16.
Sayers, Henry, L/Sgt. (C), d. of w., 9/8/18.
Sayers, William Richard, L/Cpl. (A), k. in a., 26/8/18.
Scarce, Ernest William, Pte. (A), k. in a., 8/10/16.
Scopes, George Lewis, Pte. (C), k. in a., 5/10/16.
Scott, Leonard Randall, Pte. (C), k. in a., 30/7/16.
Scrivens, William Frederick, Pte. (D), k. in a., 27/3/18.
Scutt, Frederick, Pte. (A), k. in a., 18/9/18.
Scutt, Thomas William, Pte. (A), k. in a., 4/8/16.
Seamark, Joseph Samuel, Pte. (B), k. in a., 9/8/18.
Sears, Henry George, Pte. (D), d., 10/2/17.
Secker, George, Pte. (D), k. in a., 29/9/18.
Secker, William, Pte. (D), d. of w., 25/8/18.
Seckham, Gerald, A/L/Sgt. (A), k. in a., 4/8/16.

Appendix C

Selby, Albert Edward, Sgt., M.M. (A), k. in a., 8/8/18.
Seldon, Herbert Alfred, Pte. (A), k. in a., 9/4/17.
Sewell, Herbert Charles, Pte. (C), d. of w., 16/4/17.
Seymour, William, Pte. (C), k. in a., 16/5/18.
Shawyer, Ernest Henry, Pte. (A), k. in a., 1/8/16.
Sheppard, Frederick, Pte. (A), k. in a., 18/9/18.
Sheppard, William John, L/Cpl. (A), k. in a., 4/3/16.
Sherman, Lawrence Shuster, L/Cpl. (A), d. of w., 5/8/16.
Shoesmith, David William, Pte. (B), k. in a., 28/3/18.
Short, Herbert, Pte. (A), d. of w., 29/3/18.
Shorten, John Daniel, Pte. (A), k. in a., 3/5/17.
Shorter, Aaron, Pte. (D), d., 1/5/18.*
Sickelmore, Charles Stanley, Cpl. (A), k. in a., 30/11/17.
Silsby, Charles, Pte. (A), d. of w., 16/4/16.
Silsby, Frederick, Pte. (A), d. of w., 5/10/16.
Simmonds, Frank, Pte. (B), k. in a., 7/7/16.
Simmons, Charles, Pte. (C), d. of w., 27/8/18.
Simmons, Harry, Pte. (D), k. in a., 5/7/17.
Simmons, Hugh, Pte. (B), k. in a., 31/7/15.
Simmons, Sidney John, Pte. (B), k. in a., 18/9/18.
Simons, Ambrose Ernest, Pte. (A), k. in a., 9/4/17.
Sims, Harry, Pte. (B), d. of w., 6/8/15.
Sinclair, Daniel, Pte. (A), k. in a., 7/7/16.
Sinclair, John, Pte. (D), k. in a., 20/1/16.
[18]Sisley, Charles Lawrence, Cpl. (D), k. in a., 7/7/18.
Skerrett, Arthur, Sgt. (D), d. of w., 14/4/16.
Skinner, Frank, Pte. (A), k. in a., 4/3/16.
Slade, James, Pte. (C), d., 3/2/17.
Small, Frank Mitchell, Pte. (B), k. in a., 3/5/17.
Smissen, George, Pte. (A), k. in a., 31/3/17.
Smith, Alfred, Pte. (B), k. in a., 20/11/17.
Smith, Arthur, Pte. (B), k. in a., 3/7/17.
Smith, Arthur Henry Thomas, Pte. (C), k. in a., 7/7/16.
Smith, Arthur William, Cpl. (C), d. of w., 24/10/15.
Smith, Bertram Frank, Pte. (D), k. in a., 18/9/18.
Smith, Harry, L/Cpl. (C), d. of w., 20/9/18.
Smith, Henry, Pte. (D), k. in a., 14/5/17.
Smith, Walter William, Pte. (B), d. of w., 24/8/18.
Smith, William, Pte. (A), k. in a., 19/10/15.
Smithers, Frederick James, Pte. (C), d., 8/8/16.*
Snell, Frederick, Pte. (C), k. in a., 21/9/18.
Soal, Arthur, Pte. (D), k. in a., 9/11/15.
Soffe, Gabriel, Pte. (D), d. of w., 10/4/17.
Souch, Frederick Henry, L/Cpl. (C), d. of w., 10/8/17.
Southon, Jesse, Pte. (A), k. in a., 5/4/18.
[19]Southon, Robert, L/Cpl. (A), k. in a., 7/7/16.
Spencely, John Henry, Pte. (C), k. in a., 11/8/18.
Springett, Frederick Richard, Pte. (B), k. in a., 25/11/17.
Squires, Arthur Edwin, Pte. (B), d., 5/3/18.
Squires, David, Pte. (A), k. in a., 9/4/17.
Squires, James Edward, Pte. (D), k. in a., 21/10/15.

Appendix C

STAMPE, Herbert William, Pte. (A), k. in a., 7/7/16.
STANLEY, John, Pte. (A), k. in a., 5/4/18.
STAPLEHURST, Ernest, Pte. (A), d. of w., 19/9/18.
STAPLEHURST, George, Pte. (A), d. of w., 6/8/16.
STARLING, Frederick Charles, Pte. (D), k. in a., 7/7/16.
STEADMAN, Charles, Pte. (A), k. in a., 7/7/16.
STEAR, Gilbert, L/Cpl. (B), k. in a., 8/4/16.
STEBBINGS, Walter Henry, Pte. (A), k. in a., 9/4/17.
STEDMAN, Arthur George, Pte. (A), k. in a., 8/10/16.
STEEDMAN, Cyril, Pte. (B), k. in a., 7/7/16.
STENNER, William George, L/Cpl. (B), k. in a., 17/3/16.
STEPHENSON, Mossetse, Pte. (A), k. in a., 26/8/18.
STEVENS, Harry, Pte. (A), k. in a., 1/8/16.
STONE, Frederick Edward, Pte. (A), k. in a., 20/5/18.
STONE, Richard William, L/Cpl. (D), k. in a., 7/10/16.
STONER, Edward, Sgt. (D), k. in a., 9/4/17.
STRUDWICK, William, Pte. (D), k. in a., 25/7/17.
STUBBS, Thomas, Pte. (C), k. in a., 7/7/16.
STURT, Harry James, L/Cpl. (B), k. in a., 7/7/16.
SUMMERFIELD, Henry, Pte. (C), d. of w., 15/4/16.
SUMMERS, Harold, Pte. (D), k. in a., 18/9/18.
SUMMONS, Arthur Stephen, Pte. (C), k. in a., 5/8/16.
SWAIN, Edward Alfred, Pte. (D), d. of w., 19/8/18.
SWAYNE, Dennis, Pte. (D), d. of w., 11/7/16.
SWIFT, Frederick, Pte. (A), k. in a., 18/9/18.
SYLVESTER, Samuel, Pte. (C), k. in a., 7/7/16.
TAYLOR, Alfred Edward, Pte. (D), d. of w., 16/10/18.*
TAYLOR, Arthur Hines, Pte. (A), d. of w., 28/3/18.
TAYLOR, Frederick, Pte. (B), k. in a., 7/7/16.
TAYLOR, George, Sgt. (D), k. in a., 4/7/17.
TAYLOR, George, Pte. (D), d. of w., 18/10/18.*
TAYLOR, George Edward, Pte. (A), k. in a., 18/3/16.
[20]TAYLOR, George Henry, Pte. (C), k. in a., 3/5/17.
TEAGUE, Eric Jonathan, Pte. (D), d. of w., 26/9/18.
TEE, James Edward, L/Cpl. (A), k. in a., 7/7/16.
TEGERDINE, John Oscar, Pte. (A), k. in a., 26/8/18.
TESTER, Harry, Pte. (A), k. in a., 30/7/17.
THACKER, Robert George, Pte. (B), d. of w., 9/10/16.
THAKE, Ernest, Pte. (C), k. in a., 18/9/18.
THIRST, William, Pte., M.M. (B), d. of w., 4/10/18.*
THOMPSON, Arthur James, Pte. (B), k. in a., 8/7/15.
TIFFIN, Fred Baxter, Pte. (C), k. in a., 26/7/15.
TILL, Ernest George, L/Cpl. (C), k. in a., 5/10/16.
TIMMINS, John Caswell, Pte. (C), k. in a., 7/7/16.
TINDELL, John Harold, Pte. (D), d. of w., 16/10/16.
TINGLEY, George Arthur, Pte. (B), k. in a., 7/7/16.
TINSLEY, Edward, Pte. (A), k. in a., 31/3/17.
TITMAN, Lewis, Pte. (C), k. in a., 18/9/18.
TOOKE, Albert, Pte. (D), d. of w., 14/12/17.
TOOMS, Frederick John, L/Sgt., M.M. (A), k. in a., 22/8/18.
TOWNSEND, Charles Arthur, Pte. (C), k. in a., 28/4/18.

Appendix C

TRILL, Charles Tower, L/Cpl. (D), k. in a., 7/7/16.
TROTMAN, Alfred John, Pte. (D), k. in a., 9/4/17.
TULLY, Arthur, Pte. (B), d. of w., 23/6/18.
TURNER, Frederick Thomas, Pte. (D), d. of w., 8/8/18.
TWIBELL, Reginald, L/Cpl. (A), k. in a., 28/7/17.
TWINE, Harold John, Pte. (B), k. in a., 7/7/16.
TWINN, Walter Wallace, Pte. (C), k. in a., 22/8/18.
TYRRELL, George Warden, Sgt. (A), k. in a., 1/8/16.
UNSTED, William, Sgt. (C), k. in a., 7/7/16.
UTTING, Edward, Pte. (C), k. in a., 18/9/18.
VENN, Edward Noah, C.S.M. (C), k. in a., 9/8/18.
VINCENT, James, Pte. (B), k. in a., 5/4/18.
VOAK, Harry, L/Cpl. (B), k. in a., 25/7/17.
VOICE, Arthur, Pte. (B), k. in a., 8/4/16
WADE, Arthur, Pte. (B), k. in a., 5/4/18.
WADY, Edward, Cpl. (B), k. in a., 7/7/16.
WAKEFORD, Harry, Pte. (B), k. in a., 8/8/18.
WAKEHAM, Peter, Pte. (D), k. in a., 28/3/18.
WALDER, Percy, Pte. (C), k. in a., 12/9/16.*
WALKER, Frederick Charles, Pte. (A), k. in a., 5/10/16.
WALKER, George Edwin, Pte. (A), k. in a., 7/7/16.
WALL, Percy Charles, Pte. (C), k. in a., 7/7/16.
WALLER, Charles Henry, L/Cpl. (D), d., 14/11/18.*
WALLER, Charles William, Pte. (A), k. in a., 7/7/16.
WALLER, Frank, Pte. (B), k. in a., 9/4/17.
21WALLS, James, L/Cpl. (B), d. of w., 28/3/16.
WALLS, John, Pte. (A), k. in a., 7/7/16.
WARE, Thomas William, Pte. (C), d. of w., 4/5/17.
WARRINGTON, Fred, Pte. (C), d. of w., 24/9/18.
WASHER, George, L/Cpl. (D), k. in a., 3/7/18.
WATSON, Alfred, Pte. (A), k. in a., 16/10/15.
WATSON, Charles John, L/Cpl. (C), d. of w., 2/3/16.
WATSON, Edward, Pte. (D), k. in a., 25/11/17.
WATTS, Andrew George, Pte. (B), k. in a., 4/3/16.
WATTS, George Frederick, Pte. (A), d. of w., 28/9/15.
WEATHERLEY, William, Pte. (D), d. of w., 30/8/17.
WEBB, Bertie Frank, Pte. (B), k. in a., 24/8/18.
WEBBER, Frederick Percy, Pte. (C), k. in a., 4/7/17.
WEBBER, Thomas, Pte. (C), d. of w., 11/4/17.
WEBSTER, Thomas, Cpl. (B), k. in a., 31/7/17.*
WEEDEN, Robert George, Pte., k. in a., 30/11/17.
WEST, Henry Edward, Pte. (D), d. of w., 23/11/17.
WEST, William, Pte. (B), k. in a., 7/7/16.
WESTGATE, James William George, Pte. (C), d. of w., 18/9/18.
WESTGATE, William, Pte. (C), d. of w., 5/5/17.
WESTON, Albert George, Pte. (C), k. in a., 7/7/16.
WHARTON, David, Pte. (A), k. in a., 24/9/18.
WHITE, Arthur Thomas, Pte. (C), d. of w., 9/8/18.
WHITEMAN, James, L/Cpl. (D), d. of w., 7/7/16.
WHITENSTALL, Albert, L/Cpl. (C), k. in a., 7/7/16.
WHITTEMORE, Frederick Arthur, Pte., M.M. and Bar (D), k. in a., 26/8/18.

Appendix C

WICKHAM, Ernest Humphrey, Pte. (B), k. in a., 25/7/17.
WIGHTWICK, Edwin Bert, Pte. (A), k. in a., 9/4/17.
WILD, George, Pte. (B), k. in a., 9/8/18.
WILDMAN, Ernest Vaughan, Pte. (B), k. in a., 5/7/16.
WILKINS, Edward, Pte. (C), k. in a., 25/7/17.
WILLIAMS, John, L/Cpl. (B), k. in a., 18/9/18.
WILLS, William Henry, Pte., d. of w., 20/4/17.*
WILSON, Fred William, Pte. (C), d. of w., 26/11/17.
WINGFIELD, John, Pte. (C), k. in a., 24/5/18.
WINKWORTH, Victor Charles, Pte. (B), k. in a., 8/4/16.
WINTER, Henry Horace, Pte. (D), d. of w., 12/8/18.
22WINTER, Robert Ernest, Pte. (C), k. in a., 8/8/18.
WISE, Edward, Cpl. (D), k. in a., 8/8/18.
WOOD, Albert, Pte. (B), d. of w., 19/3/16.
WOOD, Leonard Daniel, Pte. (A), k. in a., 9/4/17.
WOOFF, Arthur Thomas, Pte. (A), k. in a., 9/4/17.
WOOLLER, Albert Stanley, Pte. (A), k. in a., 7/7/16.
WORTH, Lewis, Cpl. (B), k. in a., 4/8/15.*
WRAPSON, William, Pte. (A), k. in a., 8/7/16.
WRIGHT, Ernest, Pte. (D), d. of w., 10/8/15.
WRIGHT, George Henry, Pte. (B), k. in a., 3/5/17.

CORRECTIONS TO OFFICIAL LIST, &c.

1. Name is given in Official List as Astell.
2. Date   ,,   ,,   30/10/16.
3. Date   ,,   ,,   8/ 3/16.
4. Date   ,,   ,,   18/ 8/18.
5. Date   ,,   ,,   8/ 8/18.
6. Date   ,,   ,,   8/ 2/17.
7. Date   ,,   ,,   22/ 8/16.
8. Given as d. (not d. of w.) in Official List.
9. Date is given in Official List as 22/12/15.
10. Name   ,,   ,,   and on Panels as Gill.
11. Date   ,,   ,,   as 4/ 5/17.
12. Date   ,,   ,,   8/ 4/16.
13. Date   ,,   ,,   30/10/16.
14. Date   ,,   ,,   28/ 8/18.
15. Date   ,,   ,,   2/ 4/18.
16. Date   ,,   ,,   29/ 7/18.
17. Date   ,,   ,,   8/ 5/17.
18. Date   ,,   ,,   9/ 7/18.
19. Date   ,,   ,,   15/ 5/16.
20. Date   ,,   ,,   3/ 5/15.
21. Name   ,,   on Panels as Waller.
22. Date   ,,   in Official List as 8/ 8/16.

The inclusion in the Official List of Kenward, Ernest Henry, Pte., d. of w., 18/9/14, must have been in error, as the battalion was not in France at that date and no such name can be found in Part II Orders; the name has, therefore, been omitted from the above list.

APPENDIX D.

HONOURS AND AWARDS GAINED BY MEMBERS OF THE BATTALION.

SUMMARY.

Bar to D.S.O.	1
D.S.O.	4
O.B.E.	1
Bar to M.C.	2
M.C.	27
Bar to D.C.M.	1
D.C.M.	17
2nd Bar to M.M.	1
Bar to M.M.	10
M.M.	118
M.S.M.	5
Foreign decorations	4
Mentions	33 (23 individuals)

NOTE.—This list is probably not entirely complete, for when a member of the battalion was wounded or sick and went to the Base he was struck off the strength and any honour subsequently awarded to him would not be recorded in our Part II Orders. As our Part I Orders and Recommendation Book have been destroyed and the *London Gazettes* do not give the numbers of the battalions, the Compilers have been obliged to leave the list in its incomplete form, with apologies to those whose names have been omitted.

From the Roll of Honour it will be seen that three more members of the battalion were awarded decorations, but their names have not been included in the list, as there is no record of their having received these honours when serving with our battalion.

Their names are :—

HARVEY, Pte. A.	(D) awarded	D.C.M.
THIRST, Pte. W.	(B) ,,	M.M.
WHITTEMORE, Pte. F. A.	(D) ,,	M.M. and Bar.

BAR TO DISTINGUISHED SERVICE ORDER

IMPEY, Lt.-Col. G. H., D.S.O.   26/ 7/18. (Also three times mentioned in despatches.)

Appendix D

DISTINGUISHED SERVICE ORDER

ANDREWS, Capt. S. A., M.C.   8/ 3/19. (Also awarded Bar to M.C.)
O'MALLEY, Capt. G. P.   1/ 2/19.
OSBORN, Lt.-Col. W. L.   14/ 4/16. (Also three times mentioned in despatches.)
THOMSON, Lt.-Col. A. L.   11/ 1/19. (Also mentioned in despatches.)

OFFICER OF THE ORDER OF THE BRITISH EMPIRE

CLARKE, Capt. and Q.M. J. E.   3/ 6/19. (Also mentioned in despatches.)

BAR TO MILITARY CROSS

ANDREWS, Capt. S. A., M.C.   1/ 2/19. (Also awarded D.S.O.)
RECKITT, Capt. G. L., M.C.   11/ 1/19.

MILITARY CROSS

BALLARD, Capt. C. W.   18/ 7/17.
BOWLBY, Capt. H. S.   26/ 9/16.
BRANSON, Lt. V. C.   1/ 2/19.
BROUGHALL, 2/Lt. H. S.   22/ 9/16.
BURDETT, Lt. S. L.   8/ 3/19.
CLARK, Lt. B. H. C.   11/ 1/19.
CLARKE, 2/Lt. T.   19/11/17.
CLEAVER, Capt. A. E. T.   22/ 9/16.
CLEMENTS, Lt. R. F.   13/ 5/18.
COXHEAD, 2/Lt. L. G.   8/ 3/19.
CUTLER, 2/Lt. E. C.   26/ 7/18.
FARROW, Lt. H. J. R.   18/ 2/18.
GORRINGE, Capt. E. C.   26/ 7/18.
HIND, Capt. R. C. D.   14/12/17. (Also twice mentioned in despatches.)

HOWE, Capt. R. M.   11/ 1/19.
JOY, C.S.M. J.   19/12/16.
LE HARDY, Capt. W. H. C.   18/ 2/18.
LOTHAM, 2/Lt. S.   11/ 1/19.
McCRACKEN, 2/Lt. N.   18/ 7/17.
NAGLE, 2/Lt. G.   14/ 4/16. (Also mentioned in despatches.)

OSBORNE, Major G. F.   26/ 7/18. (Also three times mentioned in despatches.)

PRINCE, Lt. G. W.   18/ 7/18.
RECKITT, Capt. G. L.   11/ 1/19. (Also awarded Bar.)
SADLER, 2/Lt. H.   22/ 9/16.
SUTTON, Lt. E. G.   -/ -/15. (Also mentioned in despatches.)

TAYLOR, Capt. H. F.   18/ 7/17.
WILLIAMS, Rev. W. J.   -/11/17.

Appendix D

BAR TO DISTINGUISHED CONDUCT MEDAL
TREVOR, Sgt. A., D.C.M., M.M. (D) 16/ 1/19. (Also awarded M.M.)

DISTINGUISHED CONDUCT MEDAL

CHEESMAN, Pte. R.	(C)	14/ 4/16.
FAIRHALL, Sgt. F. C.	(B)	17/ 9/17.
HEAD, Sgt. E. J.	(C)	16/ 1/19.
HIGHGATE, Pte. E., M.M.	(B)	12/ 3/19. (Also awarded M.M. and 2 Bars.)
HODGES, Sgt. G.	(C)	22/ 9/16. (Also awarded Italian Bronze Medal.)
KING, Sgt. J.	(A)	8/11/15.
LANGLEY, Sgt. G.	(C)	14/ 4/16.
MOSS, Cpl. E. W.	(A)	22/ 3/18.
PAGE, R.S.M., H.	(B)	20/ 6/16.
PREVETT, Sgt. R.	(B)	22/ 9/16.
RANSOM, Sgt. F. J., M.M.	(B)	5/13/18. (Also awarded M.M. and French Croix de Guerre.)
SANDERSON, Sgt. J. W.	(C)	11/ 1/16.
SHORT, L/Cpl. H.	(C)	14/ 4/16. (Also awarded Long Service Medal.)
TONEY, Cpl. E.	(D)	1/ 5/18.
TREVOR, Sgt. A., M.M.	(D)	5/11/18. (Also awarded Bar to D.C.M., and M.M.)
WARD, Sgt. G.	(B)	22/ 9/16.
WEST, Sgt. C., M.M.	(B)	12/ 3/19. (Also awarded M.M.)

2ND BAR TO MILITARY MEDAL
HIGHGATE, Pte. E., M.M. (B) 11/ 2/19. (Also awarded D.C.M.)

BAR TO MILITARY MEDAL

AUNGIER, Pte. H., M.M.	(B)	19/ 2/17.
BUCKMAN, Sgt. S., M.M.	(A)	11/ 2/19.
CORNWELL, L/Sgt. P. W., M.M.	(C)	23/ 7/19.
EMERY, Pte. C., M.M.	(A)	11/ 2/19.
GRISTON, Pte. P., M.M.	(A)	11/ 2/19.
GROVES, Pte. A. L., M.M.	(D)	11/ 2/19.
HIGHGATE, Pte. E., M.M.	(B)	11/ 2/19. (Also awarded D.C.M. and 2nd Bar to M.M.)
HORNE, Sgt. A. W., M.M.	(A)	15/ 6/17.
SIMMONDS, Sgt. J., M.M.	(B)	11/ 2/19.
WILSON, Pte. J., M.M.	(D)	5/ 1/17.

MILITARY MEDAL

AMSBURY, Pte. J.	(B)	23/ 7/19.
AUNGIER, Pte. H.	(B)	23/ 8/16. (Also awarded Bar.)
BAKER, Pte. F.	(D)	11/ 2/19.
BAKER, Sgt. W.	(D)	15/ 6/17.

Appendix D

MILITARY MEDAL—continued

Bankes, Sgt. E. R.	(B)	12/ 9/16.
Barber, Pte. H.	(D)	23/ 7/19.
Bartholomew, Pte. G.	(D)	18/ 7/17.
Barwick, L/Cpl. W. R.	(D)	11/ 2/19.
Beale, Sgt. A. W.	(A)	12/ 9/16.
Beale, Pte. T. H.	(B)	9/ 7/17.
Bird, Pte. J.	(D)	12/ 9/16.
Bishop, Pte. C.	(A)	11/ 2/19.
Bone, Pte. H.	(D)	11/ 2/19.
Booker, Cpl. P.	(B)	11/ 2/19.
Brackpool, Pte. H.	(B)	11/ 2/19.
Bridger, Pte. P. W.	(C)	9/ 7/17. (Also mentioned in despatches.)
Britt, Pte. F.	(B)	23/ 7/19.
Brown, Pte. C. E.	(B)	1/ 9/16.
Buckman, Cpl. S.	(A)	19/ 3/18. (Also awarded Bar.)
Bull, Pte. J.	(D)	23/ 7/19.
Burch, Cpl. T.	(A)	13/ 9/18.
Burchell, L/Cpl. H.	(B)	11/ 2/19.
Butcher, Cpl. W.	(C)	1/ 9/16.
Carpenter, Pte. J.	(B)	11/ 2/19.
Carr, Pte. W.	(B)	18/ 7/17.
Clayton, Pte. H.	(B)	18/ 7/17.
Coates, Pte. R.	(B)	12/12/17.
Cooper, L/Cpl. E.	(A)	19/ 3/18.
Cornwell, L/Sgt. P. W.	(C)	13/ 3/19. (Also awarded Bar.)
Cosham, Pte. H. E.	(C)	1/ 9/16.
Covey, Pte. A.	(A)	11/ 2/19.
Dancy, Pte. F.	(A)	11/ 2/19.
Dendy, L/Cpl. E.	(A)	19/ 3/18.
Dewell, Cpl. F.	(C)	11/ 2/19.
Dinnage, Cpl. W.	(C)	19/ 3/18.
Donald, Pte. M.	(B)	11/ 2/19.
Dudman, L/Cpl. E.	(A)	12/ 9/16.
Eade, Pte. W. J.	(D)	25/ 4/18.
Elphick, L/Sgt. J. A.	(A)	23/ 7/19.
Emery, Pte. C.	(A)	9/ 7/17. (Also awarded Bar.)
Evans, Sgt. A. J.	(A)	12/ 9/16.
Evans, Pte. J.	(A)	2/ 4/18.
Glenister, Pte. H.	(A)	19/ 9/16.
Goddard, Pte. J. H.	(D)	19/ 9/16.
Golds, Sgt. W.	(C)	19/ 3/18.
Goodyer, Pte. L.	(D)	11/ 2/19.
Gratwicke, Pte. F.	(D)	12/ 9/16.
Griston, Pte. P.	(A)	13/ 9/18. (Also awarded Bar.)
Groves, Pte. A. L.	(D)	25/ 4/18. (Also awarded Bar.)
Harman, Pte. E.	(D)	12/ 9/16.
Hayes, C.S.M. J.	(D)	19/ 9/16.
Hayward, Pte. W. H.	(C)	12/ 2/17.
Hendry, L/Cpl. W.	(B)	12/ 9/16.

Appendix D

MILITARY MEDAL—continued

Highgate, Pte. E.	(B)	18/ 7/17.	(Also awarded D.C.M. and 2 Bars to M.M.)
Holder, Pte. B.	(A)	13/ 9/18.	
Horne, Sgt. A. W.	(A)	19/ 9/16.	(Also awarded Bar.)
Isted, Pte. S.	(C)	9/ 7/17.	
Josland, Pte. A. E.	(D)	25/ 4/18.	
Knope, Pte. H.	(D)	11/ 2/19.	
Lawrence, Pte. H. J.	(B)	12/ 9/16.	
Lawrence, Sgt. R.	(A)	19/ 9/16.	
Lee, Sgt. A.	(D)	23/ 7/19.	(Also awarded M.S.M. and mentioned in despatches.)
Leppard, Cpl. C. H.	(B)	11/ 2/19.	
Lister, Sgt. E.	(B)	23/ 7/19.	
Maguire, L/Cpl. J.	(B)	23/ 7/19.	
Marshall, Sgt. C.	(D)	23/ 7/19.	
Maughan, L/Cpl. H.	(D)	18/ 7/17.	
Mayes, L/Cpl. C. P.	(D)	19/ 9/16.	
Moore, Pte. F.	(A)	11/ 2/19.	
Morris, Pte. O. C.	(A)	13/ 9/18.	
Munt, Sgt. C.	(B)	23/ 7/19.	
Mustchin, Pte. W.	(A)	11/ 2/19.	
Newport, L/Cpl. H. W.	(A)	19/ 9/16.	
Nichols, Pte. F. V.	(B)	19/ 9/16.	
Onions, L/Sgt. W.	(C)	23/ 7/19.	
Osborne, Sgt. W. J.	(D)	16/ 8/17.	
Packham, Cpl. F.	(B)	11/ 2/19.	
Paine, Pte. E.	(C)	11/ 2/19.	
Parsons, Sgt. A.	(B)	23/ 7/19.	
Peacock, Sgt. A. N.	(B)	12/ 9/16.	
Peacock, Sgt. J. G.	(D)	12/ 9/16.	
Peck, Pte. J.	(D)	11/ 2/19.	
Penticost, Pte. J.	(A)	15/ 6/17.	
Pepper, Pte. S.	(A)	11/ 2/19.	
Phillips, L/Cpl. T.	(D)	16/ 7/18.	
Picton, Cpl. F.	(D)	12/ 9/16.	
Porteous, Pte. D. R.	(D)	25/ 4/18.	
Porter, Cpl. E.	(D)	19/ 3/18.	
Preston, Sgt. G. W.	(C)	18/ 7/17.	
Randall, Pte. J.	(D)	16/ 7/18.	
Ranger, Cpl. C.	(D)	23/ 7/19.	
Ransom, Sgt. F. J.	(B)	2/ 4/18.	(Also awarded D.C.M. and French Croix de Guerre.)
Reed, L/Cpl. F. J.	(B)	11/ 2/19.	
Richold, C.S.M. A.	(C)	19/ 9/16.	
Rovery, Sgt. L.	(C)	19/ 9/16.	
Saunders, L/Cpl. J.	(A)	23/ 7/19.	
Scott, Pte. P.	(A)	15/ 6/17.	
Selby, Sgt. A. E.	(A)	19/ 9/16.	
Selsby, Pte. J. R.	(B)	19/ 9/16.	
Simmonds, Sgt. J.	(B)	11/ 2/19.	(Also awarded Bar.)

Appendix D

MILITARY MEDAL—continued

SLAUGHTER, Pte. F.	(C)	23/ 7/19.
SMITH, Pte. J.	(B)	15/ 6/17.
SMITH, Pte. W.	(B)	16/ 7/18.
SQUIRES, L/Cpl. A.	(A)	23/ 7/19.
TAYLOR, Pte. A.	(C)	13/ 9/18.
TOOMS, Sgt. F. J.	(A)	11/ 2/19.
TREVOR, Sgt. A.	(D)	16/ 7/18. (Also awarded D.C.M. and Bar.)
TULETT, Sgt. C.	(D)	11/ 2/19.
TULITT, Pte. W.	(B)	11/ 2/19.
TURTON, L/Cpl. A.	(B)	12/ 9/16.
WAGHORN, Pte. T.	(B)	11/ 2/19.
WEST, Sgt. C.	(B)	23/ 7/19.
WHITBREAD, Cpl. E.	(A)	23/ 7/19.
WHITE, Pte. P. A. C.	(C)	19/ 9/16.
WILMSHURST, Pte. J.	(A)	11/ 2/19.
WILSON, Pte. J.	(D)	1/ 9/16. (Also awarded Bar.)
WOOLVEN, L/Cpl. G.	(D)	11/ 2/19.
WRIGHT, Cpl. G. W.	(C)	11/ 2/19.

MERITORIOUS SERVICE MEDAL

AYLMORE, Sgt.-Dr. A.	(D)	4/ 6/18.
COLEMAN, C.Q.M.S. C.	(C)	4/ 6/18.
HANLON, C.Q.M.S. P.J.	(D)	4/ 6/19. (Also twice mentioned in despatches.)
LEE, Sgt. A.	(D)	4/ 6/18. (Also awarded M.M. and mentioned in despatches.)
LONG, R.Q.M.S. W.	(A)	4/ 6/17. (Also mentioned in despatches.)

FRENCH CROIX DE GUERRE

RANSOM, Sgt. F. J., D.C.M., M.M.	(B)	10/10/18. (Also awarded D.C.M. and M.M.)

BELGIAN CROIX DE GUERRE

GRIFFITHS, Sgt. C.	(A)	12/ 7/18.

ITALIAN BRONZE MEDAL FOR MILITARY VALOUR

HODGES, Sgt. G., D.C.M.	(C)	25/ 5/17. (Also awarded D.C.M.
BUDGEN, C.Q.M.S. W. H.	(B)	12/ 9/18. (Also twice mentioned in despatches.)

MENTIONS IN DESPATCHES

BIRKETT, Major R. M. (B. and H.Q.), 1/1/16.
BRIDGER, Pte. P. W. (C), 15/5/17. (Also awarded M.M.)
BUDGEN, Sgt. W. H. (B), 15/5/17 and 14/12/17. (Also awarded Italian Bronze Medal.)
CLARKE, Capt. J. E. (Q.M.), 4/1/17. (Also awarded O.B.E.)
HALL, Cpl. H. (D), 7/4/18.

Appendix D

MENTIONS IN DESPATCHES—*continued*

HANLON, C.Q.M.S. P. J. (D), 4/1/17 and 28/12/18. (Also awarded M.S.M.)
HIND, Capt. R. C. D. (Transport), 4/1/17 and 28/12/18. (Also awarded M.C.)
HYGATE, Cpl. H. P. (B), 7/4/18.
IMPEY, Lt.-Col. G. H. (D. and H.Q.), 30/4/16, 7/4/18, and 28/12/18. (Also awarded Bar to D.S.O.)
JONES, Sgt. T. (A), 1/1/16.
LEE, Sgt. A. (D), 15/5/17. (Also awarded M.M. and M.S.M.)
LONG, R.Q.M.S. W. (A), 4/1/17. (Also awarded M.S.M.)
NAGLE, Capt. G. (A), 30/4/16. (Also awarded M.C.)
NUTLEY, C.S.M. A. (C), 1/1/16.
OSBORN, Lt.-Col. W. L. (H.Q.), 1/1/16, 30/4/16, 4/1/17 (Brevet). (Also awarded D.S.O.)
OSBORNE, Major G. F. (D. and H.Q.), 30/4/16, 4/1/17, and 24/5/18. (Also awarded M.C.)
RABY, Q.M.S. W. (D), 14/12/17.
SANSOM, Lt.-Col. A. J. (H.Q.), 15/5/17.
SUTTON, Lt. E. G. (B), 1/1/16. (Also awarded M.C.)
THOMSON, Lt.-Col. A. L. (H.Q.), 28/12/18. (Also awarded D.S.O.)
THOMSON, Capt. A. M., R.A.M.C. (M.O.), 30/4/16.
WILTON, Lt. J. R. (C and Signals), 30/4/16.
WOODHAMS, Capt. G. (B), 1/1/16 and 30/4/16.

APPENDIX E.

OFFICERS AND SENIOR N.C.O.s WHO PROCEEDED OVERSEAS WITH THE BATTALION IN MAY, 1915.

BATTALION HEADQUARTERS, &c.

Commanding Officer	Lt.-Col. W. L. Osborn.
Second-in-Command	Major J. L. Sleeman.
Adjutant	Capt. R. J. A. Betham.
Quartermaster	Lt. J. E. Clarke
Transport Officer	Lt. R. C. D. Hind.
Machine-gun Officer	Lt. C. D. Jay.
Medical Officer	Capt. A. M. Thomson, R.A.M.C., attd.
Regimental Sgt.-Major	R.S.M. F. C. J. Coley (B).
Regimental Q.-M.-Sgt.	Q.M.S. W. Long (A).
Orderly Room Sgt. (at Base)	Q.M.S. J. Dunlop (C).
" " (with Bn.)	Sgt. W. Baker (A).
Sgt. Drummer	Sgt.-Dr. A. Aylmore (D).
Cook Sgt.	Sgt. W. Raby (D).
Machine-gun Sgt.	Sgt. E. C. Hulkes (B).
Mess Sgt.	Sgt. E. Harris (A).
Pioneer Sgt.	Sgt. R. Sparrow (B).
Provost Sgt.	Sgt. G. Pannick (C).
Scout and Sniper Sgt.	Sgt. F. J. Russell (C).
Shoemaker Sgt.	Sgt. F. Maudling (B).
Signal Sgt.	Sgt. C. Lord (B).
Transport Sgt.	Sgt. A. Lee (D).

A COMPANY

Officer Commanding	Capt. J. G. Bussell.
Second-in-Command	Capt. H. S. Bowlby.
Platoon Commanders	Lt. R. T. May (No. 3).
	2/Lt. G. Nagle (No. 4).
	2/Lt. H. S. Stocks (No. 2).
Coy. Sgt.-Major	C.S.M. T. Solomon.
Coy. Q.-M.-Sgt.	C.Q.M.S. R. Whapham.
Platoon Sgts.	Sgts. W. E. Chalk (1), E. N. Venn (2), J. E. Vinall (3), and W. Yeo (4).

B COMPANY

Officer Commanding	Major R. M. Birkett.
Second-in-Command	Capt. L. F. Cass.

Appendix E

B COMPANY—*continued*

Platoon Commanders	-	Lt. N. J. Cox (No. 6).
		Lt. R. J. Richardson (No. 5).
		2/Lt. E. G. Sutton (No. 8).
		2/Lt. D. F. Woodford (No. 7, and Bn. Bombing Officer).
Coy. Sgt.-Major	- -	C.S.M. H. Page.
Coy. Q.-M.-Sgt.	- -	C.Q.M.S. H. L. Faircloth.
Platoon Sgts. -	- -	Sgts. J. Hayes (5), F. J. Ransom (7), E. Read (6), and E. Simmins (8).

C COMPANY

Officer Commanding	- -	Capt. J. A. Thompson.
Second-in-Command	- -	Capt. G. F. Osborne.
Platoon Commanders	-	Lt. C. W. Beale (No. 9 and Bn. Scout and Sniping Officer).
		Lt. A. K. Trower (No. 11).
		2/Lt. G. A. Thompson (No. 12).
		2/Lt. J. R. Wilton (No. 10 and Bn. Signals Officer).
Coy. Sgt.-Major	- -	C.S.M. A. Nutley.
Coy. Q.-M.-Sgt.	- -	C.Q.M.S. A. Richold.
Platoon Sgts. -	- -	Sgts. J. P. Catchpole 10), J. Sanderson (12), B. Songhurst (9), and F. Taylor (11).

D COMPANY

Officer Commanding	- -	Capt. G. H. Impey.
Second-in-Command	- -	Capt. G. Woodhams.
Platoon Commanders	-	Lt. G. L. Reckitt (No. 14).
		Lt. R. G. Wells (No. 16).
		2/Lt. F. H. Bickerton (No. 15).
		2/Lt. D. L. Cox (No. 13).
Coy. Sgt.-Major	- -	C.S.M. A. F. Lusted.
Coy. Q.-M.-Sgt.	- -	C.Q.M.S. G. Burr.
Platoon Sgts. -	- -	Sgts. P. J. Hanlon (13), J. Joy (14), H. Rowe (15), and J. Turner (16).

Regimental Mascot - - "Harold."

Note.—Capt. S. G. Evans and 2/Lt. C. H. May also proceeded overseas with the Division, the former as Staff Captain, 36th Brigade, and the latter with the 9th Motor M.-G. Battery.

The following officers remained in England to form our casualty reserve :—2/Lts. W. D. Champneys, B. T. M. Hebert, T. A. Hill, E. G. C. Richards, G. G. Stocks, and W. K. Sutton. Hill, Richards and Stocks rejoined in France before the end of 1915.

APPENDIX F.

NAMES AND SERVICE OF OFFICERS WHO SERVED WITH THE BATTALION.

ALLAN, W. D. (C); joined, 22/4/16 as 2/Lt.; w., 7/7/16.
ANDREWS, S. A. (A); joined, 13/8/18 as Capt., M.C.; bar to M.C., 1/2/19; D.S.O., 8/3/19; demob., 11/2/19.
ARMITAGE, F. G. (B); joined, 4/11/18 as Lt.; demob., 7/2/19.
ASHBY, T. P. (C); joined, 30/8/18 as 2/Lt.; k. in a., 5/9/18.
ATKINSON, G. H. (B); joined, 15/4/17 as 2/Lt.; Lt., 11/1/18; w., 27/3/18.
AXELL, W. T. (D); joined, 30/8/18 as 2/Lt.; w., 18/9/18.
BABONEAU, C. A. (B); joined, 27/8/16 as 2/Lt.; to 36th T.M.B. early 1917.
BALLARD, C. W. (A and C); joined, 8/8/16 as 2/Lt.; Lt., 10/8/16; Capt., 6/7/17; M.C., 18/7/17; k. in a., 25/11/17.
BEALE, C. W. (C, and Scouts and Snipers); joined, England; 2/Lt., 26/9/14; Lt., 29/1/15; overseas with Bn., 31/5/15; k. in a., 3/3/16.
BEETON, E. C. (C); joined, England, 12/8/15; Capt. R. Sussex Regt.; to 2nd Bn., Sept., 1914. (Now Major, retd.)
BENNETT, A. (C); joined, 21/10/18 as 2/Lt.; to 1-4th Bn., 2/3/19.
BENNETT, H. R. H. (B); joined, 29/8/18 as 2/Lt.; w., 5/9/18.
BETHAM, R. J. A. (Adjutant and Second-in-Command); joined, England, 12/8/15; Lt., R. Sussex Regt.; T/Capt., 29/10/14; overseas with Bn., 31/5/15; attd. 12th Div. H.Q., 11/3/16; T/Major, 10/8/16; rejoined, 10/8/16; sick, 26/9/16. (Now Major, retd.)
BICKERTON, F. H. (D); joined, England; 2/Lt., 26/4/15; overseas with Bn., 31/5/15; to M.G.C., 1/2/16. (Later with R.F.C.)
BINGEN, E. A. (D); joined, 2/8/17 as 2/Lt.; w., 25/11/17. (Later with R.F.C.)
BIRKETT, R. M. (B, and Second-in-Command); joined, England, 12/8/15; Capt., R. Sussex Regt.; T/Major, 29/10/14; overseas with Bn., 31/5/15; despatches, 1/1/16; attd. 36th Brigade, 22/10/15; rejoined, 11/11/15; to 12th Div. School, 18/11/15; rejoined, 19/1/16; to 12th Div. School, 7/2/16; to command 2/17th London Regt., 27/2/16. (Now Col., D.S.O., commanding 133rd Inf. Brigade.)
BLUNDEN, E. C. (D); joined, 28/11/18 as Lt., M.C.; demob., 15/2/19.
BORLASE, W. J. (B and D); joined, 22/4/16 as Capt.; w., 7/7/16.
BOURNE, R. H. (A); joined, 23/9/18 as 2/Lt., R.A.S.C., attd.; k. in a., 25/10/18.
BOURNE, S. N. (A); joined, 14/12/15 as 2/Lt.; sick, 9/3/16; rejoined, 15/4/17; to bomb course, England, 29/4/17; rejoined, 10/7/17 as Lt.; to R.F.C., 24/11/17.

Appendix F

BOWLBY, H. S. (A, C, and Adjutant); joined, England; 2/Lt., 22/8/14; Lt., 29/10/14; Capt., 4/2/15; overseas with Bn., 31/5/15; M.C., 26/9/16; Adjutant, 6/7/17; Major, 30/7/18; to Senior Officers' Course, England, 2/10/18; rejoined, 1/1/19; demob., 23/3/19.

BOWLLER, H. C. (D); joined, 15/11/16 as 2/Lt.; w. (acc.), 9/3/17.

BOYS, S. C. (A); joined, 7/5/18 as Lt.; k. in a., 23/6/18.

BRADLEY, J. (B); joined, 8/10/18 as 2/Lt.; d. of w., 26/10/18.

BRANSON, V. C. (A); joined, 15/8/18 as 2/Lt.; Lt., 1/9/18; M.C., 1/2/19; w., 5/9/18; rejoined, 24/10/18; demob., 11/2/19.

BRAUN, C. L. (A); joined, 18/11/15 as Lt.; sick, 28/11/15.

BROUGHALL, H. S. (A); joined, 12/6/16 as 2/Lt.; Lt., 8/7/16; M.C., 22/9/16; to R.F.C., 2/9/16. (Now Squadron-Leader, R.A.F.)

BROWN, J. C. (B); joined, 13/5/18 as 2/Lt.; to H.A.C., 29/6/18.

BROWNING, R. S. (A and D); joined, 29/6/16 as 2/Lt.; w., 4/8/16; rejoined, 5/10/18 as Lt.; to 1/4th Bn., 4/3/19.

BUCKINGHAM, T. H. (A); joined, 4/12/18 as Lt.; demob., 30/4/19.

BUCKLER, E. F. (M.O.); joined, 15/7/16 as Lt., R.A.M.C., attd.; to R.A.M.C., Nov., 1916.

BULLOCK, A. D. (D); joined, 8/5/17 as 2/Lt.; prisoner of war, 25/7/17.

BURDETT, S. L. (A and Assistant Adjutant); joined, 29/6/16 as 2/Lt.; w., 7/7/16; rejoined, 15/3/17; Lt., 1/7/17; M.C., 8/3/19; demob., 30/1/19.

BURLEY, C. P. (B); joined, 5/5/18 as 2/Lt.; k. in a., 8/8/18.

BUSSELL, J. G. (A and D); joined, England, Sept., 1914; Lt. R. of O.; Capt., 9/9/14; overseas with Bn., 31/5/15; k. in a., 28/6/15.

BUTLER, T. H. (C); joined, 21/10/18 as 2/Lt.; to 1/4th Bn., 27/3/19.

CALDECOTT, R. G. (C); joined, 7/6/17 as 2/Lt.; to 12th Bn., 9/7/17.

CAMPBELL, W. F. (A); joined, 2/8/17 as Capt.; sick, 5/4/18.

CAMPBELL-JOHNSTON, M. (D); joined, 20/3/18 as Capt.; special employment, 14/5/18.

CARR, H. A. (Commanding Officer); joined, 5/8/16 as Lt.-Col., D.S.O., from 4th Worcesters; to command 1/8th Worcesters, 9/10/16.

CASS, L. F. (A and B); joined, England, April, 1915, as Capt.; overseas with Bn., 31/5/15; k. in a., 13/12/15.

CHAMPNEYS, W. D. (B); joined, England; 2/Lt., 22/8/14; to 10th Bn., 31/5/15; to Grenadier Guards, 1915.

CHAPMAN, G. (B); joined, 21/10/18 as 2/Lt.; to 1/4th Bn., 2/3/19.

CHRISTIE, D. F. (C); joined, 13/3/16 as 2/Lt.; w., 7/7/16.

CLARK, B. H. C. (A); joined, 2/4/18 as Lt.; M.C., 11/1/19; sick, 30/10/18.

CLARKE, J. E. (Quarter-Master); joined, England, 19/8/14; Lt., R. Sussex Regt., 25/8/14; overseas with Bn., 31/5/15; w., 29/10/15; rejoined, 23/1/16; despatches, 4/1/17; Capt., 25/8/17; O.B.E., 3/6/19; to 2nd Bn., 7/2/19. (Now Capt., retd.)

CLARKE, T. (A and B); joined, 8/8/16 as 2/Lt.; to prisoner of war Coy., 8/12/16; rejoined, 31/8/17; M.C., 19/11/17; Lt., 8/2/18; to England, 25/5/18.

CLAYTON, C. (C); joined, 28/10/16 as 2/Lt.; w., 19/2/17; rejoined, 20/12/17; Lt., 5/2/18; w., 7/8/18.

Appendix F

CLEAVER, A. E. T. (C); joined, 3/7/16 as A/Capt.; 2nd R. Scots Fus., attd.; M.C., 22/9/16; w., 7/7/16.
CLEMENTS, R. F. (D); joined, 28/10/16 as 2/Lt.; Lt., 5/2/18; M.C., 13/5/18; k. in a., 14/8/18.
CLEMETTS, H. (D); joined, 8/9/18 as 2/Lt.; w., 22/9/18.
COHEN, D. T. (D); joined, 2/8/17 as 2/Lt.; w. (acc.), 21/8/17; d. of w., 20/11/17.
COLLINS, J. S. (A); joined, 7/3/18 as Lt.; k. in a., 5/4/18.
COMPTON, C. (C); joined, 27/5/18 as 2/Lt., M.M.; sick, 31/5/18.
COOKE, H. F. (B); joined, 9/6/16 as 2/Lt.; k. in a., 4/8/16.
CORNFORD, R. (D); joined, 29/4/16 as 2/Lt.; w., 7/7/16. (Later with 22nd Squadron, R.F.C.; k. in a., 17/8/17.)
COUSENS, H. S. (A); (attached England, early 1915 as Lt.); joined, Dec., 1915, as Lt.; w., 3/3/16; rejoined, 4/8/16 as Capt.; to Senior Officers' Course, England, 7/7/17; rejoined, 2/10/17; to General List, 29/9/18.
COX, D. L. (D); joined, England; 2/Lt., 17/12/14; overseas with Bn., 31/5/15; w. (acc.), 24/10/15. (Later with R.F.C.)
COX, N. J. (B); joined, England; 2/Lt., 13/11/14; Lt., 22/3/15; overseas with Bn., 31/5/15; k. in a., 23/8/15.
COXHEAD, L. G. (B); joined, 8/9/18 as 2/Lt.; M.C., 8/3/19; to 1/4th Bn., 4/4/19.
CUTLER, E. C. (D); joined, 8/7/17 as 2/Lt.; M.C., 26/7/18; w., 27/3/18.
DADSWELL, C. I. (D); joined, 12/12/15 as 2/Lt.; k. in a., 7/7/16.
D'ALTON, R. (C); joined, 13/7/16 as 2/Lt.; w., 4/8/16.
DAUNT, B. (D); joined, 8/9/18 as 2/Lt.; k. in a., 21/9/18.
DAVIS, S. J. (B); joined, 29/7/18 as Lt.; w., 8/8/18.
DAY, J. C. (D); joined, 18/6/16 as 2/Lt.; to 36th T.M.B., 3/8/16. (Later with 52nd Squadron, R.F.C.; k. in a., 9/5/17.)
DIXON, P. S. (C); joined, 22/2/18 as 2/Lt.; Lt., 25/4/18; k. in a., 7/8/18
DRAGE, F. (D); joined, 22/2/18 as 2/Lt.; sick, 25/3/18.
DUMBRELL, J. H. (A); joined, 29/12/17 as Lt.; sick, 18/3/18. (Now Capt., R. Sussex Regt.)
DUNLEVY, J. (C); joined, 1/9/16 as 2/Lt.; w., 3/5/17.
EDGAR, T. H. (A); joined, 31/3/18 as Lt.; to M.G.C., 18/6/18.
EDWARDS, T. E. (A); joined, 4/12/18 as 2/Lt.; to 1/4th Bn., 2/3/19.
ELLIS, E. S. (A. and Adjutant); joined, 13/4/18 as Capt., M.C.; Adjutant, 30/7/17; w., 26/10/18; rejoined, 11/11/18; demob., 6/2/19.
ERICSON, E. C. (C); joined, 8/9/18 as 2/Lt., M.M.; k. in a., 18/9/18.
EVANS, S. G. (A); joined, England, 4/9/14; Lt., Spec. Res.; to 36th Brigade as Staff Capt., Dec., 1914. (Later Capt., M.C.)
EVE, C. W. (A); joined, 7/2/18 as 2/Lt.; to England, six months' duty, summer, 1918, and retained there.
FARROW, H. J. R. (C and D); joined, 15/11/16 as 2/Lt.; Lt., 4/4/17; M.C., 18/2/18; to England, six months' duty, 15/1/18; rejoined, 27/5/18; A/Capt., 20/9/18; w., 18/9/18.
FIELD, J. M. (A); joined, March, 1916; k. in a., 11/4/16.
FINNEMORE, H. J. (A); joined, 28/3/17 as 2/Lt.; to R.F.C., 20/11/17. (Later d. of w., 27/3/18.)
FITZSIMONS, T. (C); joined, 29/6/16 as 2/Lt.; k. in a., 4/8/16.

Appendix F

Flowers, J. A. (B); joined, 9/6/16 as 2/Lt.; to 9th Bn., 30/6/16. (Later k. in a. with 9th Bn., 1/9/16.)
Forster, T. (A); joined, 13/5/18 as 2/Lt.; to 11th Manchesters, 25/11/18.
Fortescue, R. H. (B); joined, 29/6/16 as 2/Lt.; w., 9/4/17. (Later Lt., M.C.)
Foster, P. G. (C); joined, 7/12/15 as 2/Lt.; w., 3/3/16; d. of w., 2/4/16.
Franklin, W. J. (D); joined, 2/9/16 as 2/Lt., E. Surrey Regt, attd.; k. in a., 5/10/16.
Fraser, H. J. (B); joined, 16/10/18 as 2/Lt.; to 1/4th Bn., 2/3/19.
Frewer, F. (D); joined, 2/8/17 as 2/Lt.; w., 20/11/17 (at duty) and 25/11/17.
Gee, G. R. D. (D); joined, 25/7/16 as 2/Lt.; to R.F.C., 22/1/17. (Later with 21st Squadron; k. in a., 4/6/17.)
Gervis, H. S. (B); joined, 28/10/16 as 2/Lt.; sick, 28/1/17.
Gilbert, A. (A and Signals); joined, 23/9/18 as 2/Lt.; to 1/4th Bn., 2/3/19.
Gleeson, G. T. (C); joined, 8/10/18 as 2/Lt.; demob., 20/2/19.
Glenister, D. S. (B); joined, 29/6/16 as 2/Lt.; w., 4/8/16.
Glenister, R. T. (C); joined, 2/8/17 as 2/Lt.; to M.G.C., 19/12/17.
Godwin, J. C. R. (B); joined, 13/3/16 as 2/Lt.; k. in a., 7/7/16.
Golds, F. (A); joined, 1/9/16 as 2/Lt., E. Surrey Regt., attd.; k. in a., 5/10/16.
Goodwin, H. C. (D); joined, 8/9/18 as 2/Lt.; w., 18/9/18.
Gordon, H. B. (B and Bombs); joined, Oct., 1915, as 2/Lt.; Lt., 15/1/16; k. in a., 7/7/16.
Goring, F. Y. (D); joined, 15/3/16 as Lt.; to 2nd Bn., 1/4/16. (Now Capt., R. Sussex Regt.)
Gorringe, E. C. (C); joined, 3/9/16 as 2/Lt.; Lt., 12/3/17; w., 3/5/17; rejoined, 19/9/17; Capt., 26/11/17; M.C., 26/7/18; k. in a., 5/9/18.
Hall, W. G. (C); joined, 29/6/16 as 2/Lt.; w., 7/7/16.
Hardy. *See* Le Hardy.
Hebert, B. T. M. (D); joined, England; 2/Lt., 1/9/14; to 10th Bn., 31/5/15; to Welsh Guards, 1915. (Later Lt., M.C.)
Hill, G. H. (B, Lewis Guns, and Assistant Adjutant); joined, 15/6/17 as 2/Lt.; w., 25/11/17; rejoined, Feb., 1918; Lt., 26/10/18; to England as A/Capt. and Adjutant of Cadre, 16/6/19.
Hill, T. A. (D); joined, England; 2/Lt., 22/8/14; to 10th Bn., 31/5/15; rejoined, Oct., 1915; to M.G.C., 1/2/16.
Hind, R. C. D. (Transport Officer); joined, England; 2/Lt., 3/10/14; overseas with Bn., 30/5/15; Capt., 10/8/16; despatches, 4/1/17 and 27/12/18; M.C., 14/12/17; to England with Cadre, 16/6/19.
Hine, W. (B); joined, 24/3/17 as 2/Lt.; sick, 30/6/17.
Hodges, F. E. D. (A); joined, 16/2/17 as 2/Lt.; w., 9/4/17.
Honeyman, G. G. (A); joined, 15/8/18 as 2/Lt.; w., 26/8/18.
Howe, R. M. (A and B); joined, 25/7/16 as 2/Lt.; w., 4/8/16; rejoined, 30/3/17; Lt., 1/7/17; Capt., 6/9/18; M.C., 11/1/19; demob., 1/2/19.
Howett, W. (B); joined, 8/9/18 as 2/Lt.; k. in a., 18/9/18.
Huggett, S. G. (A); joined, 30/8/18 as 2/Lt.; k. in a., 18/9/18.

Appendix F

IMPEY, G. H. (D, Second-in-Command, and Commanding Officer); joined, England, Aug., 1914; Capt., R. Sussex Regt.; overseas with Bn., 31/5/15; T/Major, 20/7/15; w., 2/10/15 (at duty); despatches, 30/4/16, 7/4/18, and 27/12/18; to command 12th Bn., 30/4/16; rejoined to command Bn. as T/Lt.-Col., D.S.O., 7/8/17; bar to D.S.O., 26/7/18; to England, 24/7/18. (Now Lt.-Col., retd.)

JAY, C. D. (A, D, and Machine Guns); joined, England; 2/Lt., 22/8/14; Lt., 11/11/14; overseas with Bn., 30/5/15; Capt., 10/6/15; to M.G.C., 15/1/16. (Later Major, D.S.O.)

JOHNSTONE, R. C. S. (B); joined, 15/3/16 as 2/Lt.; w., 15/4/16.

JONES, A. A. (A); joined, 6/2/18 as 2/Lt.; sick, 25/3/18.

KEMP, E. A. (A and Assistant Adjutant); joined, 3/11/16 as Lt.; Adjutant, 12th Div. Reinforcement Wing, April, 1917; rejoined, August, 1918; demob., 1919.

KENDERDINE, J. H. B. (A and C); joined, 7/6/18 as 2/Lt.; w., 18/9/18; rejoined, Oct., 1918; to 1/4th Bn., March, 1919.

KENWARD, R. (A); joined, 17/5/16 as 2/Lt.; k. in a., 7/7/16.

KNOX, J. L. (C); joined, 15/1/17 as 2/Lt.; k. in a., 20/11/17.

LATHAM, C. (A); joined, 21/10/18 as 2/Lt.; demob., 11/2/19.

LAVENDER, H. R. (A); joined, 15/8/18 as 2/Lt.; k. in a., 26/8/18.

LAWRENCE, T. E. (C); joined, 21/8/18 as 2/Lt.; d. of w., 24/9/18.

LEDGER, R. J. (D and Bombs); joined, 8/8/16 as 2/Lt.; w. (acc.), 9/3/17; d. of w., 11/3/17.

LE DOUX VEITCH, D. G. (D); joined, 29/6/16 as 2/Lt.; k. in a., 4/8/16.

LE HARDY, W. H. C. (A); joined, 8/5/17 as Capt.; M.C., 18/2/18; to 36th Brigade as Staff Capt., 2/1/18. (Now Lt.-Col. commanding 23rd London Regt., T.F.)

LEWIS, J. V. (C); joined, 29/8/18 as 2/Lt.; demob., 19/4/19.

LOTHAM, S. (C); joined, 6/2/18 as 2/Lt.; w., 27/3/18; rejoined, 30/3/18; M.C., 11/1/19; w., 9/8/18.

LYONS, A. J. (D); joined, 12/5/18 as 2/Lt.; w., 18/9/18.

MCCRACKEN, N. (B); joined, 23/11/16 as 2/Lt.; M.C., 18/7/17; to England, six months' duty, 5/2/18; Lt., 26/3/18; rejoined, 27/5/18; w., 21/9/18.

MAGRATH, J. S. (—); joined, England, 9/8/14; 2/Lt. 3rd R. Sussex Regt.; to 3rd Bn., Sept., 1914.

MANLEY, H. D. (B); joined, 16/8/17 as 2/Lt.; k. in a., 27/3/18.

MARGARY, I. D. (A); joined, 29/6/16 as 2/Lt.; sick, 25/1/17; rejoined, 15/6/17; Lt., 1/7/17; w., 13/8/17; rejoined, 23/11/18; demob., 30/1/19.

MARTIN, B. (D); joined, 1/9/16 as 2/Lt.; w., 5/10/16.

MATTHEWS, J. L. (A); joined, 9/1/17 as 2/Lt.; attd. Div. H.Q. as Wireless Officer, Oct., 1917; d., 28/12/17.

MAY, C. H. (B); joined, England; 2/Lt., 12/9/14; to 9th Motor M.G. Battery, Nov., 1914. (Later Major, M.C., Tank Corps.)

MAY, R. T. (A); joined, England; 2/Lt., 12/9/14; Lt., 22/3/15; overseas with Bn., 31/5/15; Capt., 14/12/15; k. in a., 7/7/16.

MENNIE, J. (B); joined, 5/5/18 as 2/Lt.; k. in a., 18/9/18.

MILLS, E. A. (M.O.); joined, 4/2/17 as Capt., R.A.M.C., attd.; to Div. H.Q. as D.A.D.M.S. (A/Major), 22/2/18.

Appendix F

MILLS, T. W. (C); joined, 2/8/17 as 2/Lt.; w., 25/11/17; rejoined, Jan., 1918; to M.G.C., 19/3/18.

MILLWARD, W. C. (B); joined, 24/3/16 as Capt.; to 11th Bn., 7/5/16. (Later Lt.-Col., D.S.O.)

MONTESOLE, E. A. (B and Lewis Guns); joined, Oct., 1915, as 2/Lt.; k. in a., 4/3/16.

MORRIS, A. J. (B); joined, 14/11/16 as 2/Lt.; w., 3/5/17; rejoined, 11/7/17; Lt., 14/5/18; w., 22/8/18.

MORSE, G. E. (A); joined, 1/9/16 as 2/Lt.; sick, 9/10/17.

MOSCROP, H. A. (C); joined, 16/10/18 as 2/Lt.; demob., 5/12/19.

MOSSOP, G. P. (B and C); joined, 8/5/17 as 2/Lt.; w., 5/4/18; rejoined 3/5/18; Lt., 1/9/18; w., 5/9/18.

MURRAY, A. (D); joined, 8/5/17 as 2/Lt.; attd. Div. H.Q. as Burial Officer, 17/6/17; rejoined, July, 1918; k. in a., 8/8/18.

MYLIUS, H. H. (C and D); joined, 29/8/18 as 2/Lt.; demob., March, 1919.

NAGLE, G. (A and Adjutant); joined, England; 2/Lt., 26/9/14; overseas with Bn., 31/5/15; w., 4/3/16; rejoined, 9/3/16; Capt., 20/3/16; M.C., 14/4/16; despatches, 30/4/16; attd. 35th Brigade, 22/6/16; rejoined, 13/7/16; Adjutant, 10/8/16; k. in a., 5/7/17.

O'MALLEY, G. P. (M.O.); joined, 22/2/18 as Capt., United States Army Medical Corps, attd.; D.S.O., 1/2/19; rejoined U.S. Army, 1919.

OSBORN, W. L. (Commanding Officer); joined, England, 19/8/14; Major, R. Sussex Regt.; T/Lt.-Col., 19/8/14; overseas with Bn., 31/5/15; despatches, 1/1/16, 30/4/16, and 1/1/17 (Brevet Lt.-Col.); D.S.O., 14/4/16; w., 7/7/16 (at duty); to command 16th Brigade, 24/7/16. (Now Brig.-Gen., C.B., C.M.G., D.S.O., Colonel of the R. Sussex Regt.)

OSBORNE, G. F. (C, D, and Second-in-Command); joined, England, Aug., 1914; 2/Lt., R. Sussex Regt.; T/Lt., 29/10/14; T/Capt., 4/2/15; overseas with Bn., 31/5/15; w., 28/8/15; rejoined, 17/2/16; w., 3/3/16; rejoined, 9/3/16; T/Major, 2/9/16; despatches, 30/4/16, 4/1/17, and 24/5/18; to Base Depot, special duty, 24/4/17; rejoined, May, 1917; M.C., 26/7/18; to Senior Officers' Course, England, 2/7/18; rejoined, 5/10/18; to England in command of Cadre, 16/6/19. (Now Major, R. Sussex Regt.)

PALEY, F. R. (B); joined, 25/5/17 as 2/Lt.; w., 27/3/18; rejoined, 21/10/18 as Lt.; demob., 1919.

PALMER, H. J. (A); joined, 7/5/18 as 2/Lt.; k. in a., 8/8/18.

PEPPER, E. G. (D); joined, 22/1/16 as 2/Lt.; w., 16/4/16.

PERCY, E. F. (B); joined, 23/9/18 as 2/Lt.; sick, 12/10/18.

PERKIN, E. N. (C and D); joined, 29/12/16 as 2/Lt.; to England, six months' duty, 21/2/18.

PHILIP, O. (C); joined, 13/11/18 as Capt., M.C., 4th E. Yorkshires, attd.; to 1/4th Bn., 26/3/19.

PHIPPS, G. A. (D); joined, 3/9/16 as 2/Lt.; w., 5/10/16; rejoined, 7/5/18 as Lt.; w., 26/8/18; rejoined, Oct., 1918; to England as A/Capt. and M.G.O. with Cadre, 16/6/19. (Since deceased.)

PHIPPS, S. J. (D); joined, 15/8/18 as 2/Lt.; w., 1/9/18.

Appendix F

PLUMMER, J. H. (—); joined, 8/9/18 as 2/Lt.; sick, 26/9/18.
PRICE, W. E. (C); joined, 30/8/18 as 2/Lt.; w., 5/9/18.
PRINCE, G. W. (A); joined, 28/10/16 as 2/Lt.; Lt., 3/12/16; M.C., 18/7/17; to England, six months' duty, Oct., 1917; rejoined, 24/5/18; w., 8/8/18. (Now Capt., R. Sussex Regt.)
PULLEN, F. (B); joined, 12/5/18 as 2/Lt., M.M.; to M.G.C. (Cavalry). 8/8/18.
READING, F. W. (D); joined, 1/9/16 as 2/Lt.; Lt., 24/2/17; w., 3/7/17; rejoined, 30/8/18; w., 18/9/18.
RECKITT, G. L. (D); joined, England; 2/Lt., 22/8/14; Lt., 11/11/14; overseas with Bn., 31/5/15; Capt., 15/1/16; w., 7/7/16; rejoined, 6/12/16; M.C., 13/5/18; bar to M.C., 11/1/19; demob., 27/3/19.
REES, A. A. (M.O.); joined, Nov., 1916, as Capt., R.A.M.C., attd.; d., 4/2/17.
RHODES, P. W. (C); joined, 24/10/18 as 2/Lt.; to 1/4th Bn., 2/3/19.
RICHARDS, E. G. C. (A); joined, England; 2/Lt., 22/8/14; to 10th Bn., 31/5/15; rejoined, Oct., 1915; Lt., 21/2/16; to 4th Coldstream Guards, 7/5/16.
RICHARDSON, R. J. (B); joined, England; 2/Lt., 22/8/14; Lt., 29/10/14; overseas with Bn., 31/5/15; w., 31/7/15; rejoined, 30/9/15; Capt., 10/1/16; w., 19/3/16 (at duty); to Training Reserve Bn., England, 27/6/16.
ROCHE, E. (C); joined, 19/3/17 as 2/Lt.; sick, 27/4/17.
ROGERS, V. E. (C); joined, 16/8/17 as 2/Lt.; w., 8/4/18 (at duty); w., 7/8/18.
ROLFE, C. F. (A); joined, 12/3/16 as 2/Lt.; w. and prisoner of war, 4/8/16.
ROOS, H. (B); joined, 1/9/16 as 2/Lt.; w., 3/10/16; rejoined, 7/5/18 as Lt.; to M.G.C., 19/7/18.
ROUSELL, W. S. (B); joined, 2/8/17 as 2/Lt.; k. in a., 8/8/18.
ROWE, E. W. T. (—); joined, England, 9/8/14; Lt., 3rd R. Sussex Regt.; to 3rd Bn., Sept., 1914.
ROWSELL, T. S. (D); joined, 10/1/18 as 2/Lt.; w., 26/8/18.
RUSSELL, Hon. V. A. F. V. (attd.); joined, 26/10/16 as Lt.-Col., 2/5th Bedfords, attd.; to command 1/5th Northumberland Fus., 10/12/16.
SADLER, H. (A); joined, 17/6/16 as 2/Lt.; w., 7/7/16; rejoined, 21/7/16; M.C., 22/9/16; sick, 23/10/16. (Later Capt.)
SAINTON, W. H. (B); joined, 16/2/17 as Lt.; A/Capt., 20/7/17; to England, six months' duty, 14/1/18.
SANSOM, A. J. (Commanding Officer); joined, 10/10/16 from VIII Corps H.Q. as Capt., 5th Bn.; Lt.-Col., 10/10/16; despatches, 15/5/17; k. in a., 5/7/17.
SHAW, —— (M.O.); joined, 9/7/16 as Capt., R.A.M.C., attd.; rejoined 38th F.A., 15/7/16.
SHILSTON, A. C. (D); joined, 23/9/18 as 2/Lt.; demob., 25/1/19.
SIMMINS, S. G. (B); joined, 13/3/16 as 2/Lt.; w., 17/3/16.
SING, C. M. (B); joined, 19/3/16 as 2/Lt.; d. of w., 7/7/16.
SKINGLEY, H. C. (C); joined, 22/4/17 as 2/Lt.; w., 25/7/17.

Appendix F

SLEEMAN, J. L. (A. and Second-in-Command); joined, England, 9/8/14; Capt., R. Sussex Regt.; T/Major, 29/10/14; overseas with Bn., 30/5/15; sick, 14/7/15. (Now Colonel, C.M.G., C.B.E., M.V.O., commanding 160th Brigade, T.F.)

SMART, A. H. (D); joined, 3/11/16 as 2/Lt.; w., 9/4/17; rejoined, 28/2/18 as Lt.; w. and prisoner of war, 27/3/18; repatriated, 29/11/18.

SMITH, V. St. G. (D); joined, 8/7/17 as 2/Lt.; Lt., 26/10/18; to 1/4th Bn., 2/3/19.

SMITH, W. (C); joined, 7/2/17 as 2/Lt.; w., 3/5/17; d. of w., 9/5/17.

SOPER, R. H. (C); joined, 29/8/18 as 2/Lt.; sick, 1/10/18.

SOUTTER, J. L. (D); joined, 7/2/18 as 2/Lt.; w., 8/8/18.

STEPHEN, R. (B); joined, 9/5/18 as 2/Lt.; w., 18/9/18.

STOCKS, G. G. (A and Assistant Adjutant); joined, England; 2/Lt., 13/4/15; sick, 19/5/15; rejoined, 14/12/15; Lt., 4/3/16; sick, 9/5/16; rejoined, 29/12/16; A/Capt., 20/7/17; sick, 26/8/17.

STOCKS, H. S. (A and Adjutant); joined, England; 2/Lt., 13/4/15; overseas with Bn., 31/5/15; Lt., 29/11/15; Adjutant, 11/3/16; w., 7/7/16.

SURRIDGE, R. R. (B); joined, 1/9/16 as 2/Lt.; w., 9/4/17.

SUTTON, E. G. (B); joined, England; 2/Lt., 12/9/14; overseas with Bn., 31/5/15; Lt., 10/6/15; M.C. for 7/9/15; despatches, 1/1/16; k. in a., 8/4/16.

SUTTON, W. K. (B); joined, England; 2/Lt., 22/3/15; to 10th Bn., 31/5/15.

SWIFT, A. W. (B); joined, 7/2/18 as 2/Lt.; w., 8/8/18.

TALBOT, G. E. P. (A); joined, 15/3/16 as Lt.; to 2nd Bn., 1/4/16.

TAYLOR, H. F. (B and C); joined, 3/12/15 as 2/Lt.; Lt., 8/7/16; Capt., 2/9/16; to Base Depot, special duty, 10/10/16; rejoined, 18/2/17; M.C., 18/7/17; to England, six months' duty, 22/11/17; rejoined, 27/5/18; attd. 36th Brigade, Sept., 1918; rejoined, 12/11/18; demob., 18/2/19.

THOMAS, S. C. (D); joined, 16/10/18 as Lt.; demob., 24/3/19.

THOMPSON, G. A. (C); joined, England; 2/Lt., 3/10/14; overseas with Bn., 31/5/15; sick, 15/10/15. (Later with R.F.C.)

THOMPSON, J. A. (C); joined, England, 12/8/14; Lt., R. Sussex Regt.; T/Capt., 29/10/14; overseas with Bn., 31/5/15; sick, 3/8/15. (Now Capt., retd.)

THOMSON, A. L. (Second-in-Command and Commanding Officer); joined, 29/1/17 as Capt., R. Sussex Regt.; T/Major, 16/4/17; w., 4/5/18 (at duty); T/Lt.-Col., 30/7/18; w., 26/8/18; rejoined, 30/8/18; D.S.O., 1/11/19; despatches, 27/12/18; to R. Sussex Regt., 4/4/19. (Now Major, R. Sussex Regt.)

THOMSON, A. M. (M.O.); joined, England; Lt., R.A.M.C., attd., 19/9/14; Capt., 1/4/15; overseas with Bn., 31/5/15; despatches, 30/4/16; k. in a., 7/7/16.

THORNTON, G. E. (B); joined, 21/8/18 as 2/Lt.; w., 23/10/18. (Now Capt., R. Sussex Regt.)

TILL, W. S. (C and Assistant Adjutant); joined, Oct., 1915, as 2/Lt.; Lt., 10/1/16; w., 4/10/16.

Appendix F

Torrens, J. R. (Second-in-Command) ; joined, 24/4/16 as Major ; sick, 11/6/16. (Since deceased.)

Trowell, W. T. (C) ; joined, 13/5/18 as 2/Lt. ; w., 13/3/18.

Trower, A. K. (C and D) ; joined, England ; 2/Lt., 22/8/14 ; Lt., 29/10/14 ; overseas with Bn., 31/5/15 ; Capt., 10/6/15 ; sick, 9/1/16 ; rejoined, 14/5/16 ; w., 4/8/16.

Uloth, A. C. W. (B and C) ; joined, 16/9/16 as 2/Lt. ; w., 4/10/16 ; rejoined, 8/9/18 as Lt., M.C. ; w., 18/9/18 ; d. of w., 19/9/18.

Uppleby, W. C. S. (B) ; joined, 8/2/18 as Capt. ; d. of w., 9/2/18.

Walkerley, G. B. (A) ; joined, 4/12/18 as 2/Lt. ; to 1/4th Bn., 2/3/19.

Ward, A. C. (C) ; joined, 16/9/16 as 2/Lt. ; to M.G.C., 15/2/17.

Waring, F. R. (A) ; joined, 25/4/16 as 2/Lt. ; k. in a., 7/7/16.

Warren, A. E. (D) ; joined, 22/4/16 as 2/Lt. ; w., 7/7/16.

Watson, L. A. F. (A) ; joined, 11/7/17 as 2/Lt. ; to England, six months' duty, 8/3/18.

Wells, R. G. (D) ; joined, England ; 2/Lt., 22/8/14 ; Lt., 22/3/15 ; overseas with Bn., 31/5/15 ; k. in a., 4/3/16.

Willard, A. E. (A, C, and D) ; joined, 26/9/16 as 2/Lt. ; Lt., 2/10/16 ; w. (acc.), 10/3/17 ; rejoined, April, 1917 ; k. in a., 4/7/17.

Williams, C. (D) ; joined, 22/4/17 as 2/Lt. ; w., 4/7/17.

Williams, W. J. (Chaplain) ; joined, 1/5/16 as C.F. 3rd Class (Capt.), attd. ; M.C., Nov., 1917 ; to England, special duty, March, 1919.

Wilton, J. R. (C and Signals) ; joined, England ; 2/Lt., 12/9/14 ; overseas with Bn., 31/5/15 ; Lt., 10/6/15 ; w., 4/3/16 ; rejoined, 29/3/16 ; despatches, 30/4/16 ; w., 7/7/16. (Later Capt., P.W. Vols.)

Wood, T. V. (A) ; joined, 13/3/16 as 2/Lt. ; k. in a., 4/8/16.

Woodford, D. F. (B and Bombs) ; joined, England ; 2/Lt., 23/12/14 ; overseas with Bn., 31/5/15 ; to R.F.C., 22/3/16.

Woodhams, G. (B and D) ; joined, England ; 2/Lt., 22/8/14 ; Lt., 29/10/14 ; Capt., 4/2/15 ; overseas with Bn., 31/5/15 ; w., 29/10/15 ; rejoined, 5/11/15 ; despatches, 1/1/16 and 30/4/16 ; k. in a., 19/3/16.

Worlledge, J. F. E. (C) ; joined, England ; 2/Lt., 1/9/14 ; relinquished commission, 1915.

Wright, F. L. (C) ; joined, 5/5/18 as 2/Lt. ; w., 4/7/18 ; rejoined, 21/7/18 ; w., 18/9/18.

Wright, H. (B) ; joined, 23/9/18 as 2/Lt. ; demob., 16/2/19.

Wright, J. A. (A) ; joined, 8/9/18 as Lt., M.C. ; k. in a., 18/9/18.

APPENDIX G.

PARTICULARS OF REUNION DINNERS.

THE ROYAL SUSSEX REGIMENT OLD COMRADES' REUNION DINNER

All ranks of all Battalions are eligible to attend.

Held annually on the nearest Saturday to the 25th September, at The Dome, Royal Pavilion, Brighton.

Tickets, price 3s. 6d.

Hon. Secretary: At the Barracks, Chichester, Sussex.

THE 7TH BATTALION THE ROYAL SUSSEX REGIMENT ANNUAL OFFICERS' DINNER

All officers of, or attached to, the 7th Battalion are eligible to attend.

Held annually on the nearest Saturday to the 31st May (Whitsun excepted), at The Junior United Service Club, London, S.W.1.

Tickets, price 10s.

Hon. Secretary: G. L. Reckitt, 2, Stone Buildings, Lincoln's Inn, London, W.C.2. (Telephone: Holborn 0596.)

THE 12TH DIVISION ANNUAL OFFICERS' DINNER

All officers who served with the 12th Division, and those who were granted commissions from the ranks of the Division, are eligible to attend.

Held annually on the Friday of the week in which the 11th November occurs.

Tickets, price 10s.

Hon. Secretary: G. L. Reckitt (address given above).

INDEX.

NOTE.—Of the Appendices, only D and E have been indexed.

A

ACE OF SPADES :—
  adopted as 12th Div. Sign, 29
  road-houses named after, 29
  sign well-known in Arras, 134
  on tanks in Battle of Cambrai, 153
ACHEUX, 94, 212, 213, 214, 215
ACHEVILLE, 254
ACHEVILLE TRENCH (Méricourt), 254
ACHICOURT, 140, 141, 142, 143
ACQ, 253
ADAMS, Sgt. C.—killed at Monchy, 140
AGNEZ-LEZ DUISANS, 116, 121, 133, 134
AGNY—trench tours at, 104, 108
AIRE, 45, 180, 181
AJAX TRENCH (Nurlu), 235
" ALADDIN "—played by 12th Div. Theatrical Troupe, 44
ALBERT :—
  in 1916, 79, 81, 82, 89
  in 1917, 180
  in 1918, 190, 191, 192, 193, 194, 202, 203, 204, 205, 206, 208, 210, 228, 229, 231
ALBERT, BATTLES OF :—
  in 1916. *See* OVILLERS
  in 1918, described, 228-230
ALBERT-BOUZINCOURT LINE, 81, 103
ALDERSHOT :—
  march to, 10
  Ramillies Barracks at, 11
  training at, 10-12
  Bn. leaves, 12, 13
ALEXANDER, Cpl. E.—killed at Cambrai, 172
ALLAN, Lt. W. D. :—
  before Ovillers, 83
  wounded at Ovillers, 93
ALLENBY, Field-Marshal Viscount—G.O.C. Third Army at Arras, 111
AMBRINES, 144
AMIENS, 79, 204, 205, 206, 208, 211, 221, 227
AMIENS, BATTLE OF :—
  secrecy observed for, 220
  objectives of, 221-222
  description of, 223-227
  casualties in, 227
  decorations in, 228
  captures in, 228
AMMUNITION—shortage of, 21, 28
AMSBURY, Pte. J.—awarded M.M., 306
ANCRE, BATTLE OF, 1918. *See* BOUZINCOURT RIDGE
ANCRE RIVER, THE, 118, 180, 192, 193, 204, 221
ANDREWS, Capt. S. A. :—
  O.C. A Coy. at Mametz, 231-232
  awarded bar to M.C. for Mametz, 233, 305
  at Nurlu, 236
  at Epehy, 242, 243-245
  awarded D.S.O. for Epehy, 251, 305

Anglia, The—mined in the Channel, 32
ANNEQUIN, 41, 42, 58, 59, 69, 71, 73, 74-76
ANNESLEY, Lt.-Col. A. C. :—
  C.O. 8th R. Fusiliers in Hohenzollern, 57
  killed at Ovillers, 86
ANSON BATTALION, THE :—
  at Aveluy Wood, 194
  at Mailly-Maillet, 214
ARLEUX, BATTLE OF. *See* SCARPE, BATTLES OF
ARMENTIÈRES :—
  trench tours at, 15-32
  shelling of, 22, 28, 32
  other references to, 17, 22, 23, 31, 44, 135, 181, 185
ARMIES, BRITISH :—
  First, at Hohenzollern, 71
    12th Div. in reserve to, 78
    at Fleurbaix, 180
    at Vimy, 1918, 253
  Second, at Armentières, 1915, 29
  Third, at Battle of Arras, 111, 118
    at Monchy, 142
    at Battle of Cambrai, 149, 158, 172
    in German offensive, 1918, 189, 192
    at 2nd Battle of Somme, 1918, 228
  Fourth, at Battle of Somme, 1916, 81, 106
    at Battle of Amiens, &c., 1918, 220, 221
    at Epehy, 251, 252
  Fifth, at Battle of Somme, 1916, 83, 101, 102, 106
    at Battle of Arras, 118
    in German offensive, 1918, 189
ARMIES, FRENCH :—
  First, 12th Div. in reserve to, 215
    at Battle of Amiens, 221
  Sixth, at Battle of Somme, 1916, 106
ARMISTICE, THE—remarks upon, 263-264
ARMY POSTAL SERVICE, THE—efficiency of, 17
ARNELL, Sgt. A.—killed at Monchy, 140
ARNELL, Pte. S.—dies in England, 1915, 10
ARQUES, 14
ARRAS, 80, 104, 109, 111-118, 121, 124, 130, 133, 134, 135, 143, 144, 189, 190, 265
  Mayor of, 130-131
ARRAS, BATTLES OF, 1917 :—
  preparations for, 110, 111-118
  objectives of, 118-119
  description of, 119-130
  decorations for, 117, 132
  casualties in, 123
ARREWAGE, 189
ASHBY, 2/Lt. T. P.—killed at Nurlu, 238
ASHENDEN, Sgt. A.—killed at Battle of Amiens, 227
ASHFORD, 10
ASTLEY, Maj. A. G.—8th R. Fusiliers, O.C. 36th M.G. Coy., 53

323

INDEX

ASTON, Maj.-Gen. Sir G. G.—*Secret Service* by, quoted, on Battle of Amiens, 220
ATHIES, 131
ATKINSON, Lt. G. H. :—
 at Battle of Scarpe, 126
 at Battle of Cambrai, 162
 wounded at Aveluy Wood, 202
AUBERS RIDGE, THE :—
 attacks upon, in 1915, 17, 182
 in 1916, 142, 182
AUNGIER, Pte. H. :—
 awarded M.M. for Pozières, 103, 306
 awarded bar for Gueudecourt, 107, 306
AUSTIN, Sgt. H. J.—killed at Arras, 123
AUSTIN, L/Cpl. J.—at Givenchy, 51
AUSTRALIANS. *See* CORPS, BRITISH, INFANTRY
AUTHUILLE, 192, 203
AVELUY, 89, 194, 195, 203, 204, 210
AVELUY WOOD :—
 operations in, described, 192-202, 218
 casualties in, 202
 decorations for, 196, 198, 201, 203
 German accounts of, 203-204
AXELL, 2/Lt. W. T.—wounded at Epehy, 250
AYLMORE, Sgt.-Dr. A. :—
 in England, 5
 overseas with Bn., 311
 at Sibiville, 110
 at Grand-Rullecourt, 134
 awarded M.S.M., 309

B

BAILLEUL, 22
BAIZIEUX, 81
BAJOLLE LINE (Loos), 79
BAKER, Pte. F.—awarded M.M., 306
BAKER, C.S.M. W. :—
 at Givenchy, 49
 awarded M.M. for Arras, 132, 306
BAKER, Sgt. W.—overseas with Bn., 311
BALDWIN, Sgt. J.—wounded at Armentières and drowned in *The Anglia*, 32
BALDWIN, Lt.-Col. R. H.— C.O. 7th E. Surreys, at Ovillers, 88
BALLARD, Capt. C. W. :—
 O.C. C Coy. at Gueudecourt, 107
 O.C. A Coy. at Arras, 119
 awarded M.C. for Arras, 132, 305
 O.C. C Coy. at Cambrai, 151
 killed at Cambrai, 160, 172
BANKES, Sgt. E. R.—awarded M.M. for Battle of Craters, 66, 307
BANTEUX, 149, 155, 156, 163, 164, 175, 176
BANTOUZELLE, 155, 176
BAPAUME—1st Battle of, 1918 *See* AVELUY WOOD
BARBER, Pte. H—awarded M.M., 307
BARKER, L/Cpl. L. M.—at Agny, 104
BARLOW, Capt. E. M.—8th R. Fusiliers, O.C. 36th T.M.B., 53
BARNETT, Sgt. —.—wounded at Arras, 117
BARRACK TRENCH AND SUPPORT TRENCH (Cambrai), 154, 162
BARRICADE, THE (Cambrai), 173
BARRIER TRENCH (Cambrai), 162, 165
BARTHOLOMEW, Pte. G.—awarded M.M. for Scarpe, 127, 132, 307
BARTLEY-DENNISS, Maj. T. V.—C.O. 5th R. Berks, at Bouzincourt Ridge, 207
BARWICK, L/Cpl. W. R.—awarded M.M., 307
BASSE NOYELLE, 255

BASSON, Sgt. A. :—
 joins Bn. from 2nd R. Sussex, 1
 killed at Armentières, 32
BATHING PARTIES :—
 at Houplines, 24, 29
 at Méricourt, 228
BATTALIONS. *See under* names of various Regiments
BATTLE SURPLUS :—
 on leaving England, 312
 for Ovillers, 81, 94
 for Arras, 116
 for Scarpe, 124
 for Cambrai, 147, 162
 at Domqueur, 216
BAUDAINS, Capt. G. la C.—9th R. Fusiliers, at Aveluy Bridge, 195
BAUDIMONT GATE (Arras), 121
BAYONET TRENCH (Gueudecourt), 106, 107
BAYONET TRENCH (Scarpe), 125, 128, 129
BAZENTIN-LE-GRAND, 192
BEALE, Sgt. A. W. :—
 awarded M.M. for Battle of Craters, 66
 killed at Arras, 123
BEALE, Lt. C. W. :—
 overseas with Bn., 312
 at Le Touquet, 19
 at Houplines, 24, 25, 31
 killed in Battle of Craters, 65
BEALE, Pte. T. H.—
 awarded M.M. for Arras, 132, 307
 killed at Aveluy Wood, 196
BEAUMONT HAMEL, 212, 214
BEAUQUESNE, 214-216
BEAURAINS, 142
BECK, Maj. E. T.—9th R. Fusiliers, at Ovillers, 87
BECORDEL-BECOURT, 180, 229, 230
BEETON, Maj. E. C.—joins Bn., 1, 3
BEHENCOURT, 220
BELGIUM—rare appearances of Bn. in, 18, 259
BELLEWAARDE, 17
BENNETT, 2/Lt. H. R. H.—wounded at Nurlu, 238
BERGUETTE, 181
BERKELEY, Rev. H. P.—consecrates Colours at Erre, 267
BERKSHIRES, THE. *See* ROYAL BERKSHIRE REGIMENT
BERNAFAY WOOD, 106
BERNEVILLE, 104
BETHAM, Maj. R. J. A. :—
 joins Bn., 1
 overseas with Bn. as Adjutant, 311
 at Le Touquet, 21
 at Hohenzollern, 59
 attached to 12th Div. H.Q., 69
BETHUNE, 37, 38, 44, 45, 46, 51, 52, 71, 73, 77, 135, 181
BETTS, Sgt. A.—joins Bn. from 2nd R. Sussex, 1
BICKERTON, 2/Lt. F. H. :—
 overseas with Bn., 312
 at Hohenzollern, 43
 transfers to M.G.C., 53
BIG WILLIE (Hohenzollern), 42
BILLING, Sgt. E. V.—killed at Mametz, 233
BILLY-MONTIGNY, 255
BINDING, RUDOLF — quoted, on German offensive, 1918, 204-205
BINGEN, 2/Lt. E. A. :—
 at Cambrai, 152, 160
 wounded at Cambrai, 172

INDEX

BIRD, Pte. J. :—
   awarded M.M. for Battle of Craters, 62, 66, 307
   killed at Ovillers, 62, 66
BIRD TRENCH (Ephey), 247, 248
BIRKETT, Col. R. M. :—
   joins Bn., 1, 3
   overseas with Bn. as O.C. B Coy., 311
   2nd in Command at Houplines, 22
   temporary C.O. at Houplines, 29
   attached to 36th Brig. H.Q., 41
   at 12th Div. School, 46, 58
   to command 2/17th London Regt., 58
   mentioned in despatches, 309
BISHOP, Pte. C.—awarded M.M., 307
BITCH TRENCH (Cambrai), 155, 156, 159, 161, 163
BLACK HORSE BRIDGE (Aveluy Wood), 192, 197
BLANGY, 114
BLEAK HOUSE (Cambrai), 159, 164, 167, 175, 176
BLEAK QUARRY (Cambrai), 156, 159
BLEAK TRENCH (Cambrai), 150
BLENDECQUES, 14
BLESSY, 52
BLUE CROSS KENNELS, THE—" Harold " demobilised through, 4, 219
BOIS DE LA HAIE (Vimy), 253
BOIS DES BŒUFS (Arras), 142
BOIS DU VERT (Monchy), 136
BOIS DU WARNIMONT (Somme), 95
BOIS GRENIER—trench tours at, described, 183-185
BOMBERS, THE BN.—at Essex Sap, 39-40
BOMBING ACCIDENTS :—
   at Fouquereuil, 40
   at Givenchy, 50
   at Lignereuil, 116
   at Beaurains, 142
BONAVIS RIDGE (Cambrai), 164, 167, 176
BONE, Pte. H.—awarded M.M., 307
BOOBY TRAPS, 255, 259
BOOKER, Cpl. P.—awarded M.M., 307
BORDER REGIMENT, THE—7th Bn., at Mailly-Maillet, 214
BORLASE, Capt. W. J. :—
   O.C. B Coy. at Ovillers, 84
   wounded at Ovillers, 93
BORRADAILE, Brig.-Gen. H. B. :—
   first G.O.C. 36th Brig., 2
   inspects Bn. at Houplines 28
BOUCHAIN, 278
BOULOGNE, 13
BOUQUEMAISON, 104
BOURLON, 150, 158
BOURNE, 2/Lt. R. H.—killed in Final Advance, 262
BOURNE, Lt. S. N.—wounded at Battle of Craters, 66
BOUZINCOURT, 103, 201, 202, 204, 206, 207, 210, 211, 216
BOUZINCOURT RIDGE :—
   German attacks on, 206-209, 217
   casualties in, 208
   British attacks on, 217-218
BOVES, 215
BOWLBY, Maj. H. S. :—
   overseas with Bn., 311
   O.C. C Coy. at Houplines, &c., 29, 59
   with battle surplus for Ovillers, 84, 94
   after Pozières, 102
   awarded M.C. for Pozières 103, 305
   presents tenor drum, 110

BOWLBY, Maj. H. S. (continued) :—
   appointed Adjutant at Monchy, 140
   at Cambrai, 163
   at Aveluy Wood, 193, 196, 202
   promoted Major, 219
   temporary C.O. at Mametz, 233
BOWLEY, Pte. C.—dies in England, 1915, 10
BOWLLER, 2/Lt. H. C.—acc. wounded at Lignereuil, 116
BOYD-MOSS, Brig.-Gen. L. B. :—
   G.O.C. 36th Brig., 44
   presents cards to Bn., 80
   at Ovillers, 83, 88
   congratulates Bn. after Ovillers, 94
   at Pozières, 100
   leaves Brigade, 108
BOYS, Lt. S. C.—killed at Bouzincourt, 216
BRACKPOOL, Pte. H.—awarded M.M., 307
BRADLEY, 2/Lt. J.—killed in Final Advance, 262
BRANSOM, Lt. V. C. :—
   awarded M.C. for Mametz, 233, 305
   wounded at Nurlu, 238
BRAY, 192, 223, 228, 229, 230
BRESLAU TRENCH AND SUPPORT TRENCH (Cambrai), 151, 156, 159
BREWERY CORNER (Festubert), 47, 51
BREWERY CROSS-ROADS (Vermelles), 36, 37
BREWSTER, Sgt. R.—killed at Battle of Craters, 66
BRIDGER, Pte. P. W. :—
   awarded M.M. for Arras, 132, 307
   mentioned in despatches, 309
BRIGADES, BRITISH, ARTILLERY :—
   62nd, mentioned in despatches, 78
   65th, at Loos, 35
   169th, at Cambrai 173
BRIGADES, BRITISH, CAVALRY :—
   8th, at Monchy, 120
BRIGADES, BRITISH, INFANTRY :—
   1st, Guards, at Loos, 34
   1st, at Loos, 37
   2nd, at Loos, 34
   5th, Gen. Osborn in command of, 215
   16th, Gen. Osborn takes command of, 95
   35th, composition of, xvii., 184
      at Loos, 38
      at Givenchy, 48
      at Quarries Sector, 74
      at Ovillers, 81, 82
      at Gueudecourt, 107
      at Arras, 116, 119
      at Monchy, 141, 144
      at Cambrai, 150, 154, 159, 164, 167, 171
      at Aveluy Wood, 193, 194, 195
      at Bouzincourt Ridge, 206, 208
      at Battle of Albert, 1918, 229
      at Fricourt and Mametz, 230, 233
      at Nurlu, 235, 236
      at Ephey, 240, 241, 243, 244
      at Courcelles, 256
   36th, composition of, xvii., 184
      Bn. posted to, 2
      G.O.C.s of, 2, 44, 108
      Capt. Evans as Staff Capt. of, 8
      marches from Folkestone to Aldershot, 10
      at Houplines, 22
      Mining Section, formed, 30
      M.G. Coy., formed, 53
      T.M. Battery, formed, 53
      at Ovillers, 83-92

INDEX

BRIGADES, BRITISH, INFANTRY (continued) :—
    inspected by H.M. The King at Senlis, 103
    at Arras, 118
    at Scarpe, 124
    at Cambrai, 150, 179
    at Aveluy Wood, 192
    at Battle of Amiens, 222, 224
    at Epehy, 240
  37th, composition of, xvii., 184
    at Loos, 38
    at Ham, 53
    at Battle of Craters, 70
    at Ovillers, 82, 83
    at Gueudecourt, 105, 106
    at Arras, 111, 113, 116
    at Monchy, 141, 144
    at Cambrai, 150, 176
    at Aveluy Wood, 193, 194
    at Mailly-Maillet, 213, 214
    at Bouzincourt, 217
    at Battle of Amiens, 225
    at Fricourt and Mametz, 230, 233
    at Epehy, 240, 247, 250
    at Château l'Abbaye, 262
  44th, at Hohenzollern, 74
  53rd, Gen. Higginson from, 212
    at Battle of Amiens, 222, 224
  54th, at Battle of Amiens, 220, 221
  74th, at La Boisselle, 84, 86, 88
  76th, at Monchy, 136
  82nd, at Armentières, 15, 16
  112th, at Monchy, 121
  141st, at Nurlu, 235
  145th, Bn. in reserve to at Bus, 95
  156th, at Château l'Abbaye, 262
  174th, at Battle of Amiens, 222
BRIQUETERIE (Somme), 230, 231, 233
BRITT, Pte. F.—awarded M.M., 307
BROUGHALL, 2/Lt. H. F. :—
  at Ovillers, 87, 89, 91
  awarded M.C. for Ovillers, 93, 305
  after Ovillers, 94
  at Pozières, 100
BROWN, Pte. C. E. — awarded M.M. for Ovillers, 93, 307
BROWNING, Lt. R. S. :—
  with battle surplus for Ovillers, 94
  wounded at Pozières, 103
  at Méricourt, 254
  O.C. A Coy. at Courcelles, 256
  at Château l'Abbaye, 260
BROWN LINE, THE (Arras). See WANCOURT-FEUCHY LINE
BRUMWELL, Rev. P. M.—editor of 12th Div. History, 39
BUCK HOUSE (Houplines), 24
BUCKLER, Capt. E. F., R.A.M.C.—Bn. M.O. after Ovillers, 94
BUCKMAN, Sgt. S. :—
  awarded M.M. for Cambrai, 173, 307
  awarded bar, 268, 306
BUCQUOY, 206
BUDGEN, Sgt. W. H. :—
  receives green card, 81
  awarded Italian Bronze Medal, 309
  mentioned in despatches, 309
BUFFS, THE (East Kent Regt.) :—
  6th Bn., relieves Bn., 214, 218
    relieved by Bn., 42, 141, 228
    at Pozières, 96, 97, 100
    at Battle of Amiens, 225
    in Final Advance, 259

BUIRE, 108
BULL, Pte. J.—awarded M.M., 307
BULLECOURT, 152, 158
BULLOCK, 2/Lt. A. D.—taken prisoner at Monchy, 140
BULLY-GRENAY, 79
BURBERRYS, LTD.—branch of, at Armentières, 15
BURBURE, 189, 190
BURCH, Cpl. T.—awarded M.M. for Aveluy Wood, 203, 307
BURCHELL, L/Cpl. H.—awarded M.M., 307
BURDETT, Lt. S. L. :—
  at Ovillers, 87
  wounded at Ovillers, 93
  at Cambrai, 162
  Ass. Adjutant at Epehy, 245, 246
  awarded M.C. for Epehy, 251, 305
BURIDON, 259
BURLEY, 2/Lt. C. P.—killed at Battle of Amiens, 227
BURR, C.S.M. G. :—
  joins Bn., 3
  overseas with Bn., 312
BURRITT, Col. R.—G.S.O.2, 12th Div., at Caudescure, 189
BURROUGHS, Sgt. C. G.—killed at Nurlu, 238
BUS-LES-ARTOIS, 94, 95
BUSNES, 189
BUSNETTES, 33
BUSSELL, Capt. J. G. :—
  joins Bn., 3
  overseas with Bn. as O.C. A Coy., 311
  killed at Le Touquet, 18, 47
  appreciation of, 18
BUTCHER, Sgt. C. W.—at Givenchy, 49
BUTCHER, Cpl. W. — awarded M.M. for Ovillers, 93, 307
BUTLER, Lt.-Gen. Sir R. H. K.—G.O.C. III Corps, congratulates 12th Div. after Epehy, 251-252
BYNG, Field-Marshal Viscount :—
  G.O.C. Third Army, at Monchy, 142
  his orders for Battle of Cambrai, 149, 158
  congratulates 12th Div. after Cambrai, 172
  his remarks on counter-attack at Cambrai, 179

C

CADRE, THE BN. :—
  embarks for England, 269
  arrives at Chichester, 269
CAESAR'S CAMP (Folkestone), 9
CAIN, Pte. " Barney "—acc. wounded at Noyelles, 41
CAMBRAI, 136, 148, 150, 158, 240
CAMBRAI, BATTLE OF :—
  training for, 145-146
  secrecy for, 145, 147, 152
  origin of, 148-149
  objectives of, 150-151
  description of attacks in, 151-162
  criticism of Higher Command in, 150, 155-156, 157-158, 162, 178
  description of counter-attack in, 163-177
  casualties in, 154, 161, 172
  decorations for, 173
  German accounts of, 154, 161-162, 175-176
  debates on, in Parliament, 177-179

INDEX

CAMBRAI ROAD, THE (Arras), 116, 118, 120, 121, 122, 134, 138, 142
CAMBRAI ROAD, THE (Battle of Cambrai), 150, 151, 153, 155, 156, 157, 164, 165, 167, 169, 173, 175, 176
CAMBRIDGESHIRE REGIMENT (T.F.), THE :—
   1/1st Bn., joins 12th Div., 184
   at Nurlu, 236, 237
CAMERON HIGHLANDERS, THE QUEEN'S OWN—
   1st Bn., at Loos, 37
   6th Bn., at Annequin, 76
   7th Bn., in Quarries Sector, 74
CAMERONIANS, THE (Scottish Rifles) :—
   2nd Bn., at Baizieux, 81
   7th Bn., at Château l'Abbaye, 262
CAMPBELL, Col. R. B.—lectures to Bn. at Lapugnoy, 77
CAMPBELL, Capt. W. F.—at Cambrai, 162, 168
CANADIANS—at Battle of Amiens, 221, 228
CANAL DU NORD, 150, 235
CANCHE RIVER, THE, 145
CANTEEN FARM (Fleurbaix), 183
CANTEENS :—
   Bn., started, 80, 110
   at Feuchy Chapel cross-roads, 134
   E.F.C. at Arras, 135
   at Vignacourt, 220
CARDS (red and green) :—
   institution of, 80
   presentation of, 80, 81, 110
CARLISLE, Lt. T. H., R.E.—at Houplines, 30
CARNOY, 180, 230, 234, 252
CARPENTER, Pte. J.—awarded M.M., 307
CARR, Lt.-Col. H. A. :—
   to command Bn., 101
   leaves, to command 1/8th Worcesters, 106
CARR, Pte. W.—awarded M.M. for Arras, 132, 307
CARTIGNY, 171, 180
CASS, Capt. L. F. :—
   overseas with Bn., 311
   O.C. A Coy. at Le Touquet, 18
   killed at Festubert, 47
CASUALTIES :—
   in England, 10, 11
   first, in France, 16
   during instructional period, 16
   during first trench tour, 19
   at Armentières, 31, 32
   at Loos, 37, 39
   at Essex Sap, 40
   from trench feet in Hohenzollern, 43
   at Battle of Loos and after, 44
   at Festubert and Givenchy, 51
   at Battle of Craters, 65-66
   in Hohenzollern and Quarries Sectors, 76
   at Ovillers, 92-93
   at Pozières, 96, 98, 103
   at Agny, 104
   at Gueudecourt, 107
   total, in Battle of Somme, 1916, 109
   at Battle of Arras, 123
   at Battle of Scarpe, 128-129
   at Spoon Trench, 140
   at Monchy, 144
   at Cambrai, 154, 161, 172
   at Aveluy Wood, 202
   at Bouzincourt Ridge, 208
   at Battle of Amiens, 227
   at Fricourt and Mametz, 233
   at Nurlu, 238
   at Epehy, 242, 245, 247, 248, 250-251
   in August and September, 1918, 251

CASUALTIES (continued) :—
   in Final Advance, 262
   total, summaries of, 279
   in main engagements, 280
   And see APPENDIX B (ii.) *and under* 12th DIVISION
CATAPULTS—use of, at Houplines, 30
CATCHPOLE, Sgt. J. P. :—
   overseas with Bn., 312
   at Houplines, 28
CATELET COPSE, 248
CATELET TRENCH, 250
CATOR, Maj.-Gen. A. B. E. — G.O.C. 37th Brig. at Arras, 111
CAUDESCURE, 189
CAVALRY, BRITISH :—
   at Hohenzollern, 55
   at Arras, 118
   at Monchy, 120
   at Cambrai, 149, 157, 177
" CAVES, THE " (Arras), 111-112
CELLE RIVER, THE, 218
CENTRAL KEEP (Festubert), 47, 51
CENTRAL KEEP (Hohenzollern), 58
CHALK, Sgt. W. E.—overseas with Bn., 311
CHAMPNEYS, 2/Lt. W. D.—remains in England with casualty reserve, 312
CHAPEL HILL (Cambrai), 175
CHAPELLE DUVELLE, 182
CHARLES, Capt. N. H. H. — Staff Capt. 36th Brigade, at Cambrai, 170
CHARMAN, Pte. —.—wounded at Ovillers, 87
CHÂTEAU DE MORTAGNE, 262
CHÂTEAU DES PRÉS (Labourse), 74
CHÂTEAU FORESTEL (Vieil Hesdin), 145
CHÂTEAU L'ABBAYE—capture of by Bn., 259-262
CHÂTEAU LE RUAGE (Houplines), 22
CHÂTEAU ROSE (Houplines), 22, 31
CHÂTEAU VAL VION (Beauquesne), 215
CHATFIELD, Pte. E. J.—wounded at Cambrai, 152
CHEESMAN, Cpl. R. :—
   awarded D.C.M. for Battle of Craters, 66, 306
   killed at Gueudecourt, 107
CHEESMAN, Cpl. W.—killed at Ovillers, 93
CHESHIRE STREET (Cambrai), 150, 151
CHESTNUT AVENUE (Epehy), 240, 249
CHEVALIER, Sgt. A.—killed at Mametz, 233
CHEVIS, Cpl. G. E.—killed at Ovillers, 89, 93
CHICHESTER :—
   Regimenal Depot at, 1
   nucleus of Bn. at, 1, 2
   cadre received at, 269
CHICHESTER PADDOCK (Arras), 80
CHICKEN RUN, THE (Houplines), 24, 26
" CHINESE " BOMBARDMENTS :—
   at Monchy, 129, 139
   described, 129-130
CHIPILLY SPUR, 221
CHOCQUES, 32, 33
CHORD, THE (Hohenzollern), 42, 44, 58, 60, 67, 70
CHRISTIE, 2/Lt. D. F.—wounded at Ovillers, 93
CHRISTMAS :—
   1914, at Folkestone, 8
   1915, at Givenchy, 50
   1916, at Sibiville, 109
   1917, at Berguette, 181
   1918, at Hornaing, 266
CHUIGNOLLES, 253
" CIRCUS, THE "—at Monchy, 141, 144

INDEX

City of Dunkirk, ss.—takes Bn. Transport and M.G. Sections overseas, 13
CLARK, Lt. B. H. C. :—
  at Battle of Amiens, 225, 226
  awarded M.C. for Amiens, 228, 305
CLARKE, Capt. and Q.M. J. E. :—
  gazetted as Bn. Q.M., 2
  overseas with Bn., 311
  at Loos, 36
  wounded at Noyelles, 41
  returns to Bn. at Ham, 52
  starts Bn. canteen, 80
  at Senlis, 94
  at Arras, 130
  at Burbure, 190
  leaves Bn. to go to 2nd R. Sussex, 268
  awarded O.B.E., 268, 305
  mentioned in despatches, 309
CLARKE, Lt. T. :—
  at Gueudecourt, 107
  at Monchy, 143
  O.C. A Coy. at Aveluy Wood, 192, 198
  awarded M.C., 305
CLAYTON, Lt. C. :—
  O.C. C Coy. at Battle of Amiens, 220
  wounded at Heilly, 223, 227
CLAYTON, Pte. H.—awarded M.M. for Arras, 132, 307
CLEAVER, Capt. A. E. T. :—
  O.C. C Coy. at Ovillers, 84, 87
  wounded and awarded M.C. at Ovillers, 93, 305
CLEMETTS, Lt. R. F. :—
  takes part in raid at Fleurbaix, 185-188
  awarded M.C. for raid, 188, 305
  at Battle of Amiens, 223, 226
  killed near Morlancourt, 227
CLEMENTS, 2/Lt. H.—wounded at Epehy, 250
CLERY, 180
CLOTHING—difficultes over supply of, 5
COATES, Pte. R.—awarded M.M. at Monchy, 140, 307
COCHENDAL, 180
COHEN, 2/Lt. D. T. :—
  acc. wounded at Achicourt, 142
  killed at Cambrai, 153, 172
COJEUL RIVER, THE, 136
COLCHESTER—training at, 2-6
COLDSTREAM GUARDS, THE—3rd Bn., at Loos, 34
COLEMAN, C.Q.M.S. C.—awarded M.S.M., 309
COLEY, R.S.M. F. C. J. :—
  joins Bn., 3
  overseas with Bn., 311
COLLINS, Lt. J. S. :—
  O.C. A Coy. at Bouzincourt Ridge, 207
  killed at Bouzincourt Ridge, 208
COMINES, 17
CONNAUGHT RANGERS, THE—6th Bn., at Battle of Craters, 59, 60
CONTAY, 211
COOKE, 2/Lt. H. F. :—
  with battle surplus for Ovillers, 94
  O.C. B Coy., killed at Pozières, 103
COOPER, L/Cpl. E. — awarded M.M. for Cambrai, 173, 307
COPE, Brig.-Gen. Sir T., Bt.—C.O. 6th Buffs at Pozières, 97, 100
CORBIE, 223
CORDELA, 257
CORK STREET (Hohenzollern), 42
CORNFORD, 2/Lt. R.—wounded at Ovillers, 93
CORNWELL, Sgt. P. W.—awarded M.M. and bar, 268, 306, 307
CORPS, AMERICAN—II., at Epehy, 250
CORPS, BRITISH :—
  I, Anzac, at Pozières, 96, 97, 98, 101
  Australian, at Battle of Amiens, 221, 227
    at Epehy, 250
  Canadian, at Battle of Amiens, 221, 227
  Cavalry, at Hohenzollern, 55
    at Arras, 118
    at Cambrai, 149
  Indian, at St. Hilaire, 45
  I, at Loos, 33
    at Hohenzollern, 44, 56, 69
  II, at Houplines, 27
    at Pozières, 96
  III, at Armentières, 14
    in Battle of Somme, 1916, 81
    at Cambrai, 147, 149, 150, 157, 163
    at Amiens, 1918, 220, 221, 226
    at Epehy, 251, 252
  IV, at Loos, 33
    at Cambrai, 149
  V, at Aveluy Wood, 192
    at Beauquesne, 215
    at Bouzincourt, 216
  VI, at Arras, 111, 118, 122
  VII, at Cambrai, 150, 158, 163
  VIII, Lt.-Col. Sansom comes from, 106
    at Vimy, 1918, 253
  X, at Ovillers, 83
  XV, at Gueudecourt, 105
    at Quiestede, 180
    at Fleurbaix, 186
  XVIII, at Monchy, 142
  XXII, at Beauquesne, 215
    at Oresmaux, 218
CORPS, FRENCH :—
  IX, 12th Div. in support to, 218
  XXXI, 12th Div. in support to, 218
Corps, German : Alpine. See under DIVISIONS
  II (Bavarian), at Loos, 76
  XIX (Saxon), at Le Touquet, 20
COSHAM, Pte. H. E.—awarded M.M. for Ovillers, 93, 307
COTTENCHY, 215
COTTESMORE TRENCH (Epehy), 247, 248
COURCELLES, 255, 256
COUSENS, Capt. H. S. :—
  wounded at Battle of Craters, 66
  O.C. A Coy. after Pozières, 102
COVEY, Pte. A.—awarded M.M., 307
Cox, Capt. D. L. :—
  overseas with Bn., 312
  at Houplines, 25
  acc. wounded at Fouquereuil, 40
Cox, Lt. N. J. :—
  overseas with Bn., 312
  killed at Houplines, 28
COXHEAD, 2/Lt. L. G. :—
  at Epehy, 242, 245
  awarded M.C for Epehy, 251, 305
CRATER, THE (Houplines), 24, 26
CRATERS, THE (Hohenzollern) :—
  A, 58, 59, 70, 72
  B, 58, 59, 63, 70
  C, 58, 59, 62, 63, 70, 72
  1, 58, 70
  2, 58, 70
  3, 58, 59, 70, 72, 73
  4, 58, 59, 60, 70, 72

INDEX

CRATERS, THE, BATTLE OF (Hohenzollern):—
  objectives of, 58
  description of, 58-70
  second phase of, 70
  casualties in, 65-66, 70
  German account of, 67-69
  decorations for, 60, 66
CRAWLEY, Cpl. J.—killed at Ovillers, 93
CREVECŒUR, 149, 177
CROMBIE, Capt. I. A.—11th Middlesex, at Ovillers, 88
CROSS BOW TRENCH (Scarpe), 129
CROSS TRENCH (Hohenzollern), 41, 42, 60, 61
CRUCIFIX CORNER (Aveluy), 89, 99
CRUCIFORM POST (Epehy), 247, 248
CRUTTENDEN, Sgt. H. J—killed at Mametz, 233
CURLEY CRESCENT (Quarries Sector), 69
CUTLER, 2/Lt. E. C.:—
  at Monchy, 142
  at Fleurbaix, 186
  wounded and awarded M.C. at Aveluy Wood, 198, 202, 203, 305

D

DADOS LOOP (Epehy), 249, 250
DADSWELL, 2/Lt. C. I.—killed at Ovillers, 93
Daily Mirror, The — provides Christmas puddings, 109
Daily Telegraph, The — provides Christmas puddings, 109
DAINVILLE, 108
D'ALTON, 2/Lt. R.—wounded at Pozières, 103
DANCY, Pte. F.—awarded M.M., 307
DAUNT, 2/Lt. B.—killed at Epehy, 248, 250
DAVIES, Maj. D., M.P.—in Parliamentary debate on Cambrai, 178
DAVIS, Lt. S. J.—wounded at Battle of Amiens, 227
DAWSON, Sgt. L.—killed at Battle of Amiens, 227
DAY, 2/Lt. J. C.—at Ovillers, 89, 94
DEAD MAN'S CORNER (Cambrai), 171
DECORATIONS:—
  awarded at Armentières, 23, 30
    for Battle of Craters, 60, 66, 80, 81
    for Ovillers, 93, 103
    for Pozières, 103
    for Gueudecourt, 107
    for Arras and Scarpe, 117, 127, 132
    for Spoon Trench, 140
    for Cambrai, 173, 188
    for raid at Fleurbaix, 188
    for Aveluy Wood, 196, 198, 201, 203
    for Amiens, 228
    for Fricourt and Mametz, 233
    for Epehy, 251
    final lists of, 267-268
  And see APPENDIX D
DEELISH AVENUE (Epehy), 248
DEELISH POST (Epehy), 242
DEMOBILISATION—methods of, criticised, 264, 265, 266
DENDY, L/Cpl. E. — awarded M.M. for Cambrai, 173, 307
DERNANCOURT, 180, 206

DE ST. CROIX, Cpl. A. N. — killed at Essex Sap, 40
DESPATCHES :—
  Bn. mentioned in, 78
  Sir D. Haig's, quoted on Cambrai, 157-158
  mentions in, 309-310
DEVIL'S TRENCH (Monchy), 129, 136, 139
DEWAR, JOHN & SONS, LTD.—periscopes provided by, 26
DEWELL, Cpl. F.—awarded M.M., 307
DINNAGE, Cpl. W. — awarded M.M. for Cambrai, 173, 307
DIVISIONS, BRITISH, CAVALRY—Dismounted, at Hohenzollern, 55
DIVISIONS, BRITISH, INFANTRY :—
  2nd Australian, at Pozières, 96, 97, 98, 101
  Guards,   at Loos, 34, 37
              at Cambrai, 177
  Lucknow,   Gen. Scott to command, 212
  New Zealand, at Mailly-Maillet, 212
  1st, 2nd R. Sussex in, 1, 34
    at Loos, 34
    front of, reconnoitred, 78
    Bn. attached to, at Maroc, 79
  2nd, front of, reconnoitred, 78
    at Aveluy Wood, 201
    Gen. Osborn in, 215
  3rd, at Arras, 111
    at Monchy, 136
  4th, at Monchy, 142, 144
  6th, Gen. Osborn goes to, 95
  8th, at Ovillers, 81, 82, 84
    in Final Advance, 254
  9th (Scottish) :—
    proceeds overseas, 12
    early fighting by, 17
    at Loos, 33, 42
  11th (Northern), at Agny, 104
  12th (Eastern) :—
    order of battle of, xvii.-xviii.
    Bn. posted to, 2
    G.O.C.s of, 2, 11, 37, 212
    marches to Aldershot, 10
    H.M. The King's message to, 12
    fortunate in time of arrival in France, 17
    adopts Ace of Spades as sign, 29
    units of, mentioned in despatches, 78
    congratulated after Pozières, 101, 102
    " the deliverers of Arras," 111
    congratulated after Arras, 122
    at Arras and Monchy, 134
    Gen. Scott's farewell order to, 212
    congratulated after Epehy, 251-252
    Gen. Higginson's farewell order to, 268-269
    casualties of, at Battle of Craters, 70
                  at Ovillers, 82, 92
                  at Pozières, 102
                  at Arras, 122
                  at Scarpe, 130
                  at Monchy, 144
                  at Cambrai, 172
                  at Aveluy Wood, 203
                  in Aug. and Sept., 1918, 251
                  during the war, 269
    captures by, at Arras, 122, 123
                  at Battle of Amiens, 238, 251

INDEX

DIVISIONS, BRITISH, INFANTRY (continued) :—
12th (Eastern) continued :—
  History of, quoted, on Essex Sap, 39
    on Battle of Craters, 59
    on attacks at Ovillers, 82, 92
    on attacks at Pozières, 97, 101, 102
    on Arras, 122-123
    on Cambrai, 155, 172, 176
    on Epehy, 251-252
  rôle of, at Ovillers, 81
    at Arras, 118
    at Monchy, 137
    at Cambrai, 150
    at Amiens, 222
    at Epehy, 240
  Theatrical Troupe of. *See* " SPADES, THE "
14th (Light) :—
  proceeds overseas, 12
  early fighting by, 17
  at Agny, 104, 108
15th (Scottish) :—
  at Loos, 33, 39
  at Hohenzollern, 74, 76
  at Arras, 111, 119, 120
16th (Irish) :—
  at Hohenzollern, 59
  gas attacks on, 76
  front of, reconnoitred, 78
17th (Northern) :—
  at Senlis, 206
  at Mailly-Maillet, 214
  at Bouzincourt, 218
18th (Eastern) :—
  8th R. Sussex in, 78
  Gen. Higginson comes from, 212
  at Bouzincourt, 217-218
  at Battle of Amiens, 220, 221, 222, 223, 224
  at Battle of Albert, 1918, 229
  at Fricourt, 230
  at Nurlu, 235
  at Epehy, 240, 251
19th (Western) :—
  at Battle of Somme, 81
20th (Light), at Cambrai, 150, 151, 167, 169
  at Méricourt, 253
21st, at Gueudecourt, 105
23rd, front of, reconnoitred, 78
27th, at Armentières, 15
29th, at Gueudecourt, 108
  at Monchy, 121
  at Cambrai, 157
32nd, at Ovillers, 89
  at Senlis, 94
33rd, at Festubert, 46
34th, at La Boisselle, 81, 82, 84
35th, at Bouzincourt, 216
37th, at Arras, 119, 120, 121
38th (Welsh), at Sailly-au-Bois, 95
  at Fleurbaix, 182, 183
  at Bouzincourt, 211
39th, Lt.-Col. Impey goes to, 77
40th, in Battle of the Lys, 183

DIVISIONS, BRITISH, INFANTRY (continued) :—
46th (N. Midland, T.F.) :—
  at the Quarries, 38
47th (2nd London, T.F.) :—
  at Aveluy Wood, 202
  at Nurlu, 234, 235, 236
48th (S. Midland, T.F.) :—
  at Sailly, 95
  Lt.-Col. Carr goes to, 106
50th (Northumbrian, T.F.) :—
  at Houplines, 31
52nd (Lowland, T.F.) :—
  at Château l'Abbaye, 262
55th (W. Lancs., T.F.) :—
  at Cambrai, 150, 163
57th (2nd W. Lancs., T.F.) :—
  at Fleurbaix, 189
58th (2/1st London, T.F.) :—
  at Battle of Amiens, 222, 223, 224, 225
  at Nurlu, 238
  at Epehy, 240, 247
  in Final Advance, 255, 256, 257
61st (2nd S. Midland, T.F.) :—
  at Cambrai, 170, 171
63rd (Royal Naval) :—
  at Aveluy Wood, 194, 202
  at Mailly-Maillet, 214
DIVISIONS, FRENCH, INFANTRY :—
  3rd, 15th, and 66th, fronts of, reconnoitred, 218
Divisions, German, Cavalry :—
  6th *(Dismounted)*, at Nurlu, 236
Divisions, German, Infantry :—
Alpine Corps :—
  at Epehy, 242, 246, 249
2nd Guards :—
  at Mametz, 231
  at Epehy, 242
2nd Marine :—
  in German offensive, 1918, 204
3rd Marine :—
  at Aveluy Wood, 203-204
  at Bouzincourt Ridge, 208
3rd (Bavarian) :—
  at Battle of Craters, 67
9th (Reserve) :—
  at Cambrai, 154, 161
  at Aveluy Wood, 204
17th (Reserve) :—
  at Spoon Trench, Monchy, 140
27th (Württemburg) :—
  at Battle of Amiens, 221
28th, at Cambrai, 175-176
34th, at Cambrai, 161
54th (Res. Württemburg) :—
  at Aveluy Wood, 203-204
232nd, at Epehy, 249
DIVISIONS, PORTUGUESE, INFANTRY—2nd, at Fleurbaix, 182, 187
DIXON, Lt. P. S.—killed at Heilly, 222, 227
DOMQUEUR, 216
DONALD, Pte. M.—awarded M.M., 307
DORKING, 10
DOUAI, 256, 257, 265
DOULIEU, 183
DOULLENS, 123, 124, 143, 190, 211
DOVER ROAD, THE, 9
DOYLE, Sir Arthur Conan—quoted, on Aveluy Wood, 196, 203
DROCOURT-QUEANT LINE, 255
DROUVIN, 79

INDEX

DRUMS, THE BATTALION'S CORPS OF :—
  in England, 5-6
  at Sibiville, 110
  wins competitions at Grand-Rullecourt, 134
  at Cambrai, 175
  at Beauquesne, 215
DUCK'S BILL, THE (Givenchy), 48
DUDMAN, L/Cpl. E.—awarded M.M. for Battle of Craters, 66, 307
DUKE OF CORNWALL'S LIGHT INFANTRY, THE—2nd Bn., at Le Touquet, 16, 17, 19
DUMP, THE. *See* FOSSE 8 DE BETHUNE
DUNLEVY, 2/Lt. J.—wounded at Battle of Scarpe, 128
DUNLOP, Q.M.S. J.—Bn. Orderly Room Sgt. at Base, 311
DURHAM LIGHT INFANTRY, THE—7th Bn., at Houplines, 31

E

EADE, Pte. W. J.—awarded M.M. for raid at Fleurbaix, 188, 307
EAST KEEP (Festubert), 47, 51
EAST SURREY REGIMENT, THE :—
  7th Bn., relieves Bn., 69
    mentioned in despatches, 78
    at Ovillers, 88
    disbanded, 184
ECLIMEUX, 146
ECOIVRES, 145
EDENBRIDGE, 10
EDUCATIONAL TRAINING—failure of, 266
EGGLETON, Pte. B.—killed at Monchy, 138
ELBOW TRENCH (Scarpe), 129
ELLIOTT-COOPER, Lt.-Col. N. B. :—
  C.O. 8th R. Fusiliers, at Battle of Scarpe, 126, 127
  at Cambrai, 164, 175
  awarded V.C., 164
ELLIS, Capt. E. S. :—
  O.C. A Coy., 219
  appointed Adjutant at Oresmaux, 219
  at Battle of Amiens, 228
  at Battle of Albert, 1918, 229
  at Epehy, 246
  at Orchies, 258
  wounded at Château l'Abbaye, 260-261, 262
ELLIS, Sgt. R. :—
  at Houplines, 30
  at Loos, 36
  at Lapugnoy, 78
ELPHICK, L/Sgt. J. A.—awarded M.M., 307
EMDEN TRENCH AND SUPPORT TRENCH (Cambrai), 151, 165 166
EMERY, Pte. C. :—
  awarded M.M. for Arras, 132, 307
  awarded bar to M.M., 268, 306
ENGLEBELMER, 201, 203
EPEHY, 148, 239, 242
EPEHY, BATTLE OF :—
  objectives in, 239-240
  description of, 241-250
  casualties in, 242, 245, 247, 248, 250-251
  German accounts of, 242-243, 249
  decorations for, 251
EPINETTE WEST KEEP (Festubert), 51
EQUANCOURT, 147
EQUIPMENT—difficulties over supply of, 5
ERICSON, 2/Lt. E. C.—killed at Epehy, 250

ERIN, 116
ESCAUT RIVER, THE, 262
ESCAUT-ST. QUENTIN CANAL, 149, 150, 155, 158, 239
ESSEX REGIMENT, THE :—
  9th Bn., relieves Bn., 103, 106, 143 228
    relieved by Bn., 73, 79
    at Hulluch, 39, 40
    at Ovillers, 88, 89
    at Gueudecourt, 107
    at Monchy, 143
    at Cambrai, 151
    at Battle of Amiens, 225
    at Epehy, 249, 250
ESSEX SAP (Hulluch)—action at, described, 39-40
ESTRÉE BLANCHE, 52, 78
EVANS, Sgt. A. J. :—
  awarded M.M. for Battle of Craters, 66, 307
  killed at Ovillers, 66, 93
EVANS, Pte. J.—awarded M.M. for Cambrai, 173, 307
EVANS, Capt. S. G. :—
  joins Bn., 3
  appointed Staff Capt. 36th Brig., 8, 182, 312
  at Folkestone, 8
EVERSLEY CROSS, 11
EVIN, 255, 256

F

FACTORY TRENCH (Gueudecourt), 105
FAIRCLOTH, C.Q.M.S. H. L. :—
  joins Bn. from 2nd R. Sussex, 1
  overseas with Bn., 312
  killed at Givenchy, 50
FAIRHALL, Sgt. F. C. :—
  awarded D.C.M. at Monchy, 140, 306
  killed at Cambrai, 172
FARNBOROUGH, 13
FARNHAM, 11
FARROW, Capt. H. J. R. :—
  at Sibiville, 110
  at Monchy, 142
  O.C. D Coy. at Cambrai, 151, 160
  awarded M.C. for Cambrai, 173, 305
  O.C. C Coy. at Epehy, 245-246
  wounded at Epehy, 250
Fatalist at War, A—by Rudolf Binding, quoted, 204-205
FAUBOURG D'AMIENS (Arras), 143
FAUBOURG DE RONVILLE (Arras), 80, 143
FAVIÈRE WOOD, 234
FERGUSSON, Gen. Sir C., Bt. :—
  G.O.C. II Corps, at Houplines, 27
  G.O.C. XVIII Corps, at Monchy, 142
FERN TRENCH (Cambrai), 168
FESTUBERT :—
  trench tours at, described, 46-48, 51-52
  compared with Fleurbaix, 182
FEUCHY CHAPEL—cross-roads at, 119, 121, 134, 142
FIELD, 2/Lt. J. M.—killed at Hohenzollern Redoubt, 72
FIELD AMBULANCES :—
  36th, at Philosophe, 37, 38
  at Landas, 264
FIELD COMPANIES. *See under* ROYAL ENGINEERS
FINS, 148
FIR SUPPORT (Epehy), 249
FISHER'S KEEP (Epehy), 239

INDEX

FITZSIMONS, 2/Lt. T. :—
    with battle surplus for Ovillers, 94
    killed at Pozières, 103
Flammenwerfer :—
    at Pozières, 99
    at Spoon Trench, Monchy, 140
FLERS, 104, 105
FLESQUIÈRES, 150, 158
FLESSELLES, 80
FLEURBAIX—trench tours at, described, 182-188
FLINES, 262, 265
FLORINGHEM, 78
FOLKESTONE :—
    Racecourse, Bn. Transport at, 7
    Bn. billeted in, 8-10
    Mayor of, letter from, 10-11
    Bn. proceeds overseas via, 13
FORCEVILLE, 94
FORSTER, 2/Lt. T.—in Battle of Amiens, 228
FORT DE MAULDE, 259
FORTESCUE, Lt. R. H. :—
    at Ovillers, 87, 89
    after Ovillers, 94
    wounded at Arras, 123
FOSSE 8 DE BETHUNE (Hohenzollern), 33, 35, 36, 42, 58, 59
FOSSE 9 DE BETHUNE (Annequin), 41, 75
FOSTER, 2/Lt. P. G.—dies of wounds after Battle of Craters, 63, 65
FOUQUEREUIL, 40, 57, 69, 79
FOURTH AVENUE (Pozières), 96, 102
FOX HILLS (Aldershot), 11
FRAMECOURT, 145
FRANKLIN, 2/Lt. W. J.—killed at Gueudecourt, 107
FRANVILLERS, 220
FRÉCHENCOURT, 81
FRÉLINGHIEN, 24, 26
FREMONTIERS, 218
FRENCH, Field-Marshal Sir J. *See* YPRES, Earl of
FRÉVENT, 146, 190
FREWER, 2/Lt. F.—wounded at Cambrai, 154, 161, 172
FRICOURT :—
    Bn. in camp at, 1916, 108
    Bn. attacks on, 1918, described, 230-231
FUNNELL, Sgt. D.—killed at Cambrai, 172
FUSILIERS. *See* ROYAL FUSILIERS

G

GAS :—
    training against, 11
    respirators and helmets, early types of, issued, 14
    box respirators issued, 108
    use of, by British, at Loos, 33
        at Givenchy, 48
        at Scarpe, 129
    by Germans, at 2nd Battle of Ypres, 11, 33
        at Hulluch, 75, 76
        at Arras, 113
        at Monchy, 140
        at Fleurbaix, 188
        at Senlis, 210
        at Mailly, 214
        at Morlancourt, 228
        at Nurlu, 235, 236
        at Epehy, 241

GEORGE, Pte. A. W.—dies in England, 1915, 10
GERMAN FORMATIONS. *See under* CORPS, DIVISIONS, REGIMENTS, &c.
GERMAN HISTORIES :—
    quoted, on Battle of Craters, 67-69
        on Ovillers, 93-94
        on Cambrai, 154, 161-162, 175-176
        on Aveluy Wood, 203-204
        on Epehy, 242-243, 249
GERMAN OFFENSIVE, 1918, THE, 189, 190, 191, 206
    And see AVELUY WOOD, BOUZINCOURT, &c.
G.H.Q. :—
    at St. Omer, 14
    at Beauquesne, 215
GIBBS, Sir Philip :—
    visits Bn., 21
    Realities of War by, quoted, 21
GILHAM, Sgt. F. S.—killed at Battle of Craters, 66
GIVENCHY (lez-la-Bassée) :—
    fighting at, in 1915, 17
    trench tours at, described, 48-51
GIVENCHY-LE-NOBLE, 116
GLENISTER, 2/Lt. D. S. :—
    with battle surplus for Ovillers, 94
    wounded at Pozières, 103
GLENISTER, Pte. H. — awarded M.M. for Pozières, 103, 307
GLOBE RESTAURANT, THE (Bethune), 44
GLOUCESTERSHIRE REGIMENT, THE—10th Bn., at Loos, 37
GLUE, Pte. C. R.—dies in England, 1915, 10
GODDARD, Pte. J. H.—awarded M.M. for Pozières, 103, 307
GODFREE, C.Q.M.S. E. — joins Bn. from 2nd R. Sussex, 1
GODWIN, 2/Lt. J. C. R.—killed at Ovillers, 93
GOLDS, 2/Lt. F.—killed at Gueudecourt, 107
GOLDS, Sgt. W. :—
    wounded at Battle of Craters, 66
    awarded M.M. at Cambrai, 173, 307
GOMMECOURT, 81
GONNELIEU, 146, 148, 151, 163, 173, 175, 176, 177
GOODWIN, 2/Lt. H. C.—wounded at Epehy, 250
GOODYER, Pte. L.—awarded M.M., 307
GORDON, Lt. H. B.—killed at Ovillers, 86, 93
GORDON HIGHLANDERS, THE :—
    1st Bn., at Monchy, 136
    8th/10th Bn., at Arras, 119
GORRE, 47
GORRINGE, Capt. E. C. :—
    wounded at Battle of Scarpe, 128
    O.C. C Coy. at Cambrai, 162, 164, 166
    at Aveluy Wood, 192, 197, 199
    awarded M.C. for Aveluy Wood, 201, 203, 305
    killed at Nurlu, 237, 238
GOUGH, Gen. Sir H. de la P. :—
    G.O.C. I Corps, at Hohenzollern, 44, 56, 57
    congratulates Bn. after Battle of Craters, 69
    G.O.C. Fifth Army, congratulates 12th Div. after Pozières, 101, 102
    accompanies H.M. The King on inspection at Senlis, 103
GOUY, 108
GOUZEAUCOURT, 148, 174, 177

INDEX

GRAND-RULLECOURT, 133, 134
GRANT, Capt. H. de B., R.A.—killed at Loos, 35
GRATWICKE, Pte. F.—awarded M.M. for Battle of Craters, 66, 307
GRAVES, Mr.—billets Bn. Transport at Newington, 7
GREEN, Brig.-Gen. E. W. B. :—
    C.O. 2nd R. Sussex Regt., visits Bn. at Verquigneul, 34
    commands " Green's Force " at Loos, 34
GREEN HOWARDS, THE—6th Bn., at Agny, 104
GRENOUILLÈRE BRIDGE (Cambrai), 176
GRESSAIRE WOOD (Morlancourt), 225
GRID TRENCH AND SUPPORT TRENCH (Gueudecourt), 105
GRIFFITHS, Sgt. C.—awarded Belgian C. de G. for Aveluy Wood, 203, 309
GRISTON, Pte. P. :—
    awarded M.M. for Aveluy Wood, 203, 307
    awarded bar to M.M., 268, 306
GROVES, Pte. A. L.—
    awarded M.M. for raid at Fleurbaix, 188, 307
    awarded bar to M.M., 268, 306
GUARDS, THE. *See under* DIVISIONS
GUEUDECOURT :—
    fighting at, described, 104-107
    casualties at, 105, 107
    decorations for, 107
GUILDFORD, 10
GUILDFORD TRENCH (Arras), 119
GUILDFORD TRENCH (Hohenzollern), 43, 56
GUNNERS' SIDING (Givenchy), 48, 50
GUN SUPPORT TRENCH (Cambrai), 151
GUN TRENCH (Scarpe), 125
GUYENCOURT (Somme), 173, 251
GUYENCOURT (sur-Noye), 215

H

HAIG, Field-Marshal Earl :—
    accompanies Gen. Joffre on inspection at Lillers, 52
    despatch by, Bn. mentioned in, 78
    congratulates 12th Div. after Pozières, 101
    inspects Bn. before Arras, 116
    correspondence of, with Mayor of Arras, 130-131
    his conduct of Cambrai operations, 149, 157-158, 178, 179
HAIRPIN, THE (Quarries Sector), 69, 70
HALDANE, Gen. Sir J. A. L. :—
    G.O.C. VI Corps, inspects Bn. at Lattre-St. Quentin, 116
    congratulates 12th Div. after Arras, 122
HALL, Cpl. H.—mentioned in despatches, 309
HALL, 2/Lt. W. G.—wounded at Ovillers, 93
HAM-EN-ARTOIS, 52, 53
HANLON, R.S.M. P. J. :—
    joins Bn. from 2nd R. Sussex, 1
    long service with Bn., 1
    overseas with Bn., 312
    at Le Touquet, 19
    at Houplines, 25
    at Hohenzollern Redoubt, 43, 57, 62
    at Givenchy, 49
    at Battle of Craters, 62
    at Pozières, 98-99
    card presented to at Sibiville, 110
    at Bouzincourt, 210
    awarded M.S.M., 309
    mentioned in despatches, 310

Hansard—quoted, on Cambrai debate, 178
HAPPY VALLEY (Scarpe), 125, 129
HARDECOURT, 230, 234, 252
HARDHAM, Sgt. C.—killed at Epehy, 251
HARDY. *See* LE HARDY
HARMAN, Pte. E.—awarded M.M. for Battle of Craters, 66, 307
" HAROLD " :—
    becomes Bn. mascot, 4
    characteristics of, 4, 80
    wounded, 4
    his medal ribbons and conduct sheet, 4
    " crimes " of, 4, 9
    disappears at Folkestone, 9
    overseas with Bn., 312
    at Vignacourt, 80
    demobilisation of, 4, 219
HARPONVILLE, 211, 212
HARRIS, Sgt. E.—overseas with Bn., 311
HARTFORD BRIDGE FLATS, 11
HARTLEY ROW, 11
HARVEY, Pte. A.—awarded D.C.M., 304
Hastings and St. Leonards Advertiser, The—provides Christmas puddings, 109
HAUTE DEULE CANAL—crossing of the, 255-257, 261
HAVRE, 14
HAVRINCOURT WOOD, 152
HAYDON, Capt. C. W. — Middlesex Regt., reconnaissance by, at Monchy, 141
HAYES, C.S.M. J.—overseas with Bn., 312
    awarded M.M. for Pozières, 103, 307
HAYWARD, Pte. W. H.—awarded M.M. for Gueudecourt, 107, 307
HAZEBROUCK, 14, 181
HEAD, Cpl. A. H.—killed at Gueudecourt, 107
HEAD, Sgt. E. J.—awarded D.C.M. for Epehy, 251, 306
HEBERT, 2/Lt. B. T. M.—remains in England with casualty reserve, 312
HÉDAUVILLE, 203, 204, 216
HEILLY, 222
HENDRY, L/Cpl. W.—awarded M.M. for Battle of Craters, 66, 307
HENENCOURT, 191, 192
HENIN-LIÉTARD, 255
HENLEY REGATTA—reminiscence of, 19
HERISSART, 218
HERMAVILLE, 144, 189
HERTFORD TRENCH (Arras), 119
HESDIN, 144
HETTON-LE-HOLE, 24
HEUDICOURT, 148, 171, 174
HEYDON, Sgt. A. J.—killed at Aveluy Wood, 202
HEYTHORP POST AND TRENCH (Epehy), 248
HIGGINSON, Maj.-Gen. H. W. :—
    takes over 12th Div., 212
    congratulatory order by, after Nurlu, 238-239
    at Epehy, 251
    leaves 12th Div., 268
HIGHGATE, Pte. E. :—
    awarded M.M. for Arras, 132, 308
    awarded D.C.M. and two bars to M.M. in last *Gazettes*, 267, 306
HILL, Lt. G. H. :—
    at Monchy, 143
    Lewis gun officer at Vieil Hesdin, 145
    wounded at Cambrai, 172
    O.C. B Coy. at Aveluy Wood, 192, 198
    Ass. Adjutant at Battle of Amiens, 228
    at Epehy, 245
    Adjutant of Bn. Cadre, 269

INDEX

HILL, Lt. T. A. :—
  remains in England with casualty reserve, 312
  transfers to M.G.C., 53
HILL SUPPORT TRENCH (Monchy), 136
HILL 70 (Loos), 33
HILL 105 (Morlancourt)—Bn. attacks on, 225, 226, 227
HIND, Capt. R. C. D. :—
  appointed Transport Officer, 7
  early experiences with Transport, 7
  overseas with Transport, 13, 311
  at Loos, 36
  temporary Q.M., 41
  starts Bn. Canteen, 80
  at Senlis, 94
  at Flers, 104
  at Arras, 121-122, 130
  at Cambrai, 170, 173-175, 180
  en route for Aveluy, 191
  at Aveluy Wood, 201-202
  at Bouzincourt, 210
  during Final Advance, 262
  Quartermaster of the Cadre, 268, 269
  awarded M.C., 305
  mentioned in despatches, 310
HINDENBURG LINE, THE :—
  German retreat to, 1917, 118, 147, 180
  in Battle of Arras, 118
  in Battle of Cambrai, 150, 151, 153, 154, 156, 164, 165, 169, 170, 172, 175
  German retreat to, 1918, 235, 239
  battles of. *See* EPEHY
HINGES, 46
HINGETTE, 46, 48, 51
HOBBS' FARM (Houplines), 23, 26
HODGES, 2/Lt. F. E. D.—wounded at Arras, 123
HODGES, Sgt. G. :—
  awarded D.C.M. for Pozières, 103, 306
  awarded Italian Bronze Medal for Arras, 132, 309
HOHENZOLLERN REDOUBT, THE :—
  an objective in Battle of Loos, 33, 35, 41
  trench tours in, described, 42-44, 53-73
  mining operations in, 55-56
  casualties in, 76
  decorations for, 60, 66, 80, 81
  And see CRATERS, THE, BATTLE OF
HOLDEN, Cpl. C.—killed at Gueudecourt, 107
HOLDER, Pte. B.—awarded M.M. for Aveluy Wood, 203, 308
HOLLINGDALE, Pte. R.—dies in England, 1915, 10
HONEYMAN, 2/Lt. G. G. — wounded at Mametz, 232, 233
HONOURABLE ARTILLERY COMPANY, THE, 72
HOOGE, 17
HOOK TRENCH (Monchy) :—
  attack on, 136
  counter-attack on, 140-141
HORNAING—Bn. billets at, after Armistice, 265-268
HORNE, Sgt. A. W. :—
  awarded M.M. for Pozières, 103, 308
  awarded bar for Arras, 132, 306
HORSE POST AND TRENCH (Epehy), 247
HOUPLINES :—
  instructional tour at, 16
  trench tours at, described, 22-31
  civilians evacuated from, 30
  howling dog at, 30
  compared with Hohenzollern, 56
                            Fleurbaix, 182
                            Bouzincourt, 216

HOUSE AVENUE (Le Touquet), 18
HOWE, Capt. R. M. :—
  wounded at Pozières, 103
  at Cambrai, 155
  O.C. B Coy. at Bouzincourt Ridge, 207
  at Battle of Amiens, 220, 226
  awarded M.C. for Amiens, 228, 305
  at Mametz, 231
HOWETT, 2/Lt. W.—killed at Epehy, 250
H.Q. FARM (Le Touquet), 17, 21
HUGGETT, 2/Lt. S. G.—killed at Epehy, 243, 244, 251
HUGHES, Maj. W. R.—D.A.Q.M.G. 12th Div., at Cambrai, 174
HULKES, Sgt. E. :—
  joins Bn. from 2nd R. Sussex, 1
  overseas with Bn. as M.G. Sgt., 311
  killed at Pozières, 103
HULLUCH, 4, 34, 35, 36, 39, 74
HULME, Cpl. J. A.—killed at Gueudecourt, 107
HUSSARS, 15TH THE KING'S ROYAL — at Hohenzollern Redoubt, 55
HYGATE, Sgt. H. P. :—
  killed at Epehy, 251
  mentioned in despatches, 310
HYTHE :—
  ranges at, 6
  precautions to repel German landing at, 6

I

IMPEY, Lt.-Col. G. H. :—
  joins Bn. from 1st R. Sussex, 3
  at Folkestone, 8
  overseas with Bn. as O.C. D Coy., 312
  at Houplines, 24, 29
  slightly wounded and arrested as a spy at Loos, 37-38
  temporary C.O., at Festubert, 46 ; at Hohenzollern, 57, 71
  at Battle of Craters, 59, 60-62
  leaves Bn. to command 12th R. Sussex, 77, 218
  wounded and awarded D.S.O. with 12th R. Sussex, 142
  returns to command Bn. at Monchy, 142
  at Vieil Hesdin, 145, 146
  at Cambrai, 148, 159, 163, 164, 169
  at Berguette, 181
  at Fleurbaix, 185, 187
  at Aveluy Wood, 192, 193, 195, 196, 197, 202
  awarded bar to D.S.O. for Aveluy Wood, 196, 203, 304
  at Bouzincourt Ridge, 207
  leaves Bn., 218
  appreciation of, 218
  mentioned in despatches, 310
INFANTRY HILL (Monchy), 136, 141
INFANTRY LANE (Monchy), 136, 138
INKERMAN BARRACKS (Woking)—2nd R. Sussex mobilises at, 1
INK TRENCH (Arras), 117
INTERNATIONAL POST (Fleurbaix), 182
IRISH AVENUE (Houplines), 23
IRISH FUSILIERS. *See* ROYAL IRISH FUSILIERS
IRISH REGIMENT. *See* ROYAL IRISH REGIMENT
ISBERGUES, 181
I SECTOR, THE (Arras)—trench tours at, described, 114, 115, 117
ISTED, Pte. S.—awarded M.M. for Arras, 132, 308
ITALY—British reinforcements sent to, 149
IZEL-LEZ-HAMEAU, 104

INDEX

J

JACOB, Field-Marshal Sir C. W.—G.O.C. II Corps, accompanies H.M. The King on inspection at Senlis, 103
Jägers :—
   at Pozières, 98
   at Epehy, 242, 243, 249
JAY, Maj. C. D. :—
   at Folkestone, 8
   overseas with Bn. as M.G.O., 13, 311
   at Houplines, 26
   at Essex Sap, 40
   transfers to M.G.C., 53
JEUDWINE, Lt.-Gen. Sir H. S. — G.O.C. 55th Div., at Cambrai, 163
JEWELL, Maj. M. F. S.—assists recruiting for Bn., 3
JOFFRE, Marshal J.—inspects 36th Brig. at Lillers, 52
JOHNSTONE, 2/Lt. R. C. S. — wounded at Hohenzollern Redoubt, 73
JONES, Kennedy, M.P.—in Parliamentary debate on Cambrai, 178
JONES, Capt. T. A.—Q.M. of 2nd R. Sussex, visits Bn. at Verquigneul, 34
JONES, Sgt. T.—mentioned in despatches, 310
JOSLAND, Pte. A. E.—awarded M.M. for raid at Fleurbaix, 188, 308
JOY, R.S.M. J. :—
   overseas with Bn., 312
   at Houplines, 31
   at Ovillers, 87, 89
   awarded M.C. for Ovillers, 93, 305
   at Pozières, 97
   at Cambrai, 163
JUNCTION KEEP (Hohenzollern), 58

K

KAISER, THE—his birthday celebrated, 52
KEMMEL, 211
KENDERDINE, Lt. J. H. B. :—
   at Epehy, 246
   wounded at Epehy, 250
   draws King's Colour at Somain, 267
KENT, Sgt. J. C.—killed at Ovillers, 93
KENWARD, 2/Lt. R.—killed at Ovillers, 93
KIGGELL, Lt.-Gen. Sir L. E.—C.G.S. during Cambrai operations, 149
KILDARE POST (Epehy), 240, 247
KING, H.M. THE :—
   attends church parade at Aldershot, 12
   his message to 12th Div., 12
   inspects 36th Brig. at Senlis, 103
KING, Pte. G.—killed at Houplines, 16
KING, Com. H. D., M.P.—in Parliamentary debate on Cambrai, 178
KING, Sgt. J. :—
   joins Bn. from 2nd Bn., 1
   patrols by at Armentières, 20, 23, 26, 27
   awarded D.C.M. and promoted, 23, 54, 306
   killed in Battle of Craters, 66
KING'S COLOUR, THE—presented to Bn. by H.R.H. The Prince of Wales at Erre, 267
KING'S REGIMENT, THE (LIVERPOOL) — 2/6th Bn., at Fleurbaix, 189
KING'S ROYAL RIFLE CORPS, THE—9th Bn., at Agny, 104

KITCHENER, Field-Marshal Earl :—
   organises the " New Armies," 1
   inspects Bn. on march to Aldershot, 10
   at Aldershot, 11
KNOPE, Pte. H.—awarded M.M., 308
KNOX, 2/Lt. J. L.—killed at Cambrai, 154, 172

L

LA BASSÉE, 33, 44, 46
LA BASSÉE CANAL, 48, 50, 51
LA BOISSELLE, 81, 84, 88, 96
LA BOUTILLERIE—trench tours at, described, 182-183, 185
LA FÈRE, 190
LAHOUSSOYE SWITCH, 220
LAKER, Pte. —.—at Bouzincourt, 210
LAMBERT, Sgt. H.—killed at Aveluy Wood, 202
LA MOTTE FARM (Château l'Abbaye), 259, 260, 261
LANCASHIRE FUSILIERS, THE :—
   1st Bn., at Gueudecourt, 107
   18th Bn., at Bouzincourt, 216
LANCASHIRE TRENCH (Hohenzollern), 58, 59
LANDAS, 259, 263, 265
LANGLEY, C.S.M. G.—awarded D.C.M. for Battle of Craters, 66, 306
LAPUGNOY, 76, 77, 78, 190
LATEAU WOOD (Cambrai), 150
LATTRE-ST. QUENTIN, 116, 122
LA VACQUERIE :—
   Bn.'s defence of, 162, 165, 166, 167, 168, 169, 170, 173, 176, 177
   reported capture of, 170
LAVENDER, 2/Lt. H. R.—killed at Mametz, 232, 233
LAVIEVILLE, 104, 191, 192
LAW, Rt. Hon. A. Bonar, M.P.—Chancellor of the Exchequer, in Parliamentary debates on Cambrai, 177
LAWRENCE, Pte. H. J.—awarded M.M. for Battle of Craters, 66, 308
LAWRENCE, Sgt. R.—awarded M.M. for Pozières, 103, 308
LAWRENCE, 2/Lt. T. E.—killed at Epehy, 250
LEACH, Lt. J. O.—11th Middlesex, at Essex Sap, 39
LEAS HOTEL (Folkestone), 8
LE BIZET, 16, 19
LE BOURGAGE, 258
LECELLES, 259
L'ECLEME, 53
LEDGER, 2/Lt. R. J. :—
   at Gueudecourt, 107
   acc. killed at Lignereuil, 116
LE DOUX VEITCH, 2/Lt. D. G. :—
   with battle surplus for Ovillers, 94
   killed at Pozières, 103
LEE, Sgt. A. :—
   appointed Transport Sgt., 7
   at Shorncliffe Station, 7
   overseas with Bn., 311
   awarded M.M., 308 ; M.S.M., 309
   mentioned in despatches, 310
LEFOREST (Artois), 257
LEFOREST (Somme), 234, 235
LE FORT, 262
LE HARDY, Capt. W. H. C. :—
   O.C. A Coy. at Scarpe, 129
   at Monchy, 141
   at Vieil Hesdin, 146

INDEX

LE HARDY, Capt. W. H. C. (continued):—
    at Cambrai, 151, 152, 155, 164, 167-168, 173
    awarded M.C. for Cambrai, 173, 305
    becomes Staff Capt. 36th Brig., 182
    during German offensive, 1918, 191, 192
LEINSTER REGIMENT, THE PRINCE OF WALES'S:—
    1st Bn., at Le Bizet, 16
        at Le Touquet, 18
LEIPZIG SALIENT (Thiepval), 84
LENS, 33, 37, 38, 44
LE PAVÉ, 150, 175
LE PLANTIN, 46, 50, 51
LEPPARD, Sgt. C. H.—awarded M.M., 308
LE PRÉ, 255
LE QUESNOY, 51
LE RUAGE, 22
LE RUTOIRE (Loos), 34, 36, 37, 38
LES BARAQUES (Cambrai), 176
LES BREBIS, 79
LES CINQ RUES (Hazebrouck), 14
LES FOSSES FARM (Monchy), 121
LES RUES DES VINGES (Cambrai), 155
LE TOUQUET:—
    instructional tour at, 16
    trench tours at, described, 17-21
    inhabitants evacuated from, 19
    compared with Festubert, 182
LE TOURET, 47
LE TRANSLOY, BATTLE OF. *See* GUEUDECOURT
LE TROU POST (Fleurbaix), 182
Letters from France—by Lt.-Col. Sansom, quoted, 120, 133
LEWES, Lt.-Col. C. G.—C.O. 9th Essex, at Essex Sap, 40
LEWIS, Sgt. C. E.—wounded at Le Touquet, 16
LEWIS GUNS:—
    replace machine-guns in Bn., 53
    organisation of, 53, 215
LIDDELL HART, Capt. B. H.—*The Real War* by, quoted, on Cambrai, 148, 163, 179
LIERAMONT, 238, 251
LIGNEREUIL, 115-116, 119
LILLE, 256, 257
LILLERS, 45, 52, 181, 189, 190
" LILLIPUTIANS, THE ":—
    at Givenchy, 49
    at Pozières, 98
LINDEN, Cpl. W.—killed at Pozières, 103
LIQUID FIRE. *See* FLAMMENWERFER
LISTER, Sgt. E.—awarded M.M., 308
LITTLE PRIEL FARM (Epehy), 240, 247, 248, 249
LITTLE WILLIE (Hohenzollern), 41, 42, 44, 58, 60
LIVENS PROJECTORS—used at Battle of Scarpe, 129
LOCRON FARM (Château l'Abbaye), 259
LONDON REGIMENT, THE :—
    2/17th (Tower Hamlets Rifles), Major Birkett to command, 58
    24th (The Queen's), at Aveluy Wood, 202
LONE TREE (Hulluch), 34, 37, 38
LONE TREE CEMETERY (Morlancourt), 222, 223
LONG, Q.M.S. W. :—
    joins Bn., 3
    overseas with Bn. as R.Q.M.S., 311
    card presented to, at Sibiville, 110
    awarded M.S.M., 309
    mentioned in despatches, 310
LONG LANE (Scarpe), 129
LONG TRENCH (Monchy) :—
    capture of, by 76th Brig., 136, 137
    capture of, by Germans, 140-141

LONGUEAU, 79
LOOS, 33, 35
LOOS, BATTLE OF :—
    lull before, 17
    preparations for, 31
    objectives of, 33
    description of, 33-40
    casualties in, 44
LORD, C.S.M. C. :—
    joins Bn. from 2nd R. Sussex, 1
    overseas with Bn. as Signals Sgt., 311
    at Houplines, 28
LOTHAM, 2/Lt. S. :—
    wounded at Aveluy Wood, 202
    at Battle of Amiens, 223, 225
    wounded at Amiens, 227
    awarded M.C. for Amiens, 228, 305
LOWER, Sgt. C.—wounded at Battle of Craters, 66
LUCE RIVER, THE, 221
" LUMBAGO WALK " (Houplines), 25
LUSTED, C.S.M. A. F. :—
    joins Bn., 3
    overseas with Bn., 312
LUXMOORE, Lt.-Col. N.—Devonshire Regt., C.O. 2nd Manchesters at Ovillers, 89
LYMINGE, 6
LYONS, 2/Lt. A. J.—wounded at Epehy, 250
LYS, BATTLE OF THE, 211
LYS FARM (Le Touquet), 17
LYS RIVER, THE, 17, 19, 22, 23, 24, 27, 31

M

McCRACKEN, Lt. N. :—
    at Arras, 117
    awarded M.C. for Arras, 117, 132, 305
    wounded at Epehy, 248, 250
MACHINE GUN CORPS, THE :—
    12th Bn., formed, xviii., 53
    36th Brigade Coy., formed, xviii., 53
        at Battle of Scarpe, 128
MACHINE GUN SECTION, THE BN. :—
    proceeds overseas, 13, 14
    at Le Touquet, 16
    more guns for, 27
    at Armentières, 32
    at Essex Sap, 39-40
    transferred to 36th Brig. M.G Coy., xviii., 53
MACKENSEN, Field-Marshal A. von, 213
MACPHERSON, Rt. Hon. J. Ian, M.P.—in Parliamentary debate on Cambrai, 178
MADGE, Sgt. W.—killed at Ovillers, 93
MAGRATH, Capt. J. S. :—
    joins Bn., 1
    leaves Bn., 3
MAGUIRE, L/Cpl. J.—awarded M.M., 308
MAIDMENT, Sgt. C.—joins Bn. from 2nd R. Sussex, 1
MAIDSTONE, 10
MAILLY-MAILLET :—
    Bn. billets at, 1916, 95
    trench tours at, 1918, described, 213-214
MAIRIE DE NIVELLE, 259
MAIRIE REDOUBT (Givenchy), 48
MAISTRE LINE (Loos), 79
MALARD WOOD (Morlancourt), 222
MALASSISE FARM (Epehy), 240, 242, 245, 247, 248
MALTZ HORN FARM (Somme), 230, 234

INDEX

MAMETZ, 108, 180, 230, 231, 232
    Bn. attacks near, described, 230-233
    casualties in, 233
    decorations for, 233
MANANCOURT, 147
MANCHESTER REGIMENT, THE :—
    2nd Bn., at Ovillers, 89
    12th Bn., at Bouzincourt, 218
MANLEY, 2/Lt. H. D.—killed at Aveluy Wood, 196, 202
MARETT WOOD (Méricourt), 225
MARGARY, Lt. I. D. :—
    with battle surplus for Ovillers, 94
    patrol by, at Monchy, 136
MARICOURT, 81, 180, 193, 231, 233, 252
MARLBOROUGH LINES (Aldershot), 11
MAROC, 79
MARSHALL, Pte.—wounded at Le Touquet, 16
MARSHALL, Sgt. C.—awarded M.M., 308
MARTIN, 2/Lt. B.—wounded at Gueudecourt, 107
MARTINPUICH, 81
MARTINSART, 194, 197, 201, 202
MASH VALLEY (Ovillers), 84, 86
MASNIERES, 157
MAUDLING, Sgt. F.—overseas with Bn., 311
MAUGHAN, L/Cpl. H. :—
    awarded M.M. for Scarpe, 127, 132, 308
    killed at Cambrai, 172
MAUREPAS, 252
MAY, Maj. C. H.—transfers to 9th Motor M.G. Battery, 312
MAY, Capt. R. T. :—
    overseas with Bn., 311
    O.C. A Coy. at Festubert, &c., 47 59, 71
    O.C. B Coy. at Quarries Sector, 71
    O.C. A Coy. at Ovillers, 84, 90
    killed at Ovillers, 90, 93
MAYES, L/Cpl. C. P.—awarded M.M. for Pozières, 103, 308
MAZINGARBE, 41
MEAULT, 180, 229
MEAUX, 205
MENNIE, 2/Lt. J.—killed at Epehy, 250
MÉRICOURT, 253
MÉRICOURT (l'Abbé), 225, 228
MERRIS, 14
MERVILLE, 185, 189
MESNIL, 194
METZ-EN-COUTURE, 175, 177
MIDDLESEX REGIMENT, THE :—
    11th Bn., relieves Bn., 162
    relieved by Bn., 42, 96, 142, 184
    Bn. shares barracks with, at Aldershot, 11
    at Houplines, 22
    at Loos, 35
    at Essex Sap, 39-40
    at Hohenzollern Redoubt, 41, 57, 59
    at Baizieux, 81
    at Ovillers, 88
    drafts for, sent to Bn., 95
    at Pozières, 96, 99
    at Gueudecourt, 105
    at Arras, 115, 118, 119, 120
    at Scarpe, 124
    at Agnez-lez-Duisans, 133
    at Beaurains, 142
    at Cambrai, 150, 161
    disbanded, 184
MILLENCOURT, 81, 94, 206

MILLS, Capt. E. A., R.A.M.C. :—
    Bn. M.O. at Arras, 113
    leaves Bn. to become D.A.D.M.S., 12th Div., 185
MILLS, 2/Lt. T. W.—wounded at Cambrai, 172
MILLS BOMBS—first issue of, 41
MINALL, Sgt. E. C.—killed at Aveluy Wood, 202
Minenwerfer. See TRENCH MORTARS
MINES :—
    blown by British, at Houplines, 27, 30, 31
        at Hohenzollern Redoubt, 55-56, 58, 59
        at Quarries Sector, 70, 72, 74
    blown by Germans, at Le Touquet, 16
        at Givenchy, 49, 50
        at Hohenzollern Redoubt, 55-56, 57, 58, 70, 72
    in Final Advance, 255, 259
MIRVAUX, 211
MITCHELL, Sgt. F.—killed at Arras, 123
MOISLAINS, 147, 235
MOLINGHEM, 182
MONCHY (le Preux) :—
    an objective at Battle of Arras, 118, 120, 121
    trench tours at, described, 134-144
    raids at, 137, 141-142, 143, 144
    casualties at, 140, 144
    other references to, 57, 127, 129, 131
" MONCHY EXPRESS, THE," 137, 143
MONDICOURT, 122, 123
MONRO, Gen. Sir C. C.—G.O.C. First Army, at Bethune and Sailly, 71
MONTAUBAN, 106, 192, 231, 234
MONT DE LA JUSTICE, 259, 260
MONTDIDIER, 221
MONT DU MOULIN (Château l'Abbaye), 259
MONT DU PROY, 259
MONTENESCOURT, 115
MONTESOLE, 2/Lt. E. A. :—
    first Bn. Lewis gun officer, 53
    killed at Battle of Craters, 63, 65
MONTGOMERY-MASSINGBERD, Gen. Sir A. A.—quoted, on Battle of Amiens, 224
MONTREUIL, 262
MONT ST. ELOI, 253
MOORE, Lt. E. A.—11th Middlesex, at Ovillers, 88
MOORE, Pte. F.—awarded M.M., 308
MOREUIL, 205
MORLANCOURT, 220, 221, 222, 225, 227, 228, 234, 252
    And see AMIENS, BATTLE OF
MORLEY, Sgt. W. L.—killed at Nurlu, 238
MORRIS, Lt. A. J. :—
    wounded at Battle of Scarpe, 128
    wounded at Battle of Albert, 1918, 229, 233
MORRIS, Pte. O. C.—awarded M.M. for Aveluy Wood, 203, 308
MOSS, Cpl. E. W.—awarded D.C.M. for Cambrai, 173, 306
MOSSOP, Lt. G. P. :—
    wounded at Bouzincourt Ridge, 208
    wounded at Nurlu, 238
" MOTHER "—9.2in. howitzer at Annequin, 41
MOTOR CAR CORNER (Le Touquet), 18

INDEX

MOTTISTONE, Viscount—quoted, on Cambrai, 176
MOUNTSTEPHENS, Cpl. A.—killed at Battle of Amiens, 227
MOUQUET FARM (Pozières), 97, 102
MUD TRENCH (Hohenzollern), 42, 43, 59, 60
MULE TRENCH (Epehy), 247, 248
MUNT, Sgt. C.—awarded M.M., 308
MURRAY, 2/Lt. A.—killed at Battle of Amiens, 223, 227
MUSTCHIN, Pte. W.—awarded M.M., 308
MYLIUS, 2/Lt. H. H. :—
   at Nurlu, 237
   at Epehy, 249-250
   at Château l'Abbaye, 261
   at Hornaing, 266

N

NAGLE, Capt. G. :—
   at Folkestone, 8
   overseas with Bn., 311
   at Le Touquet, 18
   O.C.A Coy. at Battle of Craters, 59, 66
   wounded at Battle of Craters, 66
   awarded M.C. and promoted for Battle of Craters, 66, 305
   O.C. A Coy. at Quarries Sector, 71
   Ass. Adjutant at Hohenzollern, 71
   attached to 35th Brig. H.Q. for Ovillers, 94
   appointed Adjutant, 101
   with battle surplus for Scarpe, 124
   killed at Monchy, 139
   appreciation of, 139-140
   mentioned in despatches, 310
NAPOLEON I.—projected invasion of England by, 13
NEALE, Capt. S. — 11th Middlesex, O.C. 36th T.M. Battery, 53
NECKLACE TRENCH (Fleurbaix)—D Coy. raid on, 185-188
" NEW ARMIES, THE " :—
   organised by Lord Kitchener, 1
   early difficulties of, 1, 5, 6
   quality of junior officers of, 4
   spirit of, 5, 11
   Sir J. French insists on divisional training for, 10
   arrival in France, effect of, 33
NEWCASTLE—men of the Bn. from, 5, 24, 34
NEWFOUNDLAND REGIMENT, THE :—
   1st Bn., at Monchy, 121
NEWINGTON, 7
NEWPORT, L/Cpl. H. W.—awarded M.M. for Pozières, 103, 308
NEWPORT TRENCH (Cambrai), 171
NEWTON, Cpl. F.—killed at Epehy, 251
NEW ZEALAND RIFLE BRIGADE, THE :—
   2nd and 3rd Bns., at Mailly-Maillet, 212
NICHOLS, Pte. F. V. :—
   presented with green card at Flesselles, 81
   awarded M.M. for Ovillers, 103, 308
NIEPPE FOREST, 189
NIVELLE, 259
NOEUX-LES-MINES, 34
NORFOLK REGIMENT, THE :—
   7th Bn., relieves Bn., 141
      relieved by Bn., 83
      at Cambrai, 164
      at Nurlu, 235
      at Courcelles, 255

NORMAN, Cpl. J. C.—killed at Gueudecourt, 107
NORTHAMPTONSHIRE REGIMENT, THE :—
   5th Bn., Pioneer Bn. of 12th Div., xviii.
      remove German guns at Loos, 37
      at Battle of Craters, 62, 70
      mentioned in despatches, 78
      efficiency of, at Arras, 113
      at Bouzincourt, 210
      appreciation of, 210
      at Epehy, 249
      build race-course at Somain, 266
NORTHAMPTON TRENCH (Hohenzollern), 42, 43, 59, 60
NORTH LANE (Epehy), 242
NORTH STREET (Fleurbaix), 185, 186
NOTRE DAME DE LORETTE, 35
NOUVEL HOUPLINES, 23, 28
NOYELLE-GODAULT, 255
NOYELLES, 38, 40, 41, 57, 69, 73
NOYE RIVER, THE, 218
NURLU :—
   Bn. attacks on, 235-238, 239, 252
   casualties in, 238
NUTLEY, C.S.M. A. :—
   overseas with Bn., 312
   mentioned in despatches, 310

O

OBSERVATION RIDGE (Arras), 118
OCKENDEN TRENCH (Epehy), 248
OFFICERS TRAINING CORPS, 1, 4
OLD COPSE (Epehy), 247
O'MALLEY, Capt. G. P., U.S. Army Med. Corps :—
   joins as Bn. M.O., 185
   awarded D.S.O. for Mametz, 233, 305
   at Orchies, 258
ONIONS, L/Sgt. W.—awarded M.M., 308
OOSTHOVE FARM (Armentières), 17
ORANGE HILL (Arras), 112, 118, 124, 129
ORCHIES, 258, 259, 265
ORESMAUX, 218, 219, 220
OSBORN, Brig.-Gen. W. L. :—
   appointed first C.O. of Bn., 2
   gazetted Lt.-Col. and joins Bn., 2
   appeal to ex-N.C.O.s by, 2, 3
   insists on purchase of necessaries for Bn., 5
   overseas with Bn., 311
   at Le Touquet, 21
   at Houplines, 28
   at Armentières, 32
   at Hohenzollern Redoubt, 42, 57, 71
   temporary G.O.C. 36th Brig. at Givenchy, 48
   at Givenchy, 50
   at Battle of Craters, 59, 60, 61
   awarded D.S.O. for Battle of Craters, 60, 305
   at Ovillers, 83, 84, 85-89, 90, 91, 92
   wounded at Ovillers, 89, 93
   at Senlis, 94
   at Sailly-au-Bois, 95
   leaves Bn. to command 16th Brig., 95
   appreciation of, 95
   revisits Bn. at Grand-Rullecourt, 133
   unable to visit Bn. at Beauquesne, 215
   mentioned in despatches, 310

INDEX

OSBORNE, Maj. G. F. :—
  joins Bn. from 1st R. Sussex, 3
  overseas with Bn., 312
  O.C. C Coy. at Houplines, 29
  wounded at Houplines, 29
  O.C. D Coy. at Battle of Craters, 59
  wounded at Battle of Craters, 66
  at Hohenzollern Redoubt, 73
  with battle surplus for Ovillers, 84
  2nd in Command after Ovillers, 94
  temporary C.O. at Pozières, 95
  2nd in command after Pozières, 101
  at Gueudecourt, 106
  at Arras, 114, 119
  temporary C.O. at Monchy, 140
  at Cambrai, 146, 157, 163, 170
  at Quiestede, 180
  at Berguette, 181
  at Aveluy Wood, 192, 199
  awarded M.C. for Aveluy Wood, 203, 305
  at Domqueur, 216
  at Orchies, 258
  in command of Bn. Cadre, 269
  mentioned in despatches, 310
OSBORNE, Sgt. W. J. :—
  awarded M.M. for Arras, 132, 308
  killed at Cambrai, 172
OSTROHOVE CAMP (Boulogne), 13
OVILLERS :—
  failure of first attacks on, 81-82
  orders for attack on, 83-85
  descriptions of attack on, 85-94
  casualties at, 85, 92-93
  honours awarded for, 93, 103
  German accounts of attack on, 93-94
  Bn. congratulated for attack on, 94
  Bn. in trenches near, 96
OWEN, Brig.-Gen. C. S. :—
  G.O.C. 36th Brig. at Agny, 108
  inspects Bn. at Sibiville, 110
  congratulates Bn. on attack at Arras, 120 and after Aveluy Wood, 206
  presents special prize for drummers, 215
  at Beauquesne, 216
  at Oresmaux, 218
  at Fricourt, 230
OWEN, Pte. T.—dies in England, 1915, 10
OXFORDSHIRE AND BUCKINGHAMSHIRE LIGHT INFANTRY, THE :—
  2nd Bn., at Aveluy Wood, 201
  5th Bn., at Agny, 108

P

PACKHAM, Cpl. F.—awarded M.M., 308
PAGE, R.S.M. H. :—
  joins Bn., 3
  overseas with Bn., 312
  wounded at Ovillers, 86, 87
  awarded D.C.M., 306
PAICE, Sgt. A. E.—killed at Cambrai, 172
PAINE, Pte. E.—awarded M.M., 308
PALEY, Lt. F. R. :—
  at Cambrai, 162
  wounded at Aveluy Wood, 196, 202
PALMER, 2/Lt. H. J. — killed at Battle of Amiens, 227
PAM PAM FARM (Cambrai), 169
PANNICK, Sgt. G. — overseas with Bn. as Provost Sgt., 311
PARIS :—
  shelled by long-range gun, 191
  railway to, freed by Battle of Amiens, 221

PARSONS, Sgt. A.—awarded M.M., 308
PASSCHENDAELE. *See* YPRES, BATTLES OF
PAYNE, Sgt. H.—at Ovillers, 87
PEACOCK, Sgt. A. N.—awarded M.M. for Battle of Craters, 66, 308
PEACOCK, Sgt. J. G.—awarded M.M. for Battle of Craters, 66, 308
PECK, Pte. J.—awarded M.M., 308
PEIZIERE, 240
PELICAN TRENCH (Cambrai) :—
  description of, 155-156
  importance of, 156
  attacks on, 158-162, 163
  casualties at, 161, 172
PELVES :—
  an objective in Battle of Scarpe, 124, 125
  Bn. attacks on, 127-128
  mill at, 125, 127
PENROSE, Lt. E.—T.O. of 36th Brig. M.G. Coy. at Cambrai, 174
PENSAM POST (Fleurbaix)—German raid on 184, 185
PENTICOST, Pte. J.—awarded M.M. for Arras, 132, 308
PEPPER, 2/Lt. E. G.—wounded at Hohenzollern Redoubt, 73
PEPPER, Pte. S.—awarded M.M., 308
PERENCHIES, 21
PERNES, 190
PERONNE, 146, 147, 148, 150, 180, 230, 231, 240, 253
PETERS, L/Cpl. —.—at Pozières, 97
PHILCOX, Cpl. T. W. — killed at Battle of Amiens, 227
PHILLIPS, L/Cpl. T. — awarded M.M. for Aveluy Wood, 203, 308
PHILOSOPHE, 37, 38
PHIPPS, Lt. G. A. :—
  wounded at Gueudecourt, 107
  wounded at Mametz, 233
  at Epehy, 249
  M.G.O. of Bn. Cadre, 269
PICK CAVE (Monchy), 138, 140, 141
PICTON, Cpl. F.—wounded and awarded M.M. at Battle of Craters, 66, 308
PIERREGOT, 211
PILKINGTON, Col. F. C.—C.O. 15th Hussars, at Hohenzollern Redoubt, 55
PINNEY'S AVENUE (Fleurbaix), 183, 185, 187
PLUMER, Field-Marshal Lord—G.O.C. Second Army, inspects Bn. at Houplines, 29
POINTS, 14, 77, 81, 85, 95 and 99 (Pozières)—
  Bn. attacks on, 96, 97
POMMIERS REDOUBT (Somme), 104, 230
PONTCEAU, 17
PONT D'ACHELLES, 22
PONT DE BRIQUES, 14
PONT DE NIEPPE, 17, 21, 32
PONT FIXE (Givenchy), 50
POPERINGHE, 95
PORTEOUS, Pte. D. R.—awarded M.M. for raid at Fleurbaix, 188, 308
PORTER, Cpl. E.—awarded M.M. for Cambrai, 173, 308
PORTUGUESE ARMY, THE — liaison with, at Fleurbaix, 182, 187
POTIN, FELIX—branch of, at Armentières, 15
POUND FARM (Newington), 7
POZIÈRES :—
  capture of, by Australian Corps, 96
  Bn. attacks at, described, 96-101
  casualties at, 96, 98, 103
  decorations awarded for, 103
  results of attacks at, 102
  during German offensive, 1918, 193

INDEX

POZIÈRES TRENCH, 96, 97
PRATT, Pte. W.—killed at Hohenzollern Redoubt, 57
PRATT, Pte. —.—at Nurlu, 237
PRESTON, Sgt. G. W. :—
  awarded M.M. for Arras, 132, 308
  killed at Cambrai, 172
PREVETT, Sgt. R. :—
  at Ovillers, 87
  awarded D.C.M. for Ovillers, 93, 306
  killed at Gueudecourt, 107
PRICE, 2/Lt. W. E.—wounded at Nurlu, 238
PRINCE, Capt. G. W. :—
  patrols by, at Arras, 115, 117
  awarded M.C. for Arras, 117, 132, 305
  O.C. A Coy. at Battle of Amiens, 220
  wounded at Amiens, 227
PRINCE OF WALES, H.R.H. THE :—
  accompanies H.M. The King on inspection at Senlis, 103
  presents King's Colour at Erre, 267
PRINCE RESERVE TRENCH (Epehy), 240, 242
PRINCESS ROYAL, H.R.H. THE — attends 12th Div. church parade at Aldershot, 12
PRINGLE, W. M. R., M.P.—in Parliamentary debate on Cambrai, 179
PROPAGANDA—German attempts at, 20
PROYART WOOD (Somme), 253
PUCHEVILLERS, 103
PULPIT, THE (Quarries Sector), 69
PULTENEY, Lt.-Gen. Sir W. P. :—
  G.O.C. III Corps, inspects Bn. at Merris, 14
  at Cambrai, 150, 158
PURPLE LINE, THE (Mailly-Maillet), 213, 214, 217, 218

Q

QUARRIES, THE (Hulluch)—attacks on, 33, 39, 40
QUARRIES SECTOR, THE :—
  trench tours in, described, 69, 70, 74
  casualties in, 76
QUARRY, THE (Hohenzollern), 42, 43, 62
QUARRY ALLEY (Hohenzollern), 62
QUARRY POST (Aveluy Wood), 192, 196, 197, 198, 199, 201
QUARRY POST (Cambrai), 159
QUARRY TRENCH (Cambrai), 150
QUEEN, H.M. THE—attends 12th Div. church parade at Aldershot, 12
QUEEN'S CROSS (Cambrai), 171
QUEEN'S PARADE (Aldershot)—inspection by Lord Kitchener on, 11
QUEEN'S ROYAL REGIMENT, THE (West Surrey) :—
  6th Bn., relieves Bn., 21, 209, 217
    relieved by Bn., 39
    drafts for, sent to Bn., 95
    at Bouzincourt Ridge, 208, 209
  7th Bn., at Nurlu, 235
  11th Bn., at Gueudecourt, 105
QUIESTEDE, 180

R

RABY, Q.M.S. W. :—
  joins Bn. from 2nd R. Sussex, 1
  long service with Bn., 1
  overseas with Bn., 311
  prepares Christmas dinners, 109
  mentioned in despatches, 310

RAIDS :—
  by British,   at Agny, 104
    at Monchy, 137, 141-142, 143, 144
    at Fleurbaix, 185-188
    at Mailly-Maillet, 214
  by Germans, at Hythe, precautions against, 6
    at Fleurbaix, 183, 184
RAILWAY RESERVE TRENCH (Hohenzollern), 58, 62
RAILWAY TRIANGLE (Arras), 124
RAIMBEAUCOURT, 257, 258
RAMILLIES BARRACKS (Aldershot), 11
RAMSAY, Cpl. —. — billeting corporal, at Sibiville, 109
RANDALL, Pte. J.—awarded M.M. for Aveluy Wood, 203, 308
RANGER, Cpl. C—awarded M.M., 308
RANSOM, Sgt. F. J. :—
  overseas with Bn., 312
  wounded at Battle of Craters, 66
  awarded M.M. for Cambrai, 173, 308
  awarded D.C.M. for Battle of Amiens, 228, 306
  killed at Epehy, 251
  awarded French C. de G., 309
RATION TRENCH (Pozières), 96, 97, 98, 99, 100, 101, 102
RAWLINSON, Field-Marshal Lord — G.O.C. Fourth Army, congratulatory order by, after Epehy, 252
READ, Sgt. E.—overseas with Bn., 312
READING, Lt. F. W. :—
  wounded at Monchy, 138
  O.C. D Coy. at Epehy, 245
  wounded at Epehy, 250
Realities of War—by Sir Philip Gibbs, quoted, 21
Real War, The — by Capt. Liddell Hart, quoted, on Cambrai, 148, 163, 178
" REAPING PARTIES " :—
  at Le Touquet, 18
  at Bouzincourt Ridge, 216
RECKITT, Capt. G. L :—
  overseas with Bn., 312
  at Houplines 31
  O.C. C Coy. at Battle of Craters, 59
  at Hohenzollern Redoubt, 73
  O.C. D Coy. at Ovillers, 84, 86
  wounded at Ovillers, 93
  O.C. D Coy. at Sibiville, 110
  at Arras, 115, 119
  at Battle of Scarpe, 128
  at Cambrai, 162, 164, 165-166, 169
  awarded M.C. for raid at Fleurbaix, 186-188, 305
  at Aveluy Wood, 192, 197, 198, 199
  at Battle of Amiens, 220, 223, 224, 226
  awarded bar to M.C. for Amiens, 228, 305
  at Raimbeaucourt, 257
  at Château l'Abbaye, 261
  remarks by, on Armistice, 263
  at Hornaing, 266
RECRUITING—early success of, 3, 4, 5
REED, L/Cpl. F. J.—awarded M.M., 308
REED LANE (Cambrai), 165, 166
REES, Capt. A. A., R.A.M.C. :—
  Bn. M.O. at Sibiville, 110
  dies at Arras, 113
REGIMENTS, BRITISH. *See under* various Regimental names

INDEX

REGIMENTS, GERMAN :—
  Guard Fusiliers :—
    at Ovillers, 87, 93
    history of, quoted, on Ovillers, 93-94
  Hohenzollern Fusiliers :—
    at Cambrai, 175
  Jäger :—
    at Pozières, 98
    at Epehy, 242, 243, 249
  Royal Bavarian Body Guard :—
    at Epehy, 242-243, 249
  18th, at Battle of Craters, 67-68
    history of, quoted, 67-68
  19th, at Cambrai, 154
  23rd, at Battle of Craters, 68
  40th (*Hohenzollern Fusiliers*) :—
    at Cambrai, 175, 176
  67th, at Cambrai, 161
  104th, at Le Touquet, 20
  110th (*Grenadiers*) :—
    at Cambrai, 175, 176
  162nd, at Spoon Trench, Monchy, 140
  246th, at Aveluy Wood, 203
  247th, at Aveluy Wood, 203-204
  248th, at Aveluy Wood, 203-204
  267th, at Fleurbaix, 187
  395th, at Cambrai, 161
  445th, at Epehy, 249
RELY, 52
RENNIE, Sgt. —.—accident to, at Sibiville, 110
RESERVE TRENCH (Hohenzollern), 58, 59, 71
RESPIRATORS. *See under* GAS
" REST "—military significance of the word, 19
REVELON RIDGE (Cambrai), 175
RIBECOURT, 149
RICHARDS, Lt. E. G. C. :—
  at Folkestone, 8
  remains in England with casualty reserve, 312
RICHARDSON, Capt. R. J. :—
  overseas with Bn., 312
  O.C. B Coy. for Battle of Craters, 59
  wounded at Quarries Sector, 70
  O.C. B Coy. at Hohenzollern, 71
  to England, 84
RICHARDSON, Sgt. —.—at Nurlu, 237
RICHOLD, C.S.M. A. :—
  joins Bn. from 2nd R. Sussex, 1
  overseas with Bn., 312
  awarded M.M. for Pozières, 103, 308
RIDGE RESERVE TRENCH (Epehy), 240, 242, 247
RIFLE BRIGADE, THE—1st Bn., at Monchy, 144
RIFLEMAN'S CRATER (Givenchy), 48
RIFLES—shortage of, 6
RIFLE TRENCH (Scarpe), 125, 126, 129
RIPPLE LANE (Cambrai), 165, 166
RIVER AVENUE (Houplines), 23, 28
RIVINGTON TUNNEL (Ovillers), 88
ROBBINS, C.S.M. W.—killed at Cambrai, 161, 172
ROBERTSON, Field-Marshal Sir W. R.—C.I.G.S., 178
ROCH, W. F., M.P.—in Parliamentary debate on Cambrai, 178
ROEUX, 125, 127
ROGERS, Lt. V. E. :—
  acc. wounded at Beaurains, 142
  at Cambrai, 162
  at Aveluy Wood, 199-201
  wounded at Heilly, 223, 227
ROHARD, Mons. E.—Mayor of Arras, 131
ROKER PARK (Sunderland)—dug-outs named after, 24

ROLFE, 2/Lt. C. F. :—
  with battle surplus for Ovillers, 94
  at Pozières, 97, 99-101
  wounded and prisoner at Pozières, 101, 103
RONVILLE CAVES (Arras), 121
ROOM TRENCH (Epehy), 247, 248
ROOS, 2/Lt. H.—wounded at Gueudecourt, 107
ROSIER, L/Cpls. A. and H.—in D Coy's football team at Sibiville, 110
ROUGE BANCS, 185
ROUGE DE BOUT (Fleurbaix), 182, 183
ROUMANIANS—German victories over, 104, 213
ROUND WOOD (Behencourt), 220
ROUSSELL, 2/Lt. W. S.—killed at Battle of Amiens, 227
ROUVROY, 254
ROVERY, Sgt. L.—awarded M.M. for Pozières, 103, 308
ROWE, Lt. E. W. T. :—
  joins Bn., 1
  leaves Bn., 3
ROWE, Sgt. H.—overseas with Bn., 312
ROWSELL, 2/Lt. T. S.—wounded at Mametz, 233
ROYAL BERKSHIRE REGIMENT, THE :—
  5th Bn., relieves Bn., 183
    relieved by Bn., 208, 213, 214, 225
    at Gueudecourt, 107
    at Arras, 119, 120, 121
    transferred from 35th to 36th Brig., 184
    at Aveluy Wood, 192, 194
    at Bouzincourt Ridge, 206, 207, 208
    at Mailly-Maillet, 214
    at Battle of Amiens, 225, 226
    at Battle of Albert, 1918, 229
    at Fricourt and Mametz, 230, 231
    at Nurlu, 237, 238
    at Epehy, 240, 248
    in Final Advance, 254, 255, 259, 262
  8th Bn., at Loos, 37
    at Franvillers, 220
ROYAL ENGINEERS, THE :—
  at Houplines, 23, 24, 27
  at Loos, 37
  at Hohenzollern Redoubt, 55, 56, 58, 64
  at Arras, 113
  at Cambrai, 151, 155
  in Final Advance, 255
  69th Field Coy., at Courcelles, 256
  70th Field Coy., mentioned in despatches, 78
  And see TUNNELLING COMPANIES
ROYAL FLYING CORPS, THE—liaison with, at Quiestede, 180
ROYAL FUSILIERS, THE (City of London Regiment) :—
  8th Bn., relieves Bn., 19, 22, 26, 44, 47, 50, 51, 57, 58, 69, 71, 72, 106, 141
    relieved by Bn., 22, 23, 50, 59, 70, 71, 108, 140, 141, 142, 159, 184
    at Houplines, 22, 26, 27
    at Loos, 35
    at Battle of Craters, 58, 59
    mentioned in despatches, 78
    at Vignacourt, 79
    at Baizieux, 81

INDEX

ROYAL FUSILIERS, THE (City of London Regiment) (continued) :—
  8th Bn. (continued) :—
    at Albert, 82
    at Ovillers, 84, 86, 87, 89
    drafts for, sent to Bn., 95
    at Pozières, 96, 97, 98
    at Gueudecourt, 105, 106
    beats Bn. at football at Sibiville, 110
    at Arras, 118, 119
    at Battle of Scarpe, 124, 125, 126, 127
    at Cambrai, 159, 164, 165, 166, 169, 173, 175
    disbanded, 184
  9th Bn., relieves Bn., 101, 162, 185
    relieved by Bn., 213, 216
    at Houplines, 22
    at Ham-en-Artois, 52
    at Battle of Craters, 58, 59
    at Lapugnoy, 77
    mentioned in despatches, 78
    at Ovillers, 84, 87, 89
    forms composite Bn. with 7th R. Sussex, 95
    drafts for, sent to Bn., 95
    at Pozières, 97, 98, 99
    at Gueudecourt, 105, 106
    at Arras, 118, 119
    at Battle of Scarpe, 124, 125, 126, 127
    at Monchy, 142, 143
    at Cambrai, 151, 154, 164, 165, 167, 168, 169, 171, 173, 175
    absorbs 8th R. Fusiliers, 184
    at Aveluy Wood, 190, 192, 193, 194, 195, 196, 197, 201
    at Bouzincourt Ridge, 206, 208
    at Mailly-Maillet, 214
    at Beauquesne, 215
    at Battle of Amiens, 222, 223, 224, 226
    at Battle of Albert, 1918, 228, 229
    at Fricourt and Mametz, 230, 231, 233, 234
    at Nurlu, 238
    at Epehy, 240, 242, 243, 247, 248, 249
    in Final Advance, 255, 258, 259, 260, 262
  10th Bn., at Colchester, 28
    at Houplines, 28
  21st Bn., at Festubert, 46
  23rd Bn., at Festubert, 46
ROYAL IRISH FUSILIERS, THE—2nd Bn., at Houplines, 16
ROYAL IRISH REGIMENT, THE—1st Bn., at Houplines, 16, 22
ROYAL PAVILION (Aldershot), 11
ROYAL SCOTS, THE (The Royal Regiment)—
  7th Bn., at Hulluch, 39
ROYAL SUSSEX REGIMENT, THE :—
  Colonel of, Maj.-Gen. Young, inspects Bn. at Aldershot, 11
  Depot of, at Chichester, 1, 2, 269
  Three Bns. of, meet on Dover Road, 9
  1st Bn., service of members of 7th Bn. with, 1, 2, 3, 4, 116
    regimental march of, 94
  2nd Bn., mobilises at Woking, 1
    provides nucleus for 7th Bn., 1
    service of members of 7th Bn. with, 1, 2, 3, 161

ROYAL SUSSEX REGIMENT, THE (continued) :—
  2nd Bn. (continued) :—
    at Loos, 34
    at Hulluch, 39
    at Lillers, 52
    at Les Brebis, 79
  3rd Bn., meets 7th and 10th Bns., 9
  4th Bn., on the Rhine, 268
  5th Bn., Lt.-Col. Sansom comes from, 106, 139
  7th Bn., *passim*
  8th Bn., surplus recruits of 7th Bn. sent to, 5
    mentioned in despatches, 78
    at Heilly, 223
  10th Bn., meets 3rd and 7th Bns., 9
  12th Bn., Lt.-Col. Impey in command of, 77, 142
    drafts sent from, 185, 247
  13th Bn., Major Torrens comes from, 77
ROYAL WEST KENT REGIMENT, THE QUEEN'S OWN :—
  6th Bn., relieves Bn., 48, 51, 57, 71, 73, 129, 130, 217
    relieved by Bn., 58, 114, 183, 185
    R. Sussex drafts sent to, 95
    Gen. Owen comes from, 108
    at Aveluy Wood, 193, 197, 199, 200, 201
    at Round Wood, 220
RUE BATAILLE (Fleurbaix), 185
RUE BIACHE (Fleurbaix), 182
RUE DE L'EPINETTE (Festubert and Givenchy), 46, 47, 48, 50, 51
RUE DELPIERRE (Fleurbaix), 183
RUE DE QUESNOY (Armentières), 16, 32
RUE DES CAILLOUX (Festubert), 47, 51
RUE DES JESUITS (Armentières), 15
RUE DU BOIS (Festubert), 46
RUE DU BOIS (Fleurbaix), 182, 183
RUE LASSON, 259
RUE MICHELET (Bethune), 44
RUMEGIES, 259
RUPPRECHT, CROWN PRINCE OF BAVARIA—quoted, on Cambrai, 176
RUSSELL, Sgt. F. J. :—
  overseas with Bn., 311
  at Le Touquet, 21
  at Houplines, 24
  wounded at Ovillers, 87, 89
  killed at Gueudecourt, 107
RUSSIANS :—
  attempted escape by two, at Arras, 115
  German victories over the, 213
RUSSIAN SAP (Hohenzollern), 62, 63, 65
RYAN, Maj. C. I.—C.O. 9th Essex, at Ovillers, 88

S

SADLEIR-JACKSON, Brig.-Gen. L. W. de V.—G.O.C. 54th Brig., at Battle of Amiens, 221
SADLER, Capt. H. :—
  " Harold " handed over to, after the war, 4
  at Vignacourt, 79
  at Ovillers, 87, 90-92
  wounded and awarded M.C. at Ovillers, 93, 305
  O.C. B Coy. after Pozières, 102
  buys filly foal, " Somme," after the war, 219
SAILLY-AU-BOIS, 95
SAILLY LABOURSE, 44, 54, 55, 57, 69, 71, 74, 76

INDEX

SAILLY-LAURETTE, 222, 225
SAILLY-LE-SEC, 222
SAILLY-SUR-LA-LYS, 183, 185
ST. AMAND, 262
ST. ELIE AVENUE (Hohenzollern), 76
ST. ELOI, 16
ST. HILAIRE, 45, 52
ST. JAMES'S PARK (Newcastle) — dug-outs named after, 24
ST. MARTIN'S PLAIN (Shorncliffe) — Bn. in camp at, 6
ST. MIHIEL, 177
ST. OMER, 14, 181
SAINTON, Capt. W. H. :—
  O.C. B Coy. at Arras, 119
  at Battle of Scarpe, 126-127
  at Cambrai, 151
ST. PIERRE-VAAST, 235
ST. POL, 109, 190
ST. QUENTIN, 149, 150, 240
ST. QUENTIN CANAL. *And see* ESCAUT-ST. QUENTIN CANAL
ST. QUENTIN CANAL, BATTLE OF. *See* EPEHY
ST. VENANT, 189
SANDERSON, C.S.M. J. :—
  overseas with Bn., 312
  awarded D.C.M., 306
SANDGATE, 9
SANDHURST, 4, 247
SANDLING :—
  Bn. hutments at, 6, 7
  training at, 6-8
SANSOM, Lt.-Col. A. J. :—
  to command Bn. at Bernafay Wood, 106
  at Sibiville, 109
  presents football cup, 110
  presents tenor drum, 110
  at Wanquetin, 111
  at Arras, 120
  at Battle of Scarpe, 124, 127, 128, 129, 130
  Letters from France by, quoted, 120, 133, 139
  killed at Monchy, 139
  appreciation of, 139
  mentioned in despatches, 310
SAPS :—
  G   (Givenchy), 49
  H   (Givenchy), 48, 49, 50
  Russian (Hohenzollern), 63
  9   (Hohenzollern), 56, 72
SARTON, 103
SAULCOURT, 173, 253
SAUNDERS, L/Cpl. J.—awarded M.M., 308
SAXONS—attempted fraternisation by, 28, 29
SAYERS, Sgt. H. T.—killed at Battle of Amiens, 227
SCABBARD TRENCH (Scarpe)—captured by B and C Coys., 125, 126, 127, 128, 129
SCARPE, BATTLES OF THE :—
  described, 124-130
  casualties in, 128-129
  decorations for, 132, 133
SCARPE RIVER, THE, 115, 118, 124, 125, 126, 150, 261
SCHRAMM BARRACKS (Arras), 143, 144
SCOTT, Maj.-Gen. Sir A. B. :—
  G.O.C. 12th Div., at Loos, 37
  editor of 12th Div. History, 39
  inspects Bn. at Fouquereuil, 39
  presents medal ribbons at L'Ecleme, 54
  at Hohenzollern Redoubt, 72
  institutes red and green cards, 80
  congratulates Bn. after Ovillers, 94

SCOTT, Maj.-Gen. Sir A. B. (continued) :—
  accompanies H.M. The King on inspection at Senlis, 103
  inspects Bn. at Sibiville, 110
  order by, after Arras, 122-123
  presents medal ribbons at Agnez, 133
  message from, after Monchy, 144
  congratulatory order by, after Cambrai, 171, 172
  after Aveluy Wood, 205
  leaves Division, 212
  appreciation of, 212
  his farewell order, 212
SCOTT, Pte. P. :—
  awarded M.M. for Arras, 132, 308
  wounded at Cambrai, 152
SCOTTISH RIFLES. *See* CAMERONIANS
SCOUTS, THE BN. :—
  at Le Touquet, 21
  at Houplines, 24, 25
SCUTT, Pte. T.—at Givenchy, 50
SECKHAM, Sgt. G.—killed at Pozières, 103
SECRECY :—
  non-observance of, before Somme, 1916, 78
  precautions for, before Cambrai, 145, 147, 152
  observed, before Amiens, 220
Secret Service—by Maj.-Gen. Sir G. Aston, quoted, on Battle of Amiens, 220
SEELY, Maj.-Gen. J. E. B. *See* MOTTISTONE, Viscount
SELBY, Sgt. A. E. :—
  awarded M.M. for Pozières, 103, 308
  killed at Battle of Amiens, 227
SELSBY, Pte. J. R. — awarded M.M. for Pozières, 103, 308
SELSEY, 3
SENLIS, 94, 103, 191, 201, 203, 204, 206, 209, 210, 211, 216, 217
SENSÉE RIVER, THE, 150
SHAW, G. Bernard—at Arras, 113
SHAW, Capt. —., R.A.M.C.—Bn. M.O. after Ovillers, 94
SHERWOOD FORESTERS, THE (Notts and Derby Regiment)—10th Bn., at Senlis, 206
SHILSTON, 2/Lt. A. C.—at Château l'Abbaye, 261
SHORNCLIFFE—Bn. training at, 6
SHORT, L/Cpl. H. :—
  awarded D.C.M. for Battle of Craters, 66, 306
  wounded at Battle of Craters, 66
SHROPSHIRE LIGHT INFANTRY, THE KING'S—6th Bn., at Méricourt, 253
SHUTE, Gen. Sir C. D.—G.O.C. V Corps, at Beauquesne, 215
SIBIVILLE, 108, 109-110, 146
SICKELMORE, Cpl. C. S.—killed at Cambrai, 172
SIGNAL COPSE (Nurlu), 235
SIGNALLING SECTION, THE BN. :—
  at Folkestone, 9
  at Le Touquet, 21
  at Houplines, 27
SIMMINS, C.Q.M.S. E.—overseas with Bn., 312
SIMMONDS, Sgt. J. :—
  green card presented to, at Flesselles, 81
  awarded M.M. and bar, 268, 306, 308
SING, 2/Lt. C. M.—killed at Ovillers, 93
SIXTH AVENUE (Pozières)—Bn. attacks on, 97

343

INDEX

SKERRETT, Sgt. A.—killed at Hohenzollern Redoubt, 71, 72
SKEY, Maj. C. O. — 8th R. Fusiliers, at Cambrai, 164, 166, 169
SKINGLEY, 2/Lt. H. C.—wounded at Monchy, 140
SLAG HEAP, THE. *See* FOSSE 8 DE BETHUNE
SLAUGHTER, Pte. F.—awarded M.M., 309
SLEEMAN, Col. J. L. :—
    proceeds from 2nd R. Sussex with nucleus of 7th Bn., 1
    at Chichester, 1, 2
    appeal to ex-N.C.O.s by, 2, 3
    purchases necessaries for Bn., 5
    as 2nd in Command, overseas with Transport and M.G. Sections, 13, 311
    at Le Touquet, 16, 21
    leaves Bn., 22
    Director of Mil. Training to N.Z. Forces, 22
SMART, Lt. A. H. :—
    wounded at Arras, 123
    wounded and captured at Aveluy Wood, 198, 202
SMELTZER, Lt.-Col. A. S.—C.O. 6th Buffs, at Battle of Amiens, 225
SMITH, Pte. J.—awarded M.M. for Arras, 132, 309
SMITH, Lt. V. St. G. :—
    at Monchy, 142
    at Fleurbaix, 186, 187
SMITH, 2/Lt. W.—dies of wounds after Battle of Scarpe, 128, 203
SMITH, Pte. W.—awarded M.M. for Aveluy Wood, 309
SMOKE :—
    used by British, at Houplines, 30, 31
    at Epehy, 241, 245
SMOKE-HELMETS. *See* GAS
SMUTS, Gen. J. C. — conducts inquiry into Cambrai operations, 178
SNEYD, Maj. F. B.—D.A.D.V.S., 12th Div., at Cambrai, 174
SNIPERS :—
    Battalion, at Houplines, 24, 25
    German, at Le Touquet, 18
        at Houplines, 25, 26, 29
        at Hulluch, 35
        at Festubert, 47
        at Hohenzollern, 57
SNOW, Lt.-Gen. Sir T. D'O. — G.O.C. VII Corps, at Cambrai, 163
SOAMES, Cpl. T. W.—wounded at Battle of Craters, 66
SOBRAON BARRACKS (Colchester), 2
SOLOMON, C.S.M. T. :—
    joins Bn., 3
    overseas with Bn., 311
SOMAIN, 267
SOMERSET LIGHT INFANTRY, THE—1st Bn., at Monchy, 142
" SOMME "—filly foal, born at Oresmaux, 219
SOMME, BATTLES OF THE :—
    1916, training for, 78-80
        description of opening of, 81-82
        casualties in, 109
        And see OVILLERS, FLERS, AND GUEUDECOURT
    1918. *See* AVELUY WOOD, BOUZINCOURT RIDGE, AMIENS, ALBERT, FRICOURT, MAMETZ
SOMME RIVER, THE, 221
SONGHURST, C.Q.M.S. B. :—
    joins Bn. from 2nd R. Sussex, 1
    overseas with Bn., 312

SONNET FARM (Cambrai), 150, 153, 159, 165, 175
SONNET ROAD (Cambrai), 151
SONNET TRENCH (Cambrai), 154
SOREL-LE-GRAND, 174
SOREL WOOD, 238
SOUCH, Pte. F. H. :—
    at Hohenzollern Redoubt, 56
    killed at Monchy, 57
SOUTH AFRICAN WAR, THE :—
    service of members of Bn. in, 1, 3
    contrasted with Great War, 13, 15
SOUTHAMPTON, 13
SOUTH LANE (Epehy), 242
SOUTTER, 2/Lt. J. L. :—
    at Fleurbaix, 186
    wounded at Battle of Amiens, 227
" SPADES, THE " (12th Div. Theatrical Troupe) :—
    at Bethune, 44
    at Arras, 135
SPANISH INFLUENZA, 217
SPARROW, Sgt. R.—overseas with Bn., 311
SPENS, Maj.-Gen. J.—first G.O.C. 12th Div., 2
SPIES :—
    rumours of, 6, 19, 30, 32
    Maj. Impey mistaken for one, at Loos, 37-38
    hunt for, at Bethune, 46
SPOON TRENCH (Monchy) :—
    attacks on, 136
    capture of, by Germans, 140
    counter-attack on, cancelled, 141
    casualties at, 140
    raid on, 143
SPOTTED FEVER—epidemic of, at Folkestone, 10
SQUIRES, L/Cpl. A.—awarded M.M., 309
STEEL HELMETS—first issue of, 40
STEENBECQUE, 189
STEENWERCK, 14, 15, 16, 17, 32
STEPHEN, 2/Lt. R.—wounded at Epehy, 250
STICKY TRENCH (Hohenzollern), 42, 43, 59, 60, 61
STOCKS, Lt. G. G. :—
    remains in England with casualty reserve, 312
    Adjutant at Battle of Scarpe, 124
STOCKS, Lt. H. S. :—
    overseas with Bn., 311
    at Le Touquet, 18
    at Houplines, 27
    appointed Adjutant at Hohenzollern, 69
    wounded at Ovillers, 86, 90, 93
STOKES MORTARS, 53
STONER, Sgt. E. :—
    at Givenchy, 49
    at Battle of Craters, 62
    killed at Arras, 123
STRETCHER-BEARERS, THE BN. :—
    at Battle of Craters, 66
    at Pozières, 100, 101
    at Mailly-Maillet, 214
    appreciation of, 268
SUBMARINES, GERMAN—precautions against, 6
SUFFOLK REGIMENT, THE :—
    2nd Bn., at Monchy, 136
    7th Bn., relieves Bn., 185
        relieved by Bn., 51, 69, 71, 124
        mentioned in despatches, 78
        disbanded, 184
    12th Bn., at Battle of the Lys, 183
SUNDERLAND—men of the Bn. from, 5, 24
SURRIDGE, 2/Lt. R. R.—wounded at Arras, 123

INDEX

Sus-St. Léger, 103
Sussex Regiment. *See* Royal Sussex Regiment
Sutton, Lt. E. G.:—
  overseas with Bn., 312
  awarded M.C. at Houplines, 30, 305
  killed at Hohenzollern Redoubt, 72
  mentioned in despatches, 310
Sutton, 2/Lt. W. K.—remains in England with casualty reserve, 312
Swallow Trench (Ephey), 250
Swift, 2/Lt. A. W.—wounded at Battle of Arras, 227
S.88 (Houplines), 23, 28
S.S.88 (Houplines), 22, 27, 29, 31

T

Tailles Wood (Morlancourt), 222
Tanks:—
  demonstration by, at Erin, 116
  at Arras, 134
  training with, for Cambrai, 146
  employment of, in 3rd Battle of Ypres, 148-149
  at Battle of Cambrai, 149, 150, 152, 153, 154, 176
  at Battle of Amiens, 223, 225
  at Battle of Albert, 1918, 229
  at Epehy, 241, 245, 246, 250
Tara Hill (Ovillers), 84
Tara-Usna Line, 101
Taylor, Pte. A.—awarded M.M. for Aveluy Wood, 203, 309
Taylor, Sgt. F.:—
  joins Bn. from 2nd R. Sussex, 1
  overseas with Bn., 312
Taylor, Capt. H. F.:—
  at Ovillers, 83, 87, 88, 89, 94
  O.C. D Coy. after Pozières, 102
  O.C. C Coy. at Arras, 119
  at Battle of Scarpe, 125, 126, 127, 128
  awarded M.C. for Scarpe, 132, 305
Telegraph Hill (Arras), 113
Territorials:—
  British, early fighting by, 17
  French, liaison with, 14
Tétard Wood (Epehy), 240, 242, 247
Thélus, 253
Thiepval, 81, 96, 97
Third Avenue (Pozières), 96
Thirst, Pte. W.—awarded M.M., 304
Thomas, Lt. S. C.—at Château l'Abbaye, 261
Thompson, 2/Lt. G. A.—overseas with Bn., 312
Thompson, Capt. J. A.:—
  joins Bn., 1
  overseas with Bn. as O.C. C Coy., 312
  leaves Bn., 29
Thomson, Lt.-Col. A. L.:—
  2nd in command, at Arras, 116
  in command of battle surplus at Cambrai, 147, 175
  C.O. at Toutencourt, 218
  at Battle of Amiens, 220, 221
  awarded D.S.O. for Amiens, 228, 305
  wounded at Mametz, 233
  at Nurlu, 235
  at Epehy, 247
  mentioned in despatches, 310

Thomson, Capt. A. M., R.A.M.C.:—
  overseas with Bn. as M.O., 311
  at Le Touquet, 16
  at Ovillers, 83, 90
  gallantry of, 16, 90
  killed at Ovillers, 90, 93
  mentioned in despatches, 310
Thornton, Capt. G. E.:—
  at Nurlu, 236, 237
  wounded in Final Advance, 262
Threlfallite—use of, at Houplines, 31
Till, Capt. W. S.:—
  at Battle of Craters, 62-65
  Acting Adjutant after Ovillers, 94
  wounded at Gueudecourt, 107
Tilloy, 131
Times, The—quoted, on debates on Cambrai operations, 178
Toney, Cpl. E.—awarded D.C.M. for raid at Fleurbaix, 188, 306
Tool Trench (Monchy), 136, 141
Tooms, Sgt. F. J.:—
  at Pozières, 99
  killed at Mametz, 233
  awarded M.M., 309
Torrens, Maj. J. R.—2nd in Command at Lapugnoy, 77
Toutencourt, 211, 218
Tower, Lt. C. C.—A.D.C. to Gen. Wing, killed at Loos, 36
" Tower Bridge " (Loos), 35
Traitoire River, The, 261
Transport, The Bn.:—
  " Harold " attaches himself to, 4
  " Harold " wounded with, 4
  formation of, 6
  efficiency of, 6, 7
  at Westenhanger, 7
  at Newington, 7
  unloading of mules by, 7
  at Aldershot, 11
  proceeds overseas, 13, 14
  at Steenwerck, 15
  at Pontceau, 17
  at Pont d'Achelles, 22
  at Armentières, 32
  en route for Loos, 32
  on Hulluch Road, 36
  at Noyelles, 41
  at Le Touret, 47
  at Givenchy, 50, 51
  at Hingette, 51
  at Chichester Paddock, Arras, 80
  at Flers, 104
  at Agnez-lez Duisans, 116
  at Arras, 114, 121-122, 130, 143
  at Mondicourt, 124
  prizes won by, at Grand-Rullecourt, 133-134
  at Cambrai, 170, 173-175, 180
  en route for Aveluy, 191
  at Aveluy Wood, 201-202
  at Bouzincourt, 210-211, 216
  at Acheux Wood, 213, 214
  filly foal born at, at Oresmaux, 219
  at Carnoy, 234
  at Nurlu, 239
  at Epehy, 246
  during Final Advance, 262
Trenches 85-89 (Houplines), 23, 24, 26, 31
Trench Feet:—
  casualties from, 43
  precautions against, 43

INDEX

TRENCH MORTAR BATTERY, 36th :—
  formed, 53
  at Battle of Scarpe, 128
TRENCH-MORTARS :—
  at Houplines, 26
  at Hohenzollern Redoubt, 56
  at Monchy, 137
TRESCAULT, 175
TREVOR, Sgt. A. :—
  awarded M.M. for Aveluy Wood, 203, 309
  awarded D.C.M. for Battle of Amiens, 228, 306
  prisoners captured by, in Battle of Albert, 1918, 229
  awarded bar to D.C.M. for Epehy, 251, 306
TROCADERO—Long Bar of the, military secrets discussed at the, 145
TROWELL, 2/Lt. W. T. :—
  at Battle of Amiens, 223, 226
  wounded at Battle of Amiens, 226, 227
TROWER, Capt. A. K. :—
  overseas with Bn., 312
  at Le Touquet, 19
  O.C. D Coy. after Ovillers, 94
  at Pozières, 98
  wounded at Pozières, 103
TUI ROAD (Fleurbaix), 184
TULETT, Sgt. C.—awarded M.M., 309
TULITT, Pte. W.—awarded M.M., 309
TUNING FORK ROAD (Festubert), 47, 48
TUNNELLING COMPANIES, R.E. :—
  New Zealand, at Arras, 113
  170th, at Hohenzollern Redoubt, 55, 56, 58
  admiration of Bn. for, 73
  German mines destroyed by, 73, 74
  mentioned in despatches, 78
TURNER, Sgt. J.—overseas with Bn., 312
TURTON, L/Cpl. A.—awarded M.M. for Battle of Craters, 66, 309
TWIN COPSES (Monchy), 129, 136, 138, 142
TWIN TRENCH (Monchy), 136
TYRRELL, Sgt. G. W.—killed at Pozières, 99, 103

U

ULOTH, Lt. A. C. W. :—
  wounded at Gueudecourt, 107
  O.C. B Coy. at Epehy, 246
  killed at Epehy, 250
UNSTED, Sgt. W.—killed at Ovillers, 93
UPPLEBY, Capt. W. C. S.—killed at Fleurbaix, 185
USNA HILL (Ovillers), 84
UZENNEVILLE, 218

V

VACANT ALLEY (Cambrai), 164, 165, 167, 168, 173
VALENCIENNES, 265
VAN SOMEREN, Lt.-Col. W. V. L. :—
  C.O. 9th R. Fusiliers, at Cambrai, 164, 165, 167
  at Aveluy Wood, 195
VARENNES, 103
VASSAS, Capt. Raoul—joins Bn. at Boulogne as interpreter, 14
VAUCELLETTE FARM (Cambrai), 148, 175
VAUDRICOURT, 79
V.C. CORNER (Fleurbaix), 182
VÉLU, 240
VENDHUILE, 269
VENN, C.S.M. E. N. :—
  joins Bn. from 2nd R. Sussex, 1
  overseas with Bn., 311
  killed at Battle of Amiens, 225, 227
VERMELLES :—
  description of, 34
  Brewery cross-roads at, 36, 37
  reserve trenches near, 38, 41
  other references to, 36, 41, 42, 44, 56, 57, 69, 70, 71, 73, 74
VERQUIGNEUL, 33, 34
VERQUIN, 33, 37, 38
VESTA TRENCH (Nurlu), 235, 236
Victoria, ss.—transports Bn. overseas, 13
VIEIL HESDIN, 145-146, 180
VIEUX CONDÉ, 262
VIGNACOURT, 79, 80, 109, 220
VILLAGE LANE (Cambrai), 154, 162, 164, 165, 167, 173
VILLAGE ROAD (Cambrai), 173
VILLERS-CAMPEAU, 268
VILLERS-GUISLAIN, 148, 171
VILLERS-PLOUICH, 170, 171, 174, 176, 177
VILLIERS, Lt.-Col. E. F.—C.O. 2nd R. Sussex at Loos, 34
VIMY RIDGE, THE, 118, 190, 253
VINALL, C.S.M. J. E.—overseas with Bn., 311
VIOLAINES, 56

W

WADEY, Cpl. E.—killed at Ovillers, 93
WAGHORN, Pte. T.—awarded M.M., 309
WALLER, Pte. —.—wounded at Le Touquet, 16
WANCOURT-FEUCHY LINE (The Brown Line) :—
  as an objective in Battle of Arras, 118, 119, 120, 121, 135
  as reserve line for Monchy Sector, 134, 140, 141, 142, 144
WANQUETIN, 110, 111, 124
WAR-CORRESPONDENTS, 21, 263
WARD, C.S.M. G.—awarded D.C.M. for Pozières, 103, 306
WARING, 2/Lt. F. R.—killed at Ovillers, 93
WARLOY, 191, 201, 202, 205, 211, 216, 217
WARREN, 2/Lt. A. E.—wounded at Ovillers, 93
WARSAW—capture of, 27
WEBB, Sgt. A. E.—at Hohenzollern Redoubt, 57
WELCH REGIMENT, THE :—
  13th Bn., at Sailly-au-Bois, 95
  14th Bn., at Fleurbaix, 182
    at Bouzincourt, 211
WELCH RIDGE (Cambrai), 168, 173, 174
WELCH TRENCH (Cambrai), 171
WELLER, Sgt. T. — joins Bn. from 2nd R. Sussex, 1
WELLS, Lt. R. G. :—
  overseas with Bn., 312
  at Houplines, 24
  killed at Battle of Craters, 61, 63, 65
WEST, Sgt. C. :—
  awarded D.C.M., 306
  awarded M.M., 309
WEST CLIFF HOTEL (Folkestone), 8
WESTENHANGER, 7
WEST FACE (Hohenzollern), 59, 60, 61, 72

INDEX

WHAPHAM, C.S.M. A. :—
  overseas with Bn., 311
  at Ovillers, 87
WHITBREAD, Cpl. E.—awarded M.M., 309
WHITE, Pte. P. A. C. — awarded M.M. for Pozières, 103, 309
WHITTEMORE, Pte. F. A.—awarded M.M. and bar, 304
WILLAN, Col. F. G.—C.O. 5th R. Berks, at Gueudecourt, 107
WILLARD, Lt. A. E. :—
  acc. wounded at Lignereuil, 116
  killed at Monchy, 138
  appreciation of, 138
WILLETT, Lt.-Col. F. W. B. — at Depot, Chichester, 269
WILLIAMS, Sgt. A. — wounded at Hohenzollern, 72
WILLIAMS, 2/Lt. C.—wounded at Monchy, 138
WILLIAMS, Capt. J. F.—T.O. of 8th R. Fusiliers at Cambrai, 174
WILLIAMS, Rev. W. J. :—
  joins Bn. at Lapugnoy, 77
  appreciation of, 77
  starts canteen at Feuchy Chapel crossroads, 134
  conducts Brigade service on Armistice Day, 264
  awarded M.C., 305
WILMSHURST, Pte. J.—awarded M.M., 309
WILSON, Pte. J. :—
  awarded M.M. for Battle of Craters, 66, 309
  awarded bar for Ovillers, 67, 93, 306
WILTON, Capt. J. R. :—
  Signals officer, at Folkestone, 9
  overseas with Bn., 312
  at Houplines, 27, 28, 29
  Acting Adjutant at Hohenzollern Redoubt, 59
  wounded at Battle of Craters, 66
  at Ovillers, 89
  wounded at Ovillers, 86, 89, 93
  mentioned in despatches, 310
WINDY CORNER (Givenchy), 50, 51
WING, Maj.-Gen. F. D. V. :—
  G.O.C. 12th Div. at Aldershot, 11
  inspects Bn. at Houplines, 28
  killed at Loos, 36

WISE, Cpl. E.—killed at Battle of Amiens, 227
WOKING—Inkerman Barracks at, 1
WOOD, Sgt. P. W.—wounded at Hohenzollern, 72
WOOD, 2/Lt. T. V. :—
  with battle surplus for Ovillers, 94
  killed at Pozières, 100, 103
WOODFORD, Capt. D. F. :—
  overseas with Bn., 312
  Bombing Officer, at Essex Sap, 39-40
WOODHAMS, Capt. G. :—
  overseas with Bn., 312
  O.C. B Coy. at Houplines, &c., 22, 59
  wounded at Noyelles, 41
  at Givenchy, 49
  killed at Quarries Sector, 70
  appreciation of, 71
  mentioned in despatches, 310
WOOLGAR, L/Cpl. —.—presented with green card at Flesselles, 81
WOOLVEN, L/Cpl. G.—awarded M.M., 309
WORCESTERSHIRE REGIMENT, THE :—
  4th Bn., Col. Carr comes from, 101
  1/8th Bn., Col. Carr goes to, 106
WORKING PARTIES :—
  at Le Bizet, 20
  at Loos, 36, 37
  at Hohenzollern Redoubt, 56, 71
  at Bully-Grenay and Maroc, 79
  before Battle of Arras, 111-113
  at Monchy, 137
  at Fleurbaix, 183
  at Mailly-Maillet, 213
WRIGHT, 2/Lt. F. L.—wounded at Epehy, 250
WRIGHT, Cpl. G. W.—awarded M.M., 309
WRIGHT, Lt. J. A.—killed at Epehy, 243, 250

Y

YEO, Sgt. W.—overseas with Bn., 311
YOUNG, Maj.-Gen. J. C.—Col. of the R. Sussex Regt., inspects Bn. at Aldershot, 11
YPRES, BATTLES OF :—
  2nd, references to, 11, 15, 17, 33
  3rd, references to, 144, 148-149
YPRES, Field-Marshal the Earl of—C. in C. in France, 10
Y RAVINE, 212

www.ingramcontent.com/pod-product-compliance
Lightning Source LLC
Chambersburg PA
CBHW050327230426
43663CB00010B/1766